THE JDC AT 100

The JDC at 100

A CENTURY OF HUMANITARIANISM

Edited by Avinoam Patt, Atina Grossmann,
Linda G. Levi, and Maud S. Mandel

WAYNE STATE UNIVERSITY PRESS
DETROIT

ISBN 978-0-8143-4234-3 (hardcover); ISBN 978-0-8143-4235-0 (ebook)

Library of Congress Control Number: 2018965069

All photographs courtesy of JDC Archives.

Wayne State University Press
Leonard N. Simons Building
4809 Woodward Avenue
Detroit, Michigan 48201-1309

Visit us online at wsupress.wayne.edu

Publication supported by the Fishman Brothers: Art, Ed, and Bob.

Contents

FOREWORD

A JDC ARCHIVES COLLEAGUE recently shared the following story:

> My great-grandfather, Isidor Simberg, was taken from his wife and daughter, my grandmother, in the Riga ghetto and never heard from again. My father is named for the grandfather that he never met. But this tragic story has a happy ending. My grandmother and great-grandmother miraculously stuck together and survived three concentration camps. After the war, my great-grandmother Rosa worked for the Joint in Berlin, and on November 3, 1947, the two of them set sail from Bremen on the S.S. Marine Tiger with help from the Joint. The proof of that is in their listed destination on the ship's manifest—"Joint, New York, NY." The Joint is a destination. The Joint is home. The Joint, in the end, is what made my family's life possible. I owe so much to the Joint and I can only hope that I can repay that in some form as one of the custodians of our organization's history.

These inspiring words and very touching personal story touch on the essence of JDC and what the organization has represented for so many over the last century.

Established in reaction to a now-renowned telegram sent by Henry Morgenthau, US ambassador to the Ottoman Empire, in August 1914, the Joint Distribution Committee for the Relief of War Sufferers was established to assist Jews in Europe and Palestine who were affected by the devastation of World War I. Jewish communities experienced calamity, revolutions, war, pogroms, and harsh poverty. It is difficult to imagine life for the Jewish communities in Poland, Romania, and Russia during World War I and in the interwar years without the extensive, life-affirming assistance provided by JDC.

The Shoah and JDC are inextricably linked. This speaks to the history of JDC's heroic attempts to save as many Jews as possible from the clutches of the Nazis in Europe. JDC saved hundreds of thousands of lives in its tireless efforts to rescue Jews from Europe. The records of JDC document the lengths taken to find countries of refuge; raise funds; lease ships; guarantee passage, care, and maintenance; and offer relief assistance. From Cuba to Shanghai, from Barcelona and Lisbon to Tangier and the Dominican Republic, JDC offered rescue and refuge to hundreds of thousands. In the displaced persons (DP) camps of Europe and on the routes to these camps from across Eastern Europe, JDC was there to assist the survivors of the Shoah (the Holocaust) and to extend a helping hand and a smile. JDC was there to help DPs establish themselves in new countries.

And along with the calamities seen by the Jewish people, there were moments of inspiration and rebirth. The establishment of the State of Israel and the rebuilding of Jewish communities in Europe in the postwar period offered hope and a future to the survivors. JDC worked closely with the fledgling government in Israel to develop services for the disadvantaged and sick, for the elderly, and for the handicapped. Indeed, JDC's imprint is found on the beginnings of many major social welfare institutions in Israel. In Europe, Africa, and Asia, JDC worked with local Jewish communities to improve the lot of the needy, the poor, and the sick and helped establish communal institutions such as homes for the elderly, kindergartens, Jewish schools, social welfare programs, health clinics, and hospitals.

JDC was the address for Jews who needed to leave their countries due to war and dislocation or for political reasons. It offered help to Hungarian Jews following the 1956 revolution, to Polish and Czech Jews in 1968, and to Soviet Jews who left the Soviet Union in the 1970s to the 1990s. And glasnost presented the opportunity to reconnect with Jews in the former Soviet Union.

The last 100 years have been witness to much tragedy for world Jewry. Jewish communities have known calamity, revolutions, war, pogroms, and the Shoah (the Holocaust). Many Jews and others have benefited from the help provided by JDC around the world. Indeed, the organization's name became well known, legendary for generations of Jews. "The Joint" was a code word for hope, for help, the 911 of the Jewish people.

In the contemporary period, JDC continues with its mission of rescue, relief, and renewal, caring for scores of thousands of survivors; working to rebuild and strengthen Jewish communal life where it had been all but extinguished; promoting innovation; and helping to strengthen Israel's social fabric.

I was approached in 2012 by a young scholar, also inspired by the work of the Joint, who proposed the idea of planning a scholars' workshop to celebrate the centennial of the American Jewish Joint Distribution Committee's global activism and humanitarian aid, which would involve historians and scholars in the 100th anniversary celebrations of the Joint in 2014. The research of these scholars demonstrates the depth and breadth of the JDC Archives and the organization's past activities. By presenting the historical aspect of JDC, historians could speak to JDC's deep, unwavering commitment to helping Jews worldwide, irrespective of their background, even through the most challenging times.

Thus was borne the idea for the scholars' workshop that took place in September 2014 and brought together twenty-five scholars from around the world whose research focuses on the work of JDC. This two-day gathering in New York City, which was also attended by a group of key JDC leaders, was an inspiring and uplifting event, generating a tremendous amount of enthusiasm and excitement. The predistributed papers indeed pointed to the new research being done on JDC, bringing together JDC leaders and the scholars whose work focuses on the Joint and enabling the group to examine JDC as a whole. The presentations focused on the analysis of the work of JDC in different locales and in every decade over the last century. The discussions grappled with the challenges addressed by the Joint, the role of prominent JDC figures across regions, the lessons learned, and more.

This encounter between JDC leadership and historians and scholars can help raise public awareness of JDC's incredible activism and foster new ideas for collaboration.

The JDC Archives is one of the most important repositories of modern Jewish history, given the depth and breadth of the organization's activity, and is committed to encouraging and assisting scholars who wish to conduct research in its historic collections. Extensive digitization of the text, photo, and other collections over the last eight to nine years has made these records even more accessible to scholars and others wishing to conduct research. The JDC Archives website can be accessed at http://archives.jdc.org.

I want to thank the Steering Committee of the scholars' workshop with whom I worked closely to plan the workshop and without whose leadership this workshop would not have happened: Atina Grossmann, Sara Halpern, Maud Mandel, Avinoam Patt, and Judith Siegel.

It has been a distinct honor to serve as an editor of this volume. It is our hope that this volume that brings together a group of the papers from this workshop will be a major contribution to university studies and to a general audience wishing to learn more about the work of the American Jewish Joint Distribution Committee.

Linda G. Levi
Director, JDC Global Archives

Introduction

Avinoam Patt, Atina Grossmann, Linda G. Levi,
and Maud S. Mandel

Since its origins in 1914, the American Jewish Joint Distribution Committee (JDC), founded to aid the victims of World War I, has played a significant role in preserving and sustaining Jewish life. As political upheaval across the globe uprooted centuries-old Jewish populations, forever changing the map of Jewish life, JDC supported refugees, helped rebuild devastated communities, and served as a global network for Jews cut off from their coreligionists through bloodshed and upheaval. The occasion of JDC's Centennial in 2014, an event that active organizations usually treat as an occasion for celebration, reminiscence, and fundraising, also offered scholars who had been using the JDC Archives for their research, without necessarily examining the institutional history documented in those archives as a specific object of research, an overdue ideal opportunity to reflect critically on the organization's transformative impact on Jewish communities around the world. In September 2014, twenty-five scholars from the United States, Western and Eastern Europe, Australia, and Israel came together to discuss JDC work across time and space. This volume draws upon select papers from that workshop and highlights innovative new research utilizing the unique and extensive resources of the JDC Archives. Given its origins in a first-time gathering of scholars devoted to the history of JDC, it offers only a partial geographical and chronological view of JDC's activities, mostly (but not entirely) focused on the turbulent decades between World War I, the impetus for its formation, and the aftermath of World War II and the Holocaust. Nonetheless, this initial collection of scholarship—treating a wide range of topics, including relief operations for Jewish victims of pogroms and impoverishment after war, revolution, and civil conflict in the young Soviet Union; aid for refugees from National Socialism in Cuba, Shanghai, Tehran, the Dominican Republic, France, and Belgium; assistance to survivors for both rebuilding and emigration after the Holocaust in displaced persons (DP) camps in Allied-occupied Germany, Poland, Hungary, and the Soviet Union; and assistance in Rome and Vienna for Soviet Jewish transmigrants in the 1970s—underscores the global impact of the organization and the hitherto unknown aspects of its history. Our volume is intended as an incitement to further research and a demonstration of how much rich historical material the JDC Archives has to offer; indeed, a second conference held in 2017 and ongoing networks have already produced further contributions on Israel, North Africa, Latin and South America, and Southern Europe. Surely much more significant work will follow on activities in other parts of the world, the complex and sometimes contentious relationships with other international Jewish organizations and movements, and non-Jewish nongovernmental organizations (NGOs) and governmental bodies.[1]

Indeed, despite the sustained transnational humanitarian work of this pioneering NGO over the past century of catastrophe and rebuilding in Jewish history, scholars have published surprisingly little devoted to the history and remarkable accomplishments of JDC. To be sure, thousands of scholars have made use of the valuable resources available in the JDC Archives, many of them newly available in digital format. Given the depth and breadth of JDC's work in over ninety countries around the world, these archives provide one of the most important repositories in the world for the study of modern Jewish history. The archives' rich holdings include the text records of the organization from its beginnings in 1914 to the present; a large photograph collection with over 100,000 photographs of JDC's work over the last century; a library with over 6,000 volumes; and audiovisual recordings, including oral histories of longtime JDC staff and lay leaders. Included in the archives are eyewitness accounts and more analytical field reports, correspondence, ship lists, annual reports, and other publications such as JDC Digests, press releases, and interwar booklets on the organization's program in each country. These records are now accessible online via the JDC Archives website at http://archives.jdc.org, which also includes online exhibits, topic guides for educators, and a names index. The digital database is searchable to the item level.

Yet despite the tremendous wealth of the archives, few scholars have comprehensively explored JDC's role on the ground—in a wide variety of regions and cultures and under dramatically differing circumstances—or critically assessed JDC's practices and impact over the past 100 years. This volume seeks to address those lacunae, not only by addressing the widespread impact of JDC but also by showcasing the richness and depth of the JDC Archives as a resource for examining crucial and understudied aspects of modern Jewish history, including global philanthropy, the interplay between local Jewish communities and the countries in which they live, the interwar and wartime campaigns for rescue and relief across Europe, the postwar reconstruction of ravaged Jewish communities, the role of JDC in Jewish migrations, and more.

Certainly, JDC itself began early on the task of documenting this history by commissioning several works championing its efforts over the past century. In 1924, H. Alsberg was assigned as historian and prepared a *History of JDC*, covering the first ten years of the organization. The Alsberg manuscript (1926) was revised by Isaac Don Levine in 1927 and by Henry Bernstein in 1928. JDC privately published Evelyn Morrissey's *Jewish Workers and Farmers in the Crimea and Ukraine* (New York, 1937) based on her four-week overseas trip to Ukraine and Crimea to observe the activities of the Agro-Joint and the network of educational, economic, and social service institutions organized around farm settlements (this is detailed in the present volume by Mikhail Mitsel). After Morrissey decided to publish this book, JDC received the devastating news of the arrests of Agro-Joint workers in 1937–1938. Indeed, many individuals mentioned in the book were arrested at that time in Stalin's Soviet Union. This probably contributed to a decision not to distribute Morrissey's book broadly once it was published. Joseph C. Hyman, secretary and executive director of JDC, authored the encyclopedic *25 Years of American Aid to Jews Overseas: A Record of the Joint Distribution Committee* (New York, 1939), which was initially published as part of Volume 41 of the *American Jewish Year Book*, published by the Jewish Publication Society and later revised for a new edition.

As this brief overview suggests, works published on JDC's history have tended to fall into four main categories: (1) those commissioned by JDC,

(2) those written by JDC activists, (3) those that focus on JDC's prominent figures (for example, the biographies of Ralph Goldman and Joseph Schwartz), and (4) those that focus on JDC's role in specific geographic areas. In addition, two volumes published in the early 1960s also addressed the work of the Joint more broadly. Historian Herbert Agar wrote *The Saving Remnant: An Account of Jewish Survival* which covered JDC's work during World War I and the interwar years in the Pale of Settlement and Poland and the rise of the Nazi Party in Germany and its impact on Jews.[2] Agar covered the Holocaust years and JDC's reconstruction activities as it helped rebuild Jewish communities in Europe, support the newly founded State of Israel, reach Jews behind the Iron Curtain, and assist Jews in the Muslim world. In addition, American historian Oscar Handlin authored *A Continuing Task: The American Jewish Joint Distribution Committee, 1914–1964* for the fiftieth anniversary of JDC, providing a shorter historical survey and analysis of the organization's humanitarian work and its impact during its first half century.[3]

The first attempt to provide a full account of JDC's work over time was by Holocaust historian Yehuda Bauer. His two volumes, *My Brother's Keeper: A History of the American Jewish Joint Distribution Committee, 1929–1939* and *American Jewry and the Holocaust: The American Jewish Joint Distribution Committee, 1939–1945*, have made major contributions to historical scholarship on the twentieth-century Jewish experience in general and provide a rich and in-depth analysis of JDC's work from 1929 to 1945.[4] Another book by Bauer, *Flight and Rescue: Bricha—The Organized Escape of the Jewish Survivors of Eastern Europe, 1944–1948* covers JDC's role in the rescue efforts bringing Eastern European Jews from the "vast graveyard" of Europe after the Holocaust to DP camps in Allied-occupied Europe and then to Palestine prior to the establishment of the State of Israel.[5] *Out of the Ashes: The Impact of American Jewry on Post-Holocaust European Jewry* also focuses extensively on JDC's role in postwar Europe.[6] Although Bauer's work provided a much-needed overview of the significant contributions of JDC over time, the broad scope of these works left open many questions about JDC's activities in specific geographic areas and regarding its comparative impact over time and place.

Following Bauer's sweeping account, more recent books by JDC employees and others have sought to fill in some of these gaps.[7] Several volumes published in recent decades focus on the organization's work in one specific place or on a more specific topic, including volumes on JDC's work in the Soviet Union and the Dominican Republic as well as newer biographies of key figures in the history of the Joint.[8] This current volume seeks to build on these recent scholarly interventions that have examined JDC in context and to begin the work of analyzing in greater detail its strengths and weaknesses, the opportunities that its leadership seized and others that it missed, the multiple constraints JDC operatives faced, and the tremendous efforts to which they went to protect and bolster Jewish life across the globe. By providing in-depth analyses of JDC's efforts across time and space, we seek not only to fill in historiographical gaps but also to provide new insight into Jewish communities and the countries in which they lived throughout the twentieth century.

JDC AS A PRISM FOR STUDYING MODERN JEWISH HISTORY

As the essays in this book demonstrate, JDC and its archives offer a critical tool for understanding the last 100 years of Jewish history. Since its establishment in 1914, when Henry Morgenthau Sr. (US ambassador to the Ottoman Empire) cabled his friend Jacob Schiff in New York asking him to raise funds for the Jews of Palestine, who had been cut off from support by the outbreak of war, JDC has been involved, in one way or another, in nearly every major world event over the last 100 years wherever Jewish communities in need could be found. As a result, a study of JDC activities provides insight into not only its myriad efforts to sustain Jewish life across the globe but also twentieth-century Jewish history more broadly, including topics as diverse as the Jewish response to crisis and catastrophe, the growing role of American Jews on the world stage, the ways in which Jews interpreted the bonds of solidarity and peoplehood, and the functioning of Jewish communities in diverse political and social contexts. Analysis of the work of JDC thus illuminates much about the dynamic relationships between Jewish communities and the societies within which they lived and continually interacted as well as the transnational global arena in which Jews moved and JDC operated.

JDC's activities since 1914 also provide a lens onto Jewish responses to some of the most important historical events of the twentieth century, including World War I; the aftermath of the Russian Revolution and Civil War; the dissolution of the Austro-Hungarian and Ottoman Empires; the creation of independent republics in interwar Europe; the development of the Yishuv in Palestine under the British Mandate; the treatment of the Jewish minority in the USSR; the persecution of Jews in Nazi Germany; the outbreak of World War II; aid to Jews in German-occupied Europe; the flight of Jewish refugees in Europe, Asia, the Middle East, Africa, and the Americas; the postwar plight of ravaged European Jewish communities and the Jewish DPs; the rebuilding of Jewish communities in Europe following World War II; Jewish communities living in North Africa and other Muslim countries; the establishment of the State of Israel and mass migration to the new state; the persecution and migration of Jews from the USSR; the fall of communism in Eastern Europe; the war in Yugoslavia (and the siege of Sarajevo); and continuing relief work during contemporary crises throughout the world from Ukraine to the Middle East.

Indeed, the twentieth century has witnessed some of the most dramatic Jewish population shifts in history, greater than the expulsion from Spain and as momentous as the destruction of the Second Temple in Jerusalem and the beginning of the "Jewish exile" in the first century CE. In the face of this disruption and as the essays in this volume document, JDC has played a pivotal role in assisting displaced Jews, aiding in migration, offering assistance to refugees, and providing support for the rebuilding of dislocated communities. Even before the European Jewish center was destroyed, mass migration westward from Eastern Europe, across Europe and reaching the Americas, began to alter the Jewish map significantly. In the aftermath of the Holocaust and with the near annihilation of European Jewry, the creation of the State of Israel led to mass migration (and expulsions) of centuries-old Jewish communities from the Middle East, North Africa, and Eastern Europe. In the last decades of the twentieth century, many of the remaining Jewish communities of the former Soviet Union relocated to Israel and North America. Although this volume provides little direct analysis of Jewish settlement in Israel given its major focus on the tensions between migration and relief and reconstruction "at home" in Europe or in far-flung refugee destinations, as well as tensions between JDC's central base in the United States and its work on the ground in vastly diverse Jewish communities, JDC projects in Israel are certainly deserving of their own separate analysis.[9] The essays in this volume nevertheless trace the shifting, sometimes conflict-ridden, relationship of JDC to settlement in Palestine and Zionist movements, just as with other strands of the global Jewish community—for example, Sephardic communities or Orthodoxy—especially in the pieces by Crago-Schneider and Patt on the DP camps, Grossmann on Iran, Glaser on Cuba and Shanghai, and Veksler on JDC support for refugees from the Soviet Union who chose not to emigrate to Israel in the 1970s.

By examining JDC's successes and failures in the context of these dramatically shifting political situations, from revolution through war and into the post–World War II period, we begin to see JDC as a transnational and yet essentially American institution trying to negotiate with foreign powers as well as Jewish organizations and multiple Jewish constituencies to provide as much useful and practical aid as possible in various crisis situations. Indeed, in the midst of the radical dislocations and transformation of Jewish tradition, Jewish practice, technological change, and secularization, JDC has continued to embody a dedication to *klal yisrael* (Jewish peoplehood) that is rooted in a tradition of *tzedakah* (charity) and modern transnational Jewish philanthropy. At the same time, an examination of twentieth-century Jewish history through the lens of JDC allows for a study of American Jewish practices of social work, fundraising, humanitarian assistance, and philanthropy and the interaction of these practices with diverse social, political, and cultural contexts.[10] For example, the first essay by Rakefet Zalashik on JDC support for Jewish communities in Eastern Europe ravaged by World War I and its aftermath of revolution, civil wars, and antisemitic persecution illustrates the young organization's sometimes dueling commitment to American "progressive" ideals of science, expertise (especially in regard to health and hygiene), and efficiency (especially in regard to professionalized organization and fundraising) on one hand and its firm belief, on the other hand, in the importance of local self-help and eventual self-sufficiency rather than traditional "charity." The organization's continual—often remarkably deft, sometimes characterized by missteps and inefficiencies—negotiation of those principles as it dealt with local conditions and partners forms a central theme of this volume and is visible in every chapter.

The essays in this volume therefore provide insight into how JDC's particular brand of apolitical or nonpartisan local engagement shaped twentieth-century Jewish life. Throughout its history, JDC's operating principles included retaining an apolitical stance and always trying to work via local Jewish communities, thereby strengthening local communities' ability to care for their own. In many ways, the history of JDC demonstrates how deeply its commitment to a putative "apolitical" stance shaped its ability to act in multiple national and political contexts—indeed, to be a political player. Research within the JDC Archives illustrates the advantages and limitations of a resolutely nonpolitical stance within extraordinarily complicated and urgent political situations and the moments when, despite this firm commitment, JDC felt it necessary to act in ways that were perceived as political. Examples of such tensions can be found in Bemporad's description of how JDC relief work in Minsk after the Bolshevik Revolution paradoxically bolstered both antireligious Communist institutions and the niches within which Jewish life and culture could survive. Sommer Schneider's and Frojimovics's pieces interestingly make similar points about the impact of JDC assistance in post–World War II Communist Poland and Hungary. Such interventions document the ways in which JDC's nonsectarian approach to Jewish politics provides a crucial lens into the Jewish encounter with Zionism, socialism, communism, fascism, and liberal democracy, often allowing a distinctively American Jewish approach to intercommunal political struggle to be transplanted to other contexts.

Methodologically, JDC's archival resources, which record the encounter between JDC and Jewish communities around the world, open up new pathways for understanding twentieth-century Jewish history. On the microlevel, these records document JDC's often seismic impact on individuals and communities large and small. On a global level, these records demonstrate how a uniquely transnational American Jewish organization (originally founded in 1914 by the leaders of an American Jewish community very much in transition itself) perceived its evolving responsibilities to Jews, regardless of political affiliation, religious denomination, or geographic location. Indeed, JDC operated on every continent—from Australia, where the relationship between the local welfare official Oscar Brand and JDC's Charles Jordan is analyzed by Suzanne Rutland—to wartime Tehran, where JDC had to negotiate with representatives of all the Allied forces, the Polish Government in Exile, local Iranian authorities, the Jewish Agency and other Zionist groups, and international aid organizations to coordinate a complex, multinational relief operation intended to assist refugee Polish Jews in the Soviet Union, as documented by Atina Grossmann. The sources also reveal that traditional models of center and periphery often need to be recalibrated; the work of JDC empowered local Jewish communities to tend to their own needs, sometimes employing American models of social work, health care, education, and the like but often adapting JDC practices to suit the local context through local relief workers.

Such research complicates the analysis of Jewish power to effect change, suggesting that even in places with limited Jewish political power, Jewish groups managed to wield "soft power," developing effective mechanisms to provide for Jews in need under extreme conditions. The volume traces remarkable continuities in such challenges, such as the ironies of supporting unpalatable Communist regimes—for example, in both postrevolutionary Minsk and post–World War II Poland and Hungary—in order to support Jewish life or the ways that JDC managed to circumvent Soviet demands for strict nonsectarianism and aid not specifically targeting Jews. JDC had to choose when and how to cooperate with local authorities and local Jewish organizations closely tied to governments or, for that matter, particular Jewish movements such as Zionism, socialism, Orthodoxy, or the more explicitly political World Jewish Congress, which at times competed for funds, resources, connections, and allegiances.

An examination of modern Jewish history through the lens of JDC work also allows us to understand the complexities of the Jewish place in the international political order. Thus, the chapters by Jaclyn Granick and Mikhail Mitsel that examine the work of JDC in the USSR or the role of JDC in providing assistance to stateless Jewish refugees during and after

World War II, as discussed by Avinoam Patt and Kierra Crago-Schneider, analyze how Jews have navigated the shifting boundaries of nation-states, the responsibilities of citizenship, and the duties of mutual assistance and Jewish peoplehood. Conversely, such research sheds light on the limits of Jewish political influence and Jewish dependence on government entities. The chapters on JDC work in the Dominican Republic, Shanghai, Tehran, and postwar Germany ask the following questions: How much can a non-partisan, apolitical, but avowedly Jewish organization do to effect change in the midst of, or in the immediate aftermath of, war? What impact did it have on work with refugees or in postconflict rebuilding? And how much does the prior experience of an organization affect the development of new and more effective strategies in new situations? How does a Jewish organization adapt its roles to changing situations? What methods were used by JDC in different circumstances to gain access to and assist Jewish communities in need? Who were the major JDC leaders and exceptional individuals who played key roles in multiple capacities and multiple places over a long period of time in the mission of rescue, relief, reconstruction, and renewal?

MODES OF OPERATION

If, as noted, the essays in this volume tell us a great deal about Jewish history in the twentieth century, they also shed significant light on JDC as an organization. Indeed, by comparing JDC operations across time and space, we begin to discern a number of broader patterns in its modes of operation that are less visible when focusing only on the local. In particular, new research on JDC points to the way the institution's core principles were operationalized on the ground in contexts where those principles could not always fully function due to a variety of pressures stemming from local governmental structures; Jewish communal organization (or lack thereof); availability of resources; and complex geopolitical contexts, including the exigencies of war and genocide. In policy and ethos, then, JDC was committed to a number of practices—forged from the American cultural, political, and social environment in which it took shape—which, while always orienting the organization's practices, also had to be flexible in light of the circumstances in which JDC workers found themselves.

JDC's philosophical commitments could certainly clash with local realities in the political arena. As noted previously, throughout its history, JDC's operating principles included retaining an apolitical stance with regard to the broader environment and with regard to Jewish intercommunal politics on the ground. Such an approach was forged out of the longer history of modern Jewish philanthropy, which—as Derek Penslar has convincingly documented—became a cornerstone of collective Jewish identity at the end of the eighteenth century as Jewish leaders began to rationalize the care of the Jewish poor through the centralization of philanthropic funds and the establishment of criteria for their receipt.[11] In the United States, such practices took on an even more highly centralized form in the late nineteenth century, when philanthropy emerged as a useful lever in the efforts to unite the increasingly diverse and divided Jewish community. Indeed, the very founding of the Joint Distribution Committee of American Funds for the Relief of Jewish War Sufferers in 1914 was a coming together of three diverse segments of the Jewish community—the German Jewish American Jewish Relief Committee, established by the American Jewish Committee; the Central Committee for the Relief of Jews established by the Union of Orthodox Congregations of America; and the labor socialist Jewish People's Relief Committee—for a common purpose: to address the crisis in Jewish communities overseas in Europe and Palestine. Following World War II, when an unprecedented economic boom brought American Jewish philanthropy into a new era, JDC had significant economic leverage that it used to promote its inclusive and apolitical approach in all places where it engaged in humanitarian interventions. Indeed, to many JDC employees, the divisions and strife that characterized postwar Jewish life in Europe seemed unnecessarily debilitating given the weakened state of the populations there because it led to the proliferation of social service agencies all competing with one another for the limited available resources. JDC thus used its economic and funding resources to encourage diverse and divided Jewish populations into conversation with each other and to create greater communal cohesion.

Research within the JDC Archives, however, illustrates the contradictions that JDC continually confronted in its wide-ranging and often daring humanitarian work. First, the broader context and the paramount mandate to provide aid for beleaguered Jews often forced JDC to work with politically compromised regimes and thereby tolerate certain political ideologies that would otherwise be objectionable in order to first and foremost further the cause of relief. As Elissa Bemporad makes clear in her essay on JDC efforts in interwar Minsk, for example, JDC cooperation with local officials meant accepting the language of the new regime and hence promoting the Bolshevization of Jewish life. The tremendous financial clout embedded in JDC relief efforts meant that the organization could be useful to politically dubious regimes. In the Dominican Republic, JDC was able, as Marion Kaplan demonstrates, to take advantage of the regime's racist purge of Haitians and desire for white settlement to negotiate a haven for some Jewish refugees from Germany and Austria escaping Nazism. In postwar Poland, as Anna Sommer Schneider documents, the Communist authorities used JDC humanitarian assistance to gain credibility in the Western world and to legitimize their power. The key paradox of this situation is, of course, self-evident: Apolitical approaches did not necessarily lead to apolitical outcomes. Indeed, whatever JDC's commitment to apoliticism, it was forced to make decisions that at times clashed with its stated commitments.

Second, local Jewish community leaders did not always accept JDC's nonsectarian and apolitical vision.[12] As Hobson Faure and Vanden Daelen make clear in their chapter on JDC activities in post–World War II France and Belgium, JDC could not help but react to internecine Jewish struggles on the ground—a reality that could give voice to those touting one ideology over another. Similarly, according to Patt and Crago-Schneider, in the DP camps in Germany after World War II, JDC officials supported Zionist groups over their rivals. Indeed, despite its avowed apoliticism, JDC was not, in fact, neutral in all matters. As Inga Veksler shows, for example, JDC staff worked closely with the Jewish Agency to encourage Soviet Jewish émigrés to go to Israel even when the latter hoped to migrate to the United States. In Iran during World War II, however, JDC, which was in fact working closely, if not always easily, with the Jewish Agency, felt it necessary to downplay that connection. JDC's stated position thus proved to be fluid at times as staff assessed the realities on the ground and came to terms with their own hopes and dreams for the Jewish future. Over time and with particular urgency during wartime crises, JDC relief efforts required careful negotiation with national governments, nongovernmental aid organizations, local authorities, and Jewish communities. JDC also had to balance rivalries within the international Jewish world and within local Jewish communities, especially challenges from Zionists and the Orthodox. Invariably, JDC had to balance its multifaceted roles as an American organization, an organ of transnational Jewry, and an apolitical nonsectarian relief organization, a tricky stance that could be challenging for JDC clients and donors but was required—and certainly perceived as absolutely necessary by the organization itself—for the success of its relief activities and especially for the all-important task of transmitting funds.

JDC's modus operandi has been to work with and through local Jewish communities in response to local needs. Its representatives focus on building relationships with all segments and groups within the local community, taking their advice and counsel on matters of approach. To be effective, JDC representatives needed to be willing to see the local point of view. Whatever JDC's own preferences, however, its employees have often found themselves compromising with local Jewish populations on a wide variety of issues. A focus on modes of funding distribution helps make the point. In principle, JDC staff were committed to the ideal that local communities should be empowered to care for their own while insisting that JDC control the distribution of its allocated resources. This policy gave JDC a framework for transitioning support to local Jewish communities while ensuring that philanthropy was delivered efficiently and without redundancy to as many who needed support as possible—a tenet of American philanthropy writ large that was a basic element of JDC philosophy and practice. This policy also strove to empower local communities to assess needs, allocate funds within their community, and initiate new programs. This approach, however, often led to struggles between JDC and the recipients of its support. Indeed, as Patt and Crago-Schneider demonstrate in their study of post–World War II DP camps, JDC control of funding and supplies could be challenged in the face of empowered aid recipients willing to test JDC at every turn. In the case of these survivors—and many other refugees who came under JDC care—self-reliance forged in war fostered distrust of agencies that, in the view of those who had survived so much loss and devastation, arrived on the scene with too little, too late. In other cases, local Jewish communities, such as in Shanghai, Tehran, or Cuba, were themselves too small or stressed to provide anywhere near the level of support that JDC could. Although JDC wished to establish national Jewish communal umbrella organizations, the local communities did not always see things this way, as in the case of postwar Belgium described by Laura Hobson Faure and Veerle Vanden Daelen. Moreover, other groups representing Jewish constituencies (such as Zionists or the Orthodox) often laid claim to JDC funding while resisting control, and at times JDC's desire to operate discreetly meant that beneficiaries could not fully recognize the organization's actual commitment or indeed might resent its apparent lack of support. JDC's preference for working behind the scenes and providing funds for initiatives that were actually carried out by other groups, whether domestic or international (such as the Jewish Agency or other relief agencies), indeed obscured the organization's considerable involvement in terms of both finances and policy—circumstances that this volume aims to reveal and illuminate.

Despite criticisms from some of those who came under JDC care, numerous others attested to the practical, efficient, and committed efforts of its employees to ensure the survival of Jewish communities throughout the world. Indeed, JDC's organizational ethos meant that in context after context, key Joint officials moved mountains to help their coreligionists in need. Whether in Shanghai, Cuba, Palestine, Iran, Poland, the Soviet Union, or countless other places, figures such as Charles Jordan, Joseph Schwartz, Laura Margolis, Joseph Rosen, Boris Bogen, Harry Viteles, Charles Passman, James Rosenberg, Sam Haber, Akiva Kohane, and Ralph Goldman—to name but some of the key JDC staff who committed their lives to this work—gave of themselves and sacrificed personal and familial comfort and stability to serve Jews in need. As is clear in several essays in this volume, the impact of these larger-than-life individuals cannot be overstated. Attentive readers will note the recurrence—at different times and in different areas of the globe—of these relief officials (and surely others) who served JDC as professionals over decades. Zhava Litvac Glaser describes the role of Laura Margolis in Cuba and Shanghai, and the work of Charles Jordan in Australia is analyzed by Suzanne Rutland. JDC's efforts stood and fell on the tireless commitment of those willing to give themselves completely to sustaining Jewish life, often at the expense of personal or family life. Many have said that the long-term commitment over decades of a very talented and dedicated cadre of JDC professionals has been one of the organization's most important assets. Their life stories deserve much more attention, especially those of the predominantly female caseworkers who were so critical to the on-the-ground humanitarian aid and policy development provided by JDC.

JDC is a unique institution. While it continues to function as an active relief organization, it has developed a major research archive based on the organization's historic collections. This dual commitment is reflected in the editorial cooperation that has made this volume possible, a cooperation among three historians who have made extensive use of the JDC Archives for their work in Jewish and Holocaust history and the director of the archives. Although this volume seeks to address new areas of research on the past century of JDC work around the world, the organization's extensive activity and the availability of archival material (much of it newly digitized) mean that there is much additional research to be done. Among the areas not covered in the present volume but deserving of further research and writing include JDC work in North Africa, Latin America (other than Sosúa), Ethiopia, and Israel and further research on the JDC headquarters in New York itself. We hope to see further research develop on the more contemporary periods of JDC's work from the 1960s onward in Europe and Israel, JDC's nonsectarian work, and its International Development Program. Scholarly study and analysis covering more recent decades not covered in this present volume could reflect on how, following glasnost, JDC sought to help rebuild Jewish community life, foster Jewish identity, and reconnect local Jews in Eastern Europe and the former Soviet Union with the global Jewish world. This analysis could also focus on JDC's work in Israel as the country absorbed vulnerable immigrant groups from Ethiopia, the former Soviet Union, Yemen, and Syria;

JDC's continuing efforts to assist the State of Israel to address social challenges such as the needs of the elderly and children at risk and find employment solutions for the ultra-Orthodox and Israeli Arabs; and the organization's work in dwindling and sometimes vulnerable Jewish communities in North Africa, Asia, and some parts of Europe. Such research could consider how JDC draws on its historical mission, methods, and relationships as it adapts to changing situations around the world. This volume only gestures at the critical role played by women as social workers, particularly in Glaser's chapter on Laura Margolis, and how that reflected both the development of the field (social work) and the particular roles that Jewish women, especially unmarried Jewish women, were carving out for themselves in Jewish and national (especially American) societies.

This volume also points to new ways of thinking about transnational Jewish history by mapping twentieth-century American Jewish history onto global Jewish history. At the very least, it is clear that JDC's impact on the strengthening of Jewish communities around the world cannot be underestimated. The impact, however, was more than structural. By building personal relationships among dedicated professionals, JDC staff were often able to bridge complex local political divisions in ways that brought together the various segments of Jewish communities: Jewish Socialists, Communists, and Zionists, the secular and the religious, all in the service of community. The biographies of these dedicated individuals have yet to be written, but we hope that scholars will take up the charge to examine the work and adventurous lives of Laura Margolis, David Guzik, and Charles Jordan, just to name a few. Such scholarship could address the nature of the interactions between JDC and other Jewish organizations as well as those between JDC and other non-Jewish relief groups and the effects of change over time and place, given that many of these remarkable individuals served JDC over decades in a wide variety of postings. An organizational history that examines the work of key agents would shed light on the interactions between Jews and non-Jews in varied settings while emphasizing the skills of highly cosmopolitan Jewish workers, fluent in multiple languages and able to adapt to varied cultural and political settings.

What can we learn about modern Jewish history from their examples? As numerous contributions demonstrate, JDC officials attempting to provide relief and resettlement assistance, especially to refugees in wartime and postwar crises, had to cope with the dual problem of societal and government antisemitism and xenophobia mixed with anxieties on the part of established Jewish communities about the arrival of possibly "asocial" and "foreign" (even if Jewish) newcomers. At the same time, when JDC operated in locales such as Shanghai, Tehran, the Dominican Republic, or Cuba, the organization's representatives had to mediate encounters between a "non-Western" locale with a small or culturally different local Jewish population on one hand and European refugees on the other hand, who—although desperate, stateless, and mostly impoverished—were nonetheless still privileged Europeans, albeit racially persecuted and, in the context of World War II, subjected to genocide.

As with any history of a venerable institution, we have aspired to provide rigorous critical analysis that also does justice to JDC's remarkable accomplishments and international reach during its past 100 years of humanitarian activism. This project reflects a collaboration between the JDC Archives and the scholarly community. As this volume's foreword, authored by the director of the JDC Global Archives, explains, the JDC Archives served as a convener of the conference that made this volume possible, bringing together a group of scholars who have used the JDC Archives to conduct research on diverse aspects of the organization's history over the last 100 years.

In marking the centennial of JDC, we present new work that highlights how much can be learned about modern Jewish history through the lens of JDC and the archives that have preserved its history—and just how much remains to be uncovered, especially beyond the dramatic events of the 1920–1950 period with World War II and the Holocaust at its center on which we have focused in this volume.

Notes

1. For one excellent review of the development of refugee relief organizations in the twentieth century, see Peter Gatrell, *The Making of the Modern Refugee*

(New York: Oxford University Press, 2013); for a review of migration in Eastern Europe, see Peter Gatrell, *A Whole Empire Walking: Refugees in Russia during World War I* (Bloomington: Indiana University Press, 2005).

2. Herbert Agar, *The Saving Remnant: An Account of Jewish Survival* (New York: Viking Press, 1960).

3. Oscar Handlin, *A Continuing Task: The American Jewish Joint Distribution Committee, 1914–1964* (New York: Random House, 1964).

4. Yehuda Bauer, *My Brother's Keeper: A History of the American Jewish Joint Distribution Committee, 1929–1939* (Philadelphia: Jewish Publication Society of America, 1974); Bauer, *American Jewry and the Holocaust: The American Jewish Joint Distribution Committee, 1939–1945* (Detroit: Wayne State University Press, 1981).

5. Yehuda Bauer, *Flight and Rescue: Bricha—The Organized Escape of the Jewish Survivors of Eastern Europe, 1944–1948* (New York: Random House, 1970).

6. Yehuda Bauer, *Out of the Ashes: The Impact of American Jewry on Post-Holocaust European Jewry* (Oxford: Pergamon Press, 1989).

7. Tom Shachtman's *I Seek My Brethren: Ralph Goldman and "the Joint"* (New York: Newmarket Press, 2001), for example, provides an account of Goldman's work as the executive vice president of JDC in the 1970s and 1980s and later as the honorary executive vice president until he passed away in 2015. Other books by JDC staff include Stanley Abramovitch, *From Survival to Revival: A Memoir of Six Decades in a Changing Jewish World* (Jerusalem: Gefen Publishing House, 2008) and Stanley Abramovitch, *Lighting Up the Soul: Stories from a Changing Jewish World* (Jerusalem: Penina Press, 2011). Abramovitch's career with JDC began in the displaced persons camps in Germany and extended over sixty years. This included serving as the country director for Iran, the Jewish education director of Europe and North Africa, the director of the Yeshivot Program in Israel, and the country director in the Muslim Republics of the former Soviet Union.

8. These include Michael Beizer, *Relief in Time of Need: Russian Jewry and the Joint, 1914–24* (Bloomington, IN: Slavica, 2015); Mikhael Mitsel, *"The Final Chapter": Agro-Joint in the Years of the Great Terror* (Kiev: Center for Jewish History and Culture, 2012); Marion Kaplan, *Dominican Haven: The Jewish Refugee Resettlement in Sosua, 1940–1945*

(New York: Museum of Jewish Heritage, 2008); Mark I. Rosen, *Mission, Meaning, and Money: How the Joint Distribution Committee Became a Fundraising Innovator* (Bloomington, IN: Universe, 2010). Of special note is a new scholarly biography by Tuvia Friling about Dr. Joseph J. Schwartz, the AJDC vice chairman from 1948 to 1974 who headed the JDC overseas headquarters in Lisbon and then Paris in the 1940s, which will soon be published in Hebrew and translated into English.

9. For research on JDC and MALBEN, see Pnina Romem, *MALBEN: Mosadot Letipul Beolim Nichshalim* [MALBEN: Institutions for the Treatment of Aged, Sick, and Handicapped Immigrants] (Zikhron Ya'akov, Israel: Itai Bahur, 2012). Unfortunately, a planned chapter on JDC work in Israel for this volume did not materialize.

10. Jaclyn Granick, *International Jewish Humanitarianism in the Age of the Great War* (monograph forthcoming), Introduction. This draws on Jaclyn Granick, "Humanitarian Responses to Jewish Suffering Abroad by American Jewish Organizations, 1914–1929" (PhD diss., The Graduate Institute of International and Development Studies, 2015). Granick critically situates JDC within the emerging historical literature on humanitarianism in her work on JDC in the Great War era.

11. Derek Penslar, *Shylock's Children: Economics and Jewish Identity in Modern Europe* (Berkeley: University of California Press, 2001), 90–123. For the impact of such efforts on key Jewish philanthropists, see Abigail Green, *Moses Montefiore: Jewish Liberator, Imperial Hero* (Cambridge, MA: Harvard University Press, 2010) and Matthew Mark Silver, *Louis Marshall and the Rise of Jewish Ethnicity in America* (Syracuse, NY: Syracuse University Press, 2013).

12. Rebecca Erbelding, *Rescue Board: The Untold Story of America's Efforts to Save the Jews of Europe* (New York: Doubleday, 2017) reveals how closely JDC worked with (and provided the majority of the funding for) the War Refugee Board after its establishment in January 1944; Richard Breitman, Barbara McDonald Stewart, and Severin Hochberg, eds., *Refugees and Rescue: The Diaries of James G. McDonald, 1935–1945* (Bloomington: Indiana University Press, 2009) demonstrates JDC involvement with US government officials throughout the period.

Medical Welfare in Interwar Europe

The Collaboration between JDC and OZE-TOZ Organizations

Rakefet Zalashik

Introduction

In the aftermath of World War I, relief organizations had a crucial role to play. The devastating effects of the events of 1914–1918 and then the Russian Civil War affected all aspects of human life, from economy to health. Western countries feared that epidemics and plagues would move from east to west, and it was especially Poland that functioned as a "cordon sanitaire."[1] Postwar Eastern Europe became the focus of rescue, relief, and reconstruction as humanitarian agencies from Western Europe and especially the United States—the latter anchored in the American Progressive Movement—strove to introduce programs and campaigns in medicine and public health. This activity had political, cultural, and humanitarian aspects.[2] American philanthropic organizations wished to transfer the "American way" to the European context through science, project management, and the rebuilding of communities.[3]

The Joint Distribution Committee (JDC) was one of the central and most influential American organizations that helped Jews in Eastern Europe during and immediately after World War I. Joining other organizations, including the Red Cross, the Young Men's Christian Association (YMCA), and the Young Women's Christian Association (YWCA), to alleviate famine and epidemics,

JDC allocated millions of dollars for this task.[4] This process involved an exchange between JDC as a "giver" and the local recipients and was influenced by the self-perception of each side, the local conditions of Jewish communities in various countries in Eastern Europe, and the political context of Jews as a minority as well as their relationships to the local national government.[5] This chapter examines the aid and collaboration between JDC and Obshchestvo Zdravookhraneniia Evreev (OZE), a Jewish medical organization, in the interwar period as a case study of Jewish transnational philanthropy and the dynamic between "givers" and "recipients" and between "center" and "periphery."

OZE, the Society for the Protection of the Health of the Jewish Population, was established on October 28, 1912, in St. Petersburg by Jewish physicians and some prominent members of the Jewish community. The association was the outcome of the attempt to find solutions to the dire physical state of Jews in Russia, many of whom suffered from poverty and poor hygienic conditions as a result of deprivation and persecution.[6] OZE's activity was essentially different from past Jewish medical and charitable aid. Believing that the source of some "Jewish diseases" was the people's ignorance and bad hygienic practices, the association strove to educate and even cure the Jewish population within the framework of social and preventive medicine.[7] OZE was modeled on the Russian *zemstvo* (local self-government) system, which was committed to making modern medical care available and desirable, abolishing the direct physician's fees, and giving public hygiene and preventive medicine a similar weight to that of medical treatment.[8] OZE envisioned assuming responsibility for the health system for the Jewish population in Russia and adopting similar methods.

The outbreak of World War I and the collapse of the Russian Empire increased the number of Jewish refugees exponentially, most of whom faced a myriad of problems. The impact on OZE was dramatic: First, OZE accelerated its activities and became a crucial agent on both the local and national levels. It expanded its activity, evolving from its primary focus of providing social and preventive medicine to Russian Jews to a transnational focus on Jews of Poland and Ukraine.[9] Second, OZE went from being a small, self-sufficient organization with a local activity and self-sustaining mechanism to, in 1916, being largely dependent on JDC's support.

Both organizations—JDC and OZE—operated with the understanding that an improvement of the situation for Jews in Russia also had to include public health and social determinants of health. OZE provided the local base for these activities while JDC provided much of the funding. Whereas OZE hoped to change the health situation among the Jews in order to enhance their political situation as a discriminated minority, JDC acted as an external philanthropic organization, providing funding and technical assistance for local initiatives that would eventually sustain themselves by means of local resources.

THE FIRST PERIOD IN RUSSIA: INITIAL CONTACT

During World War I, JDC directed significant emergency funds and rescue activities toward the Jews in Russia. During the war and in its immediate aftermath, JDC's aid focused on basic needs such as shelter, food, and hygiene. Within short order, however, it began to initiate a new phase of longer-term rehabilitation and reconstruction in the communities in Russia and Ukraine.[10] In this phase, JDC encouraged the formation of self-help agencies that would take over the work it had initiated between 1914 and 1921. One of these organizations was OZE, which enjoyed during the war the same privileges of the general Red Cross, receiving supplies from the Russian Army. As a result, OZE was able to send rescue teams to open kitchens, hospitals, and orphanages and to distribute soap to secure the physical existence of hundreds of thousands of war refugees.[11] The urgency of OZE's activities during the war led to its expansion: Within less than five years of existence, OZE grew from a small group of forty-five employees to, by the end of 1917, a large organization with 600 permanent workers and 15,000 members. It was active in 107 towns and cities, and its facilities included 27 children's homes, 5 children's kitchens, 50 soup kitchens, 60 ambulatory stations, and 6 hospitals.[12] Thus, when JDC initially planned to liquidate its activities in Russia after the end of World War I, it saw OZE as a reliable and professional organization in the field of medicine to work on its behalf.

However, the Bolshevik Regime was not interested in the activity of independent minorities and nationally defined organizations, instead wishing that these organizations would be controlled by the state. The collaboration between the Bolsheviks and JDC representatives took a quantum leap because of the inability of the Soviet health-care system and the Jewish relief organizations to adequately respond to the pogroms in Ukraine and Belorussia from 1918 until 1921.[13] OZE, like other Jewish relief organizations, hoped that JDC would help OZE establish a legal status vis-à-vis the Russian authorities. As a result, Evobshchestkom (or, in Yiddish, *Yidgezkom*), the Jewish Social Committee for Relief among the Victims of Pogroms and Counterrevolution, was founded in the autumn of 1920 to connect the Bolshevik authorities, JDC, and Jewish relief organizations such as OZE. Evobshchestkom was dissolved in 1924.

OZE failed to obtain official recognition and in 1921, after nine years of activity, the Russian government banned OZE, making it difficult for the organization to continue its medical activities in the country.[14] After OZE was liquidated in Russia, it could continue its activities informally within the activity of JDC as an international relief organization. Two district offices of OZE remained in the former Russian territory, in Vilna and Bialystok, which became Poland territories in 1921. Later, another office was revived in Lithuania. By the autumn of 1922, another OZE office managed to partly reestablish its activities through the Nansen Mission and the Jewish Help Conference.[15]

At this point, the involvement of JDC and especially its representative, Boris Bogen, as well as its financial support, became even more crucial in OZE's attempt to be legalized by the Soviet authorities. From 1923 onward, OZE acted through the Soviet-based offices of the JDC-OZE Committee, supervised by the Soviet health authority (Narkomzdrav). For this, JDC and OZE signed a collaboration agreement valid for two years until 1925, according to which JDC was to allocate funds for OZE's activities in Russia.

Another opportunity for OZE was the famine of 1921–1922 in the southern area of Ukraine, which also brought epidemics. At this point, the nationalized Jewish health-care facilities were dysfunctional because of their lack of money. The Bolsheviks' solution was to lease the facilities to the Jewish communities and let them operate these with private funding. OZE then tried to reassert its control over its former facilities with the help of JDC, with partial success.[16]

Despite great efforts, the reestablishment of OZE in Russia with the support and assistance of local JDC offices had only very limited success. The Russian authorities were not willing to delegate relief to OZE and other Jewish organizations, and JDC representatives were not fully convinced that such intermediaries were necessary.[17]

In reality, the main operations of OZE and its sister organization, Towarzystwo Ochrony Zdrowia Ludności Żydowskiej (TOZ), took place outside of Russia. In March 1922, OZE moved its main offices to Berlin, which became the headquarters of the organization, and established the Oeuvre de Secours aux Enfants (OSE) World Union in 1923. In 1922, JDC and OZE agreed that in Berlin OSE, through its former workers in St. Petersburg, Moscow, Kiev, and Odessa, would carry out medical work and children's relief to combat epidemics and take care of Jewish children.[18] JDC allocated a generous budget for this work—almost $2 million in today's value—as a one-time expense and a budget for the next six months: organizing and maintaining twenty clinics ($32,000), ten hospitals with thirty beds each ($18,000), and stations for children ($63,000). During these years, OZE engaged in diverse sociomedical activities and became an important player in Jewish public health, focusing primarily on children's health and welfare.[19] It conducted broad educational campaigns, delivering lectures in community centers and schools; publishing articles in Jewish journals, professional medical periodicals, and books; and publishing a wide array of propaganda posters and flyers.[20]

The Expansion to Poland: The Collaboration between TOZ and JDC as a Case Study

In 1921, a sister organization of OZE was established in Poland under the name TOZ, the Society for Safeguarding the Health of the Jewish Population.[21] The organization had been active earlier in Vilna[22]; however, its Polish branch was a direct outgrowth of a previous collaboration that had already begun in 1920 between JDC and local Jewish Polish activists.[23]

In March 1920, JDC organized a medical commission, headed by Dr. Harry Plotz, that was sent to Eastern Europe to determine public health needs and recommend activities. The main tasks of the health program were the construction and repair of sanitary bathhouses, the reopening and refurbishing of hospitals and dispensaries, the organization of feeding stations, the vaccination of children against smallpox, and the conducting of campaigns against epidemics.[24] Plotz, who was then a young Jewish physician at the beginning of his career (he later became an infectious disease expert specializing in typhus), recommended that JDC become deeply involved in an anti-typhus campaign within Jewish communities, as the disease was prevalent all over Poland and was being used as a tool for antisemitic propaganda and violence against Jews.[25] Plotz planned to bring to Poland fifteen young, energetic physicians from the United States to organize the local medical framework among the Polish Jewish communities. He estimated the need for a $2 million budget for one year for medical treatment and the need for a public health campaign throughout the country—although in the end only half a million dollars was collected.

Plotz tried to initiate a massive public health campaign in the Warsaw area in collaboration with local Jewish physicians and prominent citizens. A meeting with the Polish health minister and JDC took place in November 1920, where it was agreed that JDC would initiate a campaign in Poland against typhus fever. The delegation, sponsored mainly by JDC, distributed literature in cooperation with the Polish government, renovated and built baths, and distributed soaps to the general public—Jews and gentiles alike. In addition, a movie was made that explained to the local population how typhus is transmitted and how it could be avoided.

The JDC campaign against typhus created the possibility for cooperation with local medical forces—TOZ among them. The partnership with local agencies such as TOZ was not only due to the need for manpower that could ensure the locals' cooperation; it was also reinforced by certain JDC medical representatives who thought that patients should be sent to local medical professionals rather than American physicians.[26] Partnering with locals also served JDC's wider goal, as Plotz articulated in the opening speech at a conference in Lemberg: "The relief work of the JDC is taking a new aspect; until now all the work and the responsibility have been so to speak monopolized by the JDC. Now, Polish Jewry is invited to participate in the work, to share in the responsibility, and to contribute financially."[27]

When the group of physicians from the United States arrived in Poland in March 1921, JDC turned to TOZ as a possible partner in maintaining JDC's medical and sanitary efforts. Nevertheless, the question of who should take responsibility for the medical and public health work was part of an ongoing discussion both within JDC and between JDC and local organizations. During these discussions, the place of TOZ as a central Jewish public health organization operating in Poland and other Eastern European countries was solidified. TOZ's centrality took place both on the local level—as an organization that knew the language and local culture of both Jewish and non-Jewish organizations—as well as on the international level in the eyes of Jews across the ocean, primarily JDC, which had already begun in 1922 to liquidate its own local health committees, converting these into branches of TOZ.[28]

A milk distribution station at a TOZ children's health center and clinic. Piotrkow, Poland, circa 1921–1922.

The collaboration between JDC and TOZ in Poland mirrored wider patterns within international philanthropy, most notably a transition from relief to reconstruction work. In contrast to charity, which expresses the engagement of individuals in concrete, direct acts of compassion and connection to other people, philanthropy aims to promote progress through advanced knowledge.[29] This type of philanthropy required a short-term investment in a project that would be sustainable once the initial funding had ended. In the case of modern philanthropy, typically the decision to support a project is made after conducting thorough surveys of local needs and after identifying local agents with whom the philanthropist can cooperate. As an investment, it has a limited duration and aims to stimulate self-help in the local community, which must be proven by the recipients.[30]

JDC not only financed the activity of TOZ in Poland but also carried out health campaigns and brought in personnel. In this way, it introduced new scientific ideas, technologies, and practices related to health and diseases as well as hygiene and preventive medicine. JDC and TOZ worked together in a fight against contagious diseases—the most urgent health matter. Fighting typhus epidemics, the worst menace during and immediately after the war, served as a laboratory in which these understandings were developed.[31] JDC understood that it needed to develop the local forces in order to execute its public health programs. The OZE-TOZ partnership needed the time and experience gained during the typhus campaign to reinforce its status within the Jewish communities and the Polish government.

1923: THE FEDERATION OF OZE

The early 1920s marked some crucial changes both within OZE and in the OZE-JDC relationships. The move to Berlin intensified "east" and "west" relationships ("givers" and "recipients"), as OZE, which built itself as the primary Jewish medical organization working in Eastern Europe, funded mainly by American JDC, was now located in Berlin. The newly created OZE Berlin, now OSE, whose personnel was composed exclusively of recent Eastern European Jewish immigrants having to work in a foreign milieu, without finance or influence, needed help from Western Jewry. The east and west relationships were manifested in another new aspect of OZE

Berlin's activity: It now dealt with the local problems of Eastern European Jews who passed through Germany on their way to the United States.[32] The move to Berlin, the new political atmosphere in Russia, and these new obligations led OZE to reorganize itself in August 1923 as an umbrella organization to include all OZE national branches as well as other Jewish medical organizations.[33] This change was crucial: Starting as an organization that acted on the local level, it now encompassed forty-eight organizations from Eastern Europe as well as from England, France, and Belgium. This change was extremely significant, as OZE had transitioned from being a local organization operating at the national level to becoming an umbrella organization for many Jewish relief organizations in Europe.

In 1923, JDC had decided to stop fully financing OZE's activities. In December 1923, Otto Warburg from Berlin wrote to Felix Warburg of JDC in New York, asking him to help OZE finance the facilities it had taken over from JDC in Russia. Felix Warburg replied that JDC would not be able to help OZE because it lacked sufficient resources and recommended that OZE return to "their pre-war basis and depend on the resources on which they had to rely before."[34]

However, the problem was not only finding funds. OZE still faced the question of its legal status in the USSR. The Soviets were willing to recognize OZE as a legitimate body under the supervision of its health department if the organization ensured the investment of around $300,000 per year in Russia. JDC representative Boris Bogen, who was respected by the local authorities, played a crucial mediating role to help OZE gain formal legal status. Bogen supervised JDC famine relief in Russia; headed the JDC office in Warsaw and later in Moscow; and was a close friend of Abram Bramson, a physician and one of OZE's leaders in Russia.[35] In this respect, his activity on behalf of OZE reflected the differences within the organization (JDC) as well as the tensions between center and periphery. In many cases, JDC activists on the ground often behaved differently than those in the headquarters in the United States. While the American headquarters could be quite harsh and confrontational with OZE (and other relief organizations), on the local level, JDC representatives tried to accommodate OZE's needs and supported—at least partially—their financial requests from the offices in New York. In the case of OZE, in spite of its growing importance as a European Jewish welfare organization, the relationship between OZE and JDC in New York did not substantially improve.

OZE Delegations to the United States: 1925 and 1929

Until 1925, OZE had no direct contact with American Jewry or with the JDC offices in New York. It was mainly communicating with JDC's local representatives in Europe and receiving budgetary support from Bernard Kahn, the European representative of JDC. In 1925, Poland and other countries in Eastern Europe experienced a severe economic crisis. To address its dire situation, OZE sent a three-member delegation headed by Dr. Moses Gran to the United States in order to enlist the cooperation of American Jews in the work of OZE.[36] The timing was not a coincidence. The agreement that JDC had signed with OZE in 1923 regarding its medical work among Jews in Russia was about to expire in April of that year.

The delegation explained to Joseph Hyman, JDC vice chairman, that "the health of the Russian Jews is at its lowest ebb; their work must be continued. The financial needs based upon a carefully prepared budget are about $700,000 for the year. The minimum amount necessary to carry on the work by the above committee is $300,000 for twelve months which is in accordance with the agreement with the Soviet Government."[37]

The tension between JDC and OZE about the continued funding of OZE's medical work in Russia had two sources. First, as mentioned earlier, OZE had only a very partial success aiding Jews in Russia due to the organization's inability to obtain legal recognition from the Soviet government. The 600,000 patients it treated in 1923 and 1924 were mainly in the bordering countries. Second, JDC struggled over whether to allocate resources to tend to Russian Jewish medical needs or to direct the money to other JDC initiatives in Eastern Europe. In a letter to Hyman, James Rosenberg, the vice president of JDC, argued that any available funds should go to Dr. Joseph Rosen for the Agro-Joint Company (which after World War I resettled Jews on farms in Crimea and Ukraine) and not to OZE.[38]

To increase its ability to raise money in the United States, the OZE delegation traveled the country meeting with various Jewish organizations. OZE delegates contacted other philanthropists and American Jewish organizations such as the Federation of Jewish Charities of Philadelphia as well as individuals within medical circles in New York and Boston.[39] The collected monies enabled OZE to renegotiate with JDC: In May 1925, Dr. Gran wrote to JDC saying that thanks to the successful fundraising campaign in the United States, OZE now needed only $50,000 from JDC to continue its activities in Russia.[40]

The campaign OZE carried out in the United States represented a serious deviation from the JDC model of philanthropy for two reasons. First, JDC perceived itself as being the main body to distribute American Jewish funds throughout Eastern Europe. The organization believed that only it could decide on priorities; independent fundraising in the United States by European bodies was thus a violation of a long-unwritten agreement. Second, the OZE visit in the spring of 1925 coincided inconveniently with JDC's own fundraising campaign. JDC feared that the OZE campaign would not only reduce donations to JDC but also reflect poorly on JDC efforts. After all, by making a pitch to American Jews, OZE had indirectly accused JDC of failing to distribute money collected from American Jewry to needy organizations in Eastern Europe that were involved in providing direct service. To resolve these problems, Felix Warburg decided to integrate OZE into the JDC campaign under the condition that it stop its own.[41]

The 1925 crisis was a "rehearsal" for what happened in 1929.[42] As a result of the crash of the American stock market and its worldwide reverberations, OZE experienced its biggest financial crisis ever. JDC, which was the central financer of its medical activity, had sharply reduced its support from $48,000 for OZE and $40,000 for TOZ in 1927 to $6,000 for OZE and $20,000 for TOZ in 1929.[43]

The drastic cut in JDC funding derived from the shift in American Jewish philanthropy at the same time that it reflected the impact of the crash; American Jewish philanthropists considered the need to return to their pre–World War I model of "charity begins at home" and radically reduced their support for Jewish needs outside the United States.[44] Another problem for

OZE was that it was no longer a humanitarian relief organization responding to a pressing crisis but rather a medical organization that attempted to implement long-term programs of social and preventive medicine. As such, it was less attractive to Jewish American philanthropists. In addition, the Jewish Agency, which was established by the World Zionist Organization in 1929, redirected American Jewish resources and attention from Eastern Europe to Palestine.[45] This new organization, which was created to raise donations for the Zionist cause from Western Jews who were not affiliated with Zionist parties, became a central partner with JDC in their fundraising efforts until 1935.

As during the crisis of 1925, in 1929, OZE decided to send a delegate to the United States—civil engineer Solomon Jacobi—hoping to find solutions for the financial crisis in America. However, this time, OZE declared emphatically that it had no intention of carrying out an independent fundraising campaign. But at the same time, Jacobi planned to establish an American OZE Committee with 2,000 local Jewish physicians. The membership fee would, he expected, create another resource for OZE's activity in Eastern Europe. Within a few weeks of activity, Jacobi managed to secure the support of prominent American Jewish activists and to establish an American committee with Milton Rosenau, a prominent physician in the field of preventive medicine and hygiene in the United States; Jacob Golub; and Emanuel Libman, a famous cardiologist. JDC viewed Jacobi's initiative with skepticism: "The result of such an attempt would be to muddy the waters of the JDC without realizing anything substantial or worthwhile on behalf of OZE."[46] Louis Marshall was also against this initiative, which would only diminish contributions to JDC by dividing resources between competing causes.

The tension between JDC and OZE increased when JDC accused OZE of taking credit for the work of TOZ and JDC. This accusation was correct—OZE was hardly active in Russia as an independent organization after 1921 while most of the activity was carried out by TOZ outside of the country. Moreover, JDC pointed out that OZE had no legal status in Russia, nor was it likely to attain such status. Only in 1930 was a solution found when Warburg agreed to allocate $7,500 to OZE and $10,000 to TOZ via JDC's overseas headquarters in Berlin.[47] OZE's illegal status in

Russia was partially solved when JDC entered into a new agreement with OZE and the Soviet government through the existing work of Rosen and the Agro-Joint in Russia.

The economic depression of 1929 strained the relationship between JDC and OZE and crystalized problems fundamental to the ways these organizations operated. It showed that the strategy of JDC to financially support organizations for a limited time could never be realized in the case of OZE and TOZ. The 1929 clashes between JDC and OZE reflect the nature of the relationships among one of the biggest American Jewish philanthropic bodies and Eastern European welfare organizations and the various tensions such a cooperation created regarding institutional, organizational, and financial issues. It demonstrates the inherent disjuncture between JDC's expectations of the Eastern European organizations it supported—namely, promoting Progressive Era scientific ideas and becoming quickly self-sufficient—and those of the recipients of the aid: the expectation from JDC to understand the particular situation of Jews in Eastern Europe and to support their needs with its monies as long as necessary.

A summer colony on the banks of the Bug River operated by the TOZ branch in Siedlce. Klimczyc, Poland, circa 1931.

Conclusion

JDC support for OZE on a substantial scale continued into the 1930s. The rise of National Socialism in Germany created new problems of urgent importance for OZE. In 1933, OZE had to move its offices from Berlin to Paris after eleven years of activity. Thanks to JDC's substantial support, during the interwar period, OZE established an impressive public health network. OZE served as an intermediary between the local contexts—Eastern European Jewish life, as expressed in both the health and non-health-related fields and its institutions and culture—and the reform ideas coming from abroad, mainly from the United States. Thanks to JDC's financial and scientific support, OZE managed to become a central organization that improved the health of Jews in Eastern Europe until the liquidation of the ghettos in World War II.

Nevertheless, the relationship between JDC and OZE-TOZ was quite challenging throughout most of the period for two main reasons. First, OZE was never fully able to totally assume the medical-sanitary work of JDC; second, OZE never managed to become fully self-sustaining. The dependency on the financial support of JDC created constant tensions between the two organizations. The competition over resources grew even greater at the end of the 1920s with the creation of the Jewish Agency, which heavily collaborated with JDC in their fundraising campaigns. Despite these tensions, JDC continued to finance many of OZE's and TOZ's activities in Eastern Europe until they were liquidated by the Nazis. Following World War II, JDC again began supporting both organizations.

The case of OZE-TOZ is a case study of modern philanthropy in the field of public health. Both JDC and OZE acted on international, national, and local levels. To understand the complexity of Jewish relief operations in Eastern Europe, it is essential to examine each level. The three levels of operation shaped the relationship between philanthropy from abroad (in this case, the American Jewish JDC) and the members of local organizations (in this case, OZE and TOZ).

The case of OZE-TOZ and JDC is a case study not only of transnational medical Jewish relief but also of an international organization originating from civil initiatives trying to promote minorities' health through fieldwork and politics. In the first half of the twentieth century, health became a central concern and played a significant role in the formation and reconceptualization of nations. It served to integrate and exclude peoples and groups, define borders, and forge identities and also played a crucial role in the development of political and social order.

NOTES

1. Marta Balinska, "The Rockefeller Foundation and the National Institute of Hygiene, Poland, 1918–45," *Studies in History and Philosophy of Science Part C: Studies in History and Philosophy of Biological and Biomedical Sciences* 31, no. 3 (2000): 419–32.

2. See, for example, Susan Gross Solomon and Nicolai Kremntsov, "Giving and Taking across Borders: The Rockefeller Foundation and Russia 1919–1928," *Minerva* 39, no. 3 (2001): 268.

3. Paul Weindling, "Public Health and Political Stabilisation: The Rockefeller Foundation in Central and Eastern Europe between the Two World Wars," *Minerva* 31, no. 3 (1993): 253–67; Paul Weindling, "Philanthropy and World Health: The Rockefeller Foundation and the League of Nations Health Organisation," *Minerva* 35, no. 3 (1997): 269–81; John Farely, *To Cast Out Disease: A History of the International Health Division of Rockefeller Foundation (1913–1951)* (Oxford: Oxford University Press, 2004), 27, 47, 239.

4. Brian Smith, *More than Altruism: The Politics of Private Foreign Aid* (Princeton, NJ: Princeton University Press, 2014), 33.

5. Solomon and Kremntsov, "Giving and Taking across Borders," 265–66.

6. Lisa Epstein, *Caring for the Soul's Home: The Jews of Russia and Health Care 1860–1914* (New Haven, CT: Yale University Press, 1995), 255; Michel Virginie, "L'action médico-sociale de l'OSE à Paris dans les années trente," *Archives Juives* 39, no. 1 (2006): 111; L. Wulman, *The Fight for the Health of the Jewish People: 50 Years of OSE* (New York: World Union OSE and the American Committee of OSE, 1968), 185.

7. On social medicine, see George Rosen, "What Is Social Medicine?" *Bulletin of the History of Medicine* 21 (1974): 674–733; Dorothy Porter, "Introduction," in *Social Medicine and Medical Sociology in the Twentieth Century*, ed. Dorothy Porter (Amsterdam: Rudopi, 1997), 1–31.

8. Samuel Ramer, "The Zemstvo and Public Health," in *The Zemstvo in Russia: An Experiment in Local Self-Government*, ed. Terence Emmons and Wayne Vucinich (Cambridge: Cambridge University Press, 1982), 279–80.

9. Anonymous, *Die Entstehung der Gesellschaft OSE und ihre Massnahmen*, Hrg. *Verband fuer Gesundgeitsschutz der Juden OSE* (Berlin: Springer, 1925), 4; Nokhum Shtif, "Di tsen yerike geshikhte fun 'OZE,'" *Folksgezunt* 2 (1923): 1–2; Jacob Joshua Golub, "OSE: Pioneer of Jewish Health," *The Jewish Social Service* 14, no. 4 (1938): 365–66. At the beginning of World War I, OZE had 17 branches and around 1,500 members in Wilno, Byalistock, Warsaw, Lodz, Odessa, Kiev, Kharkov, Kishinev, and elsewhere. In 1916, it maintained 223 facilities, caring for 300,000 refugees.

10. Joseph C. Hyman, "Twenty-Five Years of American Aid to Jews Overseas: A Record of the Joint Distribution Committee," *The American Jewish Year Book* 41 (1939–1940): 143–44.

11. Avraham Kotik, "Di Velt Milkhum un Poiln," *Folksgezunt* 2–3 (1923): 8.

12. Shtif, "Di tsen yerike geshikhte fun 'OZE,'" 2.

13. Sofiya Grachova, "Pathologies of Civility: Jews, Health, Race and Citizenship in the Russian Empire and the Bolshevik State, 1830–1930" (PhD diss., Harvard University, 2014), 277.

14. JDC Archives, Records of the New York Office of the American Jewish Joint Distribution Committee, 1921–1932, Folder 235, Lithuania Medical 1921.

15. Anonymous, "Inermeditsinish Sanitere tetikhkeyt fun OZE in di Ukrayn," *Buletin fun tsentral biro fun der gezelshaft fur ferhitn di gezundhayt fun der idisher bafelkerung* 2, no. 2 (Berlin: OZE, June 1923).

16. Grachova, "Pathologies of Civility," 279.

17. Grachova, "Pathologies of Civility," 278.

18. Lazar Gourevitch, *Twenty Five Years of OSE, 1912–1937* (Paris: Paris OSE, 1937), 95–96.

19. Anonymous, "Inermidizinish Sanitare tetikayt fun 'OZE' in di Ukrain," *Buletin fun zentrale biro fun gezelshaft far ferhiten di gezundhait fun der idisher bafelkerung "OZE"* 2, no. 2 (Berlin: OZE, June 1923); Leo Yaffe, "Fun der nonter fergangenhait. Tsu der geshikhte fun litvishen 'OZE,'" *A Yovel Arbait Farn Falks-Gezunt* (Vilna: OZE, 1934), 120.

20. Krysia Fisher, ed. *The Society for the Protection of Jewish Health: Fighting for a Healthy New Generation*. New York: YIVO Institute for Jewish Research, 2005. Exhibition catalog.

21. Max Hirsh, *Di oyfgabn fun "TOZ": Oyfn gebit fun higyene-propaganda* (Vilna, 1937).

22. Rakefet Zalashik and Nadav Davidovitch, "Taking and Giving: The Case of the JDC and OZE in Lithuania 1919–26," *East European Jewish Affairs* 39, no. 1 (2009): 57–68.

23. On the racialization of typhus as Judenfieber, see Paul Weindling, *Epidemics and Genocide in Eastern Europe: 1890–1945* (Oxford: Oxford University Press, 2000).

24. JDC Archives, Records of the New York Office of the American Jewish Joint Distribution Committee, 1919–1921, Folder 260, Letter from Dr. Harry Plotz to Felix M. Warburg, October 20, 1920.

25. Ibid., Folder 260, Letter from Dr. Harry Plotz to Felix M. Warburg, October 20, 1920.

26. Ibid., Folder 255.1, Report on the Medico-Sanitary Conditions by Dr. William Wovschin, July 15, 1920, to March 7, 1921, March 25, 1921.

27. JDC Archives, Records of the New York Office of the American Jewish Joint Distribution Committee, 1921–1932, Folder 357, Letter from Dr. Harry Plotz to the Joint Distribution Committee, Subject: Lemberg Conference, July 1, 1921.

28. Golub, "OSE: Pioneer of Jewish Health," 396.

29. Robert Gross, "Giving in America: From Charity to Philanthropy," in *Charity, Philanthropy, and Civility in American History*, ed. Lawrence Friedman and Mark McGarvie (Cambridge: Cambridge University Press, 2002), 30–32.

30. Farely, *To Cast Out Disease*, 4.

31. Nadav Davidovitch and Rakefet Zalashik, "'Air, Sun, Water': Ideology and Activities of OZE (Society for the Preservation of the Health of the Jewish Population) during the Interwar Period," *Dynamis* 28 (2008): 127–49.

32. Ferban Khronik, "OZE," *Folksgezunt* (November 1929): 362.

33. Otto Neustaetter, Kataolg der Ausstellung veranstaltet vom Berliner Central-Buero der "OSE." The conference was accompanied by an exhibition, which aimed to supply information about the miserable situation

of the Jews in Eastern Europe as a result of the war. It was organized by Dr. Otto Neustaetter, the former director of the Museum for Hygiene in Dresden. The hope was that the exhibition would awaken the interest of the Western public and lead to concrete action.

34. JDC Archives, Records of the New York Office of the American Jewish Joint Distribution Committee, 1921–1932, Folder 481, Letter from Felix M. Warburg to Professor O. Warburg, December 27, 1923.

35. Grachova, "Pathologies of Civility," 87.

36. JDC Archives, Records of the New York Office of the American Jewish Joint Distribution Committee, 1921–1932, Folder 481, Letter from OSE to the Executive Committee, Joint Distribution Committee; ibid., Folder 253, Russia Relations Joint Archive, New York, April 4, 1925.

37. JDC Archives, Records of the New York Office of the American Jewish Joint Distribution Committee, 1921–1932, Folder 481, Letter from Dr. M. Gran et al. to the Executive Committee, April 4, 1925.

38. Ibid., Folder 481, Letter from James N. Rosenberg to Joseph C. Hyman, Subject: OSE, April 7, 1925; "James Rosenberg, Back from Russia, Tells about the Jewish Settlements," Jewish Telegraphic Agency, accessed December 17, 2015, http://www.jta.org/1926/06/29/archive/james-rosenberg-back-from -russia-tells-about-the-jewish-settlements. Rosenberg was a great supporter of Jewish settlements on Russia. In 1926, he went on a two-month tour of Jewish colonies in Russia and reported enthusiastically: "The land settlement in Russia is so successful that even Orthodox Jews who never knew anything about farming are eager to settle on the land, as evidenced by their applications made to the offices of the Agro-Joint."

39. JDC Archives, Records of the New York Office of the American Jewish Joint Distribution Committee, 1919–1921, Folder 253.

40. JDC Archives, Records of the New York Office of the American Jewish Joint Distribution Committee, 1921–1932, Folder 481, Letter from Dr. M. Gran, OZE Delegation, to the Executive Committee, May 12, 1925.

41. JDC Archives, Records of the New York Office of the American Jewish Joint Distribution Committee, 1921–1932, Folder 253, Russia Relations Joint Archive, New York, Felix Warburg, Memorandum, October 11, 1925.

42. This part is based on Rakefet Zalashik, "Jewish American Philanthropy and the 1929 Crisis: The Case of OZE-TOZ and the JDC," in *Mapping the Jewish World*, ed. Hasia Diner and Gennady Estraikh (New York: New York University Press, 2013), 93–106.

43. JDC Archives, Records of the New York Office of the American Jewish Joint Distribution Committee, 1921–1932.

44. Zosa Szajkowski, "Budgeting American Jewish Overseas Relief (1919–1939)," *American Jewish Historical Quarterly* 59, no. 1 (1969): 83–88; Zosa Szajkowski, "'Reconstruction' vs. 'Palliative Relief' in American Jewish Overseas Work (1919–1939)," *Jewish Social Studies* 32, no. 2 (1970): 111–47.

45. Yigal Elam, *HaSokhnut HaYehudit: Shanim Rishonot 1919–1931* (Jerusalem: Mossad Bialik, 1990).

46. JDC Archives, Records of the New York Office of the American Jewish Joint Distribution Committee, 1921–1932, Folder 102A, Letter from Joseph C. Hyman to Messrs. Warburg, Rosenberg, Baerwald, Bressler, Jouan, and Wise, Subject: OSE-TOZ, October 18, 1932.

47. JDC Archives, Records of the New York Office of the American Jewish Joint Distribution Committee, 1921–1932, Folder 102A, Letter from Warburg to Rosenau, January 20, 1929.

2

JDC in Minsk

The Parameters and Predicaments of Aiding Soviet Jews in the Interwar Years

Elissa Bemporad

Writing from Berlin in 1923, historian Elias Tcherikower described the experience of Russian Jews during World War I, the Bolshevik Revolution, and the ensuing Civil War as one of unprecedented turmoil. It was, he added, "one of the worst catastrophes that had ever affected the fate of the greatest Jewish center in the world, . . . which was shattered into pieces, broken in its economic foundation," and devastated by hundreds of pogroms carried out in the towns and shtetlekh on the Eastern Front by the major combatants in the conflict.[1] The violence and devastation unleashed by war and revolution also enveloped the city of Minsk and its Jewish population. A historic Jewish center since the sixteenth century, Minsk was located in the heart of the Pale of Settlement, densely populated by Jews, the area where the majority of Soviet Jews lived until the eve of World War II. Over the course of the eighteenth and nineteenth centuries, the city had developed into a prominent center of Jewish religious scholarship and Haskalah (Jewish enlightenment); during the later part of the nineteenth century, Minsk became a stronghold of Jewish socialism, Bundism, and different shades of radical Zionism. Beginning in 1915, thousands of war refugees in search of a safe haven fled to Minsk as its population grew from approximately 100,000 to 140,000; its Jewish population rose to 67,000 in 1917. In the words of a contemporary, the number of refugees "who went from home to home begging for help, or simply stood on the streets was unbelievable."[2] In some instances, synagogues abstained from holding holiday services and used their buildings to shelter the large number of destitute Jewish refugees pouring into the city.[3] The socioeconomic and political havoc in Minsk increased during 1917–1920, which saw a frantic sequence of ruling powers, starting with the Bolsheviks, followed by the Germans and again the Bolsheviks and ending with the Polish occupation. According to most accounts, the worst stage of this political frenzy coincided with the Polish-Soviet War and the eleven-month presence of Polish troops in the city.[4] On July 11, 1920, Rabbi Yechezkel Abramski described Polish brutality against the Jews as follows:

> Miserable, I walk through the ruined streets, without the strength to keep my head up, buried under the burden of destruction, freshly spilled blood and cries of orphans . . . theft and murder in every section of the city and in every neighborhood touched by the Polish army, I doubt that the world will ever believe that such horrendous crimes were committed by human beings. Who will believe that [the Polish] nation . . . began its independent existence with such horrifying actions from the middle-ages. Can one believe that people elegantly dressed . . . with European manners, act like the Haydamaks [Cossack bands], killing, looting and starting up fires against people, horses and the luggage of those who try to flee Minsk?[5]

The return of the Bolsheviks and the vigorous Sovietization of the city and its inhabitants, which included arrests and systematic property requisition, led to renewed violence and intensified the socioeconomic collapse. In late 1920, a prominent local Zionist activist remarked that

> [o]ur [Zionist] . . . activities are being hounded . . . our elementary school . . . was taken from us. The teachers and many of the students left the school because a decree was issued forbidding the teaching of Hebrew. . . . Some of our teachers are living in great poverty and don't even have bread.[6]

In October 1921, a Jewish Communist confirmed the sense of despair and the commotion that had enveloped the city:

> . . . the population is in a state of chaos because of the looting and violence. . . . [C]ity stores are empty or closed. . . . One pound of bread costs 1.500 rubles, a pound of butter 20.000 rubles . . . there is no wood. . . . I turn to the Central Bureau [in Moscow] with a personal request. I know it is not appropriate, but I have no other choice. I have no coat, no blanket and . . . no warm clothing [which] makes it impossible for me to work . . .[7]

The intensity of the destruction produced by the combination of World War I, the Polish-Soviet War, the Bolshevik rise to power, and the Civil War was so immeasurable and so great that it led to an unprecedented need for reconstruction and humanitarian relief. With their lives disrupted by the bloody events, thousands of Minsk residents, Jews, and non-Jews alike—including refugees, orphans, students, actors, writers, and religious and political activists categorized as *lishentsy* (disenfranchised) and deprived of voting rights by the Bolshevik Regime[8]—required assistance like never before. This chapter will examine the social, cultural, and religious activities that the Joint Distribution Committee (JDC) sponsored in the 1920s and early 1930s in Minsk, the only Jewish city in the Soviet landscape of urban centers that became the capital of a republic. Here, the new political and administrative hub of the Belorussian Soviet Socialist Republic intersected with a historic Jewish center of religious, cultural, and political life in the Pale of Settlement. This unique intersection influenced both the modus operandi of JDC and the nature of its support.

It seems necessary to make two comments before exploring some of the extraordinary welfare and cultural enterprises supported by JDC in Minsk during the interwar period. First, by engaging in rescue and relief activities and (at least on paper) conforming to the nonsectarian principle agreed upon with Soviet authorities, JDC actively supported the creation of a new Soviet Jewish way of life, the essence of which was communism. In the specific Soviet context, this inevitably implied promoting the Bolshevization of Jewish life and the institutions actively cooperating with the Soviets and accepting some of the tenets of the new regime. Second, JDC's official and unofficial activities in the city were closely and inextricably intertwined. The more JDC engaged in official forms of relief and welfare and funded Soviet cultural institutions, the more it could secretly—unbeknownst to Soviet authorities—sponsor underground endeavors. Amid prolific and fairly successful official activities sanctioned by the Soviet state, JDC representatives could carve out some leeway and generate new opportunities to sustain underground initiatives.

OFFICIAL ACTIVITIES

The Sovietization of Minsk involved a drastic onslaught on Jewish life. Shortly after taking over the city, in July 1920, the Bolsheviks dismantled most Jewish religious, political, and educational institutions and organizations that had formed the core of Jewish life before the revolution; the institutions were closed down and their buildings requisitioned. Zionist publications were liquidated. The Bund, which had functioned as an independent party until March 1921, was forced to merge with the Communist Party. Bringing communism to the "Jewish street" also involved taking over existing "bourgeois" institutions and incorporating them into Bolshevik organizations. Following the party's official position on prerevolutionary society, the knowledge and experience of the professional "bourgeois" workforce— the *spetsy* (specialists)—would need to be exploited in order to build the new Communist civilization. In May 1921, the Minsk branches of prominent prerevolutionary Jewish communal institutions were placed under the supervision of the Jewish Section of the People's Commissariat for Nationality Affairs (Narkomnats) and their administration transferred to the Soviet agency's locale.[9] But Communist supervision did not necessarily entail state funding. To the contrary, supervised by Soviet authorities but excluded from the state financial budget, the activities of these "bourgeois" institutions became contingent upon foreign relief funds, especially aid from JDC.[10]

In Minsk, JDC supported and funded a vast number of welfare, medical, cultural, and business enterprises throughout the city. Hundreds of war refugees still needed to be fed daily as late as 1923.[11] Local organizations and institutions faced a dearth of medical supplies. According to a 1922 report on relief activities in Belarus, from November 1, 1921, to January 15, 1922, 634 refugees died in the hospital in Minsk.[12] JDC provided assistance to university students—most of whom happened to be Jewish—who had no access to food and lived in deplorable conditions: With as many as ten students lodging together in one small room with no ventilation, they slept on boards with no linen or blankets in temporary housing across the city.[13] Local Jewish religious leaders were quick to reach out to JDC. The chief rabbis in five university cities—including Minsk—appealed for funds to support a kosher kitchen for an average of fifty university students per town at the rate of 12 rubles a month per student (or 36,000 rubles per year). The subvention, argued the rabbis, would enable them to keep in close touch with those young Jews who were "destined to influence the future of Jewish life in Russia."[14]

Relief was also provided to university professors (Belorussian State University was established in the city in 1921). Upon inspecting the recently founded Minsk university, JDC Director for Russia Boris D. Bogen noted that "the shabbiness with which the professors dressed provided enough evidence that they were badly in need of clothes."[15] JDC arranged the distribution of food purchased by the Minsk Relief Society, the New York Minsk *landsmanshaft* established at the beginning of the century to provide assistance to destitute Jews in and around the city. Keeping to the Soviet principle of nonsectarian help, the food for the needy city population was distributed by the two local rabbis—Rabbi Eliezer Rabinowitz and Rabbi Yehoshua Tsimbalist—in cooperation with the neutral party of the Minsk Quaker Unit. In 1921, for example, the Quakers (who were mostly connected to the Quaker organization, the American Friends Service Committee) helped out as distributing agents among the population of the cities and towns of Belarus, allocating supplies furnished by JDC in the amount of $100,000.[16]

In 1923, JDC paid to heat the locale of the Jewish Section of the Belorussian Drama Studio, thus providing material support to young Jewish activists.[17] In agreement with the Social Security Department,

Distribution of shoes to children of Jewish homes by JDC. Minsk, Belarus, circa 1923.

JDC allocated $2,000 to build a new Jewish old-age home in the city, which would accommodate Jews only. Inaugurated on November 1, 1923, the Jewish Minsk old-age home was the only institution of its kind in the USSR, where elderly Jews had a separate home distinct from non-Jewish institutions.[18] Finally, the American organization subsidized at least eight facilities in Minsk—including public kitchens; children's homes; and a number of vocational schools for teachers, shoemakers, and metalworkers.[19] In spite of the nonsectarian agreement with Soviet authorities, most of the JDC subsidy recipients were Jewish. In 1927, for example, of the four professional-technical facilities in Minsk that received funding from JDC to train skilled workers, three had a significant majority of Jewish students, while one—the Sholem Aleichem School of Agriculture—operated in Yiddish only and enrolled exclusively Jewish students.[20] JDC was able to break away, at least in part, from its official commitment to nonsectarian help also because of the large percentage of Jews living in the city (they made up more than 40% of the urban population). The higher rates of literacy of Jews compared to Belorussians made them more likely to enroll in JDC-funded vocational schools for teachers or artisans, which were, incidentally, sectors with a higher concentration of Jews. Finally, the Soviet policy of disenfranchising those involved in "bourgeois" activities before the revolution primarily affected the Jewish urban population, which could turn for aid almost exclusively to JDC.

Most "bourgeois Jewish elements" who, during the 1918 Red Terror campaign of mass killings and systematic oppression, managed to escape arrest and death but did not succeed in fleeing the USSR were classified under the new Soviet category of *lishentsy* and became disenfranchised.[21] In light of their prerevolutionary socioeconomic status and occupations as merchants, peddlers, and small business owners, more Jews than non-Jews faced legal restrictions under the new regime. According to one source, 40% of Jews and 5% of non-Jews were disenfranchised in the Minsk province. With no bread cards and having been expelled from cooperatives and other industrial enterprises, many *lishentsy* often had to rely exclusively on the support of JDC, which made every effort to resettle them on land or absorb their children into new factories and industrial plants.[22] As an American Jew noted after his trip to Minsk in the late 1920s, "Wherever I met a Jew and asked him what his source of livelihood was, I got the same answer: American . . . money."[23] Others dealt with their loss of income by turning to profiteering and black marketing, which often led to arrest by Soviet authorities.[24] Their children were last on the list for school matriculation and stood little chance of entering government service because of the parents' status of "non-working element."[25]

Besides lack of food and housing (only trade union members had access to co-op stores and housing allotment), disenfranchised "bourgeois" Jews had no right to free medical services. If a family member fell ill, she would not be treated in the city hospitals unless she paid high fees.[26] The status of the *lishentsy* prompted a group of Jewish Minsk doctors to come together and establish, in mid-1926, with the support of JDC, a new medical organization: Evreiskoe Meditsinskoe Sanitarnoe Obshchestvo (EMSO), or the Jewish Medical and Sanitary Society. The founders intended for it to complement the general City Committee for Mutual Aid, which refused to provide medical services for the "bourgeois non-working elements" out of commitment to the principles of communism. Disregarding the nonsectarian precondition for JDC relief support in the Soviet Union, EMSO assisted the Jewish Minsk poor and *lishentsy* only. When the doctors first organized themselves, setting up their own administration and regulations, they operated independently from Soviet agencies and beyond the supervision of the official Jewish institution—namely, the Evsektsiia, the Jewish Section of the Communist Party.[27] EMSO was so successful that one year after its establishment, the Minsk District Party Committee was still trying to figure out who had authorized the doctors to organize the society.

In addition to performing medical services, the doctors lectured on health and hygiene issues in clubs and movie theaters across the city.[28] The society had its own clinic, and it also provided financial support for those in need. A Jewish Red Army soldier turned to EMSO when his parents could no longer support his two brothers, who were enrolled in a local Soviet Jewish school. In the same appeal, soldier Levin asked EMSO to pay for his mother's dental plate, as the family did not have adequate means to buy her the missing teeth.[29] Intended as a Jewish organization, EMSO began to offer medical treatment to the poor of other ethnic groups only in late 1928.[30]

Fearing that an organization that operated outside the Bolshevik sphere of control might start offering medical assistance to the working class as well—and therefore spoil its "immaculate nature with bourgeois lies"—Communists began to attack it.[31] In late 1927, Jewish Communists warned that Mizrachi leaders had joined the society and that "EMSO . . . could turn into the old Kahal." To avoid this, the Evsektsiia struggled to ensure Communist influence on the society, encouraging party members to join its administration.[32] At the end of that year, nine Communists joined the fourteen doctors (who were non-party members) on the board of directors.[33] By November 1928, the number of Communist and non-Communist board members was roughly equal, with twelve non-party members and eleven party members.[34]

Among the Jewish organizations established under the Soviets, EMSO was, in many ways, unique. In sheer disregard of official Soviet guidelines of nonsectarianism and internationalism, which were strictly applied by the Bolsheviks to other social service and philanthropic organizations, EMSO was established solely as a Jewish institution with the purpose of bringing assistance to the outcast Jewish population of Minsk. Although the Jewish Medical and Sanitary Society eventually came under the Evsektsiia's influence, it outlived the Jewish Section of the Communist Party of Belorussia (CPB), liquidated in 1930, by one year. It existed in the city until 1931, where it functioned primarily as a clinic for the Jewish poor. The fact that a group of Jewish doctors—relying on the support of JDC—organized EMSO without consulting with the Evsektsiia and obtaining its authorization suggests that grassroots organizations were still possible in the 1920s. EMSO doctors relied on preexisting social networks to establish and operate their society. At least during the New Economic Policy (NEP) years from 1921 to 1928, these networks escaped full control from the party and the state. EMSO also availed itself of the fact that many members of the medical intelligentsia and the health-care system in Minsk were Jewish; some of them had been active in the local branch of the Society for the Protection of the Health of the Jewish Population (Obshchestvo Zdravookhraneniia Evreev [OZE]), which was liquidated by the Soviets in the early 1920s. EMSO's existence (however brief) reminds us once again that the Bolsheviks did not hold sway over society as a whole during the 1920s. EMSO was also one of the few Jewish organizations that did not adhere, at least in the beginning, to the principles of Soviet nationality and language policy. Like other prerevolutionary Jewish societies established by the Russian Jewish intelligentsia, EMSO's language was not Yiddish—the Soviet-designated Jewish national language—but Russian. After all, the Jewish doctors who had founded it and devoted themselves to the interests of the Jewish population of Minsk spoke Russian as their primary language. As Soviet influence over EMSO grew, the language of correspondence, meeting minutes, and literature progressively shifted to Yiddish.[35] This enterprise remains a revealing example of the scope of prerevolutionary social networks and modes of action within the constraints of the new system.[36]

In Support of Sovietization: JDC and the Soviet Nationality Policy

JDC supported the creation and operation of an impressive network of Soviet Jewish institutions. By January 7, 1924, Minsk boasted 10 Yiddish-language elementary schools with 2,505 students and 141 teachers, 8 orphanages with 602 children and 77 teachers, 7 kindergartens with 400 children and 34 teachers, a 4-year Jewish agricultural educational farm, and a Jewish Pedagogical Training College with 175 students and 29 teachers.[37] All of these institutions functioned in Yiddish. In some places, Soviet Yiddish schools operated with higher standards than other Soviet schools, including Belorussian Soviet schools, thanks to the financial support they received from JDC until the early 1930s.[38]

Considered by local authorities as one of the main instruments to spread communism among Jewish youth, the Jewish Pedagogical Training College (*Evpedtekhnikum* in Russian and *Yidpedtekhnikum* in Yiddish) deserves close attention. Established in November 1921, the four-year secondary school produced a new cadre of "Red teachers" who served as instructors in preschool, elementary, and adult educational institutions in Minsk and in the surrounding cities and shtetlekh of the Belorussian Republic.[39] The founders of the Evpedtekhnikum set up the new Soviet Jewish

Physics class in Yiddish at the Jewish section of the Unified Professional School. Minsk, Belarus, 1928–1929. This was a program of JDC's Reconstruction Department.

institution in a two-story brick building located at the intersection between Rakovskaia and Zamkovaia Street or, as local Jews used to call it in Yiddish, *Shlos gas* (Castle Street). This had been the building of the city's Talmud Torah, the traditional Jewish school built by the local Jewish community for the education of the poorest children in Minsk.[40] Because of its location in a densely populated Jewish area, the former Talmud Torah was the ideal venue for disseminating communism among Jews. In September 1933, the Evpedtekhnikum petitioned the Minsk municipal administration, demanding to take over the building of a nearby synagogue. In need of additional space to set up a new dormitory for its growing student population, the Evpedtekhnikum took over the Bricklayer House of Prayer on Zamkovaia Street, located just one block away from the historical building of the former Talmud Torah.[41]

During the 1921–1922 academic year, 133 students—mostly from indigent families—enrolled in the Pedagogical Training College, many relocating from different districts in Belarus and Ukraine.[42] With the goal of creating a Jewish proletarian culture, the Evpedtekhnikum's curriculum included Yiddish, math, physics, geography, gymnastics, chemistry, music (classical, workers' songs, and folk songs), mechanics, and agronomy. Belorussian was introduced during the second year of study. The social and cultural events organized by the institution in 1922 included an evening commemorating the anniversary of writer Y. L. Peretz's death, with an audience of more than 500 people; a lecture by Ester Frumkin on Communist ethics; and a lecture by the literary critic Moshe Litvakov on modern Yiddish literature.[43] The Evpedtekhnikum was thus conceived as a Sovietizing institution for Jews that would create a cadre of Communist teachers for the Yiddish schools of Belarus, therefore spreading communism among younger generations of Jews. By supporting it, JDC—which covered the total costs for the students' room and board—participated in the Soviet experiment and even promoted (at least to some degree) the Soviet nationality policy.[44] Far from being enthusiastic about the Bolshevik experiment, JDC leaders understood that support of Soviet institutions— and, by association, of communism—was indispensable and a calculated cost of doing business in the USSR. But most importantly, JDC leaders recognized that their willingness to fund official Soviet institutions enabled them to engage in clandestine assistance with unofficial activities.

Unofficial Work: Subsidizing Underground Religious Educational Institutions

Despite its official support for communism and Communist institutions, JDC applied a nonpartisan principle to the Jewish community and provided assistance to religious Jews and their non-Soviet institutions, mostly through underground channels. The support for Jewish religious education was also perhaps undertaken as a way to counterbalance the sponsoring of Soviet-sanctioned activities and was intended as compensation for the public rejection of what the Communists deemed "bourgeois" and nationalist expressions of Jewish life. In turn, Jewish Communist activists who became aware—or at least suspicious—of JDC-sponsored unofficial activities voiced their concerns to Soviet authorities, emphasizing, for example, that one of the "real counterrevolutionary forces in Russia . . . is JDC, its goal [being] to restore the Jewish communities and support the counterrevolution among Jews."[45]

In the 1920s and early 1930s, JDC managed to guarantee some support (both officially and unofficially) to religious Jews, sending parcels with matzah flour and kosher meat products. This was semi-legal—not publicly advertised, but tolerated by the Soviet state. Through the creation of a Russian Matzah Fund Committee, JDC made matzah and matzah flour available during Passover throughout most of the 1920s and early 1930s in major Soviet cities, including Minsk. In early 1929, the Soviet government approved the import of 50 carloads of matzah (albeit at a prohibitive duty fee), which guaranteed Passover bread for 20,000 families. The American kosher food company Manischewitz even agreed to retail matzah at 10¢/lb, instead of 17¢/lb, for the USSR only.[46] According to the instructions of Dr. Joseph Rosen, the JDC executive in Soviet Russia, 10% of the matzah flour was shipped directly to Leningrad, 20% to Moscow, and 25% to Minsk.[47] In early 1932, the Manischewitz Company was in the process of concluding another agreement with the Soviet government allowing the import of matzah and the delivery of matzah parcels to predesignated addresses.[48]

But what seems most impressive was JDC's support for underground religious education, especially in light of Soviet regulations about religion, which were considered the chief cause for perpetuating "bourgeois" and counterrevolutionary behavior among Soviet citizens.[49] This started in Minsk shortly after the 1922 Soviet ban on all existing heders, yeshivas, and Talmud Torahs. In 1924, Rabbi Tsimbalist established an underground yeshiva in the women's section of the Shoavei Mayim synagogue, also located on Zamkovaia Street near the former Talmud Torah building, which had been taken over by the Evpedtekhnikum. With seventy students, the Minsk yeshiva was the largest one of its kind in the Soviet Union.[50] It attracted students from the Soviet territory as well as from neighboring Poland. Born in Lodz in 1913, Moshe-Zvi Neriyah, who would later become a prominent rabbinic figure in the Yishuv and State of Israel, left his native Poland in 1926 to study Torah in the Minsk yeshiva, at a time when Jewish religious education was officially considered obsolete in Soviet cities.[51]

The Shoavei Mayim yeshiva was only one aspect of the larger underground educational system set up and coordinated by Tsimbalist through the support of JDC. Minsk soon became the city with the largest number of yeshivas in the Soviet Union. Besides the advanced Talmudic academy directed by Tsimbalist, there were at least three middle-level yeshivas and two lower-level yeshivas. A *yeshiva ketanah* (lower-level yeshiva) was set up on Staro-Vilenskaia Street, with twenty pupils whose ages ranged between twelve and fifteen. Ten students came from outside Minsk. Not only was the yeshiva tuition free, the students were also provided meals. Minsk families would invite them over for the Sabbath and serve herring and challah.[52] There were 400 pupils studying in the Minsk underground heders in 1926, most of them officially enrolled in a Soviet school as well.[53] By 1929, the number was still significant and amounted to 324.[54] During the 1920s, a well-organized Tifereth Bachurim organization, or religious youth league, existed in Minsk. It attracted mainly young workers, clerks, and a few university students who would convene at night after work, listen to lectures or engage in conversations on religious topics, get together for prayer and Torah study, and engage in religious propaganda to increase the organization's constituency. If in Leningrad there were 30 members in the local Tifereth

Bachurim, 46 in Moscow, 35 in Gomel, and 20 in Kiev, the religious youth league in Minsk counted 200 members.[55] As Moshe-Zvi Neriyah observed, "Rabbis from other cities in Russia would come to Minsk and be surprised by what they saw. Something of this nature in a time like this? How is that possible? They never imagined that there was still such a place. After all, such activity is connected to the dangers of arrest and deportation. From where does one find the courage and strength to do such things?"[56]

Both yeshivas and heders enjoyed clandestine financial support from JDC, which covered up to 30% of their budgets for religious education.[57] Few parents committed to providing a religious education for their children could afford to pay, given the duress of the economic situation and the outlawing of a large percentage of private trade and business. Expenses not only included the teacher's salary but also covered a monthly wage for a "guard" to watch over the heder or the yeshiva while in use. In case a teacher was arrested, JDC would provide financial assistance for the family while he was in prison.[58] The existence of such an elaborate network of clandestine religious institutions, with its hundreds of courageous accomplices, depended on the intersection of two factors. On the one hand, Minsk had been a large center of Jewish religious scholarship since the late eighteenth century. Therefore, those committed to imparting a religious education to the younger generation despite the separation between church and state mandated by the Soviet constitution could rely on preexisting institutions and organizations and were not in need of building the foundations from scratch. On the other hand, JDC was able to efficiently provide financial assistance for clandestine endeavors also by virtue of Minsk's nature as the new political, administrative, and bureaucratic center of a Soviet republic. The transformation of the city produced an intensification of Communist activities. But it also allowed official JDC activities to thrive there: The new Soviet capital saw a higher concentration of official institutions, often serving as a lighthouse to spread Communist ideology to the surrounding cities and towns of Belorussia. This gave JDC personnel the opportunity to consolidate the organization's support for official institutions and at the same time provide secret assistance to the unofficial "counterrevolutionary" activities. Although JDC did not coordinate the clandestine efforts—which were mostly initiated by local leaders and Minsk residents—it provided crucial support for what was going on anyway and, in some cases, became the catalyst for what could otherwise not have existed.

JDC's success in subsidizing underground religious educational institutions throughout the 1920s and early 1930s (Tsimbalist's yeshiva was closed down in 1932) can be ascribed, in part, to the relative success and vitality of its official activities. The more diverse, multifaceted, and elaborate the official activities were, the more they opened up a fertile realm of possibilities for unofficial endeavors. Not always conforming to the Soviet principle of nonsectarian help, JDC's official activities included supporting EMSO (and providing relief to Jewish social outcasts) and sponsoring Soviet Jewish cultural enterprises (and thus participating in the Sovietization process and the implementation of the Soviet nationality policy among Jews). To be sure, the relative success of JDC in a place like Minsk was determined to a large degree by the nature of the city itself: A historic Jewish center long before the establishment of the Soviet Union, located in the heart of the Pale of Settlement, densely populated by Jews, Minsk carried on some of the cultural traditions of a Lithuanian Jewish city. This undoubtedly provided some degree of infrastructure, resources, and a cultural framework that enabled JDC to accomplish some of its hidden goals, such as sustaining and providing for Jewish traditional life in Communist Russia. In other words, the significant—albeit temporary—achievements attained by JDC resulted from the interplay between the nature of the place in which the initial plan for sponsored activities was undertaken and the ability to adapt to the specific local reality that JDC workers and leaders devised in that particular place. Indeed, place mattered even within the constraints of the Bolshevik system, and it substantially informed JDC activities in any urban—or, for that matter, rural—setting in the Soviet Union.

NOTES

1. Elias Tcherikower, ed., *In der tkufe fun revolutsye: memuarn, materyaln, dokumentn* (Berlin: Yidishe literarishe farlag, 1924), 1–6.

2. Grigory Aronson, "Minsk unter daytshisher okupatsye," *Di tsukunft* 43, no. 1 (1938): 31.

3. See Moshe Levinson, "Chazonim ve-chazonut be-Minsk," in *Minsk ir va-em: korot, maasim, ishim, havai*, vol. I, ed. Sh. Even-Shoshan (Tel Aviv: Irgun yotse Minsk u-venotecha be-Yisrael, 1985), 115.

4. Natsionalnyi arkhiv respubliki Belarusi (NARB), f. 6, op. 1, d. 133, l. 26.

5. Tsentralniy Nauchnyi Arkhiv Natsionalnoi Akademii Nauk Belarusi (TsNANANB), f. 72, op. 1, d. 4, l. 67.

6. Quoted in Arn Rozin, "Ha-yeshuv ha-yehudi," *Minsk ir va-em*, 95.

7. Rossiski gosudarstvennyi arkhiv sotsialno-politicheskoi istorii (RGASPI), f. 445, op. 1, d. 9, ll. 25–26.

8. *Lishentsy* were citizens disenfranchised from Soviet electoral rights. From the Russian *lishchit'* (to deprive), this new political category designated all *byvshie liudi* (former people) of nonproletarian background and connected to the "bourgeois putrefaction," as Lenin put it. This category therefore included members of the prerevolutionary elite, former officers or high-ranking bureaucrats in the Tsarist state service, religious functionaries, and those who profited from hired labor ("exploiters"). *Lishentsy* typically became outcasts: Even if only one member had been disenfranchised, the entire family experienced restricted access to housing, education, and medical assistance.

9. Natsionalnyi arkhiv respubliki Belarusi (NARB), f. 42, op. 1, d. 72, l. 44.

10. Rossiski gosudarstvennyi arkhiv sotsialno-politicheskoi istorii (RGASPI), f. 445, op. 1, d. 64, ll. 10, 16. For JDC staff members in Minsk, see JDC Archives, Records of the New York Office of the American Jewish Joint Distribution Committee, 1921–1932, Folder 457, Minsk, List of Staff Members, June 1923.

11. JDC Archives, Records of the New York Office of the American Jewish Joint Distribution Committee, 1921–1932, Folder 459, Report from Edward Rosenblum (JDC Minsk) to Dr. Boris Bogen (JDC Moscow), 5, October 25, 1923.

12. Ibid., Folder 500, Report on the Work in White Russia, 2, May 5, 1922.

13. Ibid., Letter from Boris Bogen, Headquarters, American Jewish JDC, Moscow, to Joint Distribution, New York, March 6, 1923.

14. Ibid., Folder 474, Letter from Waldemar Haffkine to Cyrus Adler, 8, November 3, 1927.

15. Ibid., Folder 500, Letter from Boris Bogen, Headquarters, American Jewish Joint Distribution Committee, Moscow, to Joint Distribution Committee, New York, Attention—Committee on Russia, Subject: Minsk Relief to Professors, March 6, 1923.

16. Ibid., Folder 500, Report on the Work in White Russia, 1, May 5, 1922.

17. Gosudarstvennyi arkhiv rossiskoi federatsi (GARF), f. 1065, op. 1, d. 367, l. 35.

18. Ibid., Folder 459, Report from Mr. Rosenblum to Boris Bogen, 6, October 25, 1923.

19. Ibid., Folder 500, JDC Report on Minsk, June 13, 1923. There were 18 children's homes in Minsk in 1923 that provided shelter to approximately 1,536 children, most of them orphans. Six of these homes were Jewish (with 542 children); 12 were Russian, Belorussian, and Polish (with a total of 994 children).

20. Ibid., Folder 485, Additional Statement to the Report of the Relief Department of the Joint USSR, December 31, 1926.

21. Vladimir N. Brovkin, *Russia after Lenin: Politics, Culture and Society, 1921–1929* (London: Routledge, 1998), 30–31.

22. Ibid., Folder 565, Statement of Industrial Activities of the JDC in Russia, August 1, 1930.

23. See Nochem Chanin, *Soviet Rusland: vi ikh hob ir gezen* (New York: Farlag Veker, 1929), 9, 11, 30–31, 51–53.

24. See, for example, Berl Nakhamkin, "A Rov zogt az men tor nit ganvenen," *Der veker* 3 (June 1925); V. D., "Peklekh far zikh," *Oktyabr* 4 (January 1928).

25. JDC Archives, Records of the New York Office of the American Jewish Joint Distribution Committee, 1921–1932, Folder 526, Louis Fischer, "Jews in Soviet Russia: A Report," *The Jewish Tribune and Hebrew Standard: The American Jewish Weekly*, 2–4, November 20, 1925.

26. Natsionalnyi arkhiv respubliki Belarusi (NARB), f. 4, op. 1, d. 700, l. 119.

27. On the Evsektsiia's opposition to the EMSO, see Natsionalnyi arkhiv respubliki Belarusi (NARB), f. 4, op. 1, d. 430, ll. 97, 104–5.

28. See, for example, *Oktyabr* 4 (May 1928).

29. Gosudarstvennyi arkhiv Minskoi oblasti (GAMO), f. 6, op. 1, d. 240, l. 32.

30. Gosudarstvennyi arkhiv Minskoi oblasti (GAMO), f. 12, op. 1, d. 850, l. 28.

31. Gosudarstvennyi arkhiv Minskoi oblasti (GAMO), f. 12, op. 1, d. 836, ll. 7–8, 23.

32. Gosudarstvennyi arkhiv Minskoi oblasti (GAMO), f. 12, op. 1, d. 561, ll. 29–30.

33. GAMO, f. 12, op. 1, d. 558, ll. 6–14, 28. By March 1927, EMSO had 2,795 members.

34. Gosudarstvennyi arkhiv Minskoi oblasti (GAMO), f. 12, op. 1, d. 850, l. 35.

35. See Gosudarstvennyi arkhiv Minskoi oblasti (GAMO), f. 12, op. 1, d. 850, l. 13, 19.

36. On the EMSO's liquidation, see V. Rokhkind, "Ufdekn bizn sof di trotskistish-bundishe kontrabande," *Oktyabr* 3–4 (July 1937).

37. Natsionalnyi arkhiv respubliki Belarusi (NARB), f. 4, op. 1, d. 816, l. 71.

38. See, for example, Albert Kaganovitch, *The Long Life and Swift Death of Jewish Rechitsa: A Community in Belarus, 1625–2000* (Madison: University of Wisconsin Press, 2013), 240–241.

39. Natsionalnyi arkhiv respubliki Belarusi (NARB), f. 42, op. 1, d. 1438, l. 6.

40. Natsionalnyi arkhiv respubliki Belarusi (NARB), f. 42, op. 1, d. 1437, ll. 53–69.

41. Natsionalnyi arkhiv respubliki Belarusi (NARB), f. 12, op. 1, d. 4, ll. 95–97.

42. Natsionalnyi arkhiv respubliki Belarusi (NARB), f. 42, op. 1, d. 1437, ll. 53–69.

43. Natsionalnyi arkhiv respubliki Belarusi (NARB), f. 42, op. 1, d. 1437, ll. 26, 56, 62ob, 63, 63ob.

44. On JDC funding of Jewish cultural activities in Moscow, see, for example, JDC Archives, Records of the New York Office of the American Jewish Joint Distribution Committee, 1921–1932, Folder 449, Letter from Boris Bogen to JDC New York, March 28, 1923.

45. Ibid., Folder 454, JDC Report, March 1923.

46. Ibid., Folder 478, Memorandum from Joseph C. Hyman to Warburg, Rosenberg, Baerwald, and Marshall, March 1, 1929.

47. Ibid., Cable from NYC JDC Committee to Berlin, March 22, 1929.

48. Ibid., Correspondence between Joseph C. Hyman and Dr. Cyrus Adler, January 15, 1932; January 18, 1932.

49. Ibid., Letter from Samarius Gouray to Dr. Hyman, December 28, 1931; ibid., Letter from Rabbi Schneersohn to Dr. Cyrus Adler, January 18, 1932.

50. For a list of Minsk yeshivas and heders and the number of students, see JDC Archives, Records of the New York Office of the American Jewish Joint Distribution Committee, 1921–1932, Folder 476, Report of the Accomplishments of the Rabbinical Board in Russia during 5688, October 22, 1929.

51. See Moshe-Zvi Neriyah, "Al ha-yeshiva be-Minsk vemashehu al ha-chayim hadatiim," *Minsk ir va-em*, vol. 2, 159–67; Asher Kershteyn, "Im gdolei ha-Torah be-Minsk," *Minsk ir va-em*, 152–58.

52. Gosudarstvennyi arkhiv Minskoi oblasti (GAMO), f. 12, op. 1, d. 1016, ll. 25–30.

53. See, for example, Gosudarstvennyi arkhiv Minskoi oblasti (GAMO), f. 320, op. 1, d. 600, ll. 3–6, 10–12.

54. JDC Archives, Records of the New York Office of the American Jewish Joint Distribution Committee, 1921–1932, Folder 476, Report of the Accomplishments of the Rabbinical Board, 3, January 22, 1929. For more on the Council of Rabbis of the USSR, see David E. Fishman, "To Our Brethren Abroad: Letters and Reports by Soviet Rabbis, 1925–1930," *Jews in Russia and Eastern Europe* 1–2, no. 54–55 (2005): 108–79.

55. JDC Archives, Records of the New York Office of the American Jewish Joint Distribution Committee, 1921–1932, Folder 476, Report of the Accomplishments of the Rabbinical Board, 12, October 22, 1929. With 250 members, the Tifereth Bachurim in Vitebsk was the largest in the Soviet Union.

56. *Rabi Yehoshua me-Horodna zatsal more tsedek ve-rosh metivtah, kobets le-zikhro* (Jerusalem, 1949), 36–37.

57. JDC Archives, Records of the New York Office of the American Jewish Joint Distribution Committee, 1921–1932, Folder 473, Survey of the Religious and Cultural Work Accomplished with the Funds Offered by the JDC in the USSR by Means of the Rebbins Committee of the USSR, 3, May 22, 1927.

58. Ibid., Folder 472, Aide-mémoire about Religious Education in Russia, 3, July 2, 1926. On JDC relief assistance to yeshiva students in Minsk, see YIVO Archives, RG 358, file 12, l. 057, Letter from Boris Bogen to JDC in New York, March 6, 1923.

3

The First American Organization in Soviet Russia

JDC and Relief in the Ukraine, 1920–1923

Jaclyn Granick

"No physician will kill a patient even if he knows that he is going to die. The situation [of the Jews in the Ukraine] is so terrible that we cannot—because we cannot save them all—refuse to save some. We must do what we can."

Frank Rosenblatt, JDC Archives, Records of the New York Office of the American Jewish Joint Distribution Committee, 1919–1921, Folder 21, Minutes of the JDC Executive Committee, March 10, 1921

The civilian population of the Ukraine was devastated in the regions along the southwestern edge of Russia, where the imperial Pale of Settlement had been located and where the Great War, the Polish-Soviet War, and the Russian Civil War had raged. Given the instability and military occupation by many different armed forces, hunger and disease were rampant. The local population suffered from cold and lack of shelter where much property had been destroyed. Moreover, the economy was in shambles, and civil society and government were weak. For the region's Jews, conditions were particularly difficult. While Jews had frequently been the victims of violent outbursts directed by troops on civilians, "the scale of the pogroms of 1919 dwarfed previous violence"[1] in the region in terms of geographical range, the number of pogroms, and the number of fatalities. Indeed, observers estimated that between 50,000 and 150,000 Jews had been killed from the wider 3 to 4 million Jews living in the Ukraine and White Russia.[2] Mortality statistics indicated such an astoundingly high rate of Jewish deaths in Russia since 1914 that one American Jewish Joint Distribution Committee (JDC) physician considered it "race suicide to a degree that threatens national annihilation."[3]

Despite the scale of Jewish suffering throughout World War I and just after, JDC had been almost helpless to reach Jews in the Ukraine and White Russia after the Russian Revolution in 1917. Although JDC busily shipped relief to places such as Poland, Romania, Vienna, and Prague, which were accessible to the Allies following the armistice between Germany and the Allies in November 1918, JDC could not access territory held by the Soviet government, which did not have formal diplomatic relations with the Allies. JDC representatives did manage to follow the Polish Army partly into the Ukraine, attending to the local Jews as the Red Army retreated. Then, in July 1920, two of these JDC relief workers, Professor Israel Friedlaender and Rabbi Bernard Cantor, were shot and died in their American uniforms as they sought to provide relief to Jews in the quickly shrinking piece of the Ukraine occupied by Poland.[4] The terrible condition of these Jews that Soviet Russia occasionally exposed when its army retreated and these tragic murders were a hint of what might await JDC—if it could ever get inside Ukraine.

This chapter tells the story of the JDC's first forays into Soviet Russia after the Russian Revolution.[5] It began with JDC representatives concluding the first agreement of any American organization with Soviet Russia, meaning that JDC was already in Soviet Russia in the summer of 1920 while the Russian Civil War and the Polish-Soviet War were still ongoing. However, this so-called Fisher-Pine Agreement did not create the opportunity for JDC to work through the Soviet bureaucracy to distribute aid to Jews as its JDC negotiators had hoped; instead, JDC unintentionally expanded the mandate of the Soviet bureaucracy itself, which in turn provoked something of an attempted internal Communist revolution within JDC. To avoid further playing into Bolshevik hands, JDC refused to cooperate with the Bolsheviks and then spent the next two years searching for a different opening, working on a small scale via the American Friends Service Committee (AFSC) in the meantime. Finally, in 1922, JDC went to the Ukraine to provide large-scale relief as part of Herbert Hoover's American Relief Administration (ARA) Russian mission.

This episode is significant for understanding JDC's work in its early years, as it illustrates the extent to which JDC was able to work through and around the limitations it faced on its humanitarian work. Although JDC remained within the letter of the law, it was hardly a benign, neutral presence—rather, its work reflected careful, creative, and strategic planning and bargaining that stretched the possibilities of humanitarian relief so that it could act on behalf of suffering Jews. So, for example, when the ARA went to Russia to answer the Soviet's call for famine relief in the Volga Region in the hopes that food relief would serve to counteract Bolshevism and anarchy, JDC managed to turn the ARA's attention to the Ukraine and provide relief there, despite the fact that no famine was occurring in the urban areas where Jews lived. This arrangement involved JDC agreeing to provide funds for the ARA to distribute on a nonsectarian basis. JDC was thus able to find a way into the Ukraine and assist suffering Jews on a large scale while sidestepping dealings with the Bolshevik government. Although the ARA sought to control JDC's actions, and despite a constant threat of antisemitism, JDC was eventually able to find ways of pursuing its own distinct goals of reconstructing Jewish life in the Ukraine. To this end, finding a number of effective proxies to primarily target Jews under a nonsectarian banner was the key tactic of JDC, including assisting pogrom victims, associating Jews in the Ukraine with famine, incorporating remittance transfers into the ARA's relief mission, and focusing on urban centers and social institutions.

CREATING A COMMUNIST GOLEM

While JDC was organizing its first overseas unit for Poland at the end of 1919 to build upon post-armistice relief that had begun that spring in Warsaw, JDC also began investigating the possibility of further operations in the Ukraine, sending Harry M. Fisher, Max Pine, and Israel Friedlaender with the unit to launch attempts to enter the Ukraine from

Warsaw.[6] For months, these JDC delegates, along with Julius Goldman as JDC's representative in Paris and the JDC office in New York, tried to get into the Ukraine, all of which resulted only in the provision of some relief to Polish-occupied or White Army–controlled parts of the Ukraine.[7] In the late spring of 1920, JDC workers were thus distributing relief supplies and organizing committees in Kiev, Rovno, Zhitomir, Tarnopol, and the surrounding areas, but that foray was brief, dangerous, and geographically limited.[8] JDC also set aside a large sum of money for the Ukraine so that supplies and funds would be ready to go as soon as it found a way to send them.[9]

The major difficulty was obtaining permission from both the Soviets and the US State Department to enter the Ukraine. Throughout 1919, American Jewish leaders sent letters to the state department, pleading for information and for the United States to undertake relief there.[10] An American Jewish Congress delegation headed to Washington, DC, for a meeting with Secretary of State Robert Lansing on the matter in December 1919, and in that same month, the US Senate passed a resolution demanding information from the state department on massacres of Jews in the Ukraine.[11] However, the Allies maintained an informal blockade on Soviet Russia until January 1920.[12] Although Hoover had made some efforts to push the Allies toward a relief plan for Soviet Russia, they were not working out.[13] In the spring of 1920, while commercial sanctions had at last been lifted, JDC still could not obtain the support it wished to enter Russia, nor was it able to convince the ARA to match its effort.[14] The American Red Cross (ARC), the AFSC, and JDC all wanted to do relief work in Soviet Russia, and they mounted a semi-coordinated campaign to convince the US State Department and the ARA.[15]

At the end of March 1920, the US State Department consented to JDC delegates entering Soviet Ukraine, although without any support or protection.[16] Still, it was not easy to find a way into Russia as private individuals—Julius Goldman held meetings with Russian representatives in Paris, Berlin, and Denmark, and the Ukraine Commission of the JDC overseas unit took exploratory trips along Soviet borders, to seemingly little effect.[17] But once the US State Department failed to offer an objection,

JDC delegates Max Pine, a labor leader, and Harry M. Fisher, a judge from Chicago, went to Reval (Tallinn, Estonia) to apply for Soviet visas and to start arranging for JDC supplies to come through the port of Reval.[18] Max Pine reached Moscow in late May, and Fisher joined soon after.[19] Maxim Litvinov's intercession after meeting with Goldman in Denmark likely helped with the authorization of their visas. The pair thus became representatives of the first American organization in Soviet Russia, opening Bolshevik Moscow's first window to the West. On June 15, 1920, Goldman cabled the JDC New York office with Fisher and Pine's delighted announcement that they had organized the "All Russian and Ukrainian Committee of All Jewish Elements for Aid of Pogrom Sufferers" and that the Ukrainian government had sanctioned it, promising transportation and the safety of shipments. They requested that JDC send clothing, milk, grains, medicine, and tools.[20] Soviet Ukraine had a contested status as a sovereign state, with its own government—it was not merely a federated republic within Soviet Russia—and thus relief to the Ukraine had to be approved in both Moscow and the Ukraine.[21]

As JDC waited for the return of Pine and Fisher, Goldman organized supplies to send through Reval, and JDC instructed Frank Rosenblatt to head to Russia.[22] Indeed, Fisher and Pine had signed an agreement with the Bolshevik government in Moscow, dubbed the Fisher-Pine Agreement by JDC. In so doing, they had created a new organization, alternatively called the All Russian Jewish Public Committee, Evobshestkom, or Yidgeskom.[23] These JDC representatives were desperate to do whatever they could to help Jews in the Ukraine and White Russia, and the terms of the agreement swung toward the benefit of the Bolsheviks. Furthermore, they had indirectly indicated US recognition of the Soviet government.[24] Fisher and Pine acknowledged these shortcomings but wrote that "this contract is justified on the basis that an extreme emergency exists in the matter of pogrom sufferers which requires extraordinary measures to be applied to it," proud that they had created an opportunity for Jewish relief work despite the hostile environment.[25] As Fisher and Pine left Eastern Europe, the first shipment of six carloads of relief supplies was delivered via Reval into Soviet Russia.[26]

The Soviet government, unwilling to condone sectarian relief, had grant-ed permission for JDC to assist those who had suffered in the pogroms because the Bolsheviks considered the pogroms part of the counterrevolu-tion and they were willing to fund victims of counterrevolution. In reality, however, not all Jews were pogrom victims—many were simply suffering from the effects of war and revolution. This formulation, however, usefully provided JDC with a highly correlated proxy for Jewish relief that was acceptable to the authorities.

Yidgeskom was not an independent organization but an arm of the party, fully part of the Bolshevik government under the Central Commissariat for Jewish Affairs in Soviet Russia. As Fisher and Pine noted in their report to JDC, government and society were synonymous. Although Yidgeskom's organizational structure did contain remnants of the prerevolutionary, private philanthropic Russian Jewish organizations EKOPO (Evreiskii komitet pomoshchi zhertvam voiny [Central Jewish Committee for the Relief of War Victims]), ORT (Obchestvo Remeslenogo Truda [Organization for Rehabilitation through Training]), OZE (Obshchestvo Zdravookhraneniia Evreev [Society for the Preservation of the Health of the Jewish Population]), they were overwhelmed in number by leftist and Communist Jewish parties. JDC was given a representative on Yidgeskom, meaning that JDC could not direct the work, but Fisher and Pine hoped that this representative would "keep the conflicting elements together" and allow JDC to stay informed. The agreement called for local Jewish social service commissions—built upon a union of existing political and civic organizations and in cooperation with general relief work—and entailed using the Russian Red Cross Society to store and move commodities. JDC was to turn over all its relief supplies to Yidgeskom, and the Soviet government was also supposed to provide funds for it, although the precise exchange rate remained a sticking point.[27]

Dr. Frank F. Rosenblatt supervised the Fisher-Pine Agreement in Soviet Russia from September 1920 to February 1921. An economist by training who leaned toward the cause of labor, Rosenblatt had been in Siberia for much of 1919, organizing JDC work on behalf of refugees and prisoners of war in the territory held by Alexander Kolchak's White Army.[28] As he tried to lay the groundwork for relief in Russia in the summer of 1920, he discovered in discussions with Soviet representatives that there were already many misunderstandings, particularly regarding the amount of money that JDC had committed.[29] JDC leaders decided in Paris that they should adhere to the Fisher-Pine Agreement but start by sending small sums of money.[30] Meanwhile, back in the United States, the JDC Committee on Russia was busy seeking US State Department approval for the Fisher-Pine Agreement, without success.[31] Rosenblatt entered Soviet Russia via Reval, the Estonian port city west of Petrograd, again without explicit US State Department approval and without an American passport.

JDC never began sending larger sums or large shipments of goods under the Fisher-Pine Agreement. After months of frustrating negotiations with Yidgeskom, Rosenblatt had more or less reached the same point as had Fisher and Pine: He realized that getting any aid to Jews in Soviet Russia would require deference to the Bolshevik government at exploitative exchange rates. Moreover, without a visible relief organization at the local level or the opening of Odessa as a closer port, it was hard to imagine how appropriations of money or goods would ever actually reach those in need. Then, when Rosenblatt refused to play Soviet politics, OZE, EKOPO, and ORT, the last vestiges of non-party participation in Jewish relief, were officially dismantled.[32] This was a significant blow to JDC, which lost its main local partners in its efforts to support independent Jewish civil society.

JDC was not only stymied by the difficulty of working as an American private organization with the Soviet government. The very organization it had created, Yidgeskom, took on a life of its own that shocked and dismayed JDC. Yidgeskom sent a representative, David H. Dubrowsky, to New York as its agent in September 1920.[33] Nothing of the sort had been discussed by Fisher and Pine. Dubrowsky set up an office and immediately began soliciting funds, goods, and remittances among American Jews, undermining and competing with JDC, even as JDC continued to operate cautiously through Yidgeskom via Rosenblatt in Russia. Dubrowsky had a penchant for writing scathing remarks and publishing private letters he had received in the Yiddish press. He started a heated argument in the press, publicly shaming JDC, which refused to cooperate with him. Meanwhile, the *landsmanshaftn* that JDC had been carefully cultivating along with the People's Relief Committee, the left-wing constituent organization of JDC in America, began to use Dubrowsky's services to send relief to Russia because JDC could not do so independently. Within the People's Relief Committee, there were calls to secede from JDC, which nearly succeeded on several occasions. Jewish organizations such as the Poale Zion and branches of the Workmen's Circle in the United States were agitating from the left for cooperation with Yidgeskom instead of JDC. It was obvious that Yidgeskom charged exorbitant exchange rates, was willing to send unsorted and used clothing, did not have the infrastructure to deliver remittances or food packages, and had no way to guarantee its accountability to donors. Clearly, the Bolshevik government was happy to exploit Jewish relief to take American dollars and open a window to the West. Yet, some prominent JDC figures such as Judah Magnes decided that the only way to reach Russian Jews was through Dubrowsky. Despite the widely recognized dubious nature of working with Dubrowsky, JDC had not presented an alternative, nor had any other organization. So, for several months, the People's Relief Committee, the Workmen's Circle, the Poale Zion in America, and the *landsmanshaftn* were the American Jewish organizations actually working toward relief in Russia, even if the results of that work are entirely unclear.[34] This all occurred while the Red Scare in the United States was ascending, with its staple canard of "Jewish Bolshevism" threatening Jewish security overall.[35] Difficulties with Dubrowsky, in the context of the Red Scare, prompted JDC to limit its cooperation with Yidgeskom.

Later, Boris Bogen, JDC's first European director and an admirably competent social worker who had created JDC's first overseas relief mission in Poland, reflected that JDC was too timid. He intimated that the organization could have done more to cooperate with Yidgeskom despite the drawbacks of this relationship.[36] Perhaps this was true, but JDC had successfully relied on the goodwill and the protection of the US State Department and the ARA during the war and in Poland, and it was unable to make a firm decision to cut off these relationships in favor of cooperation with the Bolsheviks, even for humanitarian purposes. As was the case with all other American humanitarian organizations that saw themselves as professional, rational, and modern, one of JDC's core operating principles was organizational neutrality. The problem was that the only two real options appeared to be (1) that no relief work would be done while JDC waited for a move by the ARA while absorbing attacks on its "anti-Communist" stance or (2) that JDC would play into the hands of Soviet propaganda and allow itself to be perceived as a Communist sympathizer, which might result in negative repercussions in a nativist, anti-Bolshevik United States. JDC sought a middle ground, ignoring Dubrowsky; working in limited ways with Yidgeskom in Soviet Russia; trying to maintain Jewish pluralism within its own structure by retaining the People's Relief Committee; and attempting to sustain its neutral, nonpolitical image with the US State Department and other American relief organizations. As a result, JDC was incapacitated when it came to Russian relief, and it simply had to swallow the public shaming in the press and even Communist accusations directed at it by the state department. In one instance, the state department saw examples of Communist propaganda that Fisher forwarded through the official diplomatic pouch, which Fisher said he was bringing back to show the US State Department and JDC. The state department scolded Felix Warburg, chairman of JDC, for allowing such a delegate to try to arrange a nonpolitical, humanitarian mission in Russia.[37] Louis Marshall, the renowned lawyer and key figure in the American Jewish Relief Committee, found himself defending JDC and placing as much distance between JDC and Dubrowsky as possible.[38]

JDC eventually found a third way to make JDC funds available to Jews in the Ukraine by asking the AFSC to extend its operations in the Ukraine on JDC's behalf. The Friends had experienced similar political problems working in Soviet Russia to those of JDC, including resistance from the US State Department. The British Friends sorted out matters, and the AFSC joined the British Friends' relief efforts in Russia in September 1920 as Rosenblatt was entering the country.[39] The AFSC took on the role of distributing relief for many organizations in Russia and acting as a clearinghouse for information regarding wider relief efforts in that country.[40] Rosenblatt came home in the spring of 1921, pleading for JDC to continue working with Yidgeskom in Russia to send $3 to $4 million dollars to buy goods that could not be found in Russia: land and farm equipment for Jewish farmers and equipment for hospitals and schools in the big cities in the Ukraine.[41] Instead, however, JDC began to work toward sending small sums for distribution by the Friends rather than through Yidgeskom.[42] Warburg wrote Bogen that he felt Rosenblatt's agreement with the Soviet government was worse than the Fisher-Pine terms and would not satisfy JDC's "many shades of contributors," especially in light of the possibility of working with the Friends.[43]

In April 1921, leaders of JDC and the AFSC met twice, and JDC expressed its hope to send its own representatives as AFSC representatives.[44] Rosenblatt felt that "only a Jew would be able to know what was necessary to alleviate the misery of the Jews, and where it should be sent." He also worried that the Friends already in Russia were afraid of adding a JDC representative "because of the theory that Jews are not cooperative and cannot work in harmony with non-Jewish members of their Unit."[45] The AFSC did agree to distribute the $100,000 appropriation of JDC money but would not allow a JDC representative to act as an AFSC representative. Still, the AFSC agreed to send money to Jewish-dominated areas in the Ukraine and White Russia that were not part of official famine areas, forcing the AFSC to struggle to maintain its appearance of equal treatment regardless of religious or ethnic affiliation.[46]

Although JDC had been planning to send millions of dollars to Russia, it was long unable to take action in a way that could bridge America and Soviet Russia. Thus, after a year and a half of actively struggling to support Jews in the Ukraine, in the summer of 1921, it had only sent some carloads of rice, condensed milk, and oil of the $100,000 in supplies it allotted for the AFSC to distribute on its behalf.[47] Although JDC delegates worked out bold agreements while in Moscow, once they returned to New York, they could not convince the JDC office in New York to bet millions on the Jewish Communists in Russia on the chance that some relief could be distributed. Yidgeskom was a golem of JDC's own creation, a Jewish arm of the party that was unreliable at best and sometimes downright hostile but that now had a full monopoly on Jewish relief in Russia. Fortunately for JDC and the Jews suffering in the Ukraine, in the summer of 1921, the

ARA and the US State Department were finally coming around to the idea of a Russian mission. JDC had waited throughout the entire Great War to go with the ARA to Poland; to make an impact in Russia, it had to endure world war, a revolution, a civil war, an interstate war, and a famine.

BACK TO NEUTRAL

When Frank Rosenblatt spoke to the JDC Executive Committee in March 1921 just after his return from Moscow, he expressed despair at the overwhelming scope of need of Jews in the Ukraine and at the inability of JDC to do anything to help. Yet he insisted that any effort, no matter how little it solved, was better than doing nothing.[48] By the summer of 1921, various left-wing Jewish groups and *landsmanshaftn* in the United States were sending money and packages through the New York office of Yidgeskom, and JDC had provided about $100,000 to the AFSC for relief in the Ukraine. Following the famine appeal of Maxim Gorky, the ARA entered Russia at last, opening an official American door (as much as the ARA might have denied it was official) to Soviet Russia just as that country was transitioning to the New Economic Policy (NEP).[49] JDC slowly transitioned into a relief role with the ARA in Russia, not committing itself fully until March 1922. But first the ARA had to be convinced that there was a famine in the Ukraine, and only then could JDC even hope to aid the Jews who were concentrated there.

The ARA signed an agreement in Riga with the Soviet government at the end of August 1921.[50] JDC did not immediately join the ARA or abandon its partnership with the AFSC. Days after the Riga agreement had been signed, Herbert Hoover held a meeting with representatives of the European Relief Council, including the ARA, the AFSC, the ARC, and JDC.[51] Following the meeting, JDC began to cooperate with the ARA mission to Russia insofar as it provided $750,000 for the Volga Region and one representative on the ARA staff, even though the ARA's original plan was to employ no Jews.[52] JDC sent the agronomist Dr. Joseph Rosen as its representative because of his technical expertise. Rosen was born to an elite family in Moscow and remained close to his family there but fled from exile in Siberia (due to radical leanings) to New York, receiving his PhD from the University of Michigan.[53] Rosen's main contribution to the ARA mission was that he paved the way for corn to be planted instead of rye. Corn could be planted two months later in the season than rye, by which time grain seed could actually reach farmers through the transportation bottleneck on the Russian railroads that plagued the ARA's relief efforts, and at a lower cost.[54] He began organizing the distribution of seeds funded by JDC and intended for Jews in the Ukraine as early as December 1921, ensuring that Jewish farmers would take part in the agricultural initiatives of the ARA in Russia and opening the door to a Jewish philanthropic focus on farming there.[55] Although he was mainly devoted to seeds, he did take part in organizing ARA relief distribution to White Russia, particularly in Minsk, with its significant Jewish population.[56] Otherwise, JDC continued during the first months of the ARA mission to Russia to work mainly through the Friends. The AFSC was in charge of distributing JDC food supplies to children in White Russia, also centered in Minsk, and JDC hoped to persuade the AFSC to include Odessa in its distributions by making an additional $150,000 contribution in February 1922.[57]

ARA food remittance package delivery began in Russia, with the intention that food would be sent to the Volga Region starting in November 1921. Remittances as a form of aid appealed to American Jews, who had been sending relief remittances to East-Central Europe since the beginning of the Great War. Many maintained a strong desire to help their families and friends who were still living in Russia, and they made up a substantial portion of what the ARA estimated to be about 2 million Russian Americans.[58] JDC sold these ARA food remittance coupons alongside its own remittance offerings through its *landsmanshaft* department and its transmission offices across the United States, ensuring their convenience for American Jews. As soon as the ARA announced that it would be delivering food remittances in Russia, it started receiving inquiries from American Jews as to whether this meant that it would deliver to the Ukraine. This reaction caused the ARA to wonder if there might be a serious famine in the Ukraine.[59]

American Jews wished to feed mainly Jews, and JDC certainly liked the idea of working with the ARA again, but in the Volga Region, the ARA was not anywhere near the Jews most needing relief. To remedy the situation, James N. Rosenberg, the new JDC director in Europe, and Walter Lyman Brown of the ARA met in London in October 1921. Rosenberg pointed out the suffering of the Jews in the Ukraine and White Russia, but Brown insisted that the ARA had to confine its necessarily limited operations to the Volga valley, "where extreme famine exists," and not the Ukraine, where the ARA was unaware of similar difficulties. Nevertheless, they agreed to carry out a full investigation of the conditions in southwest Russia, and the ARA agreed to extend its food remittance work to the Ukraine if it received enough remittances aimed there.[60] As a result of Rosenberg's October negotiations with Brown and the flood of inquiries about remittance deliveries in the Ukraine that the ARA had received from American Jews, Colonel William Haskell, the head of the ARA Russian mission, sent two ARA men to investigate the Ukraine in January 1922.[61] The pair found evidence of a severe famine, estimating that there were 1.1 million adults in need, but they also found that the famine was not taking place in the regions of the Ukraine with a dense Jewish population.[62] Following the discovery of a famine in the Ukraine, the ARA renegotiated the Riga contract to add relief in the Ukraine.[63] The ARA's investigation and resulting negotiations to conduct famine relief in the Ukraine were both fortuitous and devastating for JDC; on one hand, the ARA had at last opened up the possibility of doing relief work in the Ukraine. On the other hand, although for once the Jews had been spared a misfortune (of famine), as a result they might still see no relief because the ARA was only targeting famine victims.

Following the ARA's new agreement to work in the Ukraine, the New York office of JDC decided in March 1922 to find a way to cooperate fully with the ARA—it was the best option available.[64] By this point, the ARA was already contemplating its departure in September, so the plan was to allow JDC to fully take over relief operations in the Ukraine, including famine and nonfamine areas, under the identity of the ARA.[65] Taking the helm of relief in the Ukraine, Colonel William Grove of the ARA reunited with Boris Bogen, with whom he had worked in Poland. Additional JDC workers joined Bogen—mostly seasoned personnel from the JDC overseas unit in Poland. Meanwhile, beginning in February 1922, JDC had embarked on a $14-million fundraising campaign in America in the hopes that much of this money would go to the budding initiative in Russia.[66]

The ARA insisted that all other American agencies work directly under it in Russia, which was especially true for JDC, which had to pretend to *be* the ARA in the districts of the Ukraine under its purview and follow the orders of Colonel Grove, the ARA's Ukrainian supervisor, even while the ARA remained active mostly in Russia proper.[67] In fact, by some measurements, such as when it came to providing food for children, JDC—acting as the ARA—distributed as much relief in the Ukraine as the ARA itself.[68] This arrangement was worrisome for JDC leaders. Rosenberg fretted that the ARA's requirements that JDC act as a nonsectarian agency whose main goal was to alleviate famine was going to be a major problem because the Jews were not in the officially designated famine areas.[69] He felt it was inadequate for donors who were contributing to a Jewish cause and to the Jews who needed relief in the Ukraine that likely not more than 20% of the supplies would go to Jews under the ARA. Furthermore, he thought, if JDC relief looked like it came from the ARA, it would not even have the side effect of contributing to goodwill toward Jews among its non-Jewish recipients.[70] Bogen felt that JDC was being asked unfairly to distribute general relief because such efforts were directing supplies to the Jews' recent enemies when no other organizations were being asked to do such a thing.[71] Rosenberg, by contrast, hoped that JDC relief efforts would work to diminish local antisemitism, if the ARA would at least permit placards and notes on packages stating plainly for all recipients that the relief was funded by Jews for nonsectarian purposes.[72] From the perspective of the ARA, however, whose goals included ending famine and promoting American values in Russia, JDC had to be willing to contribute substantial funding for all of the Ukraine and work in the famine zones in order to justify being part of the ARA mission.

Despite its reservations, JDC agreed to provide a first donation of $1.5 million worth of foodstuffs for ARA's work across the Ukraine in the summer of 1921, of which 50% would be geared toward relief in Jewish areas.[73] This funding made JDC the largest private donor to the ARA and a larger donor than either the British or French governments to Russian famine relief coordinated through the International Committee of the Red Cross and the League of Nations.[74] JDC-ARA relations were marked by ongoing tension over how much control the ARA maintained between the nonsectarian and explicitly Jewish missions of the organizations, by personality clashes, and by differing views of how to combat antisemitism both within the ARA and among the population being served.[75] Significantly, JDC did not want to focus only on feeding people because rehabilitating Jewish civil society was a fundamental goal of JDC and could not be achieved through food alone. JDC's vision of relief work had much in common with the vision of minority rights recently established in Paris: that Jewish lives would have to be revitalized through collective Jewish institutional life. Bogen recommended that JDC (as the ARA) focus on supporting Jewish social institutions such as orphanages, old people's homes, and hospitals, none of which were reached by Yidgeskom, which was intent on only relieving victims of pogroms. He further suggested that the ARA concentrate on refugees as a category because refugees included non-Jewish famine refugees and Jews, and targeting them all would achieve the goal of reaching many Jews while appearing to be nonsectarian.[76] Rosenberg consistently viewed the model of the Friends' cooperation with the ARA, which allowed the Friends to operate openly and autonomously without being subsumed by the ARA, as a goal to which JDC should aspire, although Lewis Strauss in New York advised that JDC would do better to simply free itself of the ARA once it had established relief in the Ukraine.[77]

According to the JDC and ARA arrangement, feeding programs to keep people from starving had to be JDC's main priority following its arrival in the spring of 1922 through the fall. Beginning April 30, 1922, adults in the Ukraine could eat in soup kitchens paid for by JDC, children ate in schools and orphanages, and students could go to specially organized kitchens.[78] JDC supplied food for both adults and children in the Ukraine on behalf of the ARA, although JDC, especially Rosenberg, was reluctant to provide extensive food supplies for non-Jewish adults. JDC and the ARA finally reached a formal compromise arrangement in June wherein half of JDC's food supplies for adults would go to the famine areas in the countryside

A group of mostly children and women waits for the opening of the JDC soup kitchen. Aleksandrovsk (now Zaporozhye), Ekaterinoslav (now Dnepropetrovsk) District, Ukraine, 1922. JDC was the largest single donor to ARA food programs in Soviet Russia, focusing resources on helping nearly 2 million Jews survive in the Ukraine while the ARA's main operations targeted famine relief in the Volga Region. Photo by J. Kogan.

where there were few Jews and the other half would go to refugees in cities outside the official famine areas.[79] Through these efforts and over the summer of 1922, JDC and the ARA in the Ukraine fed 800,000 children and 800,000 adults in some fashion.[80] In addition, the Friends in Minsk quietly continued to feed and clothe both Jewish and non-Jewish children at institutions in their districts in White Russia from the money that JDC had appropriated for the organization.[81]

More importantly, after JDC concluded its agreement with the ARA in the spring of 1922, the ARA had begun delivering remittances to the Ukraine, which became the main ARA operation in the Ukraine. Food remittances were a package system that allowed individuals in the United States to send food directly to their loved ones abroad in an efficient, reliable, standardized way. Although they resembled typical immigrant remittances sent home through the international banking system, they had become institutionalized into humanitarian relief activities due to disruptions in banking caused by the Great War, and they continued to be used by relief organizations well after the war, expanding from delivering cash to including commodities.[82] Because American Jews came out to buy food remittances in force for family and friends living in Soviet Russia and because the ARA restricted the amount of aid that JDC could otherwise provide to Jews, these food remittances were crucial.[83] From the ARA's perspective, however, food remittances were already a sensitive issue without adding a Jewish component. Because food remittances had to be purchased by Americans and addressed directly to specified individuals in Russia, they operated to the benefit of the bourgeoisie and intelligentsia who had connections abroad—those very classes that the Soviet government least wanted to support.[84]

JDC took pains to convince the ARA that remittance delivery had to continue for humanitarian reasons, and it accepted the fact that it would have to pay vast sums to the ARA and acquiesce to providing food to non-Jews in order for remittances to continue unabated.[85] The "vast majority" of ARA food remittances—75% to 90% of them—were purchased by American Jews, and the ARA, not JDC, received a quarter of the cost of each package to fund its broader efforts to feed hungry children.[86] In 1922 and 1923, JDC and the ARA delivered over 40,000 food packages to Jews in Russia, and JDC estimated that about $10 million worth of these reached Jews in Russia.[87] By consciously mobilizing immigrants in the United States to send food remittances and by including the free delivery of these remittances by JDC in the ARA-JDC agreement, JDC was able to ensure that a significant amount of food went to hungry Jews in the Ukraine, making up, at least in part, for the fact that JDC workers in the field had very little room to maneuver.[88] JDC even tried to build on this success and win back *landsmanshaft* support from Dubrowsky by allowing the *landsmanshaftn* to send bulk foodstuffs to their hometowns and appoint a committee there to distribute the food.[89] This new option added up to another $1.5 million in relief, even if it provoked endless complications and griping.[90]

JDC men working under the auspices of the ARA still found ways to move their work toward Jewish relief as much as possible despite ARA and Soviet resistance. Although JDC was subject to the supervision of Colonel Grove of the ARA in the Ukraine, Bogen's long-standing friendly relationship with him dating back to Poland paid off.[91] Within months of his arrival, Bogen remarked on how Jewish institutions, such as trade schools and hospitals, seemed to be reviving.[92] Materials were now coming in through Odessa and could bypass the long journey via Reval and through Russia. The ARA was running a medical operation in the cities of the Ukraine focused on distributing medical supplies that was a satisfactory arrangement from JDC's perspective, despite its limited scope. Bogen was optimistic and felt Jews were not discriminated against in relief, despite some evidence to the contrary. For example, the wave of 1919 pogroms in the Ukraine had not yet receded into a distant past, the NEP bolstered both persistent conflation by locals and authorities between Bolsheviks and Jews as well as accusations of Jews acting as speculators, and local Ukrainians were suspicious of the ARA and the way it seemed associated with both Jews and capitalism.[93] Nonetheless, Bogen credited the same NEP for a remarkable turnaround, although he also felt sure that JDC had saved thousands from starvation.[94] Another promising sign: When the ARA marked its soup kitchens with signs saying that they were supported by the Jewish Joint Distribution Committee at JDC's insistence in the summer of 1922, the signs were at first torn down whenever they were left unguarded and the government ordered them to be taken down. However, the situation quickly normalized, and the placards ceased to be an item of discussion.[95]

As the ARA made plans to leave Russia, JDC sought to remain and work on projects that would go beyond immediate relief needs and provide a future for the 2.45 million Jews that JDC estimated remained in Russia.[96] Thus, JDC began negotiating a new contract with the ARA just a couple of months after having finally settled on a mutually satisfactory one.[97] Negotiations started poorly, with the ARA trying to dump its entire Ukraine activity, nonsectarian principles and all, on JDC, but the new September agreement gave JDC more latitude. The new arrangement transformed JDC into an ARA affiliate directed by Bogen for the purposes

This Russian poster of the American Relief Administration (ARA) was used in the Ukraine during the feeding program carried out by JDC and the ARA. Zaporozhye, Ukraine, 1922. The text reads as follows: "Food Distribution in This Kitchen through the Intermediary of American Relief Administration is a Voluntary Gift of the American People. (signed) Chairman of ARA—Herbert Hoover. In cooperation with the American Jewish Distribution Committee."

of feeding hungry children, put a JDC medical representative on the ARA medical team, and permitted Joseph Rosen to launch JDC reconstructive efforts separately from ARA's relief work.[98] This newfound semi-autonomy, combined with sudden favor from the Soviet government, suggested that JDC might instead finally be able to sign an independent agreement with the Soviets similar to that of the Friends, the Young Men's Christian Association (YMCA), and the Mennonites.[99] Bogen and the Soviets negotiated a provisional agreement in September 1922, and Joseph Rosen concluded it in December.[100] To be sure, there were problems with this new status. One JDC leader worried about the ramifications of an American Jewish organization recognizing the Soviet government but ultimately concluded that taking action was better than returning to inactivity.[101]

Under the new agreement, JDC could support Russian Jews as long as its efforts had no religious overtones.[102] There were further downsides: JDC still often had to work through government agencies and Yidgeskom.[103] Although JDC's primary strategy was to subsidize institutions to make them self-supporting, the Soviets would not always cooperate, not least because the Soviets continued to resist attempts to revive civil society.[104] The ARA child-feeding program also remained insufficient for Jewish children, focused as it was on nonsectarian famine relief.[105]

Nevertheless, in 1923, JDC operated mostly independently in the Ukraine, with Bogen still cooperating with a shrinking ARA that was pulling out of Russia. Able to reveal itself as JDC instead of acting under the ARA's name and nonsectarian programs, JDC emblazoned its name on its offices, warehouses, and automobiles.[106] JDC was able to start a long-awaited clothing remittance program, buy food locally in cooperation with the Soviet government instead of having it shipped from the United States, and work on its own in White Russia alongside the Friends.[107] Most importantly, however, JDC activities could now be concentrated on "one ultimate aim, namely, the revival of Jewish social agencies which existed prior to the war, and adjustment of the Jews to the new conditions of social and political equality in Russia."[108] In other words, JDC could at last work on some reconstructive projects in addition to feeding the hungry, including rebuilding Jewish medical institutions, creating loan cooperatives, and helping refugees.[109] Joseph Rosen was on hand to help start a new kind of reconstructive effort, too. After his recent successes with the ARA's agricultural efforts, he turned his attention fully to helping Russia's Jews.[110] JDC began planning in the summer of 1922 to distribute grain, straw, vegetable seeds, and farm tools to the tune of $100,000 to existing Jewish farm colonies in the Ukraine to ensure their survival.[111] In August 1922, Rosen obtained the consent of President Rakowsky of the Ukrainian Republic allowing JDC to continue work in the Ukraine, with or without the ARA.[112] A ship with seeds, oil, and machinery (including tractors) as per Rosen's specifications sailed from New York to Odessa in December 1922, and a team of workers also traveled to Russia in late December to help with their distribution for the 1923 spring sowing.[113]

CONCLUSION

The perils of working in the new Soviet state had become abundantly clear as JDC tried repeatedly to reach the Ukraine after the Great War. JDC delegates Friedlaender and Cantor were murdered on the job, the Fisher-Pine Agreement contributed more to the growth of the party and its control over Jewish life than to helping Russian Jews, and the AFSC could only provide limited assistance to suffering Jews. JDC finally returned to the familiarity of working with the Americans of the ARA rather than working directly with the perplexing and vexing Soviets. The ARA gave JDC the protection and access it needed, so JDC forged a productive, if troubled, collaboration. Furthermore, in a climate within both the Western humanitarian and Soviet spheres that discouraged "sectarian" (i.e., explicitly Jewish) relief, JDC had to be resourceful about finding ways to help the Jews who had suffered through long years of war, antisemitic violence, and deprivation. To make Jewish relief tenable in these dangerous conditions, JDC found several ways to focus on Jews—inexplicitly. And so, although JDC never intended to conduct famine relief, by assisting the ARA physically and financially with this effort, it could help Jews by also pushing for targeting urban areas, social institutions, and refugees and by ensuring the continued existence of a remittance program. Under the ARA in Russia, JDC provided about $8 million—almost a third of the total ARA budget of $26 million. Over $3.5 million of that went directly to the ARA's nonsectarian general feeding and clothing programs, some went to the Friends, and over $4 million was distributed through JDC representatives in the ARA.[114]

Bogen was pleased with the results of the effort he and the rest of JDC had invested in American Jewish relief to Soviet Russia. It was sobering, however, that the degree to which JDC was able to help Jews in Russia paled in comparison to what the organization was able to accomplish in Poland while, according to JDC's own reports, the situation was actually far worse in the Ukraine than in Poland. There was too little relief, too late; Jewish cultural and religious life had withered; and JDC's reputation had suffered. But the seeds of a reconstructive project to create Jewish agricultural colonies in Crimea in cooperation with Russian Jewish organizations, facilitated by agronomist Joseph Rosen, were planted and would become the main focus of JDC's attention in Russia in the coming years.[115]

Notes

1. Henry Abramson, *A Prayer for the Government: Ukrainians and Jews in Revolutionary Times, 1917–1920* (Cambridge, MA: Harvard University Press, 1999), 110.

2. JDC Archives, Records of the New York Office of the American Jewish Joint Distribution Committee, 1919–1921, Folder 21, Minutes of JDC Executive Committee, March 10, 1921; JDC Archives, Records of the New York Office of the American Jewish Joint Distribution Committee, 1921–1932, Folder 488, Correspondence from J. N. Rosenberg to the JDC New York Office, April 4, 1922.

3. JDC Archives, Records of the New York Office of the American Jewish Joint Distribution Committee, 1919–1921, Folder 255.1, Report on the Medico-Sanitary Conditions by Dr. William Wovschin, July 15, 1920, to March 7, 1921, March 25, 1921.

4. Michael Beizer, "Who Murdered Professor Israel Friedlaender and Rabbi Bernard Cantor: The Truth Rediscovered," *American Jewish Archives Journal* 55, no. 1 (2003): 63–113; Michael Beizer, *Relief in Time of Need: Russian Jewry and the Joint, 1914–24* (Bloomington: Slavica Publishers, Indiana University, 2015), 77–91.

5. Michael Beizer's recent *Relief in Time of Need* also provides much-needed coverage of JDC's work in Soviet Russia during these initial, hesitant years up until the agreement that led to the creation of the Agro-Joint in 1924, primarily using a detailed study of Russian and Ukrainian archives. The subject has otherwise been neglected in the historical literature, and this chapter was written without reference to Beizer's then-unpublished monograph.

6. JDC Archives, Records of the New York Office of the American Jewish Joint Distribution Committee, 1919–1921, Folder 68.1, Correspondence from A. Lucas to O. Rosalsky, November 20, 1919; ibid., Folder 68.1, Draft Press Release on Polish Unit, January 12, 1920.

7. Ibid., Folder 247.2, Report on Ukraine by Leo Gerstenzang, April 15, 1920; ibid., Folder 45, Relief Work Organized in Soviet Russia, June 1, 1920.

8. Ibid., Folder 247.2, Cable from J. Goldman to the JDC New York Office, May 25, 1920; ibid., Folder 247.2, Report on Volhynia by Voorsanger and Spivak, June 9, 1920; ibid., Folder 247.2, On the Condition of Jews in Ukraine by Kass and Leff, July 20, 1920; ibid., Folder 247.2, Information Service Letter, October 4, 1920. JDC actually had a district office with a warehouse and garage headed by Abraham Shohan of the overseas unit in Rovno that coordinated efforts in areas of the Ukraine accessible from Poland.

9. Ibid., Folder 247.2, Newsletter, May 10, 1920; ibid., Folder 19.1, Meeting of the JDC Executive Committee, 29–31, February 26, 1920.

10. National Archives and Records Administration (NARA), College Park, MD, General Records of the Department of State, RG 59, 860E.4016/6, Correspondence in 1919; National Archives and Records Administration (NARA), College Park, MD, General Records of the Department of State, RG 59, 860E.48/a-17, Correspondence in 1919–1920.

11. JDC Archives, Records of the New York Office of the American Jewish Joint Distribution Committee, 1919–1921, 860E.4016/6, Correspondence between B. Richards and R. Lansing, December 3, 1919; December 5, 1919; ibid., 860E.4016/18, Correspondence from L. Marshall to Secretary B. Colby, May 21, 1920; ibid., 860E.4016/9–17, December 1919.

12. Zosa Szajkowski, *The Mirage of American Jewish Aid in Soviet Russia, 1917–1939*, vol. 4, *Jews, War, and Communism* (self-pub., 1977), 9–12.

13. Harold Henry Fisher, *The Famine in Soviet Russia, 1919–1923: The Operations of the American Relief Administration* (Stanford, CA: Stanford University Press, 1935), 1–48; Bertrand M. Patenaude, *The Big Show in Bololand: The American Relief Expedition to Soviet Russia in the Famine of 1921* (Stanford, CA: Stanford University Press, 2002), 34–38.

14. Szajkowski, *American Jewish Aid in Soviet Russia*, 15–20.

15. JDC Archives, Records of the New York Office of the American Jewish Joint Distribution Committee, 1919–1921, Folder 247.2, Memorandum of Conversation with Alex Wardwell by J. L. Magnes, January 27, 1920.

16. Ibid., Folder 248, Correspondence from F. Polk to L. Marshall, March 25, 1920.

17. Ibid., Folder 247.2, Correspondence from J. Goldman to F. Warburg, March 9, 1920; ibid., Folder 247.2, Interview of Dr. J. Goldman and Hetty

Goldman with Mr. Litvinov, April 24, 1920; ibid., Folder 247.2, Report from Judge Harry M. Fisher and Max Pine, April 6, 1920.

18. Ibid., Correspondence from H. Fisher and M. Pine to the JDC New York Office, May to July 1920.

19. Ibid., Folder 19.2, JDC Minutes of Executive Committee, June 10, 1920.

20. Ibid., Folder 247.2, Cable from J. Goldman to the JDC New York Office, June 15, 1920.

21. Patenaude, *Big Show in Bololand*, 100–101.

22. JDC Archives, Records of the New York Office of the American Jewish Joint Distribution Committee, 1919–1921, Folder 18, To the JDC, July 1, 1920.

23. The second version is a Russian acronym, the third is Yiddish, and they are sometimes rendered in English with differing systems of transliteration. I will refer to this body as the Yidgeskom.

24. JDC Archives, Records of the New York Office of the American Jewish Joint Distribution Committee, 1919–1921, Folder 248, Correspondence from J. Goldman to H. Lehman, September 15, 1920.

25. Ibid., Folder 247.2, Report of Commission Appointed by the JDC to Investigate the Conditions of and Establish a Relief Committee for the Jewish War Sufferers in Russia and Ukraina, July 20, 1920.

26. Ibid., Information Service Letter, October 20, 1920.

27. Ibid., Folder 247.2, Report of Commission Appointed by the JDC to Investigate the Conditions of and Establish a Relief Committee for the Jewish War Sufferers in Russia and Ukraina, July 20, 1920.

28. Michael Beizer, "Restoring Courage to Jewish Hearts: Frank Rosenblatt's Mission in Siberia in 1919," *East European Jewish Affairs* 39, no. 1 (2009): 35–56.

29. JDC Archives, Records of the New York Office of the American Jewish Joint Distribution Committee, 1919–1921, Folder 247.2, Cable from F. Rosenblatt to the JDC New York Office via J. Goldman, August 25, 1920.

30. Ibid., Folder 251.2, Correspondence from J. Goldman to H. Lehman, September 19, 1920.

31. Ibid., Folder 27.3, Chairman Report on Soviet Russia, August 11, 1920.

32. Ibid., Folder 247.2, Correspondence from F. Rosenblatt to F. Warburg, December 8, 1920; ibid., Folder 249.2, Agreement, July 29, 1921; ibid.,

Folder 21, Minutes of the JDC Executive Committee, March 10, 1921; Szajkowski, *American Jewish Aid in Soviet Russia*, 54–56.

33. See Szajkowski, *American Jewish Aid in Soviet Russia*, 21–59. Zosa Szajkowski made a detailed study of the messy situation, carefully examining JDC, People's Relief Committee, Judah Magnes, Yiddish press, and US State Department records to piece together the story. Yidgeskom's archives were not available at the time he wrote the manuscript. I summarize his findings here, having myself seen many of the documents to which he makes reference in the NARA, the JDC Archives, and the People's Relief Committee collections at the archives of the American Jewish Historical Society, the Central Archives for the History of the Jewish People (CAHJP), and the Judah Magnes Papers at CAHJP.

34. To my knowledge, no one has looked at the papers now available in the Soviet Archives, nor in papers of the aforementioned organizations (as well as the Friends of Soviet Russia) to try to determine objectively if the Dubrowsky relief route did actually provide relief in some way or if the money sent was mostly absorbed by the Soviet government.

35. Jonathan D. Sarna, *American Judaism: A History* (New Haven, CT: Yale University Press, 2004), 215; Zosa Szajkowski, *The Impact of the 1919–20 Red Scare on American Jewish Life*, vol. 2, *Jews, War, and Communism* (New York: Ktav, 1974); Robert K. Murray, *Red Scare: A Study in National Hysteria, 1919–1920* (Minneapolis: University of Minnesota Press, 1955), 91–95.

36. Boris David Bogen and Alfred Segal, *Born a Jew* (New York: Macmillan, 1930), 272–74.

37. JDC Archives, Records of the New York Office of the American Jewish Joint Distribution Committee, 1919–1921, Folder 248, Correspondence from N. Davis to F. Warburg, September 18, 1920.

38. NARA, Records of the Department of State, RG 59, 861.48/1325, L. Marshall's Report on JDC and Dubrowsky Relationship, December 9, 1920.

39. Szajkowski, *American Jewish Aid in Soviet Russia*, 60–62.

40. JDC Archives, Records of the New York Office of the American Jewish Joint Distribution Committee, 1919–1921, Folder 73.2, Clearing House for Russian Relief, Information Bulletin No. 1, April 19, 1921; ibid., Folder 259, Correspondence from H. Lehman to J. Norton, June 18, 1921.

41. Ibid., Folder 21, Minutes of JDC Executive Committee, March 10, 1921.

42. Ibid., Folder 21, Minutes of JDC Executive Committee, April 5, 1921; ibid., Folder 249, Correspondence from A. Kahn to D. Dubrowsky, April 11, 1921; ibid., Folder 14, Record of Administration Committee, June 2, 1921.

43. Ibid., Folder 249.1, Cable from F. Warburg to B. Bogen, April 6, 1921.

44. Ibid., Folder 73.2, Correspondence from F. Rosenblatt to J. Becker, April 22, 1921; ibid., Folder 73.2, Conference held in Philadelphia in the Office of the AFSC, April 28, 1921.

45. Ibid., Folder 249.1, Correspondence from F. Rosenblatt to J. Becker, April 8, 1921; American Jewish Archives (AJA), Cincinnati, OH, Boris D. Bogen Papers, MS-3, Box 1, Folder 4, Correspondence from F. Rosenblatt to H. L. Goldstein, May 2, 1921.

46. JDC Archives, Records of the New York Office of the American Jewish Joint Distribution Committee, 1919–1921, Folder 259, Interview with the Friends in London, May 7, 1921; ibid., Correspondence from F. Rosenblatt to J. Norton, June 23, 1921; ibid., Correspondence from J. Norton to F. Rosenblatt, June 28, 1921; Szajkowski, *American Jewish Aid in Soviet Russia*, 63–65.

47. JDC Archives, Records of the New York Office of the American Jewish Joint Distribution Committee, 1921–1932, Folder 91b, JDC Executive Director to AFSC, August 19, 1921; ibid., Folder 91b, Correspondence from W. Thomas to F. Warburg, November 20, 1921.

48. JDC Archives, Records of the New York Office of the American Jewish Joint Distribution Committee, 1919–1921, Folder 21, Minutes of the JDC Executive Committee, March 10, 1921.

49. Patenaude, *Big Show in Bololand*, 37–48.

50. Patenaude, *Big Show in Bololand*, 39. The ARA representatives negotiated with the same Maxim Litvinov with whom Goldman had spoken in Denmark. Litvinov was "the assistant people's commissar of foreign affairs, a formidable negotiating talent with ample experience at playing a weak hand."

51. JDC Archives, Records of the New York Office of the American Jewish Joint Distribution Committee, 1921–1932, Folder 488, Minutes of the European Relief Council, August 24, 1922. Felix Warburg, James N. Rosenberg (the

new European director of JDC), and Lewis Strauss (serving on the JDC's Committee on Russia in New York) represented JDC.

52. Patenaude, *Big Show in Bololand*, 50–51.

53. Yehuda Bauer, *My Brother's Keeper: A History of the American Jewish Joint Distribution Committee, 1929–1939* (Philadelphia: Jewish Publication Society of America, 1974), 57–58; Jonathan L. Dekel-Chen, *Farming the Red Land: Jewish Agricultural Colonization and Local Soviet Power, 1924–1941* (New Haven, CT: Yale University Press, 2005), 2–4, 26; Matthew Mark Silver, *Louis Marshall and the Rise of Jewish Ethnicity in America: A Biography* (Syracuse, NY: Syracuse University Press, 2013), 491.

54. JDC Archives, Records of the New York Office of the American Jewish Joint Distribution Committee, 1921–1932, Folder 488, Correspondence from J. N. Rosenberg to the JDC New York Office, April 4, 1922; Patenaude, *Big Show in Bololand*, 152–63.

55. JDC Archives, Records of the New York Office of the American Jewish Joint Distribution Committee, 1921–1932, Folder 483, Correspondence from B. Bogen to JDC Committee on Russia, December 5, 1921. The story of Jewish farming in Russia is closely examined by Dekel-Chen in *Farming the Red Land*.

56. Ibid., Folder 488, Distribution in White Russia by Cornell Hewson, February 20, 1922.

57. Ibid., Folder 91b, Correspondence from W. Thomas to F. Warburg, November 20, 1921; ibid., Folder 91b, Correspondence from W. Thomas to F. Warburg, January 9, 1922; ibid., Folder 91b, Correspondence from F. Warburg to W. Thomas, January 20, 1922; ibid., Folder 91b, Correspondence from W. Thomas to L. Strauss, January 3, 1923; ibid., Folder 457, The American Jewish Joint Distribution Committee in Russia, 4, January 1, 1924. The AFSC did not expand into the Ukraine, and it used only $50,000 of the second JDC contribution, ending its operations in White Russia in the fall of 1923.

58. Herbert Hoover, "Food Drafts for Russia," *ARA Bulletin* 2, no. 18 (1921).

59. Patenaude, *Big Show in Bololand*, 96–101.

60. JDC Archives, Records of the New York Office of the American Jewish Joint Distribution Committee, 1921–1932, Folder 488, Memorandum of Discussion between Rosenberg and Brown, October 20, 1921.

61. Ibid., Folder 488, Correspondence from W. L. Brown to W. Haskell, October 27, 1921; ibid., Folder 488, Correspondence from J. N. Rosenberg to W. L. Brown, February 1, 1922.

62. Ibid., Folder 488, Correspondence from J. N. Rosenberg to F. Warburg, March 17, 1922; ibid., Folder 488, Correspondence from J. Rosen to the JDC New York Office, March 21, 1922.

63. Fisher, *Famine in Soviet Russia*, 246–66; Patenaude, *Big Show in Bololand*, 96–101.

64. JDC Archives, Records of the New York Office of the American Jewish Joint Distribution Committee, 1921–1932, Folder 447, Minutes of the JDC Executive Committee, March 14, 1922; ibid., Folder 488, the JDC New York Office to J. N. Rosenberg, March 16, 1922; ibid., Folder 488, Cable on the ARA-JDC Conference, March 28, 1922.

65. Ibid., Folder 488, Correspondence from H. Hoover to W. L. Brown and W. Haskell, March 14, 1922; ibid., Folder 488, Correspondence from J. N. Rosenberg to the JDC New York Office, April 4, 1922.

66. Ibid., Correspondence from J. N. Rosenberg to W. L. Brown, February 1, 1922.

67. Ibid., Correspondence from J. N. Rosenberg to the JDC New York Office, March 17, 1922; ibid., Agreement Reached at Moscow between Representatives of the American Relief Administration and the Joint Distribution Committee, June 19, 1922; Patenaude, *Big Show in Bololand*, 51.

68. Frank Macy Surface and Raymond L. Bland, *American Food in the World War and Reconstruction Period: Operations of the Organizations under the Direction of Herbert Hoover, 1914 to 1924* (Stanford, CA: Stanford University Press, 1931), 914–15.

69. JDC Archives, Records of the New York Office of the American Jewish Joint Distribution Committee, 1921–1932, Folder 488, Correspondence from J. N. Rosenberg to F. Warburg, March 17, 1922.

70. Ibid., Folder 488, Correspondence from J. N. Rosenberg, F. Rosenblatt, and J. Rosen to the JDC New York Office, March 20, 1922; ibid., Folder 488, Correspondence from J. N. Rosenberg to the JDC New York Office, April 4, 1922.

71. Bogen and Segal, *Born a Jew*, 291.

72. JDC Archives, Records of the New York Office of the American Jewish Joint Distribution Committee, 1921–1932, Folder 488, Correspondence from J. N. Rosenberg to the JDC New York Office, March 18, 1922; ibid., Folder 488, Correspondence from J. N. Rosenberg to the JDC New York Office, April 4, 1922.

73. Ibid., Folder 488, J. N. Rosenberg to the JDC New York Office, April 4, 1922.

74. Surface and Bland, *American Food in the World War*, 145, 259; Kimberly Lowe, "The Red Cross and the New World Order, 1918–1924" (PhD diss., Yale University, 2013), 272–73.

75. Patenaude, *Big Show in Bololand*, 181; JDC Archives, Records of the New York Office of the American Jewish Joint Distribution Committee, 1921–1932, Folder 488.

76. Bogen and Segal, *Born a Jew*, 300; JDC Archives, Records of the New York Office of the American Jewish Joint Distribution Committee, 1921–1932, Folder 488, Correspondence from L. Strauss to J. N. Rosenberg, May 23, 1922; ibid., Folder 488, Correspondence from J. N. Rosenberg to L. Strauss, May 25, 1922.

77. JDC Archives, Records of the New York Office of the American Jewish Joint Distribution Committee, 1921–1932, Folder 488, Correspondence from J. N. Rosenberg to B. Bogen, June 6, 1922.

78. Ibid., Folder 457, Condensed Report of the Relief Activities of the JDC in Russia, November 1, 1922, to October 31, 1923; November 8, 1923.

79. Ibid., Folder 488, Conference of Herter, Logan, Kahn, and Rosenberg, June 3, 1922; ibid., Folder 488, Description of Plan Agreed Upon by JDC and ARA, June 9, 1922.

80. Ibid., Folder 488, Moscow News Item, July 25, 1922.

81. Ibid., Folder 91b, Friends International Service, November 11, 1922.

82. Jaclyn Granick, "Waging Relief: The Politics and Logistics of American Jewish War Relief in Europe and the Near East, 1914–1918," *First World War Studies* 5, no. 1 (2014): 58–60; Sébastien Farré, *Colis de Guerre: Secours Alimentaire et Organisations Humanitaires (1914–1947)* (Rennes, France: Presses Universitaires de Rennes, 2014), 66–67.

83. Patenaude, *Big Show in Bololand*, 96–101.

84. Margaret A. Trott, "Passing through the Eye of the Needle: American Philanthropy and Soviet Medical Research in the 1920s," in *Rockefeller Philanthropy and Modern Biomedicine: International Initiatives from World War I to the Cold War*, ed. William H. Schneider (Bloomington: Indiana University Press, 2002), 134.

85. JDC Archives, Records of the New York Office of the American Jewish Joint Distribution Committee, 1921–1932, Folder 488, Correspondence from J. N. Rosenberg to F. Warburg, June 3, 1922.

86. Ibid., Correspondence from J. N. Rosenberg to the JDC New York Office, April 4, 1922; ibid., Description of Plan Agreed Upon by JDC and ARA, June 9, 1922.

87. Ibid., Folder 457, Condensed Report of the Relief Activities of the JDC in Russia, November 1, 1922, to October 31, 1923, 2, November 8, 1923; ibid., Folder 457, The American Jewish Joint Distribution Committee in Russia, 3, January 1, 1924.

88. Ibid., Folder 488, Correspondence from H. Bernheim to C. Adler, July 5, 1922.

89. AJA, Bogen Papers, MS-3, Box 3, Folder 2, Correspondence from I. M. Naishtut to B. Bogen, May 4, 1922; AJA, Bogen Papers, MS-3, Box 1, Folder 5, Correspondence among I. M. Naishtut, L. Strauss, B. Bogen, and H. Hoover, June 7, 1922; AJA, Bogen Papers, MS-3, Box 1, Folder 6, Correspondence from B. Bogen to E. Morrissey, June 20, 1923; JDC Archives, Records of the New York Office of the American Jewish Joint Distribution Committee, 1921–1932, Folder 488, Conference of Herter, Logan, Kahn, and Rosenberg, June 5, 1922.

90. JDC Archives, Records of the New York Office of the American Jewish Joint Distribution Committee, 1921–1932, Folder 489, How Your Contributions Are Helping, October 20, 1922; ibid., Folder 448, Essential Points in Dr. Bogen's Letters, September 19, 1922.

91. Ibid., Folder 488, Correspondence from W. Grove to J. N. Rosenberg, June 24, 1922; ibid., Correspondence from W. Grove to L. Strauss, July 8, 1922; ibid., Folder 489, Correspondence from L. Strauss to W. Grove, August 10, 1922; ibid., Folder 449, Report of Committee on Russia from Minutes of the Executive Committee, October 24, 1922.

92. Ibid., Folder 448, Correspondence from B. Bogen to L. Strauss, August 14, 1922.

93. Patenaude, *Big Show in Bololand*, 51, 90–91, 181, 600, 633; Fisher, *Famine in Soviet Russia*, 429, 437–38; JDC Archives, Records of the New York Office of the American Jewish Joint Distribution Committee, 1921–1932, Folder 449, Correspondence from L. Strauss to B. Bogen, October 4, 1922; ibid., Folder 479, Extract from Minutes of Dinner Meeting, December 5, 1922.

94. JDC Archives, Records of the New York Office of the American Jewish Joint Distribution Committee, 1921–1932, Folder 448, Correspondence from B. Bogen to H. Lehman, August 31, 1922.

95. Ibid., Folder 488, Agreement Reached at Moscow between Representatives of the American Relief Administration and Joint Distribution Committee, June 19, 1922; ibid., Folder 457, Report of Morris Wolf and M. J. Rosenau, 6, August 22, 1922; ibid., Folder 449, Correspondence from L. Strauss to B. Bogen, October 4, 1922; Fisher, *Famine in Soviet Russia*, 275.

96. Ibid., Folder 457, Condensed Report of the Relief Activities of the JDC in Russia, 2, November 1, 1922, to October 31, 1923; ibid., Folder 457, The American Jewish Joint Distribution Committee in Russia, 38, January 1, 1924.

97. Ibid., Folder 489, Agreement Regarding Operations in the Ukraine and White Russia between the Joint Distribution Committee and the American Relief Administration, August 14, 1922; ibid., Folder 489, L. Marshall, H. Lehman, J. N. Rosenberg, and L. Strauss Cable to W. Grove and B. Bogen, August 18, 1922.

98. Ibid., Correspondence from J. N. Rosenberg to W. L. Brown, September 14, 1922; ibid., Folder 448, Correspondence from L. Strauss to B. Bogen, August 29, 1922; ibid., Folder 449, Report of Committee on Russia from Minutes of the Executive Committee, October 24, 1922; ibid., Minutes of Meeting between Representatives of the American Relief Administration and the American Jewish Joint Distribution Committee, December 11, 1922.

99. Ibid., Folder 456, Supplement to Agreement between American Mennonite Relief and Ukrainian Socialist Soviet Republic, October 20, 1921; ibid., Agreement between Russian Socialist Federative Soviet Republic and

the Society of Friends of England and America, October 25, 1922; ibid., Folder 448, Correspondence from B. Bogen to L. Strauss, September 11, 1922; AJA, Bogen Papers, MS-3, Box 1, Folder 5, Correspondence from L. Strauss to the JDC New York Office, October 20, 1922.

100. AJA, Bogen Papers, MS-3, Box 1, Folder 5, Correspondence from J. Rosen to L. Strauss, November 27, 1922; JDC Archives, Records of the New York Office of the American Jewish Joint Distribution Committee, 1921–1932, Folder 456, Temporary Agreement between Joint Distribution Committee (JDC) and Russian Government (RSFSR), September 22, 1922.

101. JDC Archives, Records of the New York Office of the American Jewish Joint Distribution Committee, 1921–1932, Memorandum from B. Kahn, November 6, 1922.

102. Bogen and Segal, *Born a Jew*, 336; JDC Archives, Records of the New York Office of the American Jewish Joint Distribution Committee, 1921–1932, Folder 449, Correspondence from C. Adler to L. Strauss, October 23, 1922.

103. JDC Archives, Records of the New York Office of the American Jewish Joint Distribution Committee, 1921–1932, Folder 457, Condensed Report of the Relief Activities of the JDC in Russia, November 1, 1922, to October 31, 1923; ibid., Folder 449, Correspondence from B. Bogen to L. Strauss, Subject: Evobshestkom, October 25, 1922.

104. Ibid., Folder 457, B. Bogen, The JDC in Russia, August 22, 1922; Patenaude, *Big Show in Bololand*, 82–86.

105. Ibid., Folder 449, Correspondence from E. Morrissey to L. Strauss, Subject: Bogen's Comments, November 20, 1922.

106. Bogen and Segal, *Born a Jew*, 335–36.

107. JDC Archives, Records of the New York Office of the American Jewish Joint Distribution Committee, 1921–1932, Folder 457, The American Jewish Joint Distribution Committee in Russia, 30, January 1, 1924; ibid., Folder 489, Final Agreement Signed by Mr. Strauss, September 25, 1922; ibid., Folder 91b, Correspondence from B. Bogen to the JDC New York Office, November 4, 1922; ibid., Folder 448, Memorandum of Matters Taken Up with Mr. Rosenberg, September 16, 1922; ibid., Folder 457, Condensed Report of the Relief Activities of the JDC in Russia, November 1, 1922, to October 31, 1923.

108. Ibid., Folder 457, B. Bogen, The JDC in Russia, August 22, 1923.

109. Ibid., Folder 457, Condensed Report of the Relief Activities of the JDC in Russia, November 1, 1922, to October 31, 1923.

110. Bogen and Segal, *Born a Jew*, 318.

111. JDC Archives, Records of the New York Office of the American Jewish Joint Distribution Committee, 1921–1932, Folder 483, Memorandum, Subject: Agreement with ORT on Seeds Signed F. Hardy, March 24, 1922; ibid., Folder 483, Correspondence from L. Strauss to J. Rosen, July 10, 1922; ibid., Folder 483, Correspondence from S. Arons to J. Hyman, Resume of the Work Done for Dr. Rosen, December 1, 1922.

112. Ibid., Folder 448, Correspondence from L. Cohan to J. N. Rosenberg and L. Strauss, August 28, 1922; ibid., Folder 448, Correspondence from Ch. Rakowsky to J. Rosen, July 20, 1922.

113. Ibid., Folder 483, Correspondence from S. Arons to J. Hyman, Shipment of Machinery and Seeds to Russia, December 26, 1922; ibid., Folder 483, Correspondence from S. Arons to J. Rosen, December 21, 1922; ibid., Folder 483, Sowing Campaign, translation from *Zwezda*, March 2, 1923. The future of this JDC reconstruction work in Russia has been finely detailed by Dekel-Chen in *Farming the Red Land*.

114. Ibid., Folder 457, The American Jewish Joint Distribution Committee in Russia, 6–7, January 1, 1924.

115. Ibid., Folder 483, Correspondence from H. Lehman to J. Rosen, September 21, 1922; ibid., Folder 483, Correspondence from J. Rosen to J. N. Rosenberg, December 4, 1922.

4

American Jewish Joint Distribution Committee Programs in the USSR, 1941–1948

A Complicated Partnership

Mikhail Mitsel

INTRODUCTION

During World War II, just a few years after relations with the Soviet Union had ruptured in 1938, the American Jewish Joint Distribution Committee (JDC or "the Joint") entered negotiations with the Soviet government, its Jewish Anti-Fascist Committee (JAC), and Soviet representatives in the United States and gained the right to renew limited assistance to Jews in the Soviet Union. Under terms agreed upon in 1943, JDC sent aid packages for Jewish refugees behind the lines, mainly to Siberia and the Asiatic republics. JDC pressed to expand its wartime aid program but was permitted by the Soviets to do so only in the form of nonsectarian aid—with the concession that the target areas have populations with some Jewish concentration. This assistance proved to be substantial and important for the Soviet Union, particularly in the emergency delivery of penicillin and scarce modern medical equipment as well as for desperate Jewish refugees, including Soviet evacuees and Polish Jewish refugees. Yet JDC's acquiescence to the provision of this nonsectarian aid as a condition for aiding needy Jews engendered constant

Packages of clothing are sent from Palestine to refugees in the Soviet Union. Tel Aviv, 1944. Photo by "Rex," Tel Aviv.

pressure and opposition toward JDC leadership from otherwise support-ive Jewish groups in the United States, including some JDC leaders who felt that "JDC . . . is the instrument for Jewish relief and rehabilitation, not the instrument of the Jews of the United States for their expression of sympathy and good will for suffering people the world over."[1]

This chapter illustrates JDC's programs in the USSR as a synthesis of successes and failures against a backdrop of constantly shifting political conditions—from the fallout of revolution, through World War II, and into the last days of Stalin's era. JDC appears to be a transnational agency but is essentially an American organization with an American ethos, trying to navigate the interests, needs, and irrational fears of a foreign power while negotiating with third-party governments, international agencies, and multiple Jewish constituencies. JDC's aim was consistent: to provide as much practical aid as possible in serial crisis conditions—from the pogroms of the early 1920s to the devastation of full-scale war and the plight of Soviet Jewish evacuees and survivors after liberation and the recrudescence of state-sponsored antisemitism in the latter part of the 1940s.

As the overseas relief arm of the organized Jewish community in America, JDC from its inception in 1914 strove to adhere to a nonpolitical stance in its work throughout the world in order to fulfill its mandate to reach Jews in need wherever they may be found. However, its work inevitably drew it into cauldrons of political ferment throughout the world, within its own country, in the international Jewish community, and in the Soviet Union.

The principal underlying tension in JDC's Soviet program during World War II was the ultimate provision of nonsectarian aid to a struggling nation versus adherence to JDC's specific raison d'etre: to serve Jews. For the Soviets, Jews comprised just one of many nationalities within the Soviet Union's borders and warranted no extraordinary help. JDC's dilemma of compromising core policy in the face of the exigencies of emergency in order to have any hope of helping Jews in the USSR only increased with the end of World War II.

Heightening this root dilemma were two insurmountable practical challenges to JDC's programs. One was the steadfast Soviet refusal to allow any visits by JDC staff—a serious violation of yet another JDC operational principle. Posing equally grave obstacles was the complete absence of reports from the field: Despite complex and repeated discussions with Soviet diplomats, the Soviet Union's JAC, and the Soviet Red Cross, no clear confirmation could be extracted that parcels with American goods sent as nonsectarian aid were reaching any Jewish survivors. This deficit of evidence would erode a portion of JDC's Jewish communal support base for the program.

After liberation, JDC was permitted to send relief packages to Jews in the western regions of the USSR. However, in short order the Stalinist regime generated a paranoiac atmosphere throughout society, with grave antisemitic overtones. In this climate, the massive relief program funded by JDC in a time of war was immediately forgotten. In January to February 1953, during Stalin's final propaganda campaign, notoriously known as the "Doctors' Plot," JDC was viciously attacked. Despite JDC's substantial good-faith programs and its record of consistent compromises, the organization ended up maligned in Soviet memory.

The complexity of implementing the aid program during World War II has to be understood in the longer-term context of JDC activity in the young Soviet Union and its relationship with both Soviet and Jewish organizations. This chapter describes the forms of JDC sectarian and nonsectarian assistance to the USSR during and immediately after World War II, the difficulties in implementing these programs, and the relationship of JDC with relevant Soviet and domestic organizations. It draws from newly accessible resources in archival repositories in countries of the former Soviet Union.

JDC AND THE AGRO-JOINT IN THE USSR DURING THE INTERWAR PERIOD

Once World War I subsided, Soviet Jews became the targets of new waves of violence unleashed by the Bolshevik Revolution, nationalism, and economic disorder. The rampant scapegoating of Jews by local mobs and bandits ravaged hundreds of Jewish communities with impunity, leaving hundreds of thousands of casualties.

During the Great Famine in the USSR in the early 1920s, JDC participated under the auspices of the American Relief Administration (ARA) in an immense US government emergency relief effort. JDC provided aid in Ukraine on a nonsectarian basis whereby, according to terms honored by JDC and the ARA, JDC established a system of free canteens in regions with a predominantly Jewish population. In the course of extensive aid missions, overseas JDC staff witnessed firsthand the abject deprivation of a significant proportion of the USSR's Jews. Under new edicts of the Bolshevik state, heads of households who did not perform accepted forms of labor were deemed parasites, and their entire families were declared *lishentsy* (déclassé). As a result, the large numbers of Jews who earned modest livings as petty tradesmen in towns and shtetls lost their rights to vote, pursue higher education, and receive subsidized medical care and other entitlements. To counter the desperate misery of these disenfranchised

Jews, JDC proposed to the Soviet government a long-term resettlement program that would move jobless Jews from traditional shtetls to new agricultural colonies in the southern Ukraine and Crimea. With the Soviet government's partnership—and financed by a small group of philanthropists organized as the American Society for Jewish Farm Settlements in Russia—JDC launched the Agro-Joint, which would operate in the USSR from July 1924 through October 1938.

The Agro-Joint created a network of economic, educational, and social service institutions, embracing farm settlements in Ukraine and Crimea, cooperative workshops, loan societies, trade schools, and medical societies, all of which, as soon as they were in working order, were taken over by the government. In June 1934, noted agronomist Joseph Rosen, an ARA veteran and an Agro-Joint founder and leader, summarized the first ten years of Agro-Joint activity. He highlighted its main achievements, taking into consideration the difficulties that had plagued the USSR during the period of forcible collectivization, industrialization, and the Great Famine: "What a tremendous change for the better has taken place in the USSR and what a potent part in the improvement of the Jewish situation the work of our organization has played."[2] The miserable state of the Jewish populations in the countries of Eastern Europe, where right-wing groups ideologically close to the Nazi party were formed and remained active, led Rosen to reflect positively on the Soviet experiment with its national minorities: "The Soviet Government has not merely actively cooperated in the work, but has actually taken the lead officially, recognizing the solution of the Jewish question as a state problem."[3]

As head of the Agro-Joint, Joseph Rosen was responsible for the realization of the program. He knew the problems and tragedies of the Soviet Union from the past decades in detail and was well informed about confrontations with local authorities, antisemitic incidents, and the incompetence of the state and regional apparatuses. He was also aware of the hunger in the Agro-Joint colonies and the arrest of Agro-Joint workers accused of "economic crimes." At the same time, Rosen saw the results of the long-standing effort directed at the transformation of the former déclassé. These former supposedly unproductive "people of air" (*luftmenschen*) who began a new life in Agro-Joint *kolkhozes* (collective farms) and colonies achieved a new social status as *kolkhozniks* and proletarians—a status conferred also on their children, enabling the new generation to enroll in universities and benefit from other social rights. As of January 1, 1937, the Agro-Joint served 133 Jewish *kolkhozes* in the Ukrainian Soviet Socialist Republic (92 in Dnepropetrovsk Oblast and 41 in Odessa Oblast) and 85 farming units in Crimea—a total of 218 collective farms in which 13,250 families lived.[4]

The Agro-Joint's viability ceased when thirty Agro-Joint employees—from directors to members of collective farms—were arrested during 1937 and 1938 and a majority of its agronomists were sentenced to death. At the time, during the Great Terror, their disappearance was shrouded in mystery. Family members were fed false accounts of the fate of their missing relatives. JDC itself had no trusted sources to turn to: Its closest Soviet colleagues themselves had been falsely implicated and purged by the regime.[5]

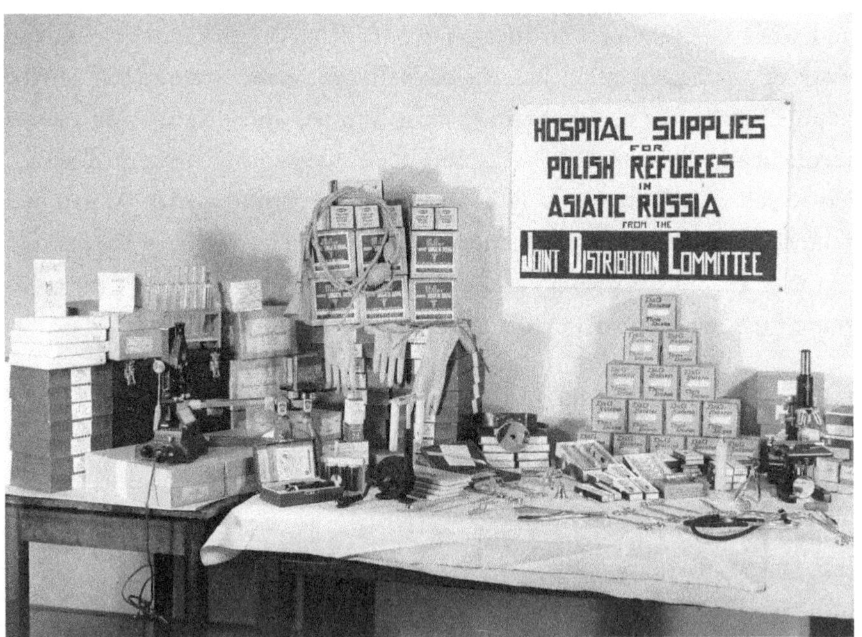

Hospital supplies sent by JDC for Polish refugees in the Asiatic Republics of the Soviet Union. New York, 1942.

Because of the grim political circumstances initiated by Stalin's regime, in October 1938, JDC signed an agreement with the Soviet government terminating Agro-Joint operations in the USSR. Jewish organizations such as ORT (Obchestvo Remeslenogo Truda [Association for the Promotion of Skilled Trades]) and the ICA (the Jewish Colonization Association [known as the ICA from its name in Yiddish]) had already been forced to terminate their activities. The closure of JDC's Moscow offices in 1938 marked the end of the activities of the last foreign Jewish organization in the USSR before it was overcome by war.

First Wartime Programs

Polish Jewish Refugees

After the German blitzkrieg attack on the USSR on June 22, 1941, approximately 2.7 million Jews caught in the prewar Soviet Union, along with the territories incorporated in 1939–1940, were unable to escape Nazi occupation; they would become victims of mass murder. Less than a million Jews from Ukraine, Belarus, and Western Russia managed to flee into the depths of the Soviet Union. They spent the war years in Kazakhstan, Uzbekistan, Kirgizia, Tajikistan, the Urals, Caucasus, and Siberia. Furthermore, they were joined by at least a quarter of a million Polish Jews who had fled east from Poland as the Nazis invaded. Those who lived in Polish areas that became Soviet after the Molotov-Ribbentrop Pact in August 1939 had become Soviet citizens with the Soviet incorporation of Western Ukraine and Belarus but evacuated to the eastern regions in panic. Polish Jews escaping areas of German occupation and moving to the east were resettled by the Soviets in labor camps in Siberia and the north of Russia and were given special refugee status. This group preserved their prewar Polish citizenship. Later, in 1941, after the Soviets entered World War II and the Soviets established a relationship with the Polish Government in Exile, this group was amnestied and was permitted to migrate to Central Asia, where the population struggled to survive on collective farms or in towns and cities.

During the last three months of 1941, Dr. Rosen began informal discussions with successive Soviet ambassadors in the United States. Rosen explored with Ambassador Konstantin Umansky—and later with Ambassador Maxim

Litvinov—whether there would be a possibility for JDC to conduct any relief activities in the USSR for the uprooted Jews. On January 27, 1942, the JDC Executive Committee decided, in light of the early conversations with Soviet representatives and the Jewish Council for Russian War Relief, to pursue the effort.[6] On February 25, 1942, JDC Chairman Paul Baerwald contacted Soviet Ambassador to the United States Maksim Litvinov with a request to allow a JDC representative to visit the USSR.[7] In short order, the Soviet diplomat conveyed a negative response from the People's Commissariat of Foreign Affairs.[8]

However, the offer of JDC assistance to refugee populations in the USSR was accepted. JDC had already been granted an opportunity to send aid to Polish Jews—citizens of prewar Poland—who had fled from the Nazis to the USSR in 1940 and were then stranded in Soviet Central Asia after the "amnesty" of the summer of 1941. The refugee aid program was defined in agreements dated July 30, 1941, between the governments of the London-based Polish Government in Exile and the USSR, permitting packages from JDC's Tehran office to be received by Polish Jews evacuated to the Asiatic Republics. During 1942–1945, JDC shipped some 10,000 such packages from Tehran each month,[9] primarily via the International Red Cross. Given the Soviet ban on aid to "sectarian" groups, this "parcel post service to refugees in Russia" had to ship relief goods to specific designated individuals (Soviet and Polish Jews alike) whose names were received at JDC offices in various locations—an activity that continued, in diminishing degrees, until 1948.[10]

In late 1941, JDC began to send medical, surgical, pharmaceutical, and food supplies via Tehran for nonsectarian distribution to Polish refugees exiled mainly in Uzbekistan and Kazakhstan. These were shipped by JDC from Philadelphia gratis via US government Lend-Lease shipments and duty free upon arrival and were distributed by representatives of the Polish Government in Exile and the Polish Red Cross. In 1942, JDC purchased medical equipment to outfit six hospitals in this region.[11] The fate of this nonsectarian aid that was sent by JDC remains unknown. That year, JDC dispatched 3,282 cases of matzah from Philadelphia for Polish Jewish refugees; the supplies arrived in Murmansk a month and a half later.[12] For more than one year, JDC routed medicines, dressings, and concentrated food products through the Polish Embassy in Kuybyshev. In all, JDC expended $118,977 in shipments to the USSR up to the time of the interruption of relations between the Soviet and Polish governments in April 1943.[13] However, even during the period that these nonsectarian shipments were permitted, JDC was always kept at arm's length by the Soviet officials—with no representation of its own permitted on the ground—and its requests to extend a direct lifeline to Soviet Jewish evacuees who had fled to the Asiatic Republics of the USSR were not addressed.

ROMANIAN DEPORTEES AND TRANSNISTRIA GHETTOS

JDC also launched a major wartime relief effort to aid Jews facing extermination in the Transnistria area of Ukraine. After the conquest of Ukraine by German and Romanian troops in July and August 1941, Romania was given the territory between the Dniester and Bug Rivers. Romanian authorities established a military administration and named the region Transnistria. Between 1941 and 1944, German and Romanian authorities murdered or caused the deaths of 150,000–250,000 Romanian and Ukrainian Jews in Transnistria. In 1942–1944, with the cooperation of the Jewish Central Committee of Romania and the International Red Cross, JDC assisted Romanian Jews deported to the notorious concentration camp in Transnistria. The first such aid arrived in February 1942, but only at the end of 1943 did it become regularized. Dispatched to the ghettos where local and deported Jews were confined, this aid took various forms: cash; over 600 cartons of clothing; and a dozen railway carloads of medicine, children's clothing, coal, soap, and salt. In November 1943, JDC purchased food in Turkey for 75,000 Jews in Transnistria.[14] In 1943–1944, thousands of Jewish orphans were moved, under JDC patronage, from Transnistria to Romania (and later to Palestine) in a method similar to that of other JDC operations to rescue children. Thus, in the first half of 1944, JDC organized transportation for 5,000 children from Transnistria to Palestine.[15]

SEPTEMBER 1943: REPRESENTATIVES OF THE SOVIET GOVERNMENT VISIT THE JDC NEW YORK OFFICE

The JDC aid operation for Jews in Central Asia was connected in complicated ways to the US alliance with the Soviet Union and efforts to secure Jewish support for the embattled Soviet Union. In the spring of 1942, in order to assist the military effort against Nazi Germany, the Soviet Information Bureau created the JAC to organize political and material support from the Jewish communities in the West.

In preparation for this, in February 1942, prominent Soviet Jewish actor/director Solomon Mikhoels[16] and journalist Shakne Epshteyn shaped an agenda for the organization-in-the-making. A preeminent goal was to organize a fundraising campaign overseas, especially in the United States, to respond to a desperate need for medication and warm clothing for the Red Army and evacuated civilians.[17] Among the JAC's priorities were the establishment of contact with "progressive" international Jewish organizations and the ideological indoctrination of the international community. The organization was meant to serve the interests of Soviet foreign policy and the Soviet military through media propaganda as well as through personal contacts with Jews abroad, especially in Britain and the United States, which was designed to influence public opinion and enlist foreign support for the Soviet war effort. Although this notion was never directly articulated, the Central Committee of the Communist Party viewed the JAC as a key to American philanthropic organizations, as it was the sole legal connection to Jews in the West.[18]

Amid an extensive Soviet information campaign in the American press and especially after the Soviet victory in the Battle of Stalingrad, members of various American Jewish organizations began to contact the Soviet Embassy in Washington and the Soviet Consulate General in New York to request a visit by representatives of the JAC. American Jewry viewed the heroism of the Red Army as a vehicle to save at least some of the Jews of Eastern Europe and initiated numerous fundraising campaigns. "We observe the marvelous and continuing progress of the Red Army," noted Albert Einstein in a letter to the JAC.[19] Professional fundraisers rightly assumed that a visit by JAC delegates would aid in conducting the fundraising drives.

On March 10, 1943, Solomon Lozovsky, vice chairman of the Soviet Information Bureau, notified Soviet Prime Minister Vyacheslav Molotov and the chairman of the Information Bureau, Aleksandr Shcherbakov, of a telegram from the Jewish Council of Russian War Relief in New York requesting a US visit by JAC Chairman Solomon Mikhoels and Vice Chairman Itzik Fefer[20]:

> Kuybyshev. Soviet Information Bureau. To Mikhoels and Fefer:
>
> We are insistently urging you to come to the USA and tour the country. Russian War Relief could collect immense sums to unite the Jewish people.
>
> The Jewish Council of Russian War Relief.[21]

Prime Minister Molotov and Soviet Information Bureau Chairman Shcherbakov conveyed their approval to Vice Chairman Lozovsky. Prior to the US trip, major Jewish organizations in the United States, Canada, Mexico, and the United Kingdom were evaluated in Moscow, and the JAC mission parameters were preapproved. A memorandum from the People's Commissariat of Foreign Affairs to the representatives of the JAC instructed them how to comport themselves in contacts with JDC and other philanthropic organizations:

> During conversations with the representatives of the organizations (Joint, Ambidzhan,[22] The Jewish Council of Russian War Relief etc.) they [members of the JAC] must not agree to any propositions without the prior approval of the People's Commissariat of Foreign Affairs, stating that all projects will be conveyed to the Jewish Anti-Fascist Committee.[23]

Every aspect of the JAC was controlled by the state. During their visit to the United States in September 1943, Solomon Mikhoels and Itzik Fefer met with Nahum Goldmann (cofounder of the World Jewish Congress) and met three times with JDC leadership in New York. They also held fundraising rallies in several US cities and met with donors. According to JDC documents, Mikhoels and Fefer were viewed not as representatives of a Jewish organization but as "representatives of the Soviet government who visited our country."[24] The first of these meetings—a confidential luncheon—took place on September 13, 1943. JDC was represented by Chairman Paul Baerwald and Treasurer James Rosenberg, who had traveled to the Soviet Union in 1927 in conjunction with the Agro-Joint program.

According to documents, the Soviet representatives attending the meeting expressed dissatisfaction concerning insufficient support from the American Jewish community for the Red Army's military efforts. The guests were generally familiar with JDC's work in Ukraine during the famine of 1921–1923, when aid had been provided on a nonsectarian basis, whereby the ARA and JDC had cooperated to set up a system of free canteens in regions with a predominantly Jewish population. However, while in the 1920s Jews had lived in certain concentrated regions of Ukraine and Belarus, by the fall of 1943, when the liberation of Ukraine was beginning, the surviving Jewish evacuees were much more dispersed, mostly in the eastern parts of the USSR, including the Asian Republics and Siberia.

During negotiations to discuss JDC assistance, Mikhoels stressed that the Soviet government would grant permission for JDC programs only on a nonsectarian basis. According to the Soviet agenda articulated by the leaders of the JAC, the idea of sending individual packages to Jews in need violated the Soviet doctrine of the equality of all people.

A second meeting took place on September 21. On this occasion, JDC's Executive Vice Chairman, Joseph Hyman, joined Paul Baerwald and James Rosenberg in representing JDC. Records uncovered to date do not contain substantive notes on this meeting. However, the State Archives of the Russian Federation preserve the memoirs of Professor Victor Lebedenko, a representative of the Soviet Red Cross in the United States, who attended the third and final meeting on September 27, where he joined JDC and JAC representatives along with Pavel Kiselev, Consul General of the USSR in New York. Details of the preparation for this meeting and certain preliminary drafts by the Soviet delegation are contained in Professor Lebedenko's report. As the text suggests, Lebedenko was not previously familiar with the work of JDC—the JAC's main negotiating partner. However, this did not prevent him from "assigning roles at the meeting with the Joint representatives":

Before their departure to London, Prof. Mikhoels and Comrade Fefer visited Ambassador Comrade Gromyko in Washington. I was invited to attend a lunch in their honor. After the official portion in the Ambassador's office, Mikhoels and Fefer reported their discussions with the Jewish philanthropic organization about the aid it wished to provide to the Jewish population of the Soviet Union. . . . The aid was to be directed to the republics of Central Asia, where during the war many Jewish evacuees were concentrated. The Joint is ready to help these regions by assisting not only the Jews, but also the entire population evacuated from the war zones. Comrades Mikhoels and Fefer were also successful at dissuading the Joint from having its representative in the USSR.

The Joint is ready to provide all aid through the Red Cross and Red Crescent of the USSR. The Joint will ask its Executive Committee to include Mikhoels as a representative of JDC. At the conclusion, it was stated that before their departure to London, I should be introduced to the president of Joint in the coming days. . . .

On Monday I met with representatives of the Joint Distribution Committee Mr. Hyman, vice-chairman; and Rosenberg, who visited the Soviet Union twice, in particular, Crimea, where he took part in providing aid to the Jewish population. After his return to the USA, he published a book on the Soviet Union, in which he speaks positively of the country. He is respected and has a great influence in his organization. His official position is Treasurer.

The third representative was Baerwald, 75 years old, a major banker, and a millionaire. He is the Chairman. Despite his mature age, he is agile and energetic. . . . They hope that Prof. Mikhoels and Fefer will be their official representatives in Moscow.[25]

Lebedenko's report reinforced JDC's assessments that the JAC representatives were indeed representing the Soviet government and not the Jewish community. Furthermore, the report underscores the Soviet desire to prevent any local JDC representation.

Following these negotiations, JDC's Emergency Administration Committee met on October 12, 1943, and after intense discussion accepted the Soviet proposal to establish a general (i.e., not exclusively Jewish) aid program in the USSR—despite JDC's inability to wrest concessions that would align its program with widely accepted operational norms that prioritized aid to Jews and preferred "on the ground" representatives.[26] This seemed to be the only way that JDC would be able to provide assistance that might reach needy Jews in the USSR.

Problematic Implementation and Differing Expectations

At the close of 1943, in preparation for that program, JDC consulted with the US State Department and the Jewish Council of Russian War Relief (JCRWR), a leading American relief organization. JDC then signed an agreement with the JCRWR designating the JCRWR as JDC's purchasing and shipping agent. JDC wanted its efforts to be coordinated with those of the US government and with the efforts of other relief organizations.

JDC's first contribution to the new nonsectarian program was $250,000 in goods, with project completion scheduled for the fall of 1944.[27] It was expected that foodstuffs (condensed milk, $76,000; egg powder, $75,000) and clothing shipped from the United States would be delivered to Soviet ports without customs and transportation fees within the USSR. Soviet areas with large populations of Jews such as Uzbekistan (evacuees and former Polish Jewish deportees) and Ukraine (survivors and returnees), which the war had affected in very different ways, were selected as the main destinations. Direct distribution in the field, irrespective of the ethnicity of the recipients, would be conducted by the Soviet Red Cross.[28] In the spring of 1944, in several towns of Ukraine—for instance, in Bershad (the Vinnitsa region)—former ghetto prisoners received aid from JDC immediately after liberation.[29] It is not clear to what extent the entirety of the shipment reached the intended recipients.

On July 21, 1944, Professor Victor Lebedenko, who represented the Soviet Red Cross in the United States, addressed a letter to JDC Chairman Paul Baerwald thanking JDC, confirming receipt of the first installment of supplies from JDC and promising to send a report as soon as possible.[30] Shortly thereafter, because of a lack of textiles, Lebedenko asked JDC on September 4, 1944, to include an additional 200,000 items in the forthcoming shipment: wool blankets, sweaters, warm jackets, skirts, and other items.[31] Lebedenko's promise to send a report never did materialize: Preparation of reports was an impossible task for strictly controlled Soviet agencies.

Beginning in 1943 and particularly as the war was gradually coming to an end, the nature of JDC's relations with the Soviet government and with the other regimes under Moscow's control became a focus of JDC's leadership. Donations to the Soviet Union during World War II largely reflected a consensus among JDC leadership, which had laid aside its standard operational guidelines for the greater end of relieving wholesale suffering. However, JDC leader James Rosenberg's perspective was unique. A longtime JDC leader for over a quarter of a century, Rosenberg was especially instrumental in such agrarian projects as the Agro-Joint, the American Society for Jewish Farm Settlement in Russia, and the Dominican Republic Settlement Association. From 1941 onward, Rosenberg worked closely with the Jewish section of the JCRWR. Similarly to those other Americans who idealistically embraced the Soviet philosophy, Rosenberg's views on the USSR and Stalin were naive: He did not fully comprehend the Soviet reality and the scope of the terror. He was sympathetic to the Soviet policy concerning the equality of all peoples while not understanding all its repercussions for JDC projects.

During World War II, James Rosenberg constantly encouraged JDC leaders to reevaluate their policies toward the USSR and provide generous donations. Despite the May 1938 Politburo decision that dictated JDC's expulsion from the USSR later that year, Rosenberg recommended that JDC again become an active organization in the USSR.

Contrary to Rosenberg, former Agro-Joint Director Joseph Rosen had been quite skeptical about the organization's possible return to the USSR. Rosen, who had been born in Russia and had worked in the USSR from 1921 to 1938, had a clearer understanding of the nature of Stalinism. In his letter to Rosenberg of December 15, 1943, Rosen offered a concise prediction of the future of JDC's endeavors in the USSR:

> I have been following with considerable interest through the press and the JDC minutes of various meetings your efforts in connection with re-establishing friendly relations with the Soviet Government, and must congratulate you on your success. I'm inclined to think that under present conditions in the USSR under the Stalin regime there will be no opportunity for any foreign organization, Jewish or non-Jewish, to carry on any work in the Soviet Union through its own staff. All you could possibly do would be to send goods and commodities to be distributed by the Russian government agencies. While this is the best possible way under present conditions, it is not quite satisfactory, as there is no assurance that the local officials, who are always of a caliber inferior to that of the authorities in Moscow but who are really the people on whom the actual execution of any program depends, will live up to your expectations and to their obligations unless at least nominally controlled by a representative of the foreign organization or government supplying the funds and commodities. I doubt whether under the Stalin regime that will be possible.
>
> . . . One cannot and should not forget that his hands are steeped in the blood of his best friends and comrades, who were intellectually and morally far superior to him and who were innocent victims of his lust for power and greatness.[32]

Given his experience with the Soviet authorities, Rosenberg believed that donations had to be provided without guarantees that any aid recipients would be Jewish. Other JDC leaders supported the view that the aid must reach at least a significant number of Jews in the territory of the Soviet Union and believed that such guarantees were necessary.

Questions surrounding Soviet aid led to sharp arguments between Rosenberg and other JDC leaders during a meeting of the Executive Committee on September 13, 1944. This difference of opinion would continue until the end of the war, and Rosenberg would remain in the minority in decisions related to deals made with the Soviets.

At the meeting of September 13, 1944, the main principles governing JDC operations during the war were enunciated:

> We have always been told that the Jews of this country have given liberally as American citizens. The JDC feels that it is the instrument for Jewish relief and rehabilitation—not the instrument of the Jews of the United States for their expression of sympathy and good will for suffering peoples the world over. The Committee felt very strongly in this matter.[33]

One month before, in August 1944, JDC Chairman Paul Baerwald had sent a letter to Andrei Gromyko, the newly appointed Soviet Ambassador to the United States, requesting a meeting. The proposed discussion points would include an increase in aid to Soviet Jewry along with the possibility of a visit to the Soviet Union by Dr. Joseph Schwartz, Chairman of JDC's European Executive Council.[34] The proposition was rejected; in his reply of September 22, 1944, Ambassador Gromyko declared the JDC initiative untimely.[35]

JDC representatives continued to be denied the right to monitor distribution in the USSR. A JDC telegram from New York of January 8, 1945, addressed to Solomon Mikhoels and Itzik Fefer at the JAC, requested that they inform JDC about the results of the delivery of goods in regions with predominantly Jewish populations.[36] The JAC, which was required to coordinate all outgoing correspondence with supervising departments of the NKVD (Narodnyi Kommissariat Vnutrennikh Del [People's Commissariat of Internal Affairs]), did not respond to the telegram.

The JAC's data would not have satisfied JDC: As feared by JDC leaders, reports from the field received by the JAC's leaders and summarized in memos addressed to Soviet Prime Minister Molotov dated May 18, 1944, and October 28, 1944, documented discrimination against Jews[37] in the distribution of relief supplies. Only a small portion of the aid reached the suffering Jewish population in Ukraine. In the October 28 letter to Molotov, Mikhoels and Epshteyn expressed the JAC's concerns: "The neglect of the Jewish population . . . is continuing and is taking on the character of a gross violation of Soviet principles."[38] These documents were obtained only many years later in the post-glasnost period. At the time, JDC could produce no evidence that the Jewish population in liberated regions of Ukraine and Belarus were receiving even limited aid; as a result, some American Jewish activists appealed to JDC to discontinue aid to the USSR.[39]

The difficult position of the Jews who had just returned to their homes in Ukraine continued to be discussed by the JAC's Presidium from October 1944 onward. In June and August 1945, Solomon Mikhoels stressed to Secretary of the Central Committee of the Communist Party Gregory Malenkov JDC's stipulation that its program be targeted to areas with large Jewish populations in Ukraine. As with previous appeals, the Presidium drew a direct connection between the USSR's fulfillment of its obligations and continued support from American Jewish organizations. In response, however, Chairman of the Department of Agitation and Propaganda of the Central Committee Georgy Aleksandrov contended that foreign organizations were using philanthropy as a means of disseminating bourgeois propaganda in the USSR.[40]

Unaware of these exchanges, by July 1945 JDC had resolved to contribute $1 million in annual aid to the USSR for 1946. It was assumed that this sum would cover the bulk of JDC's expenses for the USSR for the new fiscal year within a global annual JDC budget of $27 million. Funds collected from American Jewry intended for the Soviet Union constituted a considerable part of the budget.

On August 20, 1945, slightly over three months after the end of the European war, Soviet Deputy Consul General Pavel Mikhailov,[41] in a letter to JDC Chairman Paul Baerwald, characterized JDC's aid to the Soviet Union during the war years:

> I wish to express my appreciation of the action of the American Jewish Joint Distribution Committee in setting aside the sum of $1,000,000 for rehabilitation work in the Soviet Union. American Jewry has repeatedly shown its friendship for the Soviet people during the past four years of war and devastation, and your action is a renewed and important demonstration of that feeling.[42]

This rare Soviet statement of appreciation details very clearly the amount of funding sent by JDC at that time for rehabilitation in the Soviet Union.

ILLUSIONS ON CRIMEA

Illustrative of the diplomatic tightrope that JDC had to navigate was a gross misunderstanding on Crimea that has not been clarified to this day.

During the three meetings between JDC and the JAC in 1943—one confidential and two official—issues regarding the return of Jewish refugees from the eastern parts of the USSR had not been raised, particularly the idea of another experiment of large-scale Jewish resettlement in Crimea. Yet despite the fact that JDC leadership thought it premature to consider sending humanitarian aid to Crimea, Mikhoels and Fefer left the United States in November 1943 believing that they were supported by American Jewry in regard to a project as ambitious as Crimean resettlement. Thus, in February 1944, the leaders of the JAC appealed to the Soviet government for the creation of a Jewish Soviet Socialist Republic in Crimea, even though JDC leadership had in fact expressed no such interest at the meetings. For Mikhoel, Fefer, and their colleagues on the JAC, such hopes turned into a tragic miscalculation.[43]

At the same time, Rosenberg once again disagreed with most other JDC officials about policy toward the Soviet Union, now in regard to restoration of a Crimean project. Rosenberg believed that JDC should begin a dialogue with Soviet Consul General Kiselev in New York and offer assistance for the mass resettlement of Jews in Crimea. Rosenberg was supported by Alexander Kahn, a JDC vice chairman, who noted that "35,000 of the Jews who had settled in the colonies in the Crimea, remained there."[44]

It is impossible to speculate on the source for these numbers. It was already known that the Crimean Jews did not survive the Holocaust, and the suggestion that 35,000 Jews might be eligible for resettlement would seem to contradict news of the mass killings of Soviet Jews published in the American press.[45]

The minutes of the JDC Executive Committee's meeting of September 13, 1944, record the predominant position within JDC's administration toward the nonexistent Crimean settlements and recall the prewar expulsion of JDC from the Soviet Union:

> Crimea. [Rosenberg] had urged that we make inquiry of Mr. Kiselev, the Soviet Consul General in New York, as to the intentions of the USSR, in the hope that the JDC might participate in rebuilding Jewish farms there. The position of the Committee was that it was premature to approach the Soviet Government re any plans for resettlement of Jews in the Crimea. Furthermore, since the JDC, the Russian Society and Agro-Joint had expended approximately $30,000,000 in a large program of settling Jews on the land in the Ukraine and the Crimea and training them for productive life, it was the general feeling that a discussion which would reopen such possibilities of aid from the American Jews at this time might lead the Soviet Government to feel that vast sums were available. In 1938, however, it will be recalled the Agro-Joint, as well as other foreign organizations, were asked to leave Russia by the Soviet authorities. To our knowledge, no outside bodies have been permitted to work in Russia since that time.[46]

In October 1945, Soviet diplomats in the United States attempted to reincarnate the idea of a Crimean resettlement project. At the beginning, using JDC's interest in opening programs in the USSR, the Soviets clearly manufactured facts regarding Holocaust survivors in Crimea in order to obtain financial support from American Jewry. Thus, Pavel Mikhailov, the

Soviet deputy consul general in New York, assured JDC that many Jews—members of collective farms—had returned to Crimea. He proposed that JDC allocate funds for a rebuilding project in Crimea that would be nonsectarian.[47] Soon thereafter, on November 5, 1945, Deputy Consul General Pavel Mikhailov met with JDC representatives. By that time, JDC had received a written request from the Soviet Red Cross with a list of equipment needed for a veterans' hospital in Crimea, nothwithstanding the fact that Soviet diplomats admitted that they had no evidence that Jews had returned to Crimea. Both the Soviet and American conferees agreed that the idea of equipping this military hospital would not completely satisfy JDC's program criteria because of the lack of a substantial Jewish population in the region. As an alternative, Mikhailov offered to move the intended project to the territory of Ukraine or Belarus,[48] as indeed happened. Thus, the war ended without any clear resolution of JDC's official relationship with the now victorious USSR, even as it was clear that JDC had been generous with its aid and had even been willing to contravene established principles mandating control over the recipients and distribution of supplies in order to offer help to those Jews who could be reached.

THE CASE OF THE "MUKACHEVO BRANCH," 1944–1946: PART I

In 1945–1946, after the war had ended, a unique and (until recently) unstudied situation developed in the Soviet Union: Local authorities permitted relief activity to be conducted by JDC in Trans-Carpathian Ukraine. Before the war, 102,000 Jews had lived in this region, then called "Subcarpathian Land" and part of Czechoslovakia. Between 1938 and 1940, Hungary gradually gained control of the region. In April 1944, the Hungarian authorities incarcerated the local Jews in a temporary ghetto and soon—from May 15 to June 7, 1944—deported the majority of them to Auschwitz. Approximately 15,000 Jews who had resided in this region survived.[49] On October 27, 1944, the Red Army captured the city of Uzhgorod (Ungvár)—marking the beginning of a de facto transition of the region to the USSR. The transitional period during which Trans-Carpathian Ukraine came under the sway of the Soviet Union lasted into 1946. The area was the sole territory adjacent to the USSR with an indigenous Jewish population that had not previously been annexed on the eve of the Soviet-German War.

During that period, hundreds of thousands of uprooted people, both Jewish and not, moved across Eastern and Central Europe. At all stages of their difficult path, including in transit camps, Jews who had survived the Holocaust and were on the move received aid from JDC.[50] One of the regions where JDC managed to provide such aid—thanks to the initiative of the local Jewish community—was Trans-Carpathian Ukraine.

Local Jewish activists in the city of Mukachevo (Munkács) took advantage of the comparatively special conditions of the transitional period in which the Sovietization of the region was enforced slowly over a relatively longer period of time. When Holocaust survivors from Auschwitz began to return home to what was then Trans-Carpathia, local Jewish activists communicated to the European leadership of JDC that the new authorities would not be opposed to the provision of aid by Jewish organizations from abroad.

With the support of its aid offices in neighboring countries (Czechoslovakia, Hungary, and Romania), JDC established a branch ("referat") to operate a survivor aid network for Trans-Carpathia staffed by the local survivors.[51]

However, the transfer of funds to the area posed a major problem. JDC attempted to utilize various channels—first via Bucharest alone, and later via Budapest and Prague—operating in each country according to its prevailing conditions. For instance, on November 17, 1945, the JDC office in Budapest, following instructions from Joseph Schwartz, the European head of JDC, who had just visited Hungary, composed the following document regarding the transfer of funds to Trans-Carpathia:

> Independent of the above allotment 25,000 dollars will be put at the disposal of the Carpathian Ukraine Committee according to a decision of Dr. Joseph Schwartz. In case of the realization of the transaction of which the Hungarian National Bank has been notified, 100,000—will be designated for the purchasing of 10,000 pairs of shoes.[52]

At the initiative of several Jews who had returned to Mukachevo in the fall of 1944, several Jewish soup kitchens, dormitories, and workshops were soon established in the region, and measures were taken to identify the property of Jews who had not returned from the camps.

The Aid Committee (referred to officially as a "Commission") functioned under the aegis of the social services section of the local provisional government. In December 1944, the organization eliminated its obviously Jewish name and continued to operate as the Commission for Aiding Returnees Who Survived the Fascist Terror. Its main beneficiaries continued to be Jews, although this was not indicated in any official documents. Between October 1944 and March 1945, the Commission provided fifty-three railway carloads of furniture, underwear, and food products and established dormitories for men and women totaling fifty beds.[53] By the spring of 1945, JDC's activity had expanded further. In addition to direct aid to local Jewish communities, packages with food and goods were sent from JDC's Tehran office, which was also sending aid to other Jewish communities in the western regions of the USSR. A letter of February 21, 1946, from representatives of the Mukachevo community reported the distribution of seventy packages, and a letter of May 3 mentioned another fifty packages. According to these letters, approximately 4,000 Jews lived in Trans-Carpathian Ukraine at the time—2,000 of whom were in need of aid.[54] These were mostly orphans who had survived Auschwitz and were in extreme need of clothing, underwear, and footwear. Some of the foodstuffs received were allocated to the soup kitchen for repatriates that was opened in Mukachevo to distribute food according to the prepared lists of the needy.

The JDC activity of the "Mukachevo Branch" was not restricted to the distribution of relief but also aimed to revive public Jewish religious life within the parameters that were possible under Soviet rule. The program was not unique: During this period, such efforts were also pursued in areas that had been included within the 1939 borders of the Soviet Union.[55] In Mukachevo, for example, the local Jewish community held a commemorative meeting on June 2, 1946, with religious services in memory of the victims of the Nazi deportations of May to June 1944.[56] Participants marched from the synagogue to the cemetery, and the ceremony concluded with praise for Comrade Stalin and the Russians—the "liberator people."[57]

Aid from the branch was one of the few factors that fostered rehabilitation among former concentration camp inmates, including children and youth. It helped them feel that they were not completely alone in the world. Much later, in her memoirs, former Auschwitz and Dachau prisoner Sonia Gershkovich noted:

> Together with Sidoniia, I traveled to Mukachevo. There we were helped by the Joint, that "hostile Zionist organization," as we were taught. We lived with a Hungarian woman, studied in school, wore school uniforms and received from the Joint everything we needed, from underwear to textbooks. We first studied in a Czech school, then in a Hungarian one. We ate in the Joint dining room—in a huge shed. The tables and benches were arranged in the shape of the Russian letter "P." The cooks were excellent, the food—tasty. I will never forget Passover 1946. It was an unforgettable holiday with [a] snow-white tablecloth, beautiful serving utensils, and a festive atmosphere. I still remember and I am grateful to the people who arranged all this.[58]

In April 1946, however, the activity of JDC branches in Uzhgorod, Mukachevo, Beregovo, and Khust was halted by a decision of the Trans-Carpathian Provincial Executive Committee. Although no information has yet been uncovered about further JDC activity in Trans-Carpathia, it is most likely that packages were still received in 1947, addressed directly to the local Jewish communities, mostly in the western Soviet regions (from Moldova to Estonia) that were able to get bulk shipment of packages for internal distribution among members.[59]

THE END OF JDC NONSECTARIAN PROGRAMS IN THE SOVIET UNION, 1946–1947

JDC's approach to Soviet aid requests was characterized by flexibility and an understanding of the special circumstances confronting a devastated nation. In November 1945, when the Soviet Red Cross requested an urgent delivery of penicillin, 50,000 packages were immediately ordered and sent by JDC from New York Harbor.[60] Deliveries of penicillin continued until the end of 1946 at a value of about $500,000.[61] In September 1946, a new project was launched: purchase of equipment for general city hospitals in Chernigov and Dnepropetrovsk in Ukraine and Mogilev and Pinsk in Belarus. During 1947, JDC support of the Soviet aid program increased to $1,500,000, with a general allocation for Eastern Europe of $8,885,000.[62] This medical project was completed by February 1948.

These new JDC programs in the USSR, which necessarily benefited a general Soviet community, did not receive the unanimous support of American Jewish communities. In correspondence with JDC Executive Vice Chairman Joseph Hyman, Rabbi Theodore Lewis, leader of the progressive synagogue in Brooklyn, was far from enthusiastic:

> My Synagogue is now actively engaged in raising funds for the current United Jewish Appeal. As one who has personally contributed and who has asked others to do so, I am fearfully disturbed by your allocation of a million dollars or more to equip seven hospitals in Russia.
>
> If the need of the Jews in Europe is as great as it is described, this huge sum belongs to them, and should not be given to a land and government which do not allow specific Jewish philanthropy nor recognize the needs of Jews as such. When hunger and disease pursue the Jewish remnant all over Europe, what excuse can there be for giving the money donated by Jews to relieve this Jewish need to the Russian government, even though the purposes are noble and high? The assurance that the hospitals are to serve centers with large Jewish populations seems to me to be of little or no consequence. Those centers are now non-existent, since they all suffered Nazi occupation and the Jewish population was massacred.[63]

In his reply to Rabbi Lewis, Joseph Hyman stated:

> The Soviet Union, for a long time, pursuant to its policy of non-discrimination among the citizens of its country, has insisted on non-sectarian relief. In essence, this is a theory with which we cannot quarrel if it is honestly and effectively applied.

Hyman disagreed with Rabbi Lewis that the Jewish population of the Soviet Union was completely massacred. Hyman reasoned:

> There are still some two million Jews in the Soviet Union who, more than all other elements of the population, suffered indescribable cruelty, havoc and difficulty. To refuse help to these people on the ground that their government wishes to treat all citizens alike through its governmental resources and means is to penalize them unjustly.[64]

In January 1947, while completing a fundraising campaign, the Board of Directors of the American Society for Russian Relief (ASRR [the successor organization to the JCRWR]) sent a report to JDC with summary data on ASRR participation in American aid to the USSR:

> The total amount of aid, both shipped and now in process, received from JDC comes to $2,080,574.
>
> Of this amount, clothing, foodstuffs, sewing machine parts, shoe repair materials and equipment, totaling $580,574.63—the original gift from JDC—have been shipped and delivered to the Soviet Union.
>
> In 1946 JDC appropriated $1,500,000 for aid to the Soviet Union. From this, penicillin valued at $950,474.65 has been purchased and shipped to the Soviet Union.
>
> Hospital programs, earmarked for the cities of Chernigov, Mogilev, Dnepropetrovsk, Voroshilovgrad, and Pinsk, are

now in the process of execution and will eventually cost $549,525.35.[65]

These documents clearly show the tremendous outlay of funds allocated by JDC for the USSR and the wide range of places to which it provided aid in Ukraine and Belarus in the postwar period.

JDC and the Peak of Stalin's Anti-Jewish Paranoia, 1947–1953

The start of the Cold War and a growing wave of state antisemitism in the USSR once again marked the end of JDC's programs. In 1947, official contact between JDC and the USSR was terminated. Infusions of JDC aid ended in 1948 and would not resume for four decades. In January 1948, on the personal order of Stalin, Solomon Mikoels was killed in Minsk by agents of Soviet State Security. Over the next eighteen months, the fifteen surviving leaders of the JAC were arrested. Three years later, in April 1952, they were placed on trial. In the indictment, the initiative to attract JDC support during World War II was termed "a criminal agreement with representatives of Jewish reactionary circles of the USA."[66] In the summer of 1952, during a closed interrogation session of the Military Collegium of the Supreme Court of the USSR, Solomon Lozovsky of the Soviet Information Bureau was compelled to present evidence supporting an indictment of Fefer for his conduct during his 1943 trip to the United States. Lozovsky recalled his personal experience preparing the JAC officials before their travel:

> When I was instructing Mikhoels and Fefer, I told them, "Don't have any conversations without the Consul or Ambassador present, and consult with Moscow to ask about all important questions." What is more, they received a telegram from Comrade Molotov with instructions to meet with Rosenberg to discuss the conditions under which the Soviet Union would accept aid proposed by the Joint. But in all of the testimonies and in the indictment, the

meeting with Rosenberg is described as criminal. Where is the crime here? Not only did they have the right to act as they did, but as Soviet people they were obligated to go and talk with a leader of the Joint, because the issue under discussion was assistance to the Soviet Union in the war against fascism.[67]

During these interrogations, the continuing mystery surrounding the Crimea resettlement issue deepened. In testimony on May 8, 1952, while recalling meetings in New York with JDC leaders, Fefer "confessed" that

Rosenberg announced, "You demand everything, but you aren't doing anything yourselves. But if you are able to raise the issue of settling Jews in the Crimea, then we will provide material assistance." He said: "The Crimea interests us not only as Jews, but as Americans, because the Crimea also means the Black Sea, the Balkan Peninsula, and Turkey." I consider myself guilty of not properly understanding the situation then, wrapped up as I was in my nationalistic yearnings and the desire to create economic circumstances favorable to the development of Jewish culture, and I considered it highly desirable to create a Jewish republic in the northern Crimea.[68]

On the basis of Fefer's testimony, well-known Russian scholar Gennady Kostyrchenko concluded that James Rosenberg may have delivered a private assurance to Mikhoels and Fefer of JDC support for a Crimean resettlement project.[69]

However, such testimony must be viewed in perspective. Fefer had been arrested in December 1948 and severely tortured both physically and psychologically during the ensuing few years. Under such a regimen, fabrication was often substituted for fact collecting. An alternative reading of Fefer's testimony would ascribe his "confessions" to the process of "socialist justice" that he was forced to endure, and his "confessions" should not be analyzed separate from that context. Clearly, these statements by Fefer—in custody by this time for three and a half years and a survivor of "methods of physical persuasion"—reflect his devastated status rather than an assurance from JDC leadership. Fefer's tragic role is intensified by the fact that he actively collaborated with the Soviet Security Services upon his arrival in the United States in 1943 for the JAC visit.[70]

The history of JDC's successes and failures in the wartime and immediate postwar Soviet Union continues to resonate in current political discourse and agitation. Records of the interrogation of Fefer during this trial have been used by some post-Soviet journalists to support the myth of JDC's interest in transforming Crimea into a Jewish Soviet Republic.

Several current newspapers in the Russian Federation periodically publish articles about JDC's post–World War II Crimean initiatives. The idée fixe is to present JDC as a military and political organization that was able to affect the American government and empower it to tear Crimea apart from the rest of the Soviet Union.

The myth concerning JDC's all-encompassing powers and its unlimited finances, never supported by facts, was propagated and brought to mass consciousness beginning in January 1953. On January 13, 1953, Stalin's propaganda apparatus published in the Soviet press the "uncovering" of a "Doctors' Plot": a JDC-financed conspiracy orchestrating Soviet physicians to murder Stalin. It is incredible to assume that an international philanthropic organization that, from Hitler's rise in 1933, had helped hundreds of thousands of European Jews to survive, resettle, and emigrate and was expert in negotiating with diverse regimes could have developed such designs in a country in which any contacts with foreign agencies were so severely circumscribed.

Press attacks throughout January to March 1953 cited JDC aid during the first famine in Soviet Russia (1921–1923) as an example of JDC's subversive activities. Soviet newspapers characterized JDC as a "dirty spy Zionist organization hiding behind the mask of philanthropy."[71] JDC's humanitarian aid to the USSR during World War II and the postwar years—over $4 million—received no mention.

THE CASE OF THE "MUKACHEVO BRANCH," 1953: PART II

The accusations of both sabotage and espionage on the instructions of JDC were first brought against those physicians who had worked in top Kremlin clinics. The same charges were later extended to ordinary doctors in the republics and provinces. In February to March 1953, weeks after the initial announcement of the arrest of the "saboteur physicians" conspiring in the "Doctors' Plot," Ukrainian authorities ordered the arrests of five former members of JDC's "Mukachevo Branch" (Alexander Pashkus, Vasilii Maizels, Albert Shaiovich, Vasilii Iavor-Grinstain, and Isaak Klain) "for nationalistic activity and on suspicion of contacts with foreign intelligence."[72] These arrests, the investigations, and the expected results—conviction and punishment—might have served as an important milestone in the careers of all the agents, investigators, and prosecutors involved in the Trans-Carpathian security apparatus. The Trans-Carpathian security forces had, in fact, rounded up the only individuals throughout the entire USSR who had actually worked with JDC over the significant period of 1944–1946.

Contemporary articles in Soviet newspapers contained clichés about JDC activities but were devoid of substantive facts. Because of this lack of information, more than a month was needed to prepare the editorial "Chto takoe Dzhoint" ("What Is the Joint?") that appeared in *Literaturnaya gazeta* on February 24, 1953.

This and other articles about JDC first appeared in the central press and were then reprinted in provincial publications. The article "Sionizm—zakliatyi vrag trudiashchikhsia" ("Zionism—the Inveterate Enemy of the Workers") appeared in the provincial newspaper *Sovetskoe Zakarpat'e* on February 6, 1953. However, in contrast with other publications, this one included local material—charges based on historical JDC activities in Trans-Carpathia—and provided ideological grounds for the accusation of Jewish nationalism. A portion of the article dealing with past JDC activities in the interwar period was rife with anti-American remarks. Included also were threatening references to "hostile local elements," the recent Slánský trial in Prague, and calls for "vigilance against enemies of the people." This publication was unique in that it was the sole text from the contemporary provincial Soviet press that was excerpted, albeit briefly and virtually incomprehensibly, in the *New York Times*. The article illustrates the vitriol with which propaganda officials linked together incomprehensible phrases, devoid of meaning, with the probable intent to incite antisemitism:

> Soviet Sees Old Plot.
>
> Newspaper Charges U.S. and Jews Collaborating in Spying
> Special to the New York Times:
> Moscow, Feb. 16—The Soviet newspaper Soviet Trans-Carpathia says the alleged plot of Zionists and Americans against the Soviet Union has a more ancient history than previously has appeared.
>
> Back in the Nineteen Twenties, the paper says, in the extreme eastern tip of Czechoslovakia, which is now a part of Russia, Zionist and American imperialists established outposts against the Soviet Union.
>
> United States Intelligence, it said, set up headquarters in Uzhgorod in charge of Benjamin Parker. With the active aid of "Jewish bourgeois organizations," a series of Zionist organizations was set up as blind for the designs of the American imperialists, the paper declared.[73]

From the perspective of Soviet domestic policy at the onset of 1953, the branch's early activity—its affiliation with JDC, its distribution of aid from abroad, and its contacts with foreigners—was considered criminal. In the atmosphere that prevailed at the very end of Stalin's rule, when officers of the provincial security apparatus endeavored to match the zeal of their Moscow colleagues, attempts were made to fabricate accusations out of thin air. In Trans-Carpathian Ukraine, however, the security officers could invoke actual historical grounds to build a case that involved Jewish "nationalists" with ties abroad.

The death of Stalin on March 5, 1953, interrupted this local plan. On April 4, *Pravda* and *Izvestiia* published "A Communique of the Ministry of Internal Affairs of the USSR" that put an end to the trial in "the Doctors' Plot." One result of this communique—and a host of open and secret decisions initiated during April 1953 by Lavrentii Beria, Minister of Internal Affairs of the USSR[74]—was a halt to the investigation of "the Joint Branch" in Mukachevo. At the first signs of the central regime's turn toward liberalization, cases against three of the five ex-members of the now-defunct JDC aid branch were summarily closed, and these arrestees were immediately released. The two others were not as fortunate: New accusations relating to general political rather than "nationalistic" activity were substituted for those linking them to JDC.

Materials from the case reveal how difficult—practically impossible—it was for the security organs to shift toward reducing repression. The end to Soviet anti-Jewish collective persecution, which had been connected by the dictator in a bizarre way to JDC activities, has been preserved in the collective memory of Soviet Jews as the "*Purimshpil* of 1953," as the death of Stalin and Purim 1953 were coincidentally the same day.

Conclusion

JDC's considerable difficulties with its partnership with the Soviet Union during World War II must be understand in the context of the organization's inability to conduct a full and open dialogue with a totalitarian regime. JDC was granted no possibility for direct contact with Soviet Jews, with the exception of a short stateside visit of the JAC representatives in 1943. In Moscow, the JAC's leaders were completely controlled by the Kremlin's curators and could never issue a substantive report. JDC was not able to control supply and distribution in the USSR, except for individual parcels or packages addressed to Jewish individuals and particular communities. JDC's negotiating partners—medium-level Soviet officials stationed in the United States—often provided JDC with fallacious information. Their goal was obvious: to maximize receipt from abroad of resources so vital to restoring the USSR's destroyed economy. And JDC, not an entirely naive player, had its own agenda: to maximize access to and aid for Jews in the Soviet Union territory.

JDC supplied the USSR with food, clothing, medicine, and medical equipment. JDC programs were conducted within broad territories over several regions—some affected and some unaffected by the war—in support of a wide variety of groups: refugees, evacuees, Holocaust survivors, war invalids. Beneficiaries in addition to the Jewish population included wounded Red Army soldiers, children, and the general population in every locality. And yet, during the "Doctors' Plot"—the final Stalinist antisemitic campaign—JDC was labeled a "spy organization" in Soviet newspapers and accused of organized conspiracy against the top Soviet functionaries. Any evidence of wartime humanitarian assistance provided by JDC was completely buried.

This chapter aims to retrieve from oblivion the subject of American Jewish wartime aid to the USSR, to identify the milestones and challenges of the programs, to cite the breadth of its geographical coverage, and to draw historical connections with events of the last decade of Stalin's era.[75]

JDC returned to the Soviet Union in 1988, fifty years after termination of the Agro-Joint program. Since the early 1990s, building on its long traditions of aid to Russia and the Soviet Union, JDC has continued its aid programs for needy Jews in the countries of the former USSR and has supported various initiatives to preserve the history of the Holocaust by sponsoring educational centers, seminars, conferences, and publications. JDC has sponsored extensive endeavors for the renewal of Jewish communities in the countries of the former Soviet Union. These activities include efforts to portray an accurate history of the role of JDC in the Soviet Union. This topic has been recruited into debates about the wartime, postwar, and Stalinist Soviet past, just as the work of JDC and its ability to aid needy Jews were totally entangled with the shifting political situation.

Notes

1. JDC Archives, Records of the New York Office of the American Jewish Joint Distribution Committee, 1933–1944, Folder 431, Memorandum, Subject: Mr. Rosenberg's Statement to the Executive Committee, 4, September 13, 1944.

2. JDC Archives, Records of the New York Office of the American Jewish Joint Distribution Committee, 1921–1932, Folder 510, Ten Years' Work of the Agro-Joint in the USSR, June 4, 1934.

3. Ibid., Folder 510, Ten Years' Work of the Agro-Joint in the USSR, June 4, 1934.

4. YIVO Archives, RG 358, File 82.

5. See Mikhail Mitsel, *"The Final Chapter": Agro-Joint in the Years of the Great Terror* (Kyiv, 2012). More than fifty-five years later, in 2005, JDC resolved to fill the historical void. In the ensuing years, JDC Archives staff conducted research within the ex-KGB archives in Kiev, Moscow, and Crimea, as well as the State Archives of the Russian Federation in Moscow. In 2012, JDC finally pieced together the fate of its workers, colleagues, and programs.

6. JDC Archives, Records of the New York Office of the American Jewish Joint Distribution Committee, 1933–1944, Folder 1056, Efforts to Extend Aid to Jews in Russia, April 3, 1944.

7. Ibid., Folder 421, Letter from Paul Baerwald to Ambassador Maxim Litvinov, February 25, 1942.

8. Ibid., Folder 421, Letter from Ambassador Maxim Litvinov to Paul Baerwald, March 2, 1942.

9. JDC Archives, Records of the New York Office of the American Jewish Joint Distribution Committee, 1945–1954, Folder 451, JDC Work in Russia, March 20, 1945.

10. See, for example, Mikhail Mitsel, *Obshchiny iudeiskogo veroispovedania v Ukraine: Kiev, L'vov: 1945–1981* [Jewish religious communities in Ukraine: Kiev and Lvov: 1945–1981] (Kiev: Judaica Institute, 1998), 157–95.

11. JDC Archives, Records of the New York Office of the American Jewish Joint Distribution Committee, 1933–1944, Folder 169, JDC Operations Today, July 1, 1943.

12. Ibid., Folder 423, Report on the Relief Accorded to Polish Citizens by the Polish Embassy in the USSR, April 1, 1943.

13. Ibid., Folder 1056, Efforts to Extend Aid to Jews in Russia, April 3, 1944.

14. Ibid., Folder 33, JDC Proceedings, December 5, 1943.

15. Ibid., Folder 74, Records of Appropriation, June 23, 1944.

16. Solomon Mikhoels (1890–1948), a Soviet Jewish actor and the artistic director of the Moscow State Jewish Theater. In 1948, Mikhoels was murdered on the orders of Stalin.

17. Joshua Rubenstein and Vladimir Naumov, eds., *Stalin's Secret Pogrom: The Postwar Inquisition of the Jewish Anti-Fascist Committee* (New Haven, CT: Yale University Press, 2001), 10.

18. Gennady Kostyrchenko, *Stalin's Secret Policy: Power and Anti-Semitism* (Moscow: Mezhdunarodnyey otnoshenia, 2015), 393.

19. JDC Archives, Records of the New York Office of the American Jewish Joint Distribution Committee, 1933–1944, Folder 430, Letter from Albert Einstein to the JAC, October 16, 1943.

20. Itzik Fefer (1900–1952), a Soviet Yiddish poet, was tried at a closed JAC trial and executed on August 12, 1952.

21. *Sovietsko-izrailskiye otnoshenia. Sbornik documentov* [Soviet-Israeli relations. Collection of documents], vol. 1 (Moscow, 2000), 68.

22. Ambidzhan, the All-American Society for Aid to Birobidzhan.

23. *Sovietsko-izrailskiye otnoshenia*, 75–76.

24. JDC Archives, Records of the New York Office of the American Jewish Joint Distribution Committee, 1933–1944, Folder 23, Meeting of the Executive Committee of the JDC, October 27, 1943.

25. State Archive of the Russian Federation, f. 9501, op. 5, d. 254–55, 258, 304.

26. JDC Archives, Records of the New York Office of the American Jewish Joint Distribution Committee, 1933–1944, Folder 62, Meeting of the Emergency Administration Committee of the JDC, October 12, 1943.

27. Ibid.

28. JDC Archives, Records of the New York Office of the American Jewish Joint Distribution Committee, 1933–1944, Folder 451, JDC Program in the USSR, 1942–1944, July 17, 1944.

29. Semen Podolski, in discussion with the author, Lvov, Ukraine, November 8, 2008.

30. JDC Archives, Records of the New York Office of the American Jewish Joint Distribution Committee, 1933–1944, Folder 431, Letter from Professor Viktor Lebedenko to Paul Baerwald, July 21, 1944.

31. Ibid., Folder 1056, Letter from Professor Viktor Lebedenko to James Rosenberg, September 4, 1944.

32. Ibid., Folder 335, Letter from Joseph Rosen to James Rosenberg, 4, December 15, 1943.

33. Ibid., Folder 431, Memorandum, Subject: Mr. Rosenberg's Statement to the Executive Committee, 4, September 13, 1944.

34. Ibid., Folder 421, Letter from Paul Baerwald to Ambassador Andrei Gromyko, August 3, 1944.

35. Ibid., Folder 802, Letter from Ambassador Andrei Gromyko to Paul Baerwald, September 22, 1944.

36. Ibid., Folder 1056, Letter from James Rosenberg to Moses Leavitt, January 8, 1945.

37. Central State Archives of Public Organization of Ukraine, f. 1, op. 23, d. 3851, p. 2.

38. Rubenstein and Naumov, *Stalin's Secret Pogrom*, 24.

39. Gennady Kostyrchenko, ed., *Gossudarstvennyi Anti-Semitism v SSSR. Ot nachala do kulminatsyi* [State antisemitism in the USSR. From the beginning to culmination] 1938–1953 (Moscow: Materik, 2005), 50–61.

40. Shimon Redlich, ed., *War, Holocaust and Stalinism: A Documented History of the Jewish Anti-Fascist Committee in the USSR* (London: Routledge, 1995), 42, 43, 248, 258.

41. Modern scholarship has revealed what JDC could not have known at the time: Mikhailov's primary wartime portfolio was resident agent in the United States of the Main Intelligence Directorate of the General Staff of the Red Army.

42. JDC Archives, Records of the New York Office of the American Jewish Joint Distribution Committee, 1945–1954, Folder 1056, Letter from Consul Pavel Mikhailov to Paul Baerwald, August 20, 1945.

43. Rubenstein and Naumov, *Stalin's Secret Pogrom*, 19–20.

44. JDC Archives, Records of the New York Office of the American Jewish Joint Distribution Committee, 1933–1944, Folder 514a, Minutes: Meeting of the Emergency Committee of the JDC, May 23, 1944.

45. Yehuda Bauer, *Out of the Ashes: The Impact of American Jews on Post-Holocaust European Jewry* (Oxford: Pergamon Press, 1989), 3.

46. JDC Archives, Records of the New York Office of the American Jewish Joint Distribution Committee, 1933–1944, Folder 431, Memorandum, Subject: Mr. Rosenberg's Statement to the Executive Committee, 4, September 13, 1944.

47. JDC Archives, Records of the New York Office of the American Jewish Joint Distribution Committee, 1945–1954, Folder 1056, Letter from Pavel Mikhailov to Paul Baerwald, October 10, 1945.

48. Ibid., Folder 802, Memorandum on Conversation with Mr. Mikhailov, Mr. Rosenberg, and Mr. Leavitt at the Russian Consulate, November 5, 1945.

49. *Encyclopedia Judaica*, 2nd ed., vol. 19 (Jerusalem: Keter Publishing, 1973), estimates that 10,000 to 15,000 Trans-Carpathian Jews survived the Holocaust.

50. See Alla Reider, *Evreiskaia obshchina Zakarpat'a, XX vek* [The Jewish community of Trans-Carpathia, the 20th century] (Uzhgorod, Ukraine: V. Padiak, 2004), 59, 100. Two Trans-Carpathian Jews who survived, Jacob Gollender (born in 1927, who was in Auschwitz and Mauthausen) and Ladislav Roth (born in 1922, who was in Mauthhausen) mentioned help from the Joint at all stages of their journeys, from their liberation from the concentration camp to their return to Trans-Carpathia.

51. All information about the repressed members of the Mukachevo Branch was collected from the interrogative file: *Archiv Upravlinnia SBU [Sluzhby bezpeky Ukrany] Zakarpatskoi olasti, arkhivno-slidcha sprava # 1746, v piaty tomach*. Archive of the SBU [Security Service of Ukraine] in the Trans-Carpathian Oblast, Archive—Investigation Case 1746 in five volumes and published by the author: Mikhail Mitsel, "The Activity of 'the Joint' in Mukachevo in 1944–1945 and the Soviet Attitude toward It in 1953," *Jews in Russia and Eastern Europe* 58, no. 1 (2007): 5–39.

52. JDC Archives, Records of the New York Office of the American Jewish Joint Distribution Committee, 1945–1954, Folder 437, Minutes of the Conferences, November 9–17, 1945.

53. Vozz'iednannia: zbirnyk archivnykh dokumentiv [Unification: Collection of archival documents] (Uzhgorod, 1999), 179, 183.

54. The file of the investigation contains original copies of letters that were evidently taken from the local archives. Vol. 2, 63, both sides.

55. Mordechai Altshuler, "Jewish Holocaust Commemoration Activity in the USSR under Stalin," *Yad Vashem Studies* 30 (2002): 271–95.

56. Archive of the SBU in the Trans-Carpathian Oblast, Archive—Investigation Case 1746, vol. 4, 45.

57. Ibid.

58. Reider, *Evreiskaia obshchina Zakarpat'a, XX vek*, 54–55.

59. Mitsel, *Obshchiny iudeiskogo veroispovedania v Ukraine*, 157–95.

60. JDC Archives, Records of the New York Office of the American Jewish Joint Distribution Committee, 1945–1954, Folder 1056, Letter from Professor Victor Lebedenko to Moses A. Leavitt, February 2, 1946.

61. Ibid., Folder 1409, Statement of Appropriations and Payments as of November 30, 1946.

62. Ibid., Folder 2278, Today's Facts and Figures on the Joint Distribution Committee, May 15, 1946.

63. Ibid., Folder 993, Letter from Rabbi Theodore Lewis to Joseph Hyman, April 25, 1946.

64. Ibid., Folder 993, Letter from Joseph Hyman to Rabbi Theodore Lewis, May 2, 1946.

65. Ibid., Folder 993, Letter from Edward Carter to James Rosenberg, January 9, 1947.

66. Rubenstein and Naumov, *Stalin's Secret Pogrom*, 484.

67. Rubenstein and Naumov, *Stalin's Secret Pogrom*, 256–57.

68. Ibid., 84.

69. Ibid., 413.

70. Ibid., 324.

71. "Vicious Spies and Killers under the Mask of Academic Physicians," *Pravda*, January 13, 1953.

72. Mitsel, "The Activity of 'the Joint' in Mukachevo," 20.

73. *New York Times*, February 17, 1953.

74. *Lavrentii Beria, Stenogramma iul'skogo plenuma TSK KPSS I drugie dokumenty* [Transcript of the July Plenum of the CC CPSU and other documents] (Moscow: MFD, 1999), 31; April 9, 1953, *Pravda* editorial "Sovetskaya sotsialisticheskaia zakonnost' neprikosnovenna" [Soviet socialist legality is uninfringeable]. A relevant document was the secret April 4 order of Beria banning the use of any means of force and physical pressure against arrestees, which signaled that force and beatings would no longer be resorted to.

75. For additional details about JDC relief programs in the USSR during World War II, see Mikhail Mitsel, "Programmy amerikanskogo evreyskogo

ob'edinennogo raspredelitel'nogo komiteta v SSSR. 1943–1947," [JDC programs in the USSR] *Vestnik Yevreyskogo universiteta* 23, no. 8 (2003): 95–122; Mikhail Mitsel, "Joint," in *Holocaust na territorii SSSR Encyclopedia*, ed. I. Altman (Moscow: ROSSPEN, 2009), 266–69. Information for this article was collected in the JDC NY Archives, the State Archives of the Russian Federation, the Central State Archives of Public Organizations of Ukraine, and the Archive of the Security Services of Ukraine in Trans-Carpathian Oblast. A sizable amount of material on wartime aid from JDC to the USSR still requires further detailed research and additional analysis.

5

DORSA and the Jewish Refugee Settlement in Sosúa, 1940–1945

Marion Kaplan

Sosúa, a small village on the northeast coast of the Dominican Republic, was what James Rosenberg, one of its founders, called a "very modest experiment" in attempting to rescue some of the persecuted Jews of Europe.[1] Shortly after the Evian Conference in 1938, in which representatives of thirty-two countries met to discuss the refugee crisis but refused to let more refugees into their lands, the Dominican dictator Rafael Trujillo made an offer of land to the newly created Intergovernmental Committee on Refugees.[2] He proposed admitting 50,000–100,000 settlers. When US experts agreed that the Dominican Republic could settle up to 29,000 families, the President's Advisory Committee contacted James Rosenberg of the American Jewish Joint Distribution Committee (JDC), the primary Jewish philanthropic organization for overseas relief and rehabilitation. Rosenberg, in conjunction with Dr. Joseph Rosen, a long-term JDC colleague, set up the Dominican Republic Settlement Association, Inc. (DORSA) under JDC's auspices. Roosevelt endorsed this venture publicly in October 1939 and hoped that this settlement would be the forerunner of similar projects in other places. The stakes at the time were very high. Those involved in the project, including experts hired to assess its progress, saw Sosúa as a "test tube experiment," "a demonstration to all of Latin America," that would open the closed doors of the Western Hemisphere for large-scale colonization by desperate refugees.[3] This chapter focuses on the two men most responsible for developing a settlement intended to rescue tens of thousands of Jews. Even if the war and US policies ultimately stymied them, allowing only several hundred Jews to find refuge in the Dominican Republic, we may ask why they thought this project could work and how their views of Jews and Dominicans helped them pursue their vision.

ROSENBERG AND ROSEN: FROM CRIMEA TO THE CARIBBEAN

James N. Rosenberg could have chosen retirement, writing art books and painting. At sixty-five, however, he embarked on one of the most important projects of his life: an attempt to save Jews in war-torn Europe. Helping European Jews was certainly not a new cause for Rosenberg; he had been assisting Soviet Jews since 1924. But very little in his childhood or younger years would have predicted this passion. Born in Pennsylvania in 1874, the son of an accountant and the grandson of a cantor, Rosenberg took a secular path. Still, he retained a sense of Jewish community, heightened by occasional and painful encounters with antisemitism, especially as an undergraduate at Columbia University.[4] After graduating from Columbia in 1898 with a law degree, Rosenberg did not find satisfaction in law. Only his work outside of law brought him real fulfillment, especially his work for JDC. Rosenberg represented JDC in Herbert Hoover's American Relief Administration project in Russia in the early 1920s. By 1924, JDC had selected Rosenberg to head its newly founded Agro-Joint (detailed in Mitsel's chapter in this volume), which spearheaded the Crimean project that was determined to settle Soviet Jews on agricultural collectives.

Similar projects had been envisioned over a hundred years earlier by proponents of the European Enlightenment, Jews, and non-Jews. Early-nineteenth-century Central and Eastern European Jews founded societies to promote "healthy" agriculture and crafts among Jews, reacting to antisemitic stereotypes that Jews, pale and hunched over, flocked to commercial trades to make money and cheat non-Jews. These vocational retraining groups remained small and ineffective. They paled in contrast to well-funded Jewish handicraft and agricultural training projects of the later nineteenth century. In 1880, the ORT (the Organization for Rehabilitation through Training) was established in Russia, providing skills training and loans to artisans and farmers. Agricultural settlement projects that were started in the 1890s, like those sponsored by the Baron de Hirsch Fund, the Jewish Colonization Association, and the Jewish Agricultural Society, also offered opportunities to Jews seeking to build a life outside Europe. These organizations helped Russian Jews settle in Argentina, Brazil, Uruguay, Bolivia, the United States, and Canada. In Argentina, they counted 33,000 Jewish farmers at the height of settlement in 1925.[5]

Nothing as large as the Agro-Joint plan in Russia, however, involving an investment of $17 million and millions of acres of land, had ever been attempted. With the cooperation of the Soviet government, which offered land grants in Crimea and southern Ukraine, the Agro-Joint aimed to make farmers out of a quarter of a million impoverished Jews whose situation as small business owners and middlemen had deteriorated under communism.[6] The Agro-Joint assisted in the cultivation of farmland and also imported approximately 1,000 American-made tractors.[7] Acclaiming the symbolic and actual importance of farming, Rosenberg hoped to "transform" Jews "from ghetto-prisoned traders into sturdy tillers of the soil, workers in shops and factories and in other productive occupations."[8] Such strong language reveals Rosenberg's internalization of antisemitic stereotypes. He also used the eugenic and gender discourse of his day uncritically, describing agricultural work as "manly," healthy, and regenerative.[9] When he "look[ed] at these bronzed young Jews, the hygienic and eugenic aspect of this work [was] one of its weightiest assets."[10] Put less heroically, American and Soviet observers agreed that the Jews "look[ed] like farmers, act[ed] like farmers, and smell[ed] like farmers."[11]

Rosenberg's close associate and the man who ran the Agro-Joint endeavors in the Soviet Union, Dr. Joseph A. Rosen, believed that agriculture would rescue Jews from not only poverty but also the unhealthy atmosphere of urban life. Rosen, a noted agronomist, had been born in Moscow in 1877 and educated in Russia, Germany, and the United States. As a Menshevik (socialist) activist, he had fled Russia and come to the United States in 1903. Rosen returned to the Soviet Union with the Agro-Joint and ran the entire Crimean project. He mediated between the Agro-Joint and a variety of Soviet scientific, political, and bureaucratic offices. Starting in Russia in

1924, he grew the Agro-Joint from an organization with about 24 agronomists and surveyors to one with over 1,000 employees by the late 1920s.[12]

Importantly for Rosen—and later for the Sosúa project—he instituted a three-part plan. First, he diversified crops in place of traditional grains and included dairy and meat production. Second, he insisted on modern machinery. Finally, his socialist ideology combined well with cost-effectiveness: He designed these farms as collectivized, cooperative settlements that could more efficiently share limited machinery, pastures, and other resources.[13] The project lasted from 1924 until the end of 1938. By then, the Stalinist government had already subjected many of the Agro-Joint's local Jewish administrators to brutal purges. In fact, Stalin's murder of some of Rosen's closest coworkers and colleagues (Samuil Lubarsky and Yeḥezkel Grower) must have haunted him—a good reason to plunge immediately into another huge undertaking: the attempt to bring 100,000 Jews to the Dominican Republic. Rosen's misjudgment of Soviet intentions and Rosenberg's naiveté, according to one historian, may have led the Agro-Joint to a fatal misunderstanding of Soviet objectives.[14]

Nazi intentions, on the other hand, seemed to be clear. As the Crimean project closed down, the situation of Jews in Germany and Austria exploded. On November 9, 1938, the November pogrom had sent tens of thousands of new refugees pouring out of Germany and Austria. One might wonder why these two men did not turn their considerable energies toward helping refugees enter Palestine. First, the British limited immigration there. From 1922 onward, Britain placed annual quotas on immigration, although those with 500 British pounds (or 8,595 Reichsmarks, approximately three months' salary for a German civil service lawyer at the time) could enter freely. Again in 1930, they further limited Jewish immigration, and in May 1939, just months after the November pogrom, the third British White Paper set a maximum of 75,000 Jewish immigrants over the next 5 years.[15] No more Jews would be admitted, except with Arab agreement, once that limit had been reached.[16] In addition, Rosenberg's "distaste of Zionism" was known and Rosen, too, stood aloof until 1943.[17] In response to their Zionist critics, who insisted that

Sosúa would detract from Palestine, Rosenberg and Rosen worried that "while . . . Palestine may prove to be an extremely important line of defense it would be a matter of unpardonable negligence to disregard other possibilities which may prove of inestimable value."[18] Indeed, the JDC had long sustained cultural and economic activities in Palestine,[19] and now considered Palestine to be one place among others that could take in refugees.[20] Not all Central European Jews fleeing Nazism could end up in Palestine.

After the end of the Crimean project, Rosenberg and Rosen barely missed a beat. While Rosenberg set up DORSA in New York, Rosen set out to investigate the Dominican Republic.[21] Rosen would direct the on-the-spot organization of the community, at least at the beginning.[22] For Rosen, negotiating with a foreign government, constructing or renovating houses, bringing in tractors, hiring agronomists, setting up cooperatives, and greeting often reluctant or bewildered new "farmers" must have felt like a repeat performance, but on a much smaller scale.

DORSA in New York had the task of coordinating all rescue and settlement efforts and pressing US government officials to expedite matters. A sixteen-person board oversaw the project, used its connections with business and government leaders, and provided help from afar. DORSA's executive secretary during its first four years, Rebecca Hourwich Reyher, an author and former suffragist, tirelessly ran the complicated and grueling day-to-day operations.[23] She corresponded with JDC representatives and Jewish community leaders in Europe, with the managers at the Sosúan office, with refugees waiting on Ellis Island, with Jews seeking escape from Europe, and with American and Dominican officials. She placed orders for supplies for Sosúa, organized board meetings, took voluminous notes, and wrote lengthy memos and minutes. She worked closely with James Rosenberg, Joseph Rosen, Leon Falk, and Maurice Hexter, all of whom served at one time or another as president or chair of DORSA. In the first two years, the New York staff grew to twelve, but as immigration slowed to a halt, the staff diminished to three full-time employees and one part-time person by mid-1943.[24]

Planning Sosúa

Negotiations

On January 11, 1940, Rosenberg made his way to the White House, stopping at the Dominican Legation Building and the US State Department first. After fifteen minutes with President Roosevelt, Rosenberg left feeling that FDR showed "[a deep interest] in the Dominican matter as a beginning of a solution of the refugee problem which he regards as an outstanding world problem."[25] JDC was well connected, as was Rosenberg. He traveled to the Dominican Republic with a small group of American officials, including Robert T. Pell, the assistant chief, Division of European Affairs, who represented the US State Department; Stephen Van Cortland Morris, the secretary of the Intergovernmental Committee on Political Refugees (IGC); Harold Linder from the Coordinating Foundation (of the IGC); and John Clancy, Rosenberg's secretary, to whom he dictated his diary of daily events. In it he chronicled every meeting, every impression, and his concerns.

In a series of notes prepared for him by a young assistant before the trip, Rosenberg learned that Sumner Welles, FDR's adviser on Latin America and Undersecretary of State since 1937, had written a book, *Naboth's Vineyard: The Dominican Republic 1844–1924.*[26] In it he identified two forces affecting Dominican history: tension at the Haitian border and a desire "that the black may be obliterated by the white."[27] A summary of the book, a few other superficial reports, and little else but his enthusiasm prepared Rosenberg for his visit to the small nation. On January 16, the Americans arrived in Ciudad Trujillo, the capital city, and were greeted by a high-level delegation.[28] On his first day in the Dominican Republic, Rosenberg also met with Joseph Rosen, who declared that settlement would be possible and that the land in and around Sosúa could sustain 500 families. The next day, both men set out to meet the dictator, Trujillo, and his wife.

Trujillo had come to power with US help. In 1916, US Marines occupied the country for eight years in an attempt to have the Dominican government pay its debts to the United States and other foreign countries. The United States trained the Dominican National Guard, including Trujillo. When the Marines left in 1924, Trujillo controlled the National Guard, which became his power base. With the support of the United States, Trujillo took over the helm of the Dominican Republic in 1930. Until 1961, he ran it as his own personal possession.[29] He terrorized and murdered opponents; broke up unions; owned vast tracts of land; held monopolies on salt; to a large degree controlled the butter, cattle, and milk industries; and became one of the world's richest men.

Yet Trujillo worried about his standing vis-à-vis Roosevelt and Washington, DC. He had good reasons to extend an invitation to Jewish refugees, reasons that neither Rosenberg nor Rosen paid attention to. First, he had ordered the massacre of between 12,000 and 20,000 Haitians in October 1937.[30] In a murderous xenophobic frenzy, Dominican troops rounded up Haitian farmers (men, women, and children) on the north-western frontier of the Dominican Republic (not far from Sosúa) and murdered them with machetes, bayonets, and clubs. Trujillo attempted to recover in US and world opinion with his gesture toward the Jews.[31] A second reason might have been that Trujillo believed that the Jews would substitute for the Haitian farmers he had killed while JDC would bring in needed capital, supplying the machinery and the subsistence of the new settlers until they got on their feet. The Dominicans would thus derive symbolic and real capital. Third, Trujillo's "obsessive concern" to "whiten" his country[32] further explains his invitation to people considered racially "inferior" in their homelands.[33]

Trujillo appeared to be "anxious" to start the process.[34] Rosenberg found himself in the position of slowing the project, of "starting small."[35] The funds for anything larger simply did not exist. As he told the publicist he hired at the end of the month, "The fundamentals are . . . that we must not emphasize but must play down 100,000 refugees, and we must stress . . . that the Dominican Republic has done a noble and fine thing and that soon there will be the beginning of a settlement of 500 families."[36] Trujillo, on the other hand, welcomed a far larger influx as long as the settlement would help the Dominican economy. He offered 26,000 acres of an abandoned United Fruit Company plantation, which he claimed to own, and "even indicated he would give it to [the Jews]."[37] Sosúa lay twelve miles from the deep-sea port of Puerto Plata. The parcel of land contained cultivable sections, grazing fields, an eight-mile beach, and a hilly area of forests. The area's sparse population appealed to Rosen, who had developed a policy in Crimea "of never moving people from the soil or making trouble."[38] Dominicans lived in scattered villages nearby.[39]

The American group spent the next weeks working out a contract with Dr. Julio Ortega,[40] the lawyer who had agreed to represent DORSA. Ortega, also the rector of the University of Santo Domingo, charged the Americans nothing, probably on the orders of Trujillo. The Americans began to travel around the area, taking soil samples and learning about Dominican agriculture. For example, Rosenberg ascertained that plantains were "easy to raise" and that the trees lasted about twenty years. They also found sweet potatoes and fruit trees in abundance. They passed coffee plantations; saw fields of rice, bananas, corn, onions, red beans, and potatoes; and learned that three crops of beans could be cultivated in one year and that "poultry thrives splendidly."[41]

But Rosenberg concluded (wrongly, it would turn out) that the "agricultural problem is the least of all." Instead, he worried whether the Northern Europeans would tolerate the climate and if their health would suffer.[42] This attitude reflected contemporary American and European racial prejudices and misconceptions. Even "experts" worried about the "unsolved mysteries of climatic and racial influence upon white settlers."[43] Apparently the success of southern farmers in the United States[44] and the existence of European Jewish settlements in Palestine[45] did not calm Rosenberg's fears. Dr. Atherton Lee, director of the US Government Agricultural Experiment Station in Mayaguez, Puerto Rico, encouraged Rosenberg, insisting that "there are many of us who have lived in the tropics most of our lives . . ." and that within a short time the refugees would be enjoying their weekends at the beach, "just as we do in . . . Miami or San Diego."[46]

The Americans attended luxurious diplomatic parties almost every evening of their two-week visit. The sixty-five-year-old Rosenberg appeared to enjoy these events, whereas the younger Rosen apologized to Trujillo for not attending with the explanation, "I'm just a rough farmer."[47] The parties served as friendly persuasion: At one such party, Rafael Paíno Pichardo, the president of Trujillo's Dominican Party, reminded Rosenberg that in Palestine "there was bloodshed. . . . But here you will not have any kind of that. Here you will be in peace and quiet. . . . You will never be a foreigner; you will be a Dominican as soon as you come over to our shores."[48] Rosenberg concluded that the attitude of the government could be "summed up as follows:—'When is the first boat load going to land? We want to see this work started.'"[49]

Yet as much as Rosenberg hoped that the settlement project would rescue desperate Jewish refugees, the political situation of the Dominican Republic worried him, although he never addressed the Haitian genocide. He reflected that "the realities are that the state is governed and strongly governed by the Generalissimo. His word is law. . . . I find at every point that the Generalissimo is all-powerful. . . . As the government now is conducted, the Legislators carry out the will of the Generalissimo."[50] Perhaps reflecting on his Soviet experiences, Rosenberg feared that the situation could turn on a dime. He and his colleagues sought advice from a number of Americans living in the capital. One such American painted a positive picture of the situation, arguing that two years earlier he would have warned them to go slowly but that now the government appeared to be "more stable." With Trujillo "tackling large economic problems," the American concluded that he had moved beyond being a "military chieftain."[51] When other local Americans concurred with this assessment, Rosenberg turned to Robert T. Pell. Pell, who had worked in the US State Department since 1928, had accompanied Rosenberg not only in his capacity as assistant chief of the Division of European Affairs but also as "personal representative of the Chairman of the American Delegation to the Intergovernmental Committee."[52] Invited to write in Rosenberg's diary, Pell noted: "[J]udging by Latin-American governments in general, the situation here is one warranting a good degree of confidence and warranting your going forward with this project."[53] Rosenberg reflected: "Maybe it all sounds too good—that gives me moments of fear."[54]

Still, this project also held out hope. Desperate Jews needed a haven, and Rosenberg had committed himself to finding one. The American government appeared to be supportive. Given the antisemitism faced by Jews around the world, Rosenberg could not have failed to be impressed by the generosity of all the Dominicans he met: "We certainly have been received and treated throughout the country as if we were visiting royalty."[55]

The DORSA Contract with the Dominican Republic

The central goal of the visit involved entering into a contract between DORSA and the Dominican government. Negotiations took time. On the fourth day of Rosenberg's visit, he received a letter from Trujillo stating his understandings:

> This property of about 26,685 acres, contains 24 dwellings, reservoir . . . has 4,950 acres of cultivated pasture. . . . I am deeply interested to cooperate in a practical way with the humanitarian plans of President Roosevelt. I hope the immigration of European refugees to the Dominican Republic will stimulate the progress of our country and will intensify the development of our natural resources as well as our industries. . . . It is, therefore . . . my pleasure to offer to the Refugee Association of which you are the esteemed President my Sosúa property as my personal contribution for the establishment there of the first refugee settlement in the Dominican Republic.[56]

Rosenberg took note of the word *contribution*, surmising that it "might not mean outright gift . . . probably means that he will turn it over to our Association for stock." Rosenberg liked this solution: "I should much prefer this business relation with him than to be in a position of always having it in the back of my mind that I have been the beneficiary of an outright gift . . ."[57] Thus, in the final negotiation, Rosenberg asked that Trujillo make him happy by taking stock for the cost of his property: "I did not want him to be more generous than the people in New York."[58] Trujillo agreed.

"Jew Tax?"

Rosenberg appreciated the courtesy with which the Dominican government had treated his delegation. When he objected to a clause in the contract, the government usually dropped it.[59] Nevertheless, he also fretted over what he called the "$500 discriminatory tax against Jews."[60] This Dominican Law 48 of December 23, 1938, limited the immigration of people from the "Mongolian race," those from "the African continent not of the Caucasian race," and foreigners who lacked "nationality." The last provision included German and Austrian Jews because when they left the German Reich, their passports declared them to be "without citizenship or nationality." Because Jews then possessed no citizenship, they had to pay the Dominican tax.[61] This tax produced almost $90,000 in revenue for the Dominican Republic in 1939 and affected those Jews who had come to the nation on their own.[62] In addition to the entry tax, the Dominican residence tax required $10 a year for Jewish residence and only $6 for non-Jews. Rosenberg spoke with Ortega to impress upon him the significance "to us in New York [that] every vestige of discrimination [be] removed from the statute books."[63] Ortega explained that the laws were passed when the Dominican Republic thought it would be flooded by penniless refugees and assured Rosenberg that it could be changed.[64] Rosenberg also told Bonetti Burgos, the secretary of state for the presidency, "Please note the assurances therein that all antisemitic discriminatory legislation in this country will be repealed. This is a point which Dr. Rosen calls 'trrrrremendously important' and so it is."[65] The legislature repealed the restrictive legislation in February 1940.

Dominican Motives

Whiteness and "Blood"

Jewish settlers represented more to the Dominican government than new farmers who would develop the economy with the help of American Jewish investment. Rosenberg and his committee learned that racial politics played a significant role. He commented in his diary:

> I get a feeling that he [Trujillo] and his entourage . . . are pretty strongly moved by a desire to increase the Dominican population of white people. . . . For example: At the dinner party given . . . by the Generalissimo and his wife . . .

I had quite a long talk with Sr. Bonetti. . . . [H]e brought
up Haiti and its immensely larger population than that of
the Dominican Republic, and emphasized the need of a
very much larger white Dominican population. "Two million
more," he said. "Our country could very easily support them.
We are a white people."[66]

Rosenberg did not, however, realize that his project assisted the government's postmassacre propaganda blitz in schoolbooks, the media, and political speeches, which stressed the Spanish European roots of its national identity and praised whiteness.[67] A few days after the signing of the DORSA contract, the censored Dominican press stated openly and directly what the Americans identified as an "undercurrent" in diplomatic circles. An editorial in *La Información* declared that "the Haitians, a black race, are immensely more prolific than our race, a race of white and mestizo people." In recognition of the "excessive population" of the former and its smaller land mass, it asked how the Dominican Republic could "defend itself against this huge danger . . ." and concluded: "The answer has been said a thousand times, by bringing a white migration. . . ."[68] Popular Dominican attitudes toward race were extremely complex, but elites spoke with one voice,[69] emphasizing whiteness as part of their overall project of national cohesion and modernization.[70]

Even as Rosenberg appeared to be sensitive to issues of "whitening," he did not allude in his diary to the massacre of Haitians less than three years earlier. He must have been aware of it. Although Dominican leaders tried to minimize the violence by referring to the bloodbath as "the incident,"[71] a well-read and politically interested lawyer like Rosenberg could not have failed to notice articles about the massacre in the *New York Times*, the *Herald Tribune*, *Life* magazine, or *The Nation*.[72] Moreover, someone as worried about the future safety of Jewish settlers might have wondered whether such a brutal regime could turn on Jews, too. Yet his diary did not mention the massacre once.

Rosenberg was caught in a quagmire of government policies and popular attitudes raging in Europe and the Dominican Republic—as well as in his own segregated country—which viewed race as stable and biological rather than socially constructed. Trying to save Jews from a murderous racism, he acquiesced to the racism of the Dominican elites. Many of the people who negotiated the DORSA contract with the regime found themselves in the uncomfortable position of opposing dictatorship in Europe while accepting it in the Dominican Republic. Perhaps Luis Hess, the DORSA interpreter who later ran the small school in Sosúa, summed up these feelings best: "[D]id we have a choice? Hitler, the German racist, persecuted us and wanted to murder us. Trujillo, the Dominican racist[,] saved our lives."[73]

Rosenberg and Rosen, first and foremost, were fixated on saving Jews. In addition, they may have been relieved that Dominicans accepted Jews at all, given the horror stories coming from Europe and anxiety about antisemitism in the United States, which surged in the late 1930s and realized its "historic peak" in 1944.[74] In fact, in every opinion poll up through early 1946, those surveyed singled out Jews as posing the greatest menace to the United States.[75] Coming from the land of, among others, the antisemitic German-American Bund and Father Charles E. Coughlin's rabid social justice movement, Rosenberg could only marvel at the reception that he and his project received: "The warmth of the welcome at every hand here is perfectly amazing to a man who has been devoting himself . . . to fighting the Coughlin anti-Semites. . . ."[76] Thus, when Dominican leaders merged Jews with "whites" or complimented Jews as a people, Rosenberg felt grateful rather than suspicious.

He embraced the Dominican elites' philosemitism, which was based on the same stereotypes that often plagued Jews. While praising Jews, philosemites used ancient anti-Jewish stereotypes of business acumen and political power but reversed these into positive characteristics— maintaining the stereotypes. Believing in Jewish genetic dispositions, Dominican elites held high expectations for Jewish involvement in their country and economy. Ortega, the DORSA lawyer, for example, explained, "As for me . . . I have Negro blood in me and Indian blood, and my wife has Jewish blood. We are not ashamed of any of those bloods; we are proud of them. But we want white people here, and we want the brains and skill of the Jewish people." Not even pausing at the word *blood*, despite Nazi

Germany's well-known obsessions with it, Rosenberg reflected: "There is . . . eagerness here—a genuine eagerness—to have us come; a respect for Jewish blood that pops out in all sorts of ways. For example, the young man whom the Generalissimo suggested for the agricultural fellowship . . . Dr. Rosen spoke with him and he tells me that the young man said proudly that he was 1/8th Jewish."[77]

Relations with the United States

Believing their own philosemitism, the Dominican elites overestimated the power of their Jewish guests in the United States and assumed that Jewish connections would achieve a better position for the Dominican Republic vis-à-vis the White House and the US State Department. Welcoming refugees came at a price. Trujillo expected a return on his investment in terms of better interactions with the US government and vigorous economic growth in Sosúa. He did not equivocate. He told Rosenberg that "he felt sure we were interested in the sound economic development of his country and I assured him we were deeply interested."[78] The Dominican press echoed the development theme as well.[79]

Meeting with Rosenberg, Trujillo discussed Dominican sugar, cocoa, and coffee production, which Rosenberg knew to be the island's chief crops (although he may not have known that Trujillo held vast investments in them).[80] Sugar, in fact, accounted for nearly half of the combined sales reported by Dominican industry in 1939 and about three-fourths of industrial employment and wages.[81] Trujillo, speaking as the head of state, yet with a huge personal fortune in this crop, announced that his government sought new markets, "preferential treatment wherever possible," and larger sugar exports to the American market.[82]

Promising to meet with "government people, the press, and American owners of Dominican sugar companies to get a better sugar quota," Rosenberg told Trujillo that he would work "as hard as I can to see whether I can produce any suggestions consistent with my proper regard to my duties as an American citizen and perhaps be helpful to you."[83] Later in the visit, he mused that "this country may perhaps have a just grievance against the USA. I do not pass on that."[84] The Dominican Republic, in fact,

bought "considerably more from the USA than it [sold] to the USA. . . .
Is it a lobby which the Cuban sugar growers arrange?" Reflecting on the
possible consequences of war to shipping and trade, Rosenberg wrote: "If
war destroys the sugar trade . . . it looks to me as if this country would be
flat on its back. . . . This is also, of course, a very serious thing from the point
of view of the settlement project."[85] He decided that he would present this
situation to people he knew, notably "Bob Wagner," the US senator from
New York. But he "made it clear to the Generalissimo that I am not a lob-
byist and cannot do more than to mention these facts to a number of men
of influence in America."[86] JDC did have connections, but not enough to
change American import policies that favored American business interests.
Upon his return to Washington, Rosenberg informed Trujillo through the
Dominican Embassy that US sugar interests in Cuba and the Philippines
precluded any changes in the quotas for Dominican sugar imports.[87]

Trujillo complained to Rosenberg that the Dominicans faced not only
a sugar quota but also opposition from Undersecretary of State Sumner
Welles regarding the Convention of 1924. This convention set up a customs receivership despised by the Dominicans because it gave the United
States the right to collect customs revenues. Indeed, the United States
played a major role in the Dominican economy. Commencing negotiations in 1936, the Dominican government finally reached an agreement
with the United States in September 1940 that allowed the Dominicans
once again to collect their own customs revenues.[88] However, the US Senate
only approved this agreement in April 1941. Hence, in early 1940, Trujillo
may have hoped that Rosenberg's connections would hasten the diplomatic process. But Rosenberg could only suggest that Trujillo needed "able
counsel" in Washington. In February, after the Sosúa contract had been
signed, Rosenberg, back in the United States, suggested that Trujillo hire
George M. Rublee, an official of the US State Department—and someone
close to Roosevelt—to work toward ending the customs receivership.[89]

Rosenberg probably did not realize that the Dominican government had
brought his Sosúa project into its already existing and considerable public
relations efforts in the United States. These included a promotional magazine; a film on the nation; the writings of two recruited Hearst newspaper

reporters; and an active Dominican lobby of businessmen, legislators, and paid lobbyists.[90] He promised to advise Trujillo regarding possible law firms[91] and to present the situation to "President Roosevelt, Secretary Hull, and to people in Congress." He felt "that when the Generalissimo was so anxious to have my friendly advice . . . I could not in all good conscience and fairness, in view of his conduct with us, conduct the issue with polite evasions."[92]

Exploring the Island, Seeking Opportunities for Refugees

His concern about Jewish refugees and their acceptance by Dominicans led Rosenberg to become better acquainted with the Jewish community in the capital. Before the refugee crisis, this community had been too small for a rabbi, a ritual circumciser, a ritual slaughterer, or even a Jewish cemetery.[93] But Rosenberg discovered that since the advent of Hitler, approximately 300 refugees had come to the city on their own.[94] Some 200 needed financial help.[95] He met the Dominican-based representative of the Jewish Telegraphic Agency. In response to Rosenberg's question "How are the native people toward you?" the man replied, "They could not be nicer. The only trouble is that they cannot find jobs for us."[96] Rosenberg then met with Abraham Staiman, a tailor and a "successful businessman," who headed the Jewish community in Ciudad Trujillo and ran JDC's relief committee there.[97] Staiman described the Dominican economy as "weak" and not able to sustain new small businesses.[98] In addition, he believed it would be very hard to start a business during the war.[99] Outside analysts saw the situation as a transfer of people from an area of political pressure to an area of economic pressure.[100]

Rosenberg worried about the effect of unemployed Jews in Ciudad Trujillo on Sosúa: "I am very much concerned to see whether we can find some way to help these people become self-supporting. We cannot risk our settlement project by creating dislike through having Jewish beggars here . . . it will simply have to be dealt with by the JDC in some way so as to avoid embarrassment or difficulty."[101] Rosenberg and his group also scouted Ciudad Trujillo for businesses that could be pursued along with farming, even though the Dominican government had insisted on farming. They wondered whether local materials could be utilized for manufacturing "cigarette cases, ash receivers, [and] boxes for ladies' jewelry . . ." In particular, Rosenberg bought native handmade articles "to bring home . . . to show some of my friends in America (perhaps the Macy people) a few of the articles which can be produced here. Maybe this will lead to some industries for my Jews."[102]

Rosenberg even donated $500 of his own money for scholarships for artists, a substantial amount in a poor country where a journalist for the Jewish Telegraphic Agency earned $40 a month. On one hand, he wanted to respond personally to the generosity of the Dominican government but, on the other hand, he hoped that the Dominicans might develop some woodworking and pottery that could lead to "the development of some industry which may be of use to this country and which may engage some of our settlers."[103] He was on the right track. A later study suggested that the settlers avoid producing greater quantities of "low-wage tropical commodities" like fruits and vegetables but try instead to acquire a higher living standard by "producing specialty products for export," such as cheese, cattle, or items manufactured from produce like chocolate or preserves.[104]

Worries and obstacles notwithstanding, Rosenberg believed that once they established the settlement they could work against any antisemitism that might arise. His experience in Russia gave him confidence regarding good relationships with neighbors: "There we worked with the Moslems and Tartars. . . . Our settlers in Russia are friends and comrades with the Russian settlers. This is because of Rosen's wisdom in helping all of these people with better seed, an occasional well digging . . . etc. Once we get started we will do the same thing here."[105]

Rosenberg's Success, Rosen's Plans, and the Settlement's Struggles

Alongside the private talks, negotiations over the contract between the Dominican government and DORSA continued. On January 30, 1940, both parties signed the contract in a ceremony attended by approximately 100 dignitaries. That day, Rosenberg cabled Franklin Roosevelt:

> Have honor to report that highly satisfactory settlement
> contract signed this morning with Dominican government.

Generalissimo Trujillo has been marvelously cooperative. . . .
Thanks again for your great help.[106]

The contract stipulated that 500 families would establish the community, with a population of 100,000 set as the final aim.[107] The "settlers and their descendants" received a guarantee to live and to pursue occupations "free of molestation or persecution or discrimination" and with "full freedom of religion and religious ceremonials." They could acquire citizenship according to Dominican law. Finally, the contract promised "equality of opportunities and of civil, legal and economic rights, as well as all other rights inherent to human beings."[108]

Immediately after the contract signing, Rosenberg sent publicity far and wide. By March, Trujillo thanked him, adding that he had received clippings "from periodicals all over the world."[109] A year later, Paramount Newsreel showed a segment on Sosúa that provided more positive press for the Dominican government and for the settlers.[110] Rosenberg targeted the *New York Times*, the *Washington Post*, and smaller magazines like *The Nation*.[111] The *Times*, in fact, ran an editorial on February 1, 1940, a day after

The signing of the DORSA agreement at the local committee offices in Sosúa. Ciudad Trujillo, Dominican Republic, 1940. (Harold F. Linder [signing], Robert Pell [behind him].) Photo by Dr. Kurt Schnitzer, Photo Conrado.

the signing, praising the contract for "bringing hope and encouragement to far larger numbers of European exiles" but also noting more soberly that it would "represent only a drop of rescue out of the oceans of misery."[112]

Rosenberg and Rosen's hopes came to fruition for only a small number of refugees. With Joseph Rosen running the settlement at first, a group of "pioneers" landed in March 1940. Happily, most immigrants had positive first impressions of Sosúa despite its complete isolation. They had a "wonderful view. Before us lay the ocean with a snow-white beach."[113] Rosen believed "our settlement in Sosua is but a tiny isle on the ocean of human misery, but it is these islets which may help bring back light out of darkness."[114]

Early on, the settlers lived in large barracks. Next door they found a smaller building that served as kitchen, dining room, and laundry room. Around them, other settlers and Dominican laborers built new houses. By the end of 1940, about 250 refugees lived in Sosúa, the majority Austrian (115) and German (96), along with a smattering of other Jewish Europeans, almost none of whom had experience or training as farmers. These barracks and a few shops created the nucleus of a village, known as Batey, and provided jobs for those who could not farm. The houses (or "homesteads") would be farmed collectively as the settlers learned how to care for crops and animals. After a day's work in the fields, settlers studied Spanish and agriculture, lessons required and provided by DORSA. Many settlers learned their "first Spanish" from the Dominican workers who helped out on the farm.

Rosen and DORSA saw these homesteaders as the essence of their "experiment." Europeans had lived in tropical and subtropical climates before, but they had depended on native labor. Rosen argued: "It is obvious that it would be unwise and impossible to build the economy of large-scale settlement of Europeans on the exploitation of native labor. Unless the European settlers are able to perform at least the major part of the necessary physical work themselves no mass settlement in these countries would be feasible." The success of the operation would hinge not only on whether Europeans could do a significant amount of work themselves but also on whether they could achieve a "sufficiently high standard of living . . . and continue that standard without outside help."[115] Rosen showed guarded optimism regarding the homesteads. He relied on the same three factors as in Crimea: (1) the mechanization of work, (2) new cash crops, and (3) cooperative production and marketing.[116] Yet the war stymied the delivery of machinery from the United States, cash crops grew slowly, and cooperative production did not increase quickly enough due to the lack of machinery. Still, by the mid-1940s, the butter and cheese factory expanded, as did a meat-processing factory that specialized in sausages, hams, and bacon. By the end of the war, in fact, the settlers had turned their entire attention to cattle, sending their independently raised farm products to their collectivized plants. *Productos Sosúa* became a nationally known brand. Relying less and less on DORSA, the settlers no longer needed its support by 1957.[117]

Despite some successes in these areas, DORSA remained stymied by its biggest problem: getting enough settlers to the Dominican Republic in the midst of war.[118] The war, the lack of transportation out of Europe, and the purposeful foot dragging of the US State Department, which slowly and grudgingly gave transit visas to refugees heading for the Dominican Republic, had slowed rescue. The United States did not want these refugees to enter its shores once the war came to an end, nor did it trust all of those who came over. A "fifth columnist" scare—concerns that German spies might come to the Western Hemisphere along with Jewish refugees and endanger the Panama Canal—also resulted in a slowdown. Additionally, the US State Department housed many anti-Semites.[119] With the attack on Pearl Harbor, the United States prohibited any further settlement. Between May 1940 and September 1947, a total of 729 refugees had lived at Sosúa. Seventy-six babies of refugees were born there.[120] However, DORSA's project and JDC's efforts in the Dominican Republic probably saved more lives. Another 300 to 350 Jewish refugees lived either in Ciudad Trujillo or scattered around the Dominican Republic, many supported by JDC. In addition, some of the 4,000 people who received Dominican visas but did not come to the island may have been saved by these papers.[121] The goal for Sosúa had changed after Pearl Harbor from rescue to creating a haven for needy survivors after the war.[122] And even that goal did not come to fruition, as survivors preferred North America or Palestine.

Three men and a young girl on horseback in the Sosúa refugee settlement, where they were taught agriculture and dairy farming. Sosúa, Dominican Republic, 1940s. Photo by Dr. Kurt Schnitzer, Photo Conrado.

Whether the project would have worked out as a viable agricultural settlement in any case is questionable. European Jews, mostly from commercial and professional backgrounds, had never intended to be farmers. That they tried to farm in Sosúa, and that some even succeeded, did not mean that they hoped their children, too, would become farmers. Many sought higher educations, professions, and a higher standard of living for their offspring. Also, young people who had grown up in German or Austrian cities had expected to work in commercial or professional careers. Many found adjustment to rural life difficult and clung to earlier dreams. In addition, many waited to hear from relatives who had remained in Europe before deciding where to live permanently. Once they realized that "the world we had left behind was gone forever, and so were all the relatives we had expected to be reunited with," one Sosúan described "a mass depression, and then we all wanted to leave and return to a world we hardly remembered. And of course the United States seemed to represent best that world we had lost."[123] Saved from the Nazi genocide by DORSA and the Dominican Republic, within fifteen years most went to North America. Many, especially the young, had learned Spanish, some had intermarried, and a few had become modestly successful farmers. Yet, like their grandparents or parents who had migrated from small German and Austrian villages and towns to larger cities, most looked to urban life for education for their children, commercial opportunities, cultural excitement, Jewish communities, and upward social mobility.[124]

On his return voyage from the Dominican Republic to the United States, James Rosenberg reflected on the month he had just spent creating a possible haven for Jewish refugees in the Dominican Republic. As exhausting as the schedule had been, he appreciated the "courage and the hope which these three weeks have given me . . ."[125] and believed that "we will do all we can to bring sunshine into darkened lives."[126] That DORSA could not do even more for refugees was certainly not for lack of trying.

NOTES

1. JDC Archives, Records of the Dominican Republic Settlement Association (DORSA), 1939–1977, Folder 35A, James Rosenberg et al., Reactions to Brooking Survey, 3, 12, September 30, 1942.
2. Telegram from Johnson, Chargé in the United Kingdom to the Secretary of State, August 12, 1938, in *Foreign Relations of the United States: Diplomatic Papers, 1938*, vol. 1 (Washington, DC: 1955), 764 [Document 840.48 Refugees/655: Telegram p. 753].
3. JDC Archives, Records of the Dominican Republic Settlement Association (DORSA), 1939–1977, Folder 35A, James Rosenberg et al., Reactions to Brooking Survey, September 30, 1942.
4. Allan L. Kagedan, *Soviet Zion: The Quest for a Russian Jewish Homeland* (New York: Palgrave Macmillan, 1994), 51.
5. Judith Laikin Elkin, *Jews of the Latin American Republics* (Chapel Hill: University of North Carolina Press, 1980), 128–33.

6. Jonathan Dekel-Chen, *Farming the Red Land: Jewish Agricultural Colonization and Local Soviet Power, 1924–1941* (New Haven, CT: Yale University Press, 2005), 206. Dekel-Chen suggests that the Agro-Joint helped about 200,000 people if one includes the farms, the industrial training centers, and the aid to plots adjacent to shtetls.

7. James N. Rosenberg, *Unfinished Business: James N. Rosenberg Papers*, ed. Maxwell Geismar (Mamaroneck, NY: Maraasia Press, 1967), 314.

8. Rosenberg, *James N. Rosenberg Papers*, 314.

9. This overview of Rosenberg's life comes from his autobiography, *On the Steppes: A Russian Diary* (New York: Knopf, 1927) and from Kagedan, *Soviet Zion*, chap. 5, quote on p. 55.

10. Dekel-Chen, *Farming the Red Land*, 27.

11. Ibid., 192.

12. Ibid., 66.

13. Ibid., 49, 65, 108–9, 161, 192.

14. Kagedan, *Soviet Zion*, chap. 5.

15. Theodore Lewis, "San Domingo," *American Jewish Chronicle*, March 1, 1940, 1. Mrs. Archibald Silverman also objected to the "cold philanthropy and feverish anti-Zionism" of the initiators of the Sosúa project and predicted that such projects would isolate Jews from Jewish centers and contacts and would produce "race suicide" for Jews. She completely ignored the British White Paper. See her article "Colonization in Sosua," *Congress Weekly*, December 19, 1941.

16. Walter Laqueur, *A History of Zionism* (New York: Schocken, 1989), 528–33.

17. "Distaste" from Yehuda Bauer, *My Brother's Keeper: A History of the American Jewish Joint Distribution Committee* (Philadelphia: Jewish Publication Society of America, 1974), 21; Rosenberg, *Unfinished Business*, 38, 340. During his first visit in 1950, he changed his mind about Israel, deciding that it was "a haven for the oppressed—for which I had searched most of my life."

18. JDC Archives, Records of the Dominican Republic Settlement Association (DORSA), 1939–1977, Folder 35A, Memorandum from Rosen to James N. Rosenberg, November 5, 1941. Rosen warmed toward a Jewish state by 1943 when he realized that "[i]f we had any kind of country of our own

we would not have to look for the 'benevolent' attitudes of the Trujillos, the Andersons, and the Warrens." See also JDC Archives, Records of the Dominican Republic Settlement Association (DORSA), 1939–1977, Folder 5, Letter from Rosen to Rosenberg, April 10, 1943.

19. JDC Archives, Records of the Dominican Republic Settlement Association (DORSA), 1939–1977, Folder 5, Letter from Rosenberg to Honorable M. de J. Troncoso de La Concha, Senate of the Dominican Republic, Office of the President, May 11, 1943. Maurice Hexter had led the colonization work in Palestine for nine years before becoming president of the Agro-Joint and a member of the DORSA board in May 1943.

20. Bauer, *My Brother's Keeper*, 135; Melvin Urofsky, *American Zionism from Herzl to the Holocaust* (New York: Bison Books, 1975), 420.

21. President's Advisory Committee on Political Refugees, Memorandum, December 19, 1939, in Stephen S. Wise Papers, Box 65 "Related to Dominican Republic" from American Jewish Historical Society.

22. JDC Archives, Records of the Dominican Republic Settlement Association (DORSA), 1939–1977, Folder 9, James Rosenberg Diary, 65.

23. *New York Times*, January 13, 1987. Reyher wrote children's books and books on Africa.

24. JDC Archives, Records of the Dominican Republic Settlement Association (DORSA), 1939–1977, Folder 5A, Report of Executive Secretary to the Chairman and the Board, May 5, 1943. Cutbacks occurred after mid-1943.

25. Ibid., Folder 9, James Rosenberg Diary, 1.

26. Sumner Welles, *Naboth's Vineyard: The Dominican Republic 1844–1924* (New York: Ayer, 1972), 909. In 1924, Welles had been envoy extraordinary and minister plenipotentiary in the Dominican Republic.

27. *Naboth's Vineyard* summarized in JDC Archives, Records of the Dominican Republic Settlement Association (DORSA), 1939–1977, Folder 42, A Brief History of Santo Domingo by Michael Bodkin for J. N. Rosenberg, January 5, 1940. See also Silvio Torres-Saillant, "Blackness and Meaning in Studying Hispaniola: A Review Essay," *Small Axe* 10, no. 1 (2006): 181–82; Silvio Torres-Saillant, "The Tribulations of Blackness: Stages in Dominican Racial Identity," *Latin American Perspectives* 25, no. 3 (1998): 129. In a brilliant examination of Dominican "blackness," Torres-Saillant reminds us that

Welles also stated that race discrimination was *unknown* in the Dominican Republic. He argues that too much has been made of the Negrophobia, imputing the governing elite's views to that of the general population.

28. JDC Archives, Records of the Dominican Republic Settlement Association (DORSA), 1939–1977, Folder 9, James Rosenberg Diary, 7.

29. The United States protected its investors' interests in sugar, coffee, cocoa, and bananas by maintaining political control of the island. In 1906, the Dominicans defaulted on loans and were forced to sign a fifty-year treaty with the United States that gave the United States the customs receivership of the Dominican Republic.

30. For 12,000, see Eric Paul Roorda, *The Dictator Next Door: The Good Neighbor Policy and the Trujillo Regime in the Dominican Republic, 1930–1945* (Durham, NC: Duke University Press, 1998); for 15,000, see Richard Lee Turits, *Foundations of Despotism: Peasants, the Trujillo Regime, and Modernity in Dominican History* (Stanford, CA: Stanford University Press, 2004). Some articles and websites refer to 20,000, such as the article by Metz cited below.

31. Turits, *Foundations*, 197.

32. Allen Metz, "Why Sosúa? Trujillo's Motives for Jewish Refugee Settlement in the Dominican Republic," *Contemporary Jewry* 11, no. 1 (1990): 6; Barbara Quackenbos, "Sosúa: Kol Haskholeh Koshoh" [Every beginning is difficult] (senior thesis, Princeton University, 1982), 9; Freda Kirchwey, "Caribbean Refuge," *The Nation*, April 13, 1940, 468.

33. Metz, "Why Sosúa?" 6, citing Bruno Lasker, "Elsewhere: An Atlas of Hope," *Survey Graphic* 29 (November 1949): 590; Metz, "Why Sosúa?" 5, citing Oden and Olivia Meeker, "Sosúa: A Unique Colony for Jewish Refugees in the Dominican Republic," *Tomorrow* 6 (May 1945): 23.

34. JDC Archives, Records of the Dominican Republic Settlement Association (DORSA), 1939–1977, Folder 9, James Rosenberg Diary, 9.

35. Ibid., 11.

36. Ibid., 113.

37. Ibid., 67–68.

38. Ibid., 30.

39. Richard Symanski and Nancy Burley, "The Jewish Colony of Sosúa," *Annals of the Association of American Geographers* 63, no. 3 (1973): 371.

40. This is Julio Ortega Frier, although Rosenberg does not use the last name.

41. JDC Archives, Records of the Dominican Republic Settlement Association (DORSA), 1939–1977, Folder 9, James Rosenberg Diary, 31, 34.

42. Ibid., 34.

43. Brookings Institution, *Refugee Settlement in the Dominican Republic: A Survey Conducted under the Auspices of the Brookings Institution* (Washington, DC, 1942), 8, 44. The report also discussed the effect of "indigenous races upon European whites."

44. Brookings Institution, *Refugee Settlement*, 333.

45. Mark Wischnitzer, "The Sosua Settlement," *ORT Economic Bulletin* II, no. 3 (1941): 2.

46. YIVO Archives, Letter from Atherton Lee to James Rosenberg, July 10, 1940, in Joseph Chamberlain Papers, Folder 83.

47. JDC Archives, Records of the Dominican Republic Settlement Association (DORSA), 1939–1977, Folder 9, James Rosenberg Diary, 65, 155.

48. Ibid., 56.

49. Ibid., 67.

50. Ibid., 39–40.

51. Ibid., 73.

52. Letter from Pell to Pastoriza with Enclosure to Trujillo [around January 1940] in USHMM Archives Microfilm, "Documentos de Inmigración Hebrea: Carta recuda, 1940," 1999.A.0251, Reel 1.

53. JDC Archives, Records of the Dominican Republic Settlement Association (DORSA), 1939–1977, Folder 9, James Rosenberg Diary, 74–75.

54. Ibid., 73.

55. Ibid., 81.

56. Ibid., 55–56.

57. Ibid., 67–68.

58. Ibid., 92.

59. Ibid., 179.

60. Ibid., 77.

61. YIVO Archives, Refugee Economic Corporation Representative Alfred Houston's Report to the REC, January 6, 1939, Joseph Chamberlain Papers, Folder 11.

62. YIVO Archives, Letter from W. A. Frey to HIAS-ICA (Paris), July 24, 1939, in HIAS-HICEM Papers, Folder 290.

63. JDC Archives, Records of the Dominican Republic Settlement Association (DORSA), 1939–1977, Folder 9, James Rosenberg Diary, 78–79.

64. Ibid., 79.

65. Ibid., 127–28.

66. Ibid., 13.

67. On propaganda, see Silvio Torres-Saillant and Ramona Hernández, *Dominican Americans* (Westport, CT: Greenwood, 1998), 143. On the timing of propaganda, see Turits, *Foundations of Despotism*, 172, who argues that the shift in propaganda to anti-Haitianism and whiteness was the "product of rather than the precursor to" the massacre. Before the massacre, the government focused on border "security," even if its motivations were racial.

68. "The Advantages of Immigration for Our Country" [in Spanish], *La Información* 8150 (February 13, 1940): 4.

69. See Torres-Saillant, "Tribulations of Blackness."

70. Ernesto Sagás, *Race and Politics in the Dominican Republic* (Gainesville: University Press of Florida, 2000), 51. Further, the elites hoped to integrate into a white, Spanish Catholic world that opposed Haitian "voodoo."

71. Kirchwey, "Caribbean Refuge," 468.

72. Roorda, *Dictator Next Door*, 134, 138.

73. "Vertreibung ins Paradies," Spiegel Online, December 26, 2006, accessed October 29, 2012, http://www.spiegel.de/panorama/zeitgeschichte/0,1518 ,456564,00.html.

74. David Wyman, *The Abandonment of the Jews: America and the Holocaust* (New York: Pantheon Books, 1984), 9.

75. Robert Rockaway, "The Roosevelt Administration, the Holocaust, and the Jewish Refugees," *Reviews in American History* 3, no. 1 (1975): 115.

76. JDC Archives, Records of the Dominican Republic Settlement Association (DORSA), 1939–1977, Folder 9, James Rosenberg Diary, 213.

77. Ibid., 213–14.

78. Ibid., 196.

79. "An American Commission from Washington is about to Arrive in the Country" [in Spanish], *La Información* 8118 (January 12, 1940): 1.

80. JDC Archives, Records of the Dominican Republic Settlement Association (DORSA), Folder 42, Barker, Kramer, and Kocher, A Brief Summary Outline of Essential Facts Contained in Report Covering Field Investigations of Settlement Possibilities Existent on Selected Lands in the Dominican Republic, Prepared at the Request of the President's Advisory Committee on Political Refugees, circa 1938. Trujillo also owned twelve of the sixteen sugar mills in the country. See also Howard Wiarda, *The Dominican Republic: A Nation in Transition* (New York: Praeger, 1969), 133.

81. Brookings Institution, *Refugee Settlement*, 169, 174–75.

82. JDC Archives, Records of the Dominican Republic Settlement Association (DORSA), 1939–1977, Folder 9, James Rosenberg Diary, 199.

83. Ibid., 189.

84. Ibid., 238.

85. Ibid., 237.

86. Ibid., 237. The situation deteriorated later, as can be seen in the March 8, 1953, edition of the *New York Times*, which reports that in 1950 Trujillo went into the sugar business, and now the sugar industry takes up a disproportionately large part of the economy in a time of falling prices. The Dominican Republic "is clamoring more and more for a larger US import quota and sugar purchases." See also JDC Archives, Records of the Dominican Republic Settlement Association (DORSA), 1939–1977; Turits, *Foundations of Despotism*, 242.

87. Metz, "Why Sosúa?" 15.

88. JDC Archives, Records of the Dominican Republic Settlement Association (DORSA), Folder 40, Charles A. Thomson, Dictatorship in the Dominican Republic, April 15, 1936.

89. Hyman J. Kisch, "Rafael Trujillo: Caribbean Cyrus," *Judaism* 29 (1980): 368.

90. Roorda, *Dictator Next Door*, 110–114.

91. JDC Archives, Records of the Dominican Republic Settlement Association (DORSA), 1939–1977, Folder 9, James Rosenberg Diary, 208.

92. Ibid., 209.

93. JDC Archives, Records of the Dominican Republic Settlement Association (DORSA), 1939–1977, Folder 554, Letter from A. Pomeranz to Federated Jewish Charities, Milwaukee, October 1, 1940, PDF available by contacting

Marion Kaplan at mk111@nyu.edu and asking for the document from May 28, 2006 (ReligCemetery). See also JDC Archives, Records of the Dominican Republic Settlement Association (DORSA), 1939–1977, Folder 554, Letter from H. Buchman to David Schweitzer, July 7, 1941, also available from Marion Kaplan, May 28, 2006 (Rabbi 7.7.41). Jews were buried in Christian cemeteries until they set up their own in the early 1940s.

94. JDC Archives, Records of the Dominican Republic Settlement Association (DORSA), 1939–1977, Folder 54, Letter from Joseph Rosen to Alexander Landesco, January 17, 1941. By January 1941—a year later—it appears that there were 300 *families*, most with "no means" in Ciudad Trujillo.

95. JDC Archives, Records of the Dominican Republic Settlement Association (DORSA), 1939–1977, Folder 9, James Rosenberg Diary, 99.

96. Ibid., 100; YIVO Archives, Refugee Economic Corporation Representative Alfred Houston's Report to the REC, January 6, 1939, Joseph Chamberlain Papers, Folder 11. Rosenberg did not seem to be aware of the Houston Report of a year earlier, which stated that soon after Evian, 150 to 160 Jewish families came to the country, remaining in Ciudad Trujillo as "commission agents" and causing "strong popular resentment on account of their unfair methods of competition." No further explanation was given.

97. YIVO Archives, Letter from A. Staiman to HIAS-JCA Emigration Association (Paris), September 18, 1939, in HIAS-HICEM Papers, Folder 290.

98. JDC Archives, Records of the Dominican Republic Settlement Association (DORSA), 1939–1977, Folder 9, James Rosenberg Diary, 103.

99. Ibid., 103.

100. Brookings Institution, *Refugee Settlement*, 52.

101. JDC Archives, Records of the Dominican Republic Settlement Association (DORSA), 1939–1977, Folder 9, James Rosenberg Diary, 101.

102. Ibid., 25, 160, 212–13.

103. Ibid., 212–13.

104. Brookings Institution, *Refugee Settlement*, 214.

105. JDC Archives, Records of the Dominican Republic Settlement Association (DORSA), 1939–1977, Folder 9, James Rosenberg Diary, 88.

106. Ibid., 127–28.

107. Brookings Institution, *Refugee Settlement*, 326. The Brookings Institution survey challenged these numbers a year later, arguing that the Dominican Republic could only absorb "5,000 *persons* [italics added]" given "existing conditions." DORSA and Atherton Lee (agricultural adviser to the US Board of Economic Warfare and a member of the Brookings survey team) strongly dissented. See "Settlement in the Dominican Republic" in Studies of Migration and Settlement: Memorandum, September 10, 1943, loaned to the staff of the "M" Project at Johns Hopkins University, Ms. 58, Milton S. Eisenhower Library, Johns Hopkins University.

108. JDC Archives, Records of the Dominican Republic Settlement Association (DORSA), 1939–1977, Folder 41, Rosenberg Letter to the Editor of the *New York Times*, February 23, 1950.

109. Ibid., Folder 40, Letter from Trujillo to Rosenberg, March 13, 1940.

110. Ibid., Folder 40, Letter from Trujillo to Rosenberg, March 13, 1940. The film was released in February 1941.

111. Kirchwey, publisher of *The Nation*, did, in fact, write an article only a few months later called "Caribbean Refuge."

112. "A Haven for Refugees," *New York Times*, February 1, 1940, 17.

113. Leo Baeck Institute Archives, Horst Wagner, Memoir (1975), 12.

114. JDC Archives, Records of the Dominican Republic Settlement Association (DORSA), 1939–1977, Folder 43, Joseph Rosen, Pamphlet No. 3: "Concerning Refugee Settlement in the Dominican Republic," A Discussion at the Lawyers' Club, New York City, September 17, 1940.

115. Ibid., Folder 40, Joseph A. Rosen, *Survey Graphic*, 2, September 1941.

116. Ibid., Folder 40, Joseph A. Rosen, *Survey Graphic*, 5, September 1941.

117. Ibid., Folder 57, Letter from James Rosenberg to George Warren (US State Department), November 27, 1957; Ibid., Folder 57, Letter from Maurice Hexter to James Rosenberg, February 5, 1958.

118. Ibid., Folder 35A, Minutes of Meeting of DORSA Directors, 4–5, June 12, 1940.

119. David Wyman, *Paper Walls: America and the Refugee Crisis, 1938–1941* (New York: Pantheon, 1985).

120. JDC Archives, Records of the Dominican Republic Settlement Association (DORSA), 1939–1977, Folder 47, Memorandum from Research

Department of JDC to Robert Pilpel, October 28, 1947. This report says that seventy-six children were born and then lists only seventy-two.

121. Ibid., Folder 35E, Letter from Walter Baum to James Rosenberg, December 15, 1947.

122. Ibid., Folder 35A, James Rosenberg et al., Reactions to Brooking Survey, 3, 12, September 30, 1942.

123. Grete Neumann-Burg, Sosúa Archive, copy available from Marion Kaplan at mk111@nyu.edu.

124. Today the settlement no longer exists, although some of its residents and their children remain (perhaps two dozen families). A synagogue offers Friday-night services once a month as well as holiday services.

125. JDC Archives, Records of the Dominican Republic Settlement Association (DORSA), 1939–1977, Folder 9, James Rosenberg Diary, 233.

126. Ibid., 242. From Rosenberg's thank-you letter of February 7, 1940, to the Dominican people and to Trujillo, reprinted in the Dominican press, added to the back of his diary.

6

Laura Margolis and JDC Efforts in Cuba and Shanghai

Sustaining Refugees in a Time of Catastrophe

Zhava Litvac Glaser

Jewish refugees line up for their midday meal at the Ward Road Home operated by JDC, whose soup kitchens in Shanghai fed 8,500 refugees twice a day. Shanghai, China, circa 1940. Photo by D. Koenig.

Throughout the course of World War II, the very future of European Jewry was in doubt. The increasing oppression by the Nazis placed an unprecedented demand on world Jewry to take action. The career of Laura

Margolis, who served in Cuba, China, and Europe with the American Jewish Joint Distribution Committee (JDC) from 1939 to 1953, is illustrative of American Jewish relief and rescue efforts during the war and postwar years.[1] Each location where she served—Cuba, Shanghai, Spain, Sweden, Belgium, and France[2]—had unique political and social contexts and demanded different strategies to provide crucial help to thousands of Jewish people as these catastrophic events unfolded.

After the Nazis rose to power in 1933, JDC concentrated on providing aid in three main areas: (1) supporting Eastern European Jews in their desperate economic and social situation, (2) providing physical and cultural sustenance for persecuted Jewish communities in Nazi-occupied areas, and (3) facilitating emigration from these areas. To help Jews escape, the organization made travel arrangements; attempted to secure visas; and provided food, housing, and medical aid to stranded refugees in havens such as Cuba and Shanghai until they could be relocated.

Neither the Cuban nor the Shanghai established Jewish communities were prepared to handle the overwhelming numbers of Jewish refugees arriving at their doors, nearly destitute and needing food, housing, and medical care. In neither location did the refugees attempt to settle and become integrated into the life of the country. Unable to obtain employment due to Cuba's restrictive employment laws, most refugees were forced to spend their days in idleness and depended completely on JDC aid for their sustenance. In Shanghai, where finances were much more scarce as the war progressed, incoming refugees used any means and skills at their disposal to eke out a living. In both locations, the refugees could not have survived without the financial assistance of JDC. In addition, in both Cuba and Shanghai, rising antisemitism became a serious problem as the war progressed and Nazi agents circulated around the world disseminating their disinformation.

In both locations, Laura Margolis's remarkable trajectory illustrates the difficulties and challenges faced by JDC working with World War II refugees. Margolis was faced with Jewish populations representing diverse ethnicities, socioeconomic statuses, ages, genders, political views, and religious observances. Her clients' geographic origins ranged from Polish to

Russian to Turkish to German to Austrian to Dutch. Their political views spanned the spectrum of Zionists, Socialists, Marxists, Communists, and more. She had to mediate among refugees who were religiously Orthodox, Conservative, Reform, and secular. She was faced with preserving the dignity of respected intellectuals who were suddenly reduced to begging on the streets. Margolis, representing JDC, aided people from all walks of life: physicians, tailors, butchers, and playwrights, all of whom were in need of assistance as they left everything behind to flee the Nazi menace. Frictions arose as religious traditionalists refused to live in close quarters with more liberal Jews, demanding preferential treatment and more costly kosher food and accommodations. Refugees of all ages and abilities were present, the older immigrants finding it far more difficult to adjust to a foreign environment and begin anew. All of this took place among people in deep psychological pain who had suddenly left families and friends, having no idea what their fate would be. The prewar attempts by JDC to facilitate emigration among refugees in Cuba and the early wartime efforts to ensure the survival of stranded refugees in the free port of Shanghai demonstrate the evolution of the efforts by Margolis and JDC to cope with the changing needs of Jewish refugees.

Laura Margolis (1903–1997), a remarkable woman at home in multiple worlds, was the appointed JDC director in both of these locations. Born in Istanbul in 1903 of Ashkenazi Jewish parents, Margolis grew up with a strong sense of social responsibility. Her maternal grandfather, Solomon Schwartz, was personal physician to the sultan of Turkey. Schwartz was also the leader of the Ashkenazi Jewish community in Istanbul and had a special concern for the Jews who had taken refuge there from persecution in Eastern Europe. Her uncle, Haïm Margaliot Kalvarisky, was a prominent Zionist. Her father, Herman, a European horticulturist and also a fervent Zionist, had lived in Palestine for a time but became convinced he could do more for the Zionist cause by relocating to Istanbul and training and preparing the refugees for immigration to Palestine. Herman Margolis married Schwartz's daughter, and in 1908 the family moved to Ohio, where others in the Margolis-Kalvarisky family had settled. Laura was raised in the strong Cleveland Jewish community led by well-known rabbi Abba

Laura Margolis was the JDC representative for Cuba from 1939 to 1941 and for Shanghai from May 1941 to September 1943. She then served JDC in Spain, Sweden, Belgium, France, and Israel. Photo likely from New York, circa 1939.

Hillel Silver. Since her teenage years, Margolis had volunteered with local welfare services. Later, she received a degree in social work from Western Reserve, now Case Western Reserve University.

Although social work was predominantly a woman's career in the 1930s, social work that crossed international borders was not. In this, Laura Margolis was a pioneer, both within JDC and for women in social work in general. Margolis's career in social welfare dated from 1930 when she was employed by the Jewish Social Service Bureau in Cleveland as a caseworker and then as supervisor of the Jewish Big Sister Association, working with "maladjusted" girls until 1934. She then became director of the Jewish Welfare Society in Buffalo, New York, where she served until she was recruited by JDC in 1939 to work in Cuba.[3]

Margolis was trained in the predominant theory of social welfare in the interwar period, which emphasized bringing order to the process of relief through a thorough evaluation of the client's need and the "weeding out" of individuals who did not qualify. Jewish social work principles and social workers, specifically in the United States, emphasized that Jewish communities must "take care of their own."[4] The training Margolis received in accepted welfare procedures and her Jewish background of communal self-sufficiency complemented each other and shaped her approach to social welfare, preparing her for the challenges she faced as a JDC official who needed to provide for a large number of refugees in an organized way and within a very limited budget under chaotic and politically complicated wartime conditions.[5]

Due to the language skills derived from her upbringing (she was able to communicate in French, Spanish, German, Turkish, Greek, and Yiddish) and her unique background and training, Margolis was the ideal candidate to work with JDC. Although she was well trained in social work theory, Margolis's substantial experience had not prepared her to deal with the refugee experiences that she encountered in Cuba and later in Shanghai. Nevertheless, she did not hesitate in accepting these foreign assignments, where she felt she could be of most help among those fleeing the Nazi terror. These people came from different social, economic, cultural, religious, and geographic backgrounds. Most had left behind their life savings, livelihoods, and loved ones and were confronted with the need to reconstruct their lives with few or no resources. The small established Jewish communities that met them were themselves divided along lines of geographic origin, political viewpoints, socioeconomic backgrounds, and levels of religious commitment. These established communities did not always welcome the refugee influx and offered relatively little by way of aid considering the enormity of the need.

CUBA: A STEPPING STONE TO FREEDOM, 1939–1941

At a time when Jews were fleeing increasing persecution and the nations of the world were closing their doors, Cuba continued to maintain a liberal immigration policy. Between 1938 and 1944, 12,000 European Jewish refugees, mostly from Germany and Austria, arrived in Cuba, most of them viewing the nation as a temporary haven in their attempts to immigrate to the United States and other countries.

Before the influx of German Jewish refugees, Cuba had a multiethnic Jewish population of between 10,000 and 12,000, composed of a mixture of Eastern and Western European, Turkish, and American Jews. Cuba established an open-door immigration policy when it achieved independence from Spain in 1898. Between 50 and 100 families of Jewish origin—many of whom were intermarried with Catholics and raised in the Catholic religion and others who were largely secular—migrated to Cuba in the late nineteenth century. When it liberated itself from US occupation in 1902, Cuba declared freedom of religion and the separation of church and state. In 1906, Romanian and other Eastern European Jews escaping from pogroms found a receptive haven there.

Just before World War I, in 1914, a group of Sephardic Jewish immigrants from Turkey arrived in Cuba. These Jews were part of a larger migration from the Middle East to the Americas due to the decline of the Ottoman Empire.[6] Another wave of Jewish immigration came between 1925 and 1935, when approximately 4,000 Eastern European Jews who spoke Russian, Polish, and Yiddish migrated to Cuba to flee persecution in their home countries.

By the early twentieth century, Cuba's culture had developed a distinctively European flavor where Jewish immigrants felt comfortable.[7] These factors, as well as Cuba's proximity to the United States and the ease of immigration, made the country attractive to Jews fleeing increasingly hostile treatment in Europe.[8] Unfortunately, the different discordant elements of the Havana Jewish communities failed to come together to establish an infrastructure to meet the dire and pressing needs. They viewed the refugees as an American problem and considered it unnecessary to shoulder any real part of the financing, administration, or social burden involved.

Although there were Jewish families of considerable wealth in Havana, the total contribution from the community in 1939 amounted to less than $10,000.[9]

As thousands of refugees continued to flood Havana, local Jewish leaders reached out to the international Jewish community for assistance, and JDC, along with the National Coordinating Committee for Aid to Refugees and Emigrants (NCC),[10] responded. The NCC, in cooperation with JDC, became the intermediary between refugees seeking entry into the United States and the American Consulate in Havana.

At the same time, thirty-five-year-old Laura Margolis was growing restless directing the Buffalo Jewish Welfare Society. At the recommendation of friends, she applied for a job with the NCC where she could use her Spanish and German language skills to work with German refugees in Cuba. In December 1938, Cecilia Razovsky, the executive director of the NCC, came across Margolis's job application and recruited her for a six-month term in Cuba to help with the immigration process.

Joseph Hyman of JDC wrote:

> . . . Miss Razovsky tried hard to secure a very competent social worker, familiar with casework and preferably with a knowledge of Spanish. This is not easy. She finally came to the conclusion that Miss Laura Margolis, Executive Director of the Buffalo Family Welfare Society, would be the right person.[11]

The Buffalo Jewish Welfare Society agreed to release Margolis from her duties for six months, and she began work as the director of the Joint Relief Committee (JRC) in Cuba on January 28, 1939.[12] Margolis faced the challenge of providing food and shelter for the thousands of Jewish arrivals while aiding their immigration efforts, all without sufficient funding. Social tensions existed between the small established Cuban Jewish community and the refugees, who were faced with longer and longer stays in Cuba as their immigration possibilities evaporated. Meanwhile, German refugees who had been forced by Nazi anti-Jewish laws to leave their worldly goods in Germany struggled with the language; the climate; and the sudden loss of their livelihoods, financial resources, and family and social environments. Among the Jewish refugees, Polish refugees were often looked down upon by the bourgeois and liberal German refugees.

Emily Perlman, the temporary JDC administrator in Cuba, was delighted to hear that Margolis had accepted the position and was hoping that the new arrival would be able to "stand the pressure" so she herself could return to the United States.[13] Perlman was worried that the JDC office would make a bad impression on Margolis upon her arrival:

> The clients overcrowd the waiting room and stand around on the balcony talking in loud voices. Then too the superintendent of the building does not care to have our clients use the elevator and the men are forced to walk up four rather steep flights. We have been looking for a house or apartment because we feel that we would attract least attention to the place and we would have plenty of room for expansion. I am terribly sorry that we will be unable to move the office before Miss Margolis arrives because I am afraid she might receive a very poor impression.[14]

When Margolis arrived in Cuba, she found an understaffed and disorganized relief operation. She had been told that there would be a man in charge,[15] and when she, who understood the complexities of working within varied local settings, learned that she would be the person overseeing local operations, she immediately requested that Cecilia Razovsky send additional staff appropriate to what she perceived as the prevailing cultural gender norms:

> I do hope you are working on the plan of getting a man worker down here as soon as possible. The administration of this office is not simply one of getting relief. It is all tied up with local immigration problems, community relationships, and interpretation to community and our committee. My impression is that there are many situations where a man be

[*sic*] much more effective than a woman because of the local Cuban attitude (Cuban women are not supposed to have too much intelligence).[16]

In the United States, the expansion of social welfare during the Depression had brought many professional women into the field. In 1930s Cuba, although there was a rising feminist movement, there were still many who held strongly to traditional Spanish gender roles that assigned women to a place in the home and not in the workplace. As a highly trained and capable professional, Margolis nevertheless saw utility in stepping back and bringing a man in to help facilitate the local situation. Her sarcastic parenthetical comment on gender roles, however, betrayed a hint of cultural superiority on her part.

Within a week of her arrival, Margolis, again relying on her training, had already begun to evaluate the finances and was disturbed at the way they had been handled before her arrival. She estimated that it would take at least a month to straighten out the bookkeeping to even begin to submit a budget.[17] She quickly learned that the funds she would receive from the United States would not be nearly sufficient to take care of the needs involved.

In attempting to tighten the finances, Margolis found that relief was being given to applicants without any kind of a home investigation to verify their claims. Home investigation was precisely part of the social work protocols in which she was trained and in which she firmly believed. She found that the existing files and records were not in any condition even to determine the number or type of clients in her caseload.[18] Margolis communicated her impression of chaos and disorganization in the relief work when she wrote to Razovsky:

> It might interest you to know that the Havana office has a reputation on the Continent already as being the one office which gives relief easily. In all my experience, I have never seen such a perfect example of how an organization was being "taken for a ride."[19]

Margolis was also forced to cope with a minimal budget and demands from ever-increasing numbers of refugees:

> I was only here a few days when I realized that if all of my energies could be devoted merely to cleaning up the "back mess," which had gained tremendous proportions, with the help of three home relief people, it would take at least several months to bring the budget down to anything approaching the Two Thousand Dollars, per week, appropriation for Cuba.[20]

Margolis, reflecting JDC's need for bureaucratic order and efficiency, immediately used her organizational skills to streamline the systems and cut expenses, putting into action a "housecleaning plan" and requiring investigations into what she called the "back mess," which she perceived as corruption among the refugees, who sometimes hid their resources in order to receive American Jewish relief. The refugees, of course, feeling a sense of panic, might well have described their actions as survival strategies rather than as "corruption," highlighting the tension between JDC's larger institutional principles and policies on one hand and the desperation of the refugees it tried to serve on the other. Margolis recruited the services of "several superior and well trained refugees,"[21] some who were on work relief and some who volunteered their services full time. Several of her recruits had experience with immigration and *Hilfsverein* (benevolent society) work in Berlin, Vienna, and Palestine, so she utilized them as paid workers and was open to learning from their experience in crisis situations.[22]

In this way, Margolis hoped to bring the budget under control and weed out those who were trying to "work the system" dishonestly while at the same time imploring JDC to provide more funds for the work. This new structure resulted in an entirely different attitude on the part of the clients as well:

> They cannot create scenes or scare us into giving emergency relief because we have a very satisfactory alternative play for

emergency relief already [*sic*] to offer them. We know that
it is becoming generally known throughout the community
that a "new wind is blowing at the JRC" so that certain relief
requests which were pending prior to the present setup, have
been withdrawn.[23]

With the help of this system, Margolis was able to cut the budget significantly, but refugees were still pouring into Cuba. The newer immigrants were making tremendous demands on the JRC's finances as they arrived with fewer and fewer resources because of Germany's increasing restrictions on Jewish economic activities throughout the 1930s.[24] Margolis constantly clashed with the New York leadership, petitioning for additional funds and personnel to help with the task at hand and bemoaning the fact that she had to send yet "another tale of woe about money. It seems all we do is cable for it and we're short again."[25]

Although the main emphasis of the JRC was on relief, there were other aspects to its work as well, such as providing help with immigration problems; efforts to unite the local Jewish community; local fundraising; and studies exploring the possibility of constructive projects such as occupational training, English-language lessons, and setting up children's camps to raise the morale of the refugees.[26] Cuban law did not permit refugees to work, and Margolis was concerned that if the refugees remained idle during their long stay, it would result in rapid demoralization. Margolis also anticipated a steady increase in the relief rolls as more immigrants were expected to arrive, and the resources of those refugees who were not yet on relief would slowly be exhausted.[27]

Exacerbating the already tense situation, Germany had dispatched Nazi agents and sympathizers in Cuba to disseminate propaganda in the press and radio targeting the rising influx of Jews. Things came to a head in May to June of 1939 with the *St. Louis* incident. Margolis was the first to sound the alarm, warning JDC headquarters that the *SS St. Louis*, a ship bearing almost 1,000 German Jewish refugees, was likely to be turned away from Cuba. Although her initial appeals were not heeded, Margolis persisted and eventually succeeded in convincing JDC leadership to send attorney Lawrence Berenson and Cecilia Razovsky to Cuba to intercede with the government. The team reported a condition of near panic, not only among the people on the boat but also among the Jewish refugees currently in Cuba, who feared that they might be deported.[28]

Historians have portrayed Berenson as a naive American who did not understand the true nature of the Cuban politics that precipitated the crisis.[29] Although the factors that led to this debacle were many and complex, the problem was brought to a head due to political machinations in the Cuban government regarding immigration. Berenson's naive optimism, believing the assurances of the Cubans that the matter would turn out well, handicapped him and prevented him from sounding a sufficient alarm to JDC and the US State Department.[30]

In a discussion about the *St. Louis* incident, JDC leadership, fearing German "refugee dumping," referred to a proliferation of conflicting claims by local Nazis based on speculation and rumor:

> . . . a Nazi program to send unfortunate people who cant [*sic*] support themselves to places where they are not wanted and then having those people seem poor, penniless, useless persons (because they can't work) and make them the nucleus for spreading antisemitism into every quarter of the world.[31]

As soon as it was definite that the *St. Louis* passengers were not allowed to disembark in Cuba and were headed back to Hamburg, JDC initiated an international effort to find a home for the refugees. They approached countries such as Haiti, Ecuador, the Dominican Republic, Mexico, and others, but they were not found feasible because the ship was too far out and could no longer return to the Americas.[32] Through the intense efforts of Morris Troper in Paris, Paul Baerwald (the JDC chairman was on temporary assignment with the President's Advisory Committee on Political Refugees in London[33]) and Harold Linder[34] in London, and James N. Rosenberg in New York, havens were found by the time the refugees docked in Antwerp[35] on June 17: Belgium took 214 refugees, Britain 287, Holland 181, and

France 224. JDC allocated $500,000 to provide for the refugees.[36] Unfortunately, those who found refuge in Belgium, Holland, and France soon found themselves once again under Nazi domination.[37]

Although JDC representatives were unsuccessful in convincing Cuba to admit the refugees, Margolis's warnings about new restrictions in Cuban immigration policy served to prevent a similar incident, as another ship of a thousand refugees had been about to sail for Cuba and was likely to be turned away.

Margolis's reports from Cuba give us firsthand insights into the changing and complex needs of the refugees. We can also discern JDC's strategies in dealing with the Cuban authorities in the midst of an ever-tightening legal environment in regard to immigration in the United States. JDC was rightfully concerned that if Cuba closed its doors because of the refugee burden that this would affect the attitude of Latin American countries such as the Dominican Republic, Argentina, and Brazil. JDC could not take that chance. Eventually acceding to Margolis's continued requests, it knowingly poured disproportionate funds (as compared with other international areas) into the effort to aid the Cuban refugees as long as it was able, with the larger goal of allowing as many to leave Hitler's clutches as was humanly possible.[38]

After the *St. Louis* incident, as Cuba tightened its immigration policies, immigration nearly stopped, and the refugees slowly began to leave for the United States and other destinations. In her time in Cuba, Margolis provided food, shelter, and vocational training to sustain 12,000 stranded refugees; assisted in managing one international incident and preventing others; and successfully navigated an immigration bottleneck. By the end of 1941, the US visas had been honored, and no more than 200 of the 12,000 who had taken refuge in Cuba remained on the island; Margolis's work in Havana was finished, and she embarked on even more complex challenges.[39]

SHANGHAI: FROM REFUGE TO IMPRISONMENT, 1941–1943

An open port that required no visas, Shanghai, which had been under Japanese control since 1937, was increasingly flooded with Jewish refugees fleeing the Nazi terror and awaiting permission to emigrate to the United States and other destinations. Unlike the Cuban refugees, most of the immigrants to Shanghai did not have visas.[40] At the time, Shanghai had a worldwide reputation as "the most pleasure-mad, rapacious, corrupt, strife-ridden, licentious, squalid and decadent city in the world."[41] Many Jewish leaders did not consider Shanghai a viable option at all,[42] but after the Evian Conference in July 1938, as the nations of the world began to close their doors to further immigration, Shanghai became just about the last choice for the immigrants. The thought of distant Shanghai as a possible refuge would have been frighteningly alarming to most German Jews, but running out of options, thousands of refugees seeking to escape from Germany and Austria sought temporary refuge there as they awaited permission to emigrate to a permanent destination.

The German, Austrian, and Polish refugees who arrived in China were not a homogeneous group. As in Cuba, they represented a variety of economic, religious, political, class, and cultural backgrounds, and rifts frequently formed between them. As the events of World War II grew more dire, certain German refugees, accustomed to a much higher socioeconomic status, were forced to grapple with turning into penniless refugees. No matter how wealthy they had been, refugees leaving Germany were now required to pay heavy exit taxes and were only permitted to take one handbag and 10 Reichsmarks out of Germany and only had an additional 150 Reichsmarks in "on-board money" to spend en route.[43] About 2,100 Polish Jews who made their way to Shanghai found assistance from the established Russian Jewish community, but there was no established German Jewish community to aid the German refugees.

Shanghai had no organized social agencies in the Western sense to provide for the flood of immigration that began in 1938, so the local Jewish communities stepped up to help.[44] In 1941, as the waves of immigration were becoming too large for them to handle, the local (Jewish) Committee for Financial Assistance to Refugees (CFA) approached JDC to send a trained social worker to open up the immigration bottleneck that had developed. Margolis's experience and efficiency in handling the Cuba emigration bottleneck had brought her to the attention of Avra Warren, the chief of the Visa Division of the US State Department, who suggested to JDC that Margolis be the staff person assigned to Shanghai.[45]

Although JDC was contributing financially, it was only at the request of the US State Department that it finally agreed to send a qualified staff member, and even then it was not to assist in the relief work but to work with the consulate to expedite emigration from Shanghai and thereby ease the strain on the local committee. This illustrates the little-known delicate cooperation between JDC and the US State Department to expedite refugee immigration to the United States during World War II. Avra Warren was familiar with JDC's work in the Dominican Republic from his work as US minister to the Dominican Republic from 1942 to 1943 and then as ambassador from 1943 to 1944.[46] He interceded on behalf of fifteen female relatives of the settlers who were stranded in Europe.[47] He was later involved in the effort to repatriate Margolis from a Japanese internment camp, suggesting that she and her coworker be classified as "representatives of a religious organization functioning in aid to their fellow members in this religious group" because such workers would have the first degree of preference, even ahead of diplomats, and could be repatriated regardless of numerical balance, with the need for an exchange.[48]

Margolis packed her things, traveled to Cleveland for one last visit with her family, and set out for the Far East.

Margolis reached Shanghai on May 12, 1941, about three years after the first wave of refugees had come. She wrote of her trip to the Far East:

> It was a great adventure. When I landed in Hong Kong, I saw a sea of Chinese faces that all looked alike to me. . . . When I had been in Buffalo there had been a lot of rice bowl dinners for Chiang-Kai-Shek's fundraising. I had been roped into some of those dinners and knew about the overseas relief program for Chiang-Kai-Shek's China—so as I was walking along the streets of Hong Kong I saw the name of that organization: The Far East Rice Bowl Dinner Campaign. I walked in [and] introduced myself as an American on my way to Shanghai. . . . We talked, and when

I got back to the hotel I found an invitation to dinner—at
the home of Mrs. Sun Yat-sen. I would be picked up in the
evening by a General [Morris] Cohen, Sun Yat-sen's former
bodyguard. . . . It was a delightful evening.[49]

When Margolis finally arrived in Shanghai, she was shocked at the stark
contrast between the extravagant luxury of the "white man" and the misery and poverty of the Chinese—whom she called "coolies"—starving to
death and lying dead in the streets.[50] Between the two extremes were the
European refugees, who suddenly found themselves in need of welfare assistance but still felt themselves, as Europeans, to be more esteemed socially
and were perceived to be more privileged than the local Chinese population.

Margolis sensed the hypocrisy of having to use scant resources to "play
the game" with the rich and influential high society of Shanghai in order to
make the contacts she needed with the American Embassy:

Life became a round of parties, one after the other. I had
flown out with a minimum of luggage and work clothes,
but there I couldn't function unless I had a different evening
gown every night. I played the game and hated every minute
of it, but I began my contacts with the American Embassy;
that was what I was sent out to do.[51]

Her dedication to help the refugees in spite of her loneliness and aversion
to "playing the game" was evident in a handwritten note she wrote to her
friend and supervisor, Robert Pilpel:

Please remember me to the staff. For all the "wining and
dining" of which there has been plenty—it's lonesome as
can be. I hate Shanghai. But I'll see it through . . .[52]

Margolis's first task as the sole representative of JDC in China was
to move as many people out of Shanghai as possible. Working with the
US State Department, she established systems to process visas and entry

permits for the émigrés, although this became increasingly difficult in light of tightening US immigration regulations. This illustrates a situation in which JDC was able to cooperate productively with the US State Department to facilitate refugee immigration.

In mid-1941, Margolis began to hear from several trusted sources that due to the state of national emergency declared by President Roosevelt in response to Germany's increasing threats of world domination, new instructions had come from Washington that would affect the issuing of visas, even if the persons should qualify. Nothing had been said officially, however. Margolis intentionally continued to work as if nothing had happened, but she felt as if she were "sitting on a volcano." The pressure of the constant demands of needy refugees was so intense that she felt that the local efforts could collapse at any moment. "We are absolutely ready to handle the job here if Washington will give us something to do," she wrote to Moses Leavitt,[53] secretary of JDC since April of 1940.[54]

Within six months of her arrival, a plan was in place to ease the immigration bottleneck, and Margolis's assignment to organize the processing of visas was completed. Although Margolis had accomplished her initial goal, despite her dislike for the venue, she decided to stay in Shanghai and turned her attention to the great need for relief work on the ground in Shanghai. The Hongkew area, where the refugees had been allowed to settle, was in ruins by mid-1941. An industrial section of Shanghai, it had sustained heavy damage in 1932[55] and 1937[56] when the forces of the Japanese Imperial Army invaded the city.[57] The Japanese occupied those parts of Shanghai that were administered by the Chinese, respecting Western treaties that created areas known as the International Settlement and the French Concession and allowing Shanghai to remain an open port. This status quo continued until World War II, when Japan joined the Axis powers and attacked Pearl Harbor (1941) and the British and Americans became enemy nationals and were imprisoned in Japanese internment camps.[58]

To provide for the influx of German and Austrian refugees, with JDC aid, five camps had been set up by a committee of the local Jewish communities that could house 2,500 refugees.[59] Made up of different waves of immigration from various locations, the Jews of Shanghai were not one community but many. In 1941, Shanghai had a Jewish population of over 25,000. The first wave of Jewish immigrants had arrived in 1845, when Shanghai became one of five new treaty ports opened at the end of the First Opium War (1839–1842). The Treaty of Nanking, which set aside ten square miles of Shanghai for foreign residence, opened up trade, and Sephardic Jews from India and Iraq under British protection migrated there to participate in the opium trade[60]; the sale of cotton yarn, paper, and flour; and other commercial activities. The Sephardic community was small in numbers—at its peak it numbered around 700—but was influential because of its wealth and international connections.

These Sephardic Jewish immigrants came to play a large part in the development of trade in China and participated in the civic councils made up of foreigners that governed the international areas of Shanghai known as the International Settlement and the French Concession.[61] By the end of the nineteenth century, many of them had achieved success in banking, public utilities, the stock exchange, real estate markets, and industrial development.[62] The most successful of the families were the Sassoons,[63] Kadoories,[64] Hardoons,[65] Ezras, and Hayims, who were able to establish branches of their family enterprises as well as purchase land in the small village of Shanghai at very low prices. These immigrants later built many of the city's major buildings, such as the Cathay Hotel, Cathay Mansions, the Metropole Hotel, Sassoon House, Grosvenor House, Hamilton House, and the Embankment Building. In 1887, this community organized Congregation Beth El, which in 1920 became the Ohel Rachel synagogue, named after Lady Rachel Sassoon, the wife of Sir Jacob Elias Sassoon. Ohel Rachel was the first of seven synagogues to be built in Shanghai.[66]

The second wave of immigration began as Russian Jews fled Czarist persecution and the pogroms of the early twentieth century. The pace of immigration increased after the Russian Revolution of 1918, when Jews fled the Communist takeover via the Trans-Siberian Railway and Harbin. Shanghai, by then a relatively modern city, attracted mostly poor, Russian-speaking immigrants who had suffered persecution after the revolution. Although the Russian immigrants were culturally different and spoke a different language, the Sephardic community extended aid to them, and in time they were able to establish retail businesses, boarding houses, and bars for the many foreign soldiers who were stationed in Shanghai. By the 1930s, they had grown to around 6,000 people—six times the population of the Sephardic Jews—and had established several synagogues of their own. This Ashkenazi community never did attain the wealth or distinction of the Baghdadi Jews,[67] but because they arrived at a time of economic growth in Shanghai, they eventually constituted a comfortable middle class, largely made up of merchants, brokers, and dealers in the import-export trade.[68] Both this Russian community and the Baghdadi community provided assistance to the growing numbers of Jewish refugees in the late 1930s to early 1940s.

In the early 1940s, 1,000 Polish Jewish refugees, including 500 yeshiva students, arrived in Shanghai, a group not often mentioned in the literature.[69]

Despite the efforts of the local Jewish community groups, the community was not equipped to handle the growing numbers of Jewish refugees arriving in Shanghai from Nazi Europe. Because the refugees' stay in Shanghai was expected to be temporary, no efforts had been made by the existing communities to improve the housing conditions. Some of the refugee camps had bunk beds lined up side by side, with men, women, and children all living together. Sanitary conditions in the barracks were poor: There were two toilets to serve 400 people; in some of the camps, the facilities were outdoors.[70]

In spite of these and other handicaps, some of the refugees were able to better their lives and indeed became self-supporting. They reconstructed entire streets with material from the ruins of Hongkew. The area around Chusan Road (now known as Zhoushan Road) became known as "Little Vienna," a sophisticated area that reflected and preserved German and Austrian culture in the midst of a Chinese city.[71] "Little Vienna" became an area where German-speaking Central European Jews would come to have a semblance of the life they had once known in Germany where it was now forever destroyed.

The refugees managed to construct a rich cultural life. The Austrian, German, and Polish Shanghai refugees produced three daily newspapers—two morning and one evening—as well as many weeklies, journals, and magazines.[72]

Refugees offered lessons in English and the sciences, and professionals such as prominent music teachers offered their skills as well.[73] Refugees played their instruments at cafés, formed orchestras,[74] and put together theater and opera performances.[75] The refugees organized educational lectures and discussion groups on many subjects,[76] schools for refugee children,[77] and various political groups that were active in the different refugee camps.[78]

However, in spite of these efforts, many lived in dire poverty. As soon as Margolis was able to tackle the relief situation, she made some immediate improvements:

> . . . I recommended an additional appropriation for an evening meal for the people in our homes . . . because the food is so poor; the people so terribly sad looking; that I didn't feel it was fair to them to let them wait, while I was investigating, and we were trying to decide what to do. In the interim, this evening meal has helped considerably. Most of the time the food is so bad, it can't be eaten. . . . This week there was a riot in the dining hall. The refugees threw all the boiled potatoes at the cook. . . .[79]

One of Margolis's favorite recollections concerned the ingenious efforts, during the Japanese occupation, to build a new, more efficient kitchen to feed the refugees. A Polish Jewish engineer had pointed out the inefficiency of the current kitchen, which was feeding 8,000 people one meal a day that consisted of one bowl of vegetable or bean soup and a 3-oz slice of bread.[80] Most of the expense was for coal to run the stove. He suggested a plan whereby for 100,000 CRB yuan (5,000 US dollars) they could have a very simple, modern, and efficient steam kitchen that could feed 10,000 people at one time for far less money. In order to do this, they would need a special type of steam boiler that could not be purchased in China. However, the Cathay Land Company, owned by Sir Victor Sassoon, a wealthy Baghdadi Jew who lived in Shanghai, possessed one of these and had not used it for many years.[81]

When Margolis approached the Cathay Land Company and asked the Sassoons to lend the boilers, the British employees refused, fearing that if they even mentioned that the boilers existed, the Japanese occupiers might confiscate them.[82] Margolis felt justified in taking possession of these boilers because she knew that sooner or later the Japanese would confiscate them anyway and they would not be of use to either the Cathay Land Company or the refugees. With the help of connections within the Gendarmerie, she procured a permit for the removal of these boilers and presented it to the Cathay Land Company, removing and transferring the boilers in the middle of the night under cover of darkness.

In December 1942, the new kitchen—erected with JDC money—was dedicated and officially opened in a ceremony at which many Japanese officials were present. These officials expressed their gratitude to the Jewish organizations that had provided for the refugees. Margolis and Emanuel (Manny) Siegel,[83] Margolis's deputy, did not attend because by that time all enemy nationals were required to wear special red armbands; anti-American and anti-British feeling was rising.[84]

In the meantime, the refugee crisis had intensified greatly when in August 1941 the Japanese transferred around 900 religious Polish Jews from Kobe, Japan, to Shanghai. The religiously observant and separatist nature of the group introduced yet another layer of communal complexity.[85] In addition to receiving money from the local Eastern European Committee (EastJewCom or EJC), the Polish immigrants were also drawing a larger proportion of JDC contributions to meet their special religious needs. This naturally raised problems of fairness. Margolis put a human face on the internecine friction between the CFA and the EJC in a report from late October 1941:

> The CFA was absolutely unprepared to house the new group.
> For the Rabbis they made room in an old Synagogue. Old
> dirty mattresses were placed on the floor, etc. About half the
> new immigration were Rabbis; and half of this group were
> Mirrer Yeshivah students and their teachers. . . .[86]

As an outsider and an American, Margolis was able to mediate somewhat, and as the provider of funds she had additional leverage. Using her diplomatic skills to negotiate between the existing local Jewish communal groups in Shanghai and the Western and Eastern European immigrants, Margolis was also able to convince everyone to acknowledge that the religious Eastern Europeans needed provisions for kosher food and a place to study and pray. Thus, a supplemental stipend was agreed upon, and separate housing for them was acquired.[87]

PEARL HARBOR CHANGES EVERYTHING

With the bombing of Pearl Harbor on December 9, 1941, JDC representatives—by now Margolis had requested and received the help of American JDC staff member Manny Siegel—immediately became enemy nationals and lost contact with the United States and access to American funding.[88]

After Pearl Harbor, Captain Koreshige Inuzuka (1890–1965), head of Jewish affairs for the Japanese Naval Landing Party, moved his offices into the Cathay Hotel, the best hotel in Shanghai, and occupied Sir Victor Sassoon's penthouse.[89] Margolis and Siegel were staying in the same hotel.[90] As the city panicked, Margolis kept a cool head and decided to approach Inuzuka personally and ask for his help. She had actually met him at some of those dinner parties and horse races she had so disliked but dutifully attended in the pre–Pearl Harbor days and had, she believed, made a favorable impression.

Margolis phoned Inuzuka, who remembered her and invited her up to his offices. Inuzuka and other officials, having read and believed the *Protocols of the Elders of Zion*, which portrayed an international Jewish conspiracy controlling the world, had decided to harness this purported "international Jewish influence" for the good of Japan.[91] Thus, he received Margolis "graciously" with a tea ceremony within two hours of her request.[92] Margolis painted a picture for Inuzuka of how dire the refugee situation would become if funds were not available and appealed for his help on a humanitarian as well as pragmatic political basis, saying, "You, as an occupying power, cannot afford to have hungry people riot."[93]

Inuzuka assured Margolis that he would allow her to borrow funds to sustain the refugees as long as the money came only from neutral parties and not from enemy countries abroad.[94] He also agreed to release for the JDC Relief Committee 5,000 sacks of cracked wheat from the Red Cross, which was more than he had done for any other charitable or civic group.[95]

In addition to needing to raise funds for the community, Margolis and Siegel were faced with a personal crisis—due to the wartime situation, their own monthly salaries from JDC had ceased. For a few weeks, their hotel allowed them to pay their bills with promissory notes, but by the first of January, they were notified that they needed to move out. The best accommodations they could find were two unheated rooms in the home of a White Russian family so far from Hongkew that it meant four hours of travel a day by train, by rickshaw, by bus, and on foot to reach the refugee community. Later, they were able to get rooms in another White Russian home, without heat and very sparsely furnished, but nearer to Hongkew.[96]

By mid-January, funds had practically run out, and the situation had reached a critical point. It was at this time that a reporter from the *Shanghai Times*, owned by a Briton and supported by Japanese money, approached Margolis. Knowing that the Japanese did not want publicity, Margolis had avoided all media. However, at great personal risk, she granted an interview to the newspaper.[97] They published it under the title "Hungry Starving Refugees in Hongkew," and various other newspapers picked up the story. The plight of the Jewish refugees in Shanghai became the subject of editorials and feature articles and was carried by radio stations, which began making appeals to the community at large for donations. Money began coming in in small amounts, and this enabled them to continue to function from day to day.[98] Eventually, Margolis was able to obtain a loan of $180,000—mostly from Joseph Shriro, a local businessman[99]—and the immediate financial pressure was temporarily relieved.[100]

The Japanese Gendarmerie, however, was furious that any news about disorder in Shanghai should get into the papers and issued an order for the arrest of Margolis and Siegel. Inuzuka was furious as well. Margolis received a call from the Japanese Consulate asking her to come and explain herself; luckily, a German Jew who had lived in Shanghai for some time knew a woman who worked with the Gendarmerie, and through her efforts the order for their arrest was canceled.[101]

In the midst of all this turmoil, Margolis continued to handle a complex set of conflicts: Tensions existed between Western European refugees and the established community of Sephardic Jews that had been there for several generations as well as the non-Jewish White Russians who had come at the time of the Bolshevik Revolution. In addition, there were class divisions and economic and religious differences and prejudices among the refugees themselves. Margolis constantly found herself in the position of mediator between these different communities, all under particular stress in a wartime situation.

Cut off from the support of JDC headquarters, Margolis realized that Shanghai Jewry was entirely on its own and would have to survive on its own resources. She reached out beyond JDC and enlisted the cooperation of groups such as the International Red Cross, the Society of Friends, and the Organization for Rehabilitation through Training (ORT). Still desperate for funds, Margolis sent cables to Jewish communities in Sweden, Turkey, Portugal, and Switzerland, asking for contributions, and received 977,716 CRB yuan (about 50,000 US dollars).

Once war with the United States broke out in full force, the Jews lost much of their perceived value in the Japanese imagination as influencers of US policy.[102] As a result, the Japanese leadership in Shanghai began to display mounting hostility toward the Jews. Increasing Nazi anti-Jewish propaganda, in an atmosphere of uncertainty, sparked wild rumors of impending anti-Jewish actions.

In 1943, the situation changed for the worse once again. The Japanese bowed to German pressure and instituted a policy of segregation: German and Austrian Jewish immigrants[103] were required to relocate into a "designated area" in Shanghai, leaving behind their homes and sometimes their livelihoods. By specifically mentioning the German and Austrian immigrants, they implicitly allowed the established Eastern European and Baghdadi Jewish communities to remain in their homes; however, recent Polish immigrants were also affected by this decree. Although there would be no barbed wire in this "designated area" and it would not be a true "ghetto" in the European sense of the word, residents could only leave with a pass issued with special permission of the hated Japanese official Kano

Ghoya.[104] The infamous Ghoya, a cruel and sadistic petty tyrant who called himself "King of the Jews," was in charge of issuing these passes and did so brutally and capriciously.[105] Joseph Bitker and others appealed to Kubota, who was in charge of refugee affairs, to replace the "beast of a man by the name of Goya [*sic*]" and secured a promise that he would be replaced. Within a month, this was done, and passes became freely available.[106] In contrast to the policies of their German ally, the Japanese did not institute severe policies and acquiesced to Jewish appeals.

Meanwhile, as Japanese antiforeign feeling escalated in Shanghai, in early 1943, Margolis and Siegel were sent to Japanese internment camps as enemy nationals. Margolis was imprisoned in an old, broken down, shelled Chinese schoolhouse in the country surrounded by barbed wire. She was assigned to a room with forty women, "a conglomeration of American missionaries, Shanghai prostitutes, widows of diplomatic corpsmen in Beijing who had been brought to Shanghai after Pearl Harbor, and others." The housing conditions were primitive—the roof leaked, the floors sagged, and it was "hellishly hot in the summer and ice cold in the winter."[107]

Around the summer of 1943, an epidemic of dysentery hit Margolis's camp. Fearing that she too might succumb to sickness, she feigned illness and was taken to Shanghai General Hospital in July 1943; freed from the internment camp, from there she was able to make contact with the local CFA Committee. Because JDC was not able to communicate with any representatives in Shanghai, Margolis was able through this channel to keep abreast of the situation in Hongkew and provide financial and logistical guidance to the local committee.[108]

Finally, in September 1943, Margolis, through the efforts of JDC in America, was repatriated in a Japanese prisoner exchange.[109] She immediately traveled with Moses Leavitt and Joseph Schwartz[110] to Washington and met personally with Secretary of the Treasury Henry Morgenthau (1891–1967) to appeal to him to allow funds to be sent to ameliorate the desperate conditions of the refugees. Following this meeting, JDC applied for and received a license from the Treasury Department to remit payments of $20,000 per month through Saly Mayer, a JDC representative in neutral Switzerland, for transmission to the Refugee Committee in Shanghai.[111]

As a result, from January 1944 until the end of the Pacific War in August 1945, life in the "restricted area" was significantly eased as funds from JDC once more began to arrive.

The Jewish communities of both Cuba and Shanghai had no formal government recognition and no general government support from Cuba, China, or the United States.[112] JDC, through Laura Margolis, stepped in to these locations and provided fundraising, religious, health and welfare services, and the organization of a representative body for external relations to confront antisemitic threats.[113] Margolis created representative bodies among the refugees, and these bodies eventually were instrumental in supplying necessities and building sorely needed social, educational, cultural, and recreational outlets for the larger refugee community.

In retrospect, it is clear that the refugees in both Cuba and Shanghai could not have survived without the help of the American Jewish community represented by JDC and specifically Laura Margolis, who served in both locations and administered American funds, bringing order to chaos and caring for the needs of the refugees. Margolis's skills and training in social welfare, along with her international upbringing and command of relevant languages, ideally suited her to function as the representative of JDC in these two critical postings. A colleague said of her: "She is an unusual human being. She has wisdom, understanding and courage. She is an extraordinarily capable organizer and administrator—in short, a rare person."[114]

Although unique in her multicultural and multilingual background, Margolis was typical of JDC staff both at home and abroad, who were trained in social work and willing to accept assignments in exotic locations. Her role as an enforcer of JDC administrative policy, which included transparency of finances and policing of eligibility for aid, was balanced with her deep commitment to sympathy for the refugees and her willingness to bend the rules and "play the high society game" if need be. Indeed, Margolis's personal courage and dedication in light of daunting and dangerous circumstances helped ensure the survival of thousands of Jewish refugees who sought and received aid in Havana and Shanghai through the efforts of the American Jewish Joint Distribution Committee.

1. The New York and Jerusalem archives of JDC contain the professional correspondence and official reports of Margolis, her coworkers, and her superiors, as well as JDC promotional materials from the period. Transcripts of oral interviews with Margolis are located at the Institute for Contemporary Jewry at Hebrew University in Jerusalem, the United States Holocaust Memorial Museum, *Het Centrum voor Onderzoek Naar de Geschiedenis der Nederlandse Joden* in the Netherlands, and the JDC Archives. The Holocaust Survivors' Film Project at Yale University in New Haven also contains a video testimony recorded by Margolis. There is also a short video documentary featuring an interview with Margolis produced by CBS News in 1968, located in the Steven Spielberg Jewish Film Archive at Hebrew University in Jerusalem. Finally, the Yehuda Bauer Collection, situated at the JDC Archives in Jerusalem, contains many of Margolis's personal papers.

2. Following her time in Cuba and Shanghai, Margolis insisted on returning to Europe even though the war was still raging; in Spain, she established an orphanage for Jewish refugee children. In Sweden, she organized shipments of supplies sent to the Theresienstadt concentration camp. In Belgium, she aided survivors as the war came to an end. In France, as the JDC Paris director, she worked for the reconstruction of the French Jewish community and helped thousands of others emigrate. In 1953, she moved with her new husband, French Socialist Zionist leader Marc Jarblum, to Israel to work with children and the handicapped through JDC's Malben organization. Margolis retired and moved to Teaneck, New Jersey, where she passed away in 1997.

3. Linda Kuzmack, "Interview with Laura Margolis," July 11, 1990, RG-50.030*0149 / 1990.422.1, United States Holocaust Memorial Museum collection of oral testimonies.

4. Herman D. Stein, "Jewish Social Work in the United States (1654–1954)," in *American Jewish Yearbook*, ed. Morris Fine, vol. 57 (New York: American Jewish Committee and Jewish Publication Society of America, 1956), 20.

5. Ibid., 19.

6. Margalit Bejarano, "Sephardic Jews in Cuba," *Judaism* 51, no. 1 (2002): 1–2.

7. Ibid., 2, 10; for more on the indigenous tribes in Cuba, see Aviva Chomsky, Barry Carr, and Pamela María Smorkaloff, *The Cuba Reader: History, Culture, Politics* (Durham, NC: Duke University Press, 2006). More than 850,000 new Europeans, mostly from Spain, arrived from 1898 through 1932; Cuba also had a population of over 300,000 Chinese and 250,000 Haitians and Jamaicans.

8. Bejarano, "Sephardic Jews in Cuba," 99.

9. See JDC Archives, Records of the New York Office of the American Jewish Joint Distribution Committee, 1933–1944, Folder 510, Letter from Joseph Hyman to Rabbi Emil Leipziger, October 1, 1940. In comparison, JDC was called on to spend almost $200,000.

10. The National Coordinating Committee for Aid to Refugees (NCC) was established (and largely funded) by JDC in 1934. (For more on the NCC, see the "Archives of the National Coordinating Committee for Aid to Refugees, 1932–1940," 1940, YIVO Archives, RG 247). The US State Department had suggested that a group be formed that would work closely with the Intergovernmental High Commission for Refugees to coordinate refugee relief work done by private organizations in the United States. The National Refugee Service (NRS) succeeded the NCC in 1939.

11. JDC Archives, Records of the New York Office of the American Jewish Joint Distribution Committee, 1933–1944, Folder 506, Letter from Joseph Hyman to David Bressler, January 12, 1939.

12. See the timeline of the Margolis assignments in JDC Archives, Records of the New York Office of the American Jewish Joint Distribution Committee, 1933–1944, Folder 130, Letter from Moses Leavitt to Roy W. McDonald, October 14, 1943.

13. JDC Archives, Records of the New York Office of the American Jewish Joint Distribution Committee, 1933–1944, Folder 506, Letter from Emily Perlman to Cecilia Razovsky, January 27, 1939.

14. Ibid. The offices were located at O'Reilly No. 11, Room 307, in Havana.

15. Ibid.

16. Ibid., Folder 506, Memorandum from Laura Margolis to Cecilia Razovsky, February 7, 1939.

17. Ibid.

18. Ibid.

19. Ibid., Folder 506, Memorandum from Laura Margolis to Cecilia Razovsky, March 24, 1939.

20. JDC Archives, Records of the New York Office of the American Jewish Joint Distribution Committee, 1933–1944, Folder 506, Memorandum from Laura Margolis to Cecilia Razovsky, March 24, 1939.

21. Ibid., Folder 506, Memorandum from Laura Margolis to Cecilia Razovsky, April 13, 1939.

22. Ibid.

23. Ibid.

24. Ibid.

25. Ibid., Folder 506, Memorandum from Laura Margolis to Cecilia Razovsky, February 15, 1939.

26. Ibid., Folder 507, Laura Margolis, Report of Activities, July 12, 1939.

27. Ibid.

28. Ibid., Folder 378, The Following Is a Brief Record of the Action Taken by the Joint Distribution Committee on Behalf of 907 Refugees Aboard the Hamburg/American Line St. Louis . . . , June 9, 1939.

29. Irwin F. Gellman, "The St. Louis Tragedy," *American Jewish Historical Quarterly* 60 (1971): 144–56.

30. Charles Paul Vincent, "The Voyage of the St. Louis Revisited," *Holocaust and Genocide Studies* 25, no. 2 (2011): 265.

31. JDC Archives, Records of the New York Office of the American Jewish Joint Distribution Committee, 1933–1944, Folder 378, The American Jewish Joint Distribution Committee, Inc., Minutes of an Informal Discussion with Reference to Cuba, June 1, 1939.

32. Ibid., Folder 378, Letter from the Executive Director to Jack Danciger, June 13, 1939.

33. Vincent, "The Voyage of the St. Louis Revisited," 265.

34. Harold Linder (1901–1981), an investment banker, joined the US State Department and became assistant secretary for economic affairs and later (1968) ambassador to Canada. Just before World War II, Linder worked in London with the Intergovernmental Committee on Refugees and after the war became a volunteer representative in the JDC London office, helping to resettle Jewish refugees.

35. "St. Louis Exiles to Be Landed at Antwerp; Troper Lauds Action by 4 Nations," *JTA*, June 15, 1939; see also "St. Louis Émigrés Head for Antwerp," *New York Times*, June 15, 1939.

36. Sarah A. Ogilvie and Scott Miller, *Refuge Denied: The St. Louis Passengers and the Holocaust* (Madison: University of Wisconsin Press, 2006); see also "Return to Europe of the St. Louis," *Holocaust Encyclopedia*, accessed January 3, 2014, http://www.ushmm.org/wlc/en/article.php?ModuleId=10005393.

37. Ogilvie and Miller have accounted for the fate of almost all of the passengers on board.

38. JDC Archives, Records of the New York Office of the American Jewish Joint Distribution Committee, 1933–1944, Folder 510, Letter from J. C. Hyman to Rabbi Emil D. Leipziger, October 1, 1940.

39. Ibid., Folder 511, "JDC in Action: Refugee Problem in Cuba," *American Hebrew*, February 21, 1941.

40. The extensive collection in the JDC Archives contains Margolis's reports and correspondence from this period. The Shanghai Collection of the YIVO Institute for Jewish Research is a rich source of context, as are the records of the Union of Sephardic congregations; HIAS-HICEM records; contemporary newspaper articles from the *Chushan Road Chatter* (a newspaper published by the refugees); contemporary issues of the *American Jewish Yearbook*; archives of the *Jewish Telegraphic Association* and the *New York Times*; personal memoirs; and additional periodicals and archives.

41. Stella Dong, *Shanghai: The Rise and Fall of a Decadent City* (New York: William Morrow, 2000), 1.

42. Avraham Altman and Irene Eber, "Flight to Shanghai, 1938–1940: The Larger Setting," *Yad Vashem Studies* 28 (2000): 53.

43. Felix Gruenberger, "The Jewish Refugees in Shanghai," *Jewish Social Studies* 12, no. 4 (1950): 330; Péter Vámos, "'Home Afar': The Life of Central European Jewish Refugees in Shanghai during World War II," *Acta Orientalia Academiae Scientiarum Hungaricae* 57, no. 1 (2004): 55–70. Some of the earliest arrivals were allowed to bring some of their possessions, including the tools and instruments of their professions in addition to their personal baggage. This practice was later stopped.

44. JDC Archives, Records of the New York Office of the American Jewish Joint Distribution Committee, 1933–1944, Folder 463, Laura Margolis, "Race against Time in Shanghai," *Survey Graphic*, March 1944.

45. Menahem Kaufman, "Transcript of Unpublished Interview with Laura Margolis Jarblum" (Jerusalem: Institute for Contemporary Jewry, The Hebrew University, 1976), 15.

46. JDC Archives, Records of the Dominican Republic Settlement Association (DORSA), 1939–1977, Folder 4, Letter from A. M. Warren to J. C. Hyman, September 5, 1942.

47. Ibid., Folder 5, Letter from Avra Warren to George L. Warren, March 30, 1943.

48. JDC Archives, Records of the New York Office of the American Jewish Joint Distribution Committee, 1933–1944, Folder 463, Letter from Marjorie Page Shauffler to Moses Leavitt, February 25, 1942.

49. Kaufman, "Interview," 16–17.

50. Ibid., 17.

51. Ibid. In her list of personal losses in Shanghai submitted to JDC upon her return, Margolis lists four "evening dresses" valued at $300. See JDC Archives, Records of the New York Office of the American Jewish Joint Distribution Committee, 1933–1944, Folder 130, Letter from Louis Rosner to Huff Prater & Company, Subject: Policy #62052 Laura Margolis, December 21, 1943.

52. JDC Archives, Records of the New York Office of the American Jewish Joint Distribution Committee, 1933–1944, Folder 461, Handwritten Letter from Laura Margolis to Robert Pilpel, June 18, 1941.

53. Ibid., Folder 488, Memorandum from Laura Margolis to Moses Leavitt, July 29, 1941.

54. American Jewish Joint Distribution Committee, *Aiding Jews Overseas* (New York: American Jewish Joint Distribution Committee, 1941), 12.

55. Hallett Abend, "Wild Turmoil in City," *New York Times*, January 31, 1932.

56. Hallett Abend, "Death Stalks Shanghai: A City Racked by War," *New York Times*, October 10, 1937.

57. JDC Archives, Records of the New York Office of the American Jewish Joint Distribution Committee, 1933–1944, Folder 463, Laura Margolis, "Race against Time in Shanghai," *Survey Graphic*, March 1944.

58. For more on the Russo- and Sino-Japanese wars, see John W. Steinberg and David Wolff, *The Russo-Japanese War in Global Perspective: World War Zero* (Leiden, Netherlands: Brill, 2005); Mark R. Peattie, Edward J. Drea, and Hans J. Van de Ven, *The Battle for China: Essays on the Military History of the Sino-Japanese War of 1937–1945* (Stanford, CA: Stanford University Press, 2011).

59. Lotte Marcus, "Survival in Shanghai," *Bulletin Igud Yotzei Sin—Association of Former Residents of China, English Supplement*, May 2010, p. 84. The camps were Alcock, Ward, Wayside, Choufung, and Pingling.

60. On Jewish participation in the opium trade, see Maisie J. Meyer, "Baghdadi Jewish Merchants in Shanghai and the Opium Trade," *Jewish Culture and History* 2, no. 1 (1999), 58–71. Opium was not illegal in England at the time and was made legal in China after the Second Opium War in 1860.

61. See Chiara Betta, "From Orientals to Imagined Britons: Baghdadi Jews in Shanghai," *Modern Asian Studies* 37, no. 4 (2003): 999–1023.

62. Maisie J. Meyer, "Baghdadi Jews in Early Shanghai," The Sino-Judaic Institute, accessed September 9, 2013, http://www.sino-judaic.org/index .php?page=shanghai_history; see also Maisie J. Meyer, "The Sephardi Jewish Community of Shanghai 1839–1939 and the Question of Identity" (PhD diss., University of London, 1994).

63. Vámos, "'Home Afar,'" 2; see also Cecil Roth, *The Sassoon Dynasty* (New York: Arno Press, 1977). The pioneer of the Sephardic Jewish community in Shanghai was Elias Sassoon (1820–1880), the son of David Sassoon (1792–1864), patriarch of the Baghdadi Jews in Bombay. The family was the most prominent family in Shanghai and was known as the "Rothschilds of the East."

64. For more on the Kadoorie family history and activities in Shanghai, see Gang Yuan Hu, *Shanghai, Hong Kong, the Kadoorie Family* (Hong Kong: Hong Kong Heritage Project, 2010).

65. For more on the Hardoon family, see Chiara Betta, *Silas Aaron Hardoon (1815–1931): Marginality and Adaptation in Shanghai* (London: The British Library, Document Supply Centre, 2006).

66. "Shanghai Jewish History," accessed July 24, 2014, http://www.chinajewish .org/SJC/Jhistory.htm.

67. "The Chronology of the Jews of Shanghai from 1832 to the Present Day," accessed June 25, 2013, http://www.jewsofchina.org/the-chronology-of -the-jews-of-shanghai-from-1832-to-the-present-day.

68. JDC Archives, Records of the New York Office of the American Jewish Joint Distribution Committee, 1933–1944, Folder 463, Laura Margolis, "Race against Time in Shanghai," *Survey Graphic*, March 1944.

69. See, for example, the United States Holocaust Memorial Museum Holocaust Encyclopedia, "Polish Jewish Refugees in the Shanghai Ghetto," accessed May 18, 2017, https://www.ushmm.org/wlc/en/article.php?Module Id=10005589.

70. Ibid.

71. Ernest G. Heppner, *Shanghai Refuge: A Memoir of the World War II Jewish Ghetto* (Lincoln: University of Nebraska Press, 1993), 84–86; Susanne Wiedemann, "Transnational Encounters with 'Amerika': German Jewish Refugees' Identity Formation in Berlin and Shanghai, 1939–1949" (PhD diss., Brown University, 2006), 17.

72. A complete list of refugee publications in Shanghai can be found in "Shanghai Collection, 1924–1950 (bulk 1939–1948) RG 243," n.d., Series IV, YIVO Institute for Jewish Research, accessed August 24, 2012; see also David Kranzler, "The History of the Jewish Refugee Community of Shanghai, 1938–1945" (Bernard Revel Graduate School, Yeshiva University, 1971), 212–19. The first Jewish daily newspaper in the Far East began publication as the *Shanghai Jewish Chronicle* in August 1939 ("Jewish Daily Started in Shanghai; Organ of Refugees," *JTA*, August 18, 1939).

73. Jonathan Goldstein and Benjamin I. Schwartz, *The Jews of China: Volume One, Historical and Comparative Perspectives* (Armonk, NY: M. E. Sharpe, 1999), 8. Wolfgang Fraenkel, a Jewish composer and performer, was the first person to introduce the "barless" music skill system to China. Many of China's composers at the time were his students.

74. For a list of orchestral and instrumental concerts, see "Shanghai Collection, 1924–1950 (bulk 1939–1948) RG 243," n.d., Series IV, folder 58, YIVO Institute for Jewish Research; see also Kranzler, "The History of the Jewish Refugee Community of Shanghai, 1938–1945," 227–33. For additional information on the impact of Jewish musicians in Shanghai, see Yating

Tang, "Reconstructing the Vanished Musical Life of the Shanghai Jewish Diaspora: A Report," *Ethnomusicology Forum* 13, no. 1 (2004): 101–18.

75. For a list of theaters and theatrical productions, see "Shanghai Collection, 1924–1950 (bulk 1939–1948) RG 243," Folders 56–57, 59, YIVO Institute for Jewish Research; see also Kranzler, "The History of the Jewish Refugee Community of Shanghai, 1938–1945," 219–23.

76. "Shanghai Collection, 1924–1950 (bulk 1939–1948) RG 243," Folder 33, YIVO Institute for Jewish Research.

77. See Kranzler, "The History of the Jewish Refugee Community of Shanghai, 1938–1945," chap. XI; Meyer, "Baghdadi Jews in Early Shanghai"; Vámos, "'Home Afar,'" 5. Baghdadi Jew Sir Horace Kadoorie (1902–1995) had a special interest in providing education to refugee children. The Kadoorie School, which opened in January 1942, had 17 teachers who taught 600 refugee children. The language of instruction was English, but Chinese and French were also taught. After the Japanese occupation, German and Japanese were introduced as well.

78. "Shanghai Collection, 1924–1950 (bulk 1939–1948) RG 243," Series II, Subseries 3, YIVO Institute for Jewish Research.

79. JDC Archives, Records of the New York Office of the American Jewish Joint Distribution Committee, 1933–1944, Folder 461, Letter from Laura Margolis to Robert Pilpel, July 17, 1941.

80. Ibid., Laura Margolis, Folder 463, "Race against Time in Shanghai," *Survey Graphic*, March 1944; Gruenberger, "The Jewish Refugees in Shanghai," 338.

81. Ibid., Folder 463, Laura Margolis, Report of Activities in Shanghai, China, from December 8, 1941, to September 1, 1943.

82. Ibid., Laura Margolis, Folder 463, "Race against Time in Shanghai," *Survey Graphic*, March 1944.

83. Manuel "Manny" Siegel, also a social worker, served with Margolis in Cuba from 1940 to 1941 and then in Shanghai from 1941 to 1945, sent there by JDC at her request. He later served as a JDC representative in Bulgaria from 1946 to 1947.

84. JDC Archives, Records of the New York Office of the American Jewish Joint Distribution Committee, 1933–1944, Folder 463, Laura Margolis,

Report of Activities in Shanghai, China, from December 8, 1941, to September 1943, September 1, 1943.

85. "Japan Deports Stranded Jewish Refugees," *JTA*, August 20, 1941.

86. JDC Archives, Records of the New York Office of the American Jewish Joint Distribution Committee, 1933–1944, Folder 462, Letter 27 from Laura Margolis to Robert Pilpel, October 26, 1941.

87. Ibid., Folder 463, Laura Margolis, Report of Activities in Shanghai, China, from December 8, 1941, to September 1, 1943; Ibid., Folder 462, Letter 27 from Laura Margolis to Robert Pilpel, October 26, 1941.

88. "JDC Representatives Marooned in Shanghai; Departure of Rabbis for Canada Prevented," *JTA*, December 9, 1941.

89. "Wartime Shanghai: A Tycoon Triumphs over the Emperor," HistoryNet, accessed June 18, 2013, http://www.historynet.com/wartime-shanghai-a -tycoon-triumphs-over-the-emporer.htm. The hotel, built by Sir Victor Sassoon and the most prestigious hotel in Shanghai, was at the entrance of Nanking Road, the commercial center of Shanghai, and in the middle of the Bund waterfront district. It was also close to the war front, with bullets often whizzing by and walls pierced by shrapnel. Now called the Fairmont Peace Hotel, it is still one of the most luxurious hotels in all of Shanghai.

90. United States Holocaust Memorial Museum, "Interview with Laura Margolis," July 11, 1990, 10, RG-50.030*0149.

91. See Marvin Tokayer, *The Fugu Plan: The Untold Story of the Japanese and the Jews during World War II* (New York: Paddington Press, 1979), 142; Pamela Rotner Sakamoto, *Japanese Diplomats and Jewish Refugees: A World War II Dilemma* (Westport, CT: Praeger, 1998), 27; David Kranzler, "Restrictions against German-Jewish Refugee Immigration to Shanghai in 1939," *Jewish Social Studies* 36, no. 1 (1974): 49–50.

92. United States Holocaust Memorial Museum, "Interview with Laura Margolis," 10.

93. Ibid. Note that Margolis had used the same threat of rioting while in Cuba to attempt to get more funds from JDC.

94. JDC Archives, Yehuda Bauer Collection, File: Shanghai 1941–1968, Memorandum from Bitker-Dicker Correspondence, February 12, 1951.

95. JDC Archives, Records of the New York Office of the American Jewish Joint Distribution Committee, 1933–1944, Folder 463, Laura Margolis, Report of Activities in Shanghai, China, from December 8, 1941, to September 1943, September 1, 1943.

96. Ibid., Folder 463, Laura Margolis, "Race against Time in Shanghai," *Survey Graphic*, March 1944.

97. Ibid.

98. Ibid., Folder 463, Laura Margolis, Report of Activities in Shanghai, China, from December 8, 1941, to September 1943, September 1, 1943.

99. "The Shriro Story," accessed September 24, 2013, http://www.shriro.com/index.php?option=com_content&view=article&id=56&Itemid=55&lang=en. The Shriro Group, founded by the Shriro family in 1906 in Harbin, China, began trading fur and leather and grew into an international commodities firm. They still exist today, with 3,500 employees in offices worldwide.

100. JDC Archives, Records of the New York Office of the American Jewish Joint Distribution Committee, 1933–1944, Folder 463, News Release: JDC Pays Loan for Funds Aiding Refugees in Shanghai, October 3, 1943.

101. Ibid., Folder 463, Laura Margolis, Report of Activities in Shanghai, China, from December 8, 1941, to September 1943, September 1, 1943.

102. Marcia R. Ristaino, *Port of Last Resort: The Diaspora Communities of Shanghai* (Stanford, CA: Stanford University Press, 2001), 191.

103. Although these Jewish people were refugees, the Japanese referred to them as "immigrants."

104. For more on Ghoya, see Tokayer, *The Fugu Plan*, 250–251; Gruenberger, "The Jewish Refugees in Shanghai," 342–43; Ristaino, *Port of Last Resort*, 199–200. He is also mentioned in many memoirs, including Heppner, *Shanghai Refuge*, and Irene Eber, *Voices from Shanghai: Jewish Exiles in Wartime China* (Chicago: University of Chicago Press, 2008).

105. For more on Ghoya, see Marvin Tokayer, *The Fugu Plan: The Untold Story of the Japanese and the Jews during World War II* (New York: Paddington Press, 1979); Felix Gruenberger, "The Jewish Refugees in Shanghai," *Jewish Social Studies* 12, no. 4 (1950): 329–48; Marcia R. Ristaino, *Port of Last Resort: The Diaspora Communities of Shanghai* (Stanford, CA: Stanford University

Press, 2001); Ernest G. Heppner, *Shanghai Refuge: A Memoir of the World War II Jewish Ghetto* (Lincoln: University of Nebraska Press, 1993); Irene Eber, *Voices from Shanghai: Jewish Exiles in Wartime China* (Chicago: University of Chicago Press, 2008).

106. JDC Archives, Yehuda Bauer Collection, File: Shanghai 1941–1968, Memorandum from Bitker-Dicker Correspondence, February 12, 1951.

107. Kaufman, "Interview," 28–30.

108. Ibid., 31; Kuzmack, "Interview," 11.

109. Siegel was not freed until the end of the war.

110. Schwartz was the JDC European director.

111. JDC Archives, Records of the New York Office of the American Jewish Joint Distribution Committee, 1933–1944, Folder 463, Letter from Moses Leavitt to the War Refugee Board, June 15, 1944.

112. JDC Archives, Yehuda Bauer Collection, File: Shanghai 1941–1968, Memorandum from Bitker-Dicker Correspondence, February 12, 1951.

113. Daniel Judah Elazar, "Jewish Communal Structures around the World," *Journal of Jewish Communal Service* 74 (1998): 120–31.

114. JDC Archives, Records of the New York Office of the American Jewish Joint Distribution Committee, 1945–1954, Folder 2352, Letter from Robert Pilpel to Ann S. Petluck, Subject: Laura L. Margolis, November 29, 1945.

7

"Joint Fund Teheran"

JDC and the Jewish Lifeline to Central Asia

ATINA GROSSMANN

SEVERAL YEARS AGO, B, a longtime audiovisual assistant at Cooper Union, listened intently as I played the *Internationale* as an opening to a lecture on the Russian Revolution and then remarked to me, "I know that song, I used to hear it as a child." Knowing that he had come to New York from Poland in 1968, I said, "Oh, in school in Poland?" He said, "No, in an orphanage in Samarkand." At which point the conversation opened, almost derailing the lecture: His mother had perished in Uzbekistan, killed by typhus, probably, he thought, in 1943 when he was three years old. His father, bereft of a mother for the children and unable to feed a toddler and a somewhat older son, had, in desperation, like many Polish Jewish refugee parents seeking to endure the war in Central Asia, brought his children to the orphanage. Indeed, he recalled, because they were both so young, he did not even realize for quite some time that he had a brother in the same institution. Eventually, his father, who had remarried, was able to retrieve the youngsters, and after the war ended, the reconstituted family was repatriated to Poland. Key to our American Jewish Joint Distribution Committee (JDC) history theme, however, is a specific memory: B, who could conjure only very limited scenes from his early childhood, vividly remembered a particular rare wonderful moment when one day a jeep from JDC pulled up at the orphanage, bringing desperately needed food and supplies. We know, however, that there were never any JDC jeeps in Uzbekistan. The Soviets did not permit entry to the American

---

A note on spelling: This chapter uses the current commonly accepted English spelling *Tehran* except when referring to or quoting sources where the name of the city is written as *Teheran*.

Jewish relief organization.[1] But packages shipped by JDC from Tehran did arrive. Probably B was remembering a truck (or maybe even a jeep?) pulling up with cartons marked with JDC insignia. And that memory, that moment of relief in all senses of the term, remained with him his entire, quite difficult, life.[2] It is, indeed, very hard to unravel the story of how that package got to—or might have gotten to—a young Polish Jewish refugee child in Samarkand. This chapter begins to explore an extraordinary and largely unknown—and unheralded—piece of JDC relief and rescue efforts during World War II.

The story of the JDC mission to aid Polish Jews from its outpost in wartime Iran is central to the fate of Eastern European, mostly Polish, Jews who survived the Holocaust. They had escaped the Final Solution in involuntary exile in the Soviet Union, first in Stalinist special camps in the Soviet interior and then in Central Asia. Of all the Polish Jews who managed to survive World War II (altogether about 330,000, a tragically small

Crates containing supplies were purchased by JDC in Palestine for shipment to Jews in the Soviet Union and sent via Baghdad and Tehran. Jerusalem, Palestine, 1945.

10% of a prewar population of approximately 3.3 million), 65% to 80% did so because they were "deported to life" within the Soviet Union in 1940 and then migrated southward to Central Asia after an "amnesty" was declared for all Poles (Jewish and not) following the German invasion in the summer of 1941.[3] After their postwar repatriation to a "vast graveyard" and continued antisemitism, many of them fled again, westward from Poland to Allied-occupied Europe. As "displaced persons," especially in the American zone of Germany, they eventually came to form the (unmarked) majority of the *She'erit Hapletah* (the surviving remnant) and would once again, under very different circumstances, encounter JDC and its aid packages.

Crucially, that only very partial rescue of refugee Jews in the USSR was achieved with the limited but significant aid of goods purchased and organized throughout the British imperial world from Australia to South Africa, India, and Palestine by the American Jewish relief organization operating out of Tehran, with the assistance of refugee German Jews and local Iranian Jews as well as the Jewish Agency and emissaries from Palestine.

In July 1941, shortly after the German invasion of the Soviet Union, with the Soviets in dire need of Allied support and the Polish Government in Exile subject to British and American pressure from its seat in London, Stalin and the exile government negotiated an "amnesty" for all imprisoned Polish citizens. The July 30 Sikorski-Maiskii Agreement allowed two key developments: the formation of a Polish army under General Władysław Anders (just released from prison in Moscow) intended to eventually fight for the fatherland in the European theater and the release of Polish citizens, Jewish and not, from the labor camps and settlements to which they had been deported from the territories occupied by the Soviets in the fall of 1939 after the Nazi-Soviet Pact.

The "amnestied" embarked on a rush south to what they imagined were better and safer conditions in the Central Asian Republics. Huddled in and around train stations, forced to keep moving when denied entry to Tashkent, the overwhelmed Uzbek capital, they were greeted instead by widespread hunger; severe overcrowding and poverty; typhus, dysentery, and cholera; crime; and despair. The general chaos and hardship were exacerbated by the upheaval of mass evacuations of Soviet citizens, particularly the cultural, technocratic, and educational elite, as well as entire industrial plants, away from the advancing front into Central Asia, a gargantuan undertaking later stigmatized in antisemitic terms as the "Tashkent Front" where "Avram speculated while Ivan fought." After "liberation" from the horrors of the camps and special settlements came another catastrophic situation in Central Asia—in some ways, conditions became even worse because now the former deportees were refugees without even the promise of bread for work. At the same time, the new arrivals also encountered an amazing variety of wartime improvisations, from evacuated universities and factories, Red Army recruiters, NKVD (Narodnyi Kommissariat Vnutrennikh Del [People's Commissariat of Internal Affairs]) agents, and lively "black markets" essential to survival. Very far from what had once been home, Polish Jews were mostly isolated from news about the horrors engulfing those who had been left behind in German-occupied Europe or on the front lines of the war. They struggled to survive on entirely unfamiliar and exotic terrain, now populated by evacuated Soviet citizens (including Soviet Jews); numerous other deportees, including Poles and Germans; local Bukharan Jews; and Muslim Uzbeks bewildered by this sudden influx of "Westerners"—who would ironically later themselves be referred to as "Asiatics" once they had returned to a postwar Europe.[4]

From 1941 to 1942 (and officially into mid-1943), all Polish refugees, Jewish and not, were at least minimally supported by the London-based Polish Government in Exile, which in turn was dependent on its British host government and private donations, including from North America, for its funding. The Government in Exile maintained an official embassy in the temporary wartime Soviet capital Kuibyshev on the Russian-Kazakh border (now Samara) as well as some 300 welfare offices throughout Central Asia.[5] Thousands of Jews, often half-starved survivors of labor camps, still Polish citizens, flocked to the Anders Army recruiting stations in the Volga region and in Kuibyshev. Initially they constituted a virtual majority of potential recruits, between 40% and 60%. Most, however, were rejected. Targets of antisemitic suspicion and branded as a potential "fifth column" for a later Stalinist takeover of Poland, Jews were subjected to humiliating inspections and insinuations that they were poor fighting material and unreliable Polish patriots. Polish Jews were thereby largely excluded from the evacuation of some 115,000 soldiers and their families to Iran—the only escape route out of the Soviet Union.

Between mid-1942 and early 1943, the situation of Polish refugees, who already had to contend with hunger, epidemics, and housing shortages, as well as the death of, and separation from, family members in Central Asia, became even more precarious. The final breakdown of steadily worsening relations between the Soviet Union and the Polish Government in Exile—ostensible anti-Nazi allies—came in April 1943, after Stalin rejected an investigation of the Katyn massacre graves that had been, in a major propaganda coup, discovered by the Germans.[6] With this crisis, Jews, who had been aided, albeit in an often discriminatory fashion, along with all other Polish refugees, by their national representatives, were now utterly on their own, behind the lines and safe from the Germans but facing dire conditions in Central Asia.

Even before this new emergency, JDC had moved to set up an operation headquartered in Tehran, which had become, since August 1941, the bustling multinational capital of an occupied nation, divided between the Soviets in the north and the British in the south, with a significant American military and civilian presence. Starting in August 1942, JDC, along with the Jewish Agency and various *landsmanshaftn* of Polish Jews in Palestine, inaugurated a modest parcel service, shipping donated food and supplies from Tehran to suffering relatives in Soviet Central Asia. Despite constraints imposed by shortages in Iran, goods began traveling through the so-called Persian Corridor, which was carrying Lend-Lease supplies to the beleaguered Soviet Union. The JDC operation began, not coincidentally, after the Anders Army arrived in Iran with over 100,000 Polish soldiers and civilians, perhaps 115,000 in all, starting with a first wave in March to April of 1942, followed by another group at the end of August. Despite bitter protests from Jewish volunteers and organizations, only a very limited number of Jews—probably around 6,000 altogether (4,000 soldiers plus women and children)—were able to join the exodus from Central Asia. They included somewhere between 700 and 1,000 "Teheran children" who endured a nightmarish journey through Uzbekistan to the port city of Krasnovodsk in Turkmenistan on the shore of the Caspian Sea about 1,000 miles west of Tashkent and then traveled by ship to the Persian port of Pahlavi (now Bandar-e-Anzali) or, in some cases, overland from Ashkabad to Mashad.[7]

The Polish Government in Exile had reported to JDC that there were some 1 million Polish refugees in the Soviet Union, 90% in Central Asia, and approximately 40% of them Jews. Relying on information from Polish Jews arriving in Tehran, JDC eventually concluded, probably correctly, that some 300,000 Polish Jews were struggling to survive in the USSR in "near catastrophic" conditions. Although their numbers were not as high as some hopeful reports had suggested, it quickly became clear that they constituted the largest group of Eastern European Jews who could still be saved and that without help they would likely perish.

Indeed, in April 1942, Maurice Barber, the American Red Cross representative in Tehran, informed his headquarters in Washington that the Polish refugees arriving from Central Asia with the Anders Army represented a humanitarian crisis that he termed "this awful holocaust." In another report to the Red Cross director for the Middle East stationed in Cairo, he characterized the refugee influx as "perhaps the greatest civilian emergency of the war."[8] In response to the urgent reports from Tehran about the condition of the Polish civilians, most of them non-Jewish women and children, and uncertain about whether perhaps an even larger number might be expected, JDC mobilized to launch arguably the most successful relief and rescue action for Eastern European Jews during World War II. From his perch as president of the Hebrew University in Jerusalem, Judah Magnes was pressing JDC to move a representative (preferably himself) directly into the Soviet Union: "Since April 1942, there ha[d] been almost continuous exchange of cables, and to a lesser extent of letters, between Dr. Magnes and the JDC in New York."[9] JDC was also eager to dispatch an emissary directly into the Soviet Union, where, as Moses Leavitt, the New York–based JDC secretary who worked with Joseph Schwartz to coordinate aid for Jews in wartime Europe, noted, "The problem of refugees in Turkestan is of much greater magnitude and has many more complicating factors" than in Iran.[10]

The New York office recognized, however, that the Soviets would neither permit JDC to operate within its borders nor allow shipments to "sectarian" communities. Building on its earlier experience in Bolshevik Russia,[11] officials devised alternative plans that called for sending packages to individual addressees via Tehran. The JDC New York office informed Magnes that in loose cooperation with the Jewish Agency, which had already directed a Mr. Szaf[f]ar (his identity is a bit unclear and he appears to have been affiliated with both the Jewish Agency and the Polish Government in Exile) to open an office in Tehran, relief activity was commencing with money transfers. The New York office transmitted $3,000 "for general relief" with an equal amount to Rabbi Bromberg, a Jewish chaplain in the Anders Army, who had been urgently requesting aid for the civilian Jewish refugees who had accompanied the evacuation from the USSR.[12] Working with several travel and shipping agencies, in particular Peltours, which had a good existing relationship with Intourist, JDC began sending parcels from Tehran into the Soviet Union starting in August 1942. Even this early effort involved complicated negotiations with multiple often conflicting and sometimes overlapping actors: the Soviet Union, Iranian authorities, the Polish Red Cross, the American Red Cross, the Jewish Agency, and the Polish Government in Exile, which was receiving and controlling valuable supplies from the Lend-Lease program passed by Congress in March 1941.

Shortly thereafter, on September 24, 1942, Eliyahu Dobkin, a delegate dispatched to Tehran by the Jewish Agency, posted a disturbing "strictly confidential" report to the World Jewish Congress on the refugees arriving from the Soviet Union. His description of a five-week mission to the city, dramatically titled "The Human Element in Teheran," echoed the alarm that had been sounded by the American Red Cross representatives, but with a specifically Jewish and Zionist focus.[13] Dobkin quickly grasped the central role of the Iranian capital as "the focal point for information issuing from Russia and especially for news about the situation of the refugees in Turkestan" (as Central Asia was often referred to in contemporary reports) and highlighted the critical role of the Polish Government in Exile, which had established its own aid outposts in Iran. Dobkin made short shrift of the hopeful rumor circulating in New York that 1 million Polish refugees remained in "Russia." One hundred forty thousand Jews had registered with the Polish "consulates" in "Turkestan," and he presumed that there were anywhere from 200,000 to 350,000 additional Polish Jews "scattered throughout the length and breadth of Russia" who were not officially counted. That said, he pointed out that "it is impossible to estimate the number of Polish Jewish refugees," a problem that bedeviled JDC as it moved to mount its relief action and that still continues to challenge researchers today as they endeavor to establish reliable statistics about the varied and shifting "far-flung" Jewish refugee population in the Soviet Union.[14]

Articulating the sentiments of most later accounts, Dobkin asserted that "Apparently we were premature in our blessing of the day when the refugees were 'fortunate' enough to escape from Hitler's maw into the haven of Soviet-Russia."[15] He acknowledged, however, that for the most part, the disastrous circumstances were a consequence of general wartime misery and not specifically directed against Jews; unquestionably, life for Jews in the Soviet Union was better than "under Hitler's rule."[16] Dobkin sought to moderate reports of mass death brought by the refugees who had made it to Palestine but conceded that even lower numbers, suggesting a 25% mortality rate, were devastating. Famine and scarcity caused suffering for all inhabitants in Central Asia, both local residents and Soviet evacuees, but were especially arduous for foreign refugees who, lacking any local knowledge, were suddenly confronting indigenous customs and arbitrary Stalinist regulations in a region already upended by wartime exigencies. All former Polish deportees, their "amnestied" status notwithstanding, were less likely to find employment than Soviet evacuees but, in Dobkin's view, Jewish Poles were particularly handicapped because urban Jews were also less able to tolerate labor on collective farms than their mostly rural Polish counterparts. Moreover, over time, their capacity to organize survival by selling their remaining possessions on the black market diminished, leaving refugee Jews with fewer and fewer options, even as they became associated, in starkly antisemitic terms, with corruption and shirking of combat—the supposed privileges of life on the "Tashkent Front."

Like American Red Cross envoy Maurice Barber, Dobkin was horrified by the state of the refugees he encountered: "Every train, every boat . . .

brings in a number of corpses" and traumatized refugees with rotting teeth and typhus. At the time of his visit, only 600 of the approximately 12,000 civilians residing in the Tehran camps were classified as Jewish, but as a hardheaded Zionist from the Yishuv, he was particularly dismayed by the poor quality of potential immigrants—the "human material"—assembled in Iran. Some were beyond saving, "not only [to] Palestine, but the world at large," having "lost their faith—in God, in themselves, and in man." Yet, despite his misgivings, he urged the Yishuv to salvage those it could. The "emaciated children" were, as he candidly noted, not necessarily true orphans but rather youngsters whose parents (or, one might add, more likely one surviving parent) had made the desperate decision to send them on with the Polish Army in the hope of saving their lives and getting them to Palestine so that "at least they [*sic*] will be spared starvation." Expressing faith in the power of the Zionist vision for a Jewish state as a source of relief and rehabilitation, he pleaded, "We must not renounce them," especially because, as he also presciently recognized, "It is very likely that they will form the majority of the survivors of the holocaust which has struck the Diasporra [*sic*]." Indeed, "perhaps they will be the only survivors."[17] JDC, for its part, committed to trying to save all of them, regardless of whether the Zionists perceived them as salvageable future citizens of a Jewish homeland.

In the late autumn of 1942, with winter approaching, conditions became ever more precarious, especially for the Teheran children quartered in tents set up on the grounds of a former Iranian military base outside of the capital. Reacting to further pressure from Magnes, who was surely aware of Dobkin's dramatic report, JDC sent its own representative to Tehran from Jerusalem via Baghdad.[18] Harry Viteles, an American employee of the Cooperative Bank in Jerusalem, produced an extraordinarily comprehensive, blunt, and thoughtful forty-seven-page "confidential" report on his "Visit to Bagdad (2/11–9/11, 1942) and Teheran (11/11–2/12, 1942)"; indeed, the text itself was a major contribution to JDC's wartime efforts and to the historical documentation of those efforts. With its usual meticulous attention to proper procedure and concern for collaboration with interested parties, JDC admonished Magnes to ensure that Viteles planned his trip carefully, with due consideration of diplomatic protocol. Viteles was to first pause in Cairo for consultations with the head of the British Near East Relief Commission, which was, along with the Polish authorities, nominally responsible for refugee relief in Tehran, while always keeping in mind that the presumably more helpful American Red Cross representatives in the Near East had pledged "every cooperation."[19] JDC immediately began exploring how best to transmit funds ("remittances") from New York to Tehran both for use on site and to support the unknown—but presumed to be in the hundreds of thousands—number of Polish Jewish refugees in Central Asia. It also aimed to support the Zionist women's organization, Hadassah, in its efforts to transfer the Teheran children, whom the British had already certified for entry, to Palestine as quickly as possible. JDC was prepared to fund the journey if the representatives on the ground in Tehran could work out how to get them there, a difficult endeavor due to the lack of cooperation from the Iraqi government, which stonewalled transit visas and thereby cut off the quickest, safest, and most direct overland route. Consistent with JDC principles prioritizing the involvement, both practical and financial, of local Jewish communities, Viteles also moved to establish a local relief committee.

As his report indicates, Viteles's tour was a sober fact-finding mission, essential to JDC planning of a larger-scale operation that could ease the situation in Tehran and increase "general relief" for the much larger number of refugees still in Central Asia. Viteles maintained a hectic schedule, meeting with "90 individuals and committees in Bagdad and Teheran," including diplomatic, military, and civil authorities of the American, British, and Polish governments; the American Red Cross; the Polish Red Cross; the Polish Delegation for Refugees; residents of the American, British, and Iranian Jewish communities; delegates of the Jewish Agency; emissaries of the Yishuv (Jewish community in prestate Palestine); and numerous refugees from both Western and Eastern Europe. Curiously, the Soviets are missing from this list, although they would be indispensable partners for the parcel delivery program.[20] In a short amount of time, with many stakeholders to consult and evaluate, he tried to investigate—and provide recommendations for—a plethora of pressing issues: What intelligence could be gained from Jews in or traveling with the Anders Army? How should funds be transferred? How could transportation to Palestine be arranged? What capacities could the local Jewish community offer? What were the practical mechanisms for delivery of supplies to Central Asia? Given the impossibility of sending an emissary directly into the Soviet Union, would it make sense to appoint a permanent JDC delegate in Tehran?

Further complicating a chaotic situation, Viteles arrived in Tehran from Baghdad on November 11, 1942, in the midst of ongoing negotiations, conducted primarily by the Jewish Agency representative, Mr. Szaf[f]ar, for the passage of refugees from Iran to Palestine. These protracted and frustrating discussions about possible transit through Iraq and the unsuccessful efforts to persuade British and American authorities to intercede with the Iraqis on behalf of the Jewish children demonstrate how powerfully geopolitical concerns—in this case, Allied fears about upsetting volatile regional relations—constrained possibilities for rescue and relief. With "too many cooks" now in play—"a criticism" Viteles noted he "often heard in the course of the inquiry"—JDC tried first to understand how to handle the multiple, conflicting, and ever-changing actors. British and Arab anxieties about Jewish emigration to Palestine limited JDC's capacity to move refugees to Palestine, and the bitter clash between the Polish Government in Exile and the Soviets—whom the Western Allies in turn could not afford to alienate—limited the possibilities for delivering aid directly to Jews in Central Asia. As Viteles pointed out in regard to the attempts to transport the Teheran children to Palestine via Iraq, "The general feeling of the American Community was 'that if the British really wished to arrange it and see the children to Palestine, it could be done.'" He added bitterly, "It's all a little confusing, but the sum total . . . clear enough. We are, as usual, the 'superfluous men'—not wanted even when we are brands plucked from the flames."[21]

With less than 1,800 of 26,000 resident Polish civilians in Tehran registered as Jews and 75% of them "certificated" for Palestine, the "serious problem," was, as Viteles realized, "the hundreds of thousands of Jewish refugees still in Russia regardless of whether they remain there or are eventually evacuated." However, "there were practically no two estimates of the number of Polish refugees in Russia which agreed" and even less clarity about the number of Jews.[22] At the end of December 1942, Henrietta K. Buchmann, the secretary of the East and Central Europe Committee of JDC in New York, was still telling American donors that 600,000 of the approximately 2 million Poles trapped in the Soviet Union were Jewish. In an indication of the extreme confusion surrounding the numbers, Viteles had a few weeks earlier referred in his report simultaneously to "hundreds of thousands" of Jews still trapped in the Soviet Union after the Anders Army evacuation, an American estimate of 1 million, 25% of them Jews, and the assumption "for the purpose of this enquiry" that there were now—a quite low figure—250,000 to 300,00 Polish refugees, including 50,000 children, "still in Russia," with Jews constituting "not less than 40% of the total number."[23] Whatever the precise figures, by the middle of November 1942, right before Viteles's arrival, with the Soviets threatening to cut off the flow of refugees, it seemed increasingly clear that even if Iran would be spared a further mass influx of refugees, large numbers were still suffering in Central Asia, with a mortality rate of between 20% and 30%, particularly afflicting the young and the old. Hence, the greater "civilian emergency" was not in Iran, where Allied, especially American, aid relatively quickly contained the Polish refugee crisis, but the one unfolding in Central Asia.

Therefore, Viteles tried both to clarify as best he could the dimensions of the crisis in Central Asia and to establish the suitability of Tehran as a base for an expanded JDC relief operation. He took extensive and careful notes on all conversations and inspected the five general Polish refugee camps—apparently mired in a corruption scandal—that housed 20,000 of the 26,000 Polish refugees, many of them children, who had been evacuated from "Russia" (as it was generally called) between March and September 1942; the adjacent Jewish children's camp; and the Alliance Israelite Universelle School, which had previously served as a hub for European Jewish aid to Persian Jews and continued to serve a critical role as a conduit for remittances and local knowledge.[24]

All of the Polish refugees were minimally—if unequally—supported by the Polish Government in Exile and supplies from the American Red Cross, with the latter providing a total of 750 tons of food, 200 tons of clothing, and 60 tons of medications—at an estimated value of about $3 million. Reflecting the rapidly changing conditions of wartime relief operations, these goods had been originally designated for distribution to Greek refugees. Two thousand refugees had settled directly in Tehran, and 1,300 non-Jewish children were placed in a (better equipped) camp in Isfahan, while, according to Viteles's information, some 735 Jewish children were "segregated in a Children's Camp" attached to a general facility.[25] Additionally, the camps housed 100 Jewish mothers with children, and altogether the number of unmarried women exceeded the number of unmarried men by 318 to 123, a result perhaps of the fact that those Jewish men in Tehran would more likely have been attached to the army and not counted as civilian refugees.[26] With characteristic concern about encouraging as much local self-sufficiency as possible, the JDC representative particularly worried about whether the Jewish refugees living outside the camps could support themselves once they had bartered or sold the belongings they had brought with them. At the same time, however, Viteles suggested that paid employment was available, "particularly for artisans, building workers and mechanics" who were willing to work at comparatively low wages for the Allied forces or in the local economy. Obliquely highlighting the contrast to Polish Government in Exile attitudes, he attested that despite some complaints, he found no evidence of discrimination against Jews among either Iranian or Allied employers.[27]

Viteles actually deemed food allotments to be adequate, which they surely were in comparison to the hunger that most refugees had suffered in the Soviet Union. Referring to the general situation of all Polish refugees—it is sometimes difficult to disentangle when he is specifically referencing Jews or Poles more generally—Viteles identified the problem as corruption, not scarcity. The refugees themselves, however, voicing grievances that would be common in the postwar displaced persons camps, were often dissatisfied, insisting "that a normal ration cannot be considered as sufficient for people who have hungered for three years."[28] Viteles strove to provide an objective assessment of generally decent conditions while also confirming discriminatory treatment of Jews by the Polish government authorities.

In general, Viteles echoed American exasperation with Polish corruption, inefficiency, and unreasonable demands, wryly noting that the American

Red Cross representative had confided that "the Poles appeared unaware of the fact that relief must be austere and that such relief is not meant to provide 'white bread, 2 eggs daily per person, meat daily, large quantities of butter, etc.'"[29] By the time JDC activity moved into full gear, after 1942, Tehran was already a center of wartime intrigue and operations, with active US involvement, and JDC's ability to gain the trust and support of American officials clearly facilitated its complex mission.

Indeed, Iran was arguably one of the most important—albeit noncombat—theaters of World War II. Alarmed by German influence in officially neutral Iran, as well as the invasion of the Soviet Union and Axis victories in North Africa, and determined to protect precious oil supplies, British and Soviet forces had moved into Iran in August 1941, dividing the country into southern and northern occupation zones. At the end of September 1941, President Roosevelt ordered the formation of a US military mission in Iran, launching what would become the Persian Gulf Command, the crucial Allied supply operation, which brought some 30,000 US uniformed personnel and thousands of civilian workers into Iran from 1942 to 1944 and shipped millions of tons of material, including some 5,000 planes and 200,000 trucks, to the Soviets. Even though neither the report from Viteles nor JDC records documenting the Tehran operation seems to highlight this presumably key factor, Viteles's JDC-sponsored mission not only followed the influx of Polish military and refugees in the spring and summer of 1942 but also occurred in the context of a growing American presence and preceded by only a few days the arrival of the first American troops at the port of Khorramshahr on December 11, 1942.[30]

JDC therefore operated in a context where the Americans, in a rehearsal of Cold War conflicts, had to navigate the competing demands of virulent Polish anticommunism, the US commitment to the Lend-Lease policy and support of the Soviet war effort, and British ambitions for semi-colonial control of southern Iran. For all their sympathy with the plight of the refugees from Central Asia, American officials were openly irritated by Polish insistence on diverting all aid intended for the Soviets to their compatriots as well as by their aggressive purchasing of scarce food and medicine, which threatened to cause political unrest and serious shortages in Iran. In any event, the Americans were not inclined to let "these Poles, a stubborn as well as gallant race,"[31] disturb their relations with either the Soviet ally or Iran. The latter was, as the US State Department clearly recognized, "vulnerable to Axis propaganda directed at all the Near Eastern countries," especially "since the Axis has already been making capital of what it calls 'soviet brutality'" in connection with the Polish refugees. "I need hardly say," an officer in the US State Department, Division of Near Eastern Affairs, added in his May 27, 1942, warning to the American Red Cross in Tehran not to make Iran a "dumping ground" for wartime refugees, "that Iran occupies a most important place in the current Near Eastern picture, and this Department is anxious to do everything possible to maintain our relations with that country on a cordial basis."[32] JDC's record—and promise—of competent and fair relief administration gave it an advantage with the Americans, who worried about the Poles' single-minded focus on their own national cause.

The Jewish refugees therefore had two crucial factors in their favor, often at odds but ultimately mutually reinforcing: on one hand, a sense of a Zionist mission fueled by the emissaries from the Yishuv and Zionist youth movement activists who had accompanied the children from Central Asia to Tehran and, on the other hand, the American funds and connections provided by JDC. Much of that financial support, however, was provided behind the scenes, without JDC aid workers actually visibly present; either Polish Government in Exile or Jewish Agency officials distributed the goods in Tehran. JDC's penchant for behind-the-scenes assistance resulted in "considerable criticism" of its failure to assist the refugees and cost it some credibility with the recipients themselves.

Acutely aware of the complex parameters of wartime geopolitics in Central Asia and the Middle East, especially the paramount importance of the open corridor to the Soviet Union both for the war effort and the survival chances of trapped Jews, JDC aimed to operate carefully and judiciously in order not to offer any grounds for expulsion from Iran. Moreover, despite Soviet warnings about closing the borders to Iran for Polish refugees, JDC still tried to prepare for the (unfulfilled) possibility that thousands more refugees might flood into occupied Iran. All the more determined to work as smoothly as possible with local institutions and leaders, Viteles organized a local committee that drew on the resources and knowledge of the Tehran Jewish community, recently enlarged—and enriched—by the arrival of Iraqi Jews fleeing the 1941 pogrom in Baghdad.[33] With the Iranians already smarting from the Allied occupation and the removal of Reza Shah Pahlavi, perceived as a potential German ally, in favor of his more pliable son, Mohammed Reza Pahlavi, Viteles underscored the political delicacy of JDC efforts. In contrast to the Jewish Agency, which was fixated on transport—especially for the children—to Palestine, JDC privileged diplomacy over ideology. Viteles particularly noted the possible negative consequences for the local Jewish community of appointing any-one who might be perceived as a permanent outside Jewish ambassador because "[t]he Iranian government . . . might not like the Jews serving a foreign organization."[34] As Viteles stressed in his confidential report, the success of the relief effort depended on JDC's "not be[ing] suspected of Zionist or any political activities."[35]

At a time when the course of the war, the possibility of more arrivals from the Soviet Union, and the future of Iranian sovereignty were all in utterly unpredictable flux, JDC worried that the openly Zionist Jewish Agency might at some point be expelled from a more independent Iran and therefore reinforced the organization's efforts to keep its (at least public) distance. This nonpartisan stance, viewed as absolutely necessary, did not, needless to say, earn the JDC plaudits from Zionist activists.[36] At the same time, the efforts by Youth Aliyah and Hadassah to transfer Jewish children to Palestine were viewed with suspicion by some, notably religious groups that deemed the Youth Aliyah Department of the Jewish Agency to be too "German, too leftish, and not sufficiently orthodox." Viteles was clearly frustrated that for religious aid groups such as *Vaad Hatzala* "the interest in the soul seems of more important consideration . . . than the physical and educational care of these children."[37] The insistence on "neutrality" strained Jewish alliances and inevitably meant that JDC was vulnerable to being seen as hostile by precisely those groups it did not specifically endorse, notably the Zionists and the Orthodox (as well as pro-Soviet groupings). With its usual realism, JDC acknowledged that "a perfect plan which would please everybody is admittedly impossible." "But," the organization insisted, "a plan which will minimize the criticism by Jewry in and out of Palestine, and to put it positively, a plan which will have the support of as large a section of the Jews in and out of Palestine, must be evolved" in order to save these traumatized "young old men and women."[38]

Difficult negotiations with all partners such as Polish Government in Exile authorities, Zionists, and the Orthodox notwithstanding, JDC was clearly determined to establish and maintain control over any Jewish relief operation. Convinced that its effectiveness depended on its nonsectarian humanitarian stance, JDC pragmatism also extended to a willingness to compromise with otherwise antagonistic players, accepting both Soviet restrictions on "sectarian" aid and demand for general relief as well as a strategic cooperation with the Polish Government in Exile. Just as many of the Jews accepted into the Anders Army served as medical personnel, much of the aid provided by JDC to be distributed by the Polish Government in Exile within the Soviet Union encompassed medical supplies. By 1942, "about 400,000 shipments of medical and surgical supplies, fitted physicians' kits, and base hospital units" had already been sent, along with more specifically targeted aid, such as "a substantial quantity of matzoh at Passover time," with hopes for arranging a similar shipment in 1943. Despite its criticism of unequal distribution practices, Viteles was still trying to ensure that JDC could support an avowedly "non-sectarian relief program under auspices of the Polish Embassy in Kuibyshev." This collaboration with the Polish Government in Exile, which lasted until relations between the USSR and the Poles fully collapsed in April 1943, provided for goods to be shipped on Soviet transports or chartered boats, without charge and duty free, to the Polish Embassy in Kuibyshev, which assumed responsibility "for distribution of such supplies through local committees they have appointed in Russia."[39]

Tensions with the Jewish Agency were, however, not only of an ideological nature but also a consequence of JDC's frustration with the unprofessional manner in which the Jewish Agency and the Zionist activists seemed to operate. Typically, the American organization was skeptical about the absence of a single "trained social worker" as well as "the lack of teachers and leaders with training, background and experience, and the absence of any strong guiding and administrative hand" among Jewish Agency staff.[40] Fearing that laxity and corruption might undermine the entire relief mission, both in Tehran and in the shipping operation, Viteles acknowledged the valid complaints about Polish antisemitism and its effects on the supply situation but also pointedly noted that "[m]ore efficient administration of the Jewish Children's Camp in the way of mending, laundering, shoe repairing shops, would have improved the situation."[41] Viteles particularly worried about proper supervision of the severely traumatized Teheran children. Hadassah's Henrietta Szold echoed the shock the children generated among so many observers, whether American or Zionist. Barber of the American Red Cross had described the "sick children" among all the young Polish refugees as "haunting shadows—literally skin and bones."[42] She desperately wanted to remove them from the demoralizing atmosphere in Tehran and the dangers of absorption into Polish groups heading toward refugee settlements in British India or Africa. Like Dobkin, she saw them as "80% parentless, many of them veritable orphans, most of them separated from their parents by a series of cruel happenings, some of them equally abandoned by desperate parents compelled by the barbarity of war to entrust their children to the mercies of the public and the only alternative promising safety." They had been "wandering in the Soviet Union for three years . . . sleeping in the woods, half naked, exposed to disease, eaten up by vermin, starved, guiltless, innocent, badly used victims of the war and the war lords."[43] David Laor, the young Hashomer Hatzair activist who had himself just escaped from Central Asia and been recruited as the director of the Jewish children's camp, also remembered his charges as "pale, gaunt and famished. They had a haunted expression in their eyes . . . They were like little battle-weary soldiers, exhausted by gunfire, expulsion, imprisonment, and wandering across Siberia's endless forgotten wastelands to Uzbekistan, Kazakhstan, and other places whose names they had never heard until they were dragged through them like beasts in cattle trucks."

However, Laor's perspective and priorities differed significantly from the professional social work practices to which JDC adhered—or at least attempted to adhere. Where JDC saw devastation and loss, he also glimpsed hope for a different future. The Zionist promise, he sensed, provided a sense of futurity that the Polish children in Soviet exile did not have; the "Polish children were actually envious of the Zhids they tormented as the onion stinkers. . . . They knew that the Jewish children would soon be on their way to Palestine, their homeland. Whereas they had left a defeated homeland and would soon be sent to another exile, never knowing when they would return home. This was a different, new encouraging feeling—Poles envying Jews."[44]

JDC professionals, however, were not convinced that devotion to the children and the Zionist cause sufficed to care for these vulnerable children. They bemoaned the shortage of clothes and sanitary arrangements and mistrusted the very practice, so central to Zionist principles of relief and rehabilitation, reflected in Laor's role—namely, a peer culture in which the caregivers were not much older than their charges and often had shared in their suffering. Laor recalled, with both bitterness and bemusement, that during one difficult meeting, Viteles even suspected him of stealing. From Viteles's point of view, however, the only stable presence was Tziporah Shertok, wife of later Israeli Minister Moshe Shertok, who had been dispatched, after some negotiation with British authorities in Palestine, from Jerusalem and served successfully as "the mother of the camp."[45]

Viteles did have good reason to fret about possible corruption and laxity. He warned about Iranian resentment of the large group of refugees on their already-occupied territory for whom Polish authorities were purchasing supplies in quantities that led to shortages and price inflation. Moreover, he observed that "the more religious and conservative section of the Iranian population was reported to be much concerned about the effect of the purported 'idleness and gay life' of the Polish refugees," especially the 2,000 who had eschewed camp life and had settled directly in Tehran. The substantial local Jewish community itself was uneasy about "the increase of immorality among the young women," including the twenty Jewish "barmaids" and "waitresses" among the 150–200 Polish Jewish refugees who had decided to try their luck outside the refugee camps in the Iranian capital. Nonetheless, the JDC representative stressed that "thus far, there has been no direct criticism against Jewish refugees; the Iranians and others always refer to Polish refugees."[46] JDC also continually prodded the local Jewish community, which had raised a remarkable $6,000 during Yom Kippur services in 1942 (and had shocked some of the Ashkenazi refugee children by picking them up in fancy cars for High Holiday services), to do its part. Ever vigilant about attending to multiple and potentially conflicting interests and needs, JDC recognized that the Iranian Jewish poor also required assistance and respected the traditional role of the Alliance Universelle in offering that aid. JDC decided therefore to supplement and extend its refugee relief work to local community support.[47]

Shortly after Viteles departed Tehran in December 1942, JDC, working closely with Szold, managed to arrange passage to Palestine for the Teheran children. JDC provided the funds and had done a considerable amount of the lengthy and vexed travel route negotiating with the Americans and British. Both allies worried that pressure on Iraq to extend itself on behalf of Jewish youth headed toward a potential future Jewish state would damage the war effort, with the British pointedly noting the opposition already generated by the occupation in Iran and colonial rule in India.[48] The children finally departed Tehran on January 3, 1943, and the now-legendary rescue—JDC's role largely hidden—succeeded after another harrowing journey on serpentine roads and through mine-infested waters, when some 1,230 children, adolescents, and accompanying adults arrived at Atlit near Haifa on February 18, 1943—just as the ghettos in their homeland were being liquidated.

As was evident in both the parcel project and the passage of the children to Palestine, JDC operated within a complex web of overlapping authorities in a country that was itself under a partial dual Soviet-British (and, in practice, US) occupation that also included the temporary presence (until August 1943) of Anders's Polish Exile Army under British command. In the midst of an escalating catastrophe facing the Jewish people in German-occupied Europe and potentially in the Soviet Union—the reports coming into Tehran were becoming increasingly ominous—JDC dealt, as it always did in its wartime efforts, with the banal and the bureaucratic. So much of the correspondence preserved in its archives concerns money, bank remittances, or acquiring proper Treasury Department licenses for sending money to foreign powers in wartime. The cables and letters are often written in standard office terms, with references to interoffice rivalries or questions about accurate bookkeeping or charging recipients for money transfers in either pounds or dollars. Letters and clippings reveal JDC's ongoing efforts to defend its umbrella role as the major nonsectarian aid organization and to convince other Jewish groups, such as *Vaad Hatzala*, which did not trust JDC to honor the needs of observant Jews, to desist from organizing their own operations or engaging in separate fundraising.

"In this time of crisis," JDC officials pleaded for the suppression of "special interests, no matter how worthy they may be" because "the needs of the largest masses must not be sacrificed."[49] JDC warned that coordination of relief work was particularly critical for the Tehran operation precisely because the "Russians" had only approved "non-sectarian" activity. After the collapse of relations with the Polish Government in Exile, which had initially overseen the relief shipments, JDC saw itself as the single agency with the means, experience, and credibility required for maintaining—and indeed expanding—the mission. JDC staff entered into sometimes tense debates— both internally and with a broader politically and religiously diverse, not to say divided, Jewish community—about whether to aid only Jews, all Poles, or the general Russian war relief campaign. Conflicts about strategy toward the Soviet Union became especially acute during and after the Jewish Anti-Fascist Committee's 1943 North American fundraising and propaganda tour.[50] JDC knew all too well that various groups had differing politics—regarding Zionism, regarding relations to Poles, and regarding the advisability of providing general aid to the USSR rather than specifically to Jews. JDC cables, letters, and reports conceal, or only hint at, the urgency and "fog of war" among JDC officials in New York, their confusion evident when they refer to the refugees in Central Asia interchangeably as "Polish Jews" and "Bukharians" or identify what would seem to be Uzbekistan as Turkistan or Turkmenistan. Nonetheless, JDC argued, all factions had to share the increasingly desperate goal of rescuing those European Jews who might still be saved.

With the "crisis" of European Jewry always looming in the background, JDC continually confronted intra-Jewish rivalries and tensions with

Zionists, Orthodox representatives, and Communist sympathizers while simultaneously negotiating with multiple other parties, including a Polish Government in Exile still active in Tehran that was understood to be, if not explicitly antisemitic or hostile, at least not particularly concerned about the fate of the Jews. Ironically, however, this relative indifference facilitated JDC's takeover of all aid operations for refugee Jews in the Soviet Union, despite the official ban on sectarian aid intended for Jews.

In 1941 and 1942, JDC was still able to work with, and through, the Polish Government in Exile, its embassy in Kuibyshev, and its network of consular offices throughout the unoccupied Soviet Union. When the Poles, who had been the main, if unsatisfactory, conduits for aid to Polish Jews, were expelled, the relief effort was left directly to JDC but under much more complex and murky protocols. The organization faced a three-pronged challenge in Tehran: to care for those Jews who had managed to find a temporary safe haven in Iran; to negotiate and finance transport to Palestine, especially for the children; and to find, fund, and funnel the packages for the "Asiatics" (the trickiest of the three).

In June 1943, after the Teheran children had been safely delivered to Palestine and with the Poles unable to cooperate with the Soviets, another American-born JDC official based in Jerusalem followed up on Viteles's tour. Charles Passman's visits in June and November 1943 established the contours of a dramatically larger relief action. Asserting its position as the only viable interlocutor with all parties, JDC formally took over authority, not only from the Poles but also from the Jewish Agency, proceeding to negotiate the conditions that sped up and increased the flow of packages. Viteles's exertions notwithstanding, from 1942 until the end of 1943, only 6,827 packages had been sent from Tehran. Passman's return trip to Tehran from Jerusalem in November confirmed the new closer and direct collaboration with Iranian and Soviet authorities. In a key move, Iran allowed expedited shipment of parcels and exemption from normally high (25%) customs duties. The Soviets, in turn, agreed to extract customs payments based only on the lower cost of supplies in their countries of origin rather than their actual inflated value in Iran. This concession was not completely honored—the Soviets apparently did extract up to some 40%

customs duties, which they felt more secure demanding at a warehouse in Tehran rather than at the border where corruption was more rampant and money and goods more likely to disappear. Nonetheless, even under these imperfect circumstances, JDC had scored a remarkable success: setting up a warehouse that acted as a virtually independent post office, thereby circumventing delays and inspections at the main facility in Tehran.

Having secured the conditions necessary for the extensive parcel project, JDC now needed to quickly and inexpensively find the supplies to fill the parcels. Goods organized by the Jewish Relief Association (JRA) in Bombay arrived in Tehran from India; supplies were also purchased and sent to Tehran from throughout the British imperial sphere—in Palestine, Egypt, South Africa, and, at least according to plans, Australia. The Bombay JRA, which included members of the Indian Jewish community as well as European refugees—comprising both Axis nationals who had been detained as enemy aliens and noninterned Polish and Hungarian Jews— was a critical source of aid, supplying large quantities of tea, although a more ambitious scheme to purchase trucks in India for quicker transport to the Soviet Union fell through. In 1944, the JRA counted 409 members and was cooperating with JDC on the Tehran program for Jewish refugees in Russia in addition to a special fund for Polish Jewish refugees in transit through, or seeking shelter in, British India.[51] Moreover, taking full advantage of its carefully cultivated good relations with the US government, JDC worked closely with the US military to acquire Lend-Lease supplies. In the spring of 1944, Charles Passman was able to state unequivocally: "The help given us by the U.S. authorities actually made possible the carrying out of our large scale, parcels-service." At the height of the campaign in 1944, 10,000 packages a month were making their way, often on Red Army trucks (some of which had been assembled by American soldiers and contractors), from Tehran into Uzbekistan.[52]

Receipts arriving in the JDC Jerusalem office proved that packages did actually arrive, even as the New York office was kept busy fielding complaints about the quality of goods (such as old clothes), slow arrival times, and corruption in the Tehran office. In fact, one of the reasons Passman undertook a second trip to Tehran at the height of the war was to investigate a bevy of complaints ranging from the heartbreaking to the bizarre. In a later example, J. A. Rosen, a decidedly skeptical voice within JDC in regard to cooperative relations with the Soviet Union, sent along a complaint published in a Canadian Jewish journal insisting that the packages contained "some phantastic undergarments which nobody has ever seen or worn in Russia and made of a kind of material which looks more like a rag than anything else" and that the precious tea from India tasted like "green poison."[53]

Undeterred by the impatience and sheer lack of understanding of some donors, especially in North America, JDC steadily collected more names for individual recipient addresses from refugees in Iran; from *landsmanshaftn* in Palestine, the United States, and elsewhere; and from the Jewish Agency. Passman was sufficiently annoyed to observe that unlike in Palestine where people were much "closer to the suffering Jews" in the Soviet Union (or by then in Poland), "the people in America are too remote and have difficulty in picturing the suffering of the Jews." Pointing out what should have been obvious, he wearily explained that Americans seemed to be "expecting the same service as they get from a first-class American merchandise concern."[54] Irate American donors apparently did not quite grasp that paying for a package to be sent to a suffering relative was not like ordering from a mail order catalog where the package arrives in perfect condition at the appointed time. Instead of earning plaudits for a daunting rescue operation, JDC staff frequently found themselves on the defensive, patiently trying to combat "bad rumors" and explain that "[w]e do our utmost to pack our parcels as well as possible." The vast majority of packages, officials insisted, did arrive, despite having "to travel long distances, very often changed from train to truck to cart . . . go[ing] through a considerable amount of rough handling."[55] Admittedly, and contrary to the intentions of a donor, they might indeed not be used by the direct addressee but would more likely be repurposed for barter on the black market that was key to survival. Here, too, JDC tried to educate its supporters about the harsh realities of life in Central Asia, noting that even the Soviet government had sanctioned "barter" on the "open market" (a euphemism for "black market") as a legitimate survival strategy. A parcel that might have cost a donor approximately $21, certainly no more than $30, could contain goods, especially luxury items like some of that "phantastical" silk underwear, worth between 1,500 and 4,000 "roubles [*sic*]" on the "open market," a truly lifesaving contribution in a situation where the price of bread had dropped to 15 "roubles [*sic*]" per kilo. In any case, JDC funded about 80% of the costs.[56]

On the larger stage, JDC's relationship to the US government was key to diplomatic maneuvering as well as access to unused Lend-Lease supplies that became more available as the tide of war turned in the Soviet Union. In a stroke of luck, and in contrast to many much more hostile US State Department consular officials, the US plenipotentiary in Tehran, Lewis G. Dreyfus Jr., proved to be particularly helpful. But the ability to take advantage of his and other US diplomatic services relied on JDC's long experience with such contacts and its experience as a political and cultural mediator. Moreover, it might not have been coincidental, although the fact goes unmentioned in JDC records, that Major Abraham Neuwirth, the officer in charge of the US medical mission, was a Jew from New York.[57]

In the midst of war, JDC officials were constantly on the move, mostly by air, throughout the Middle East and eventually liberated Europe, from Paris to Stockholm, to Rome, Athens, to Istanbul, Cairo, Jerusalem, and back to Tehran. As the archives clearly document, JDC relief work would not have been possible without the benefit of American military and diplomatic contacts. JDC's status as an essentially American nongovernmental organization facilitated close cooperation with American diplomatic officials, especially consular and embassy employees in Istanbul, Tehran, and Cairo along with the Intergovernmental Committee on Refugees established in 1938 and the War Refugee Board when it was finally set up by President Roosevelt in January 1944. The extensive cable traffic between New York, Jerusalem, Paris, and the Middle East, essential to perilously belated and feverish plans for rescue and relief as well as remittance of funds, seems to have gone almost exclusively via diplomatic pouch to "c/o American consulate," or embassy, or even to specific officials. The British mission in Tehran also channeled some money, ironically to the Jewish Agency representative. A few key players wore more than one hat, acting, for example, as representatives of the Jewish Agency and of the Polish Government in Exile. JDC itself mostly relied on US contacts in the Foreign Service or

Treasury Department, which provided the necessary licenses for money transfers to intermediaries in Tehran, most prominently the director of the Alliance Universelle School, who received funds (ostensibly for his Institute) and redirected them to the package program.

These facts do relativize, albeit in surely marginal ways, the dominant story of the US government's, and especially the US State Department's, indifference and downright hostility to the fate of the Jews. The story of the JDC effort in Tehran reasserts the limited but real efficacy of individual and organizational initiative and reframes the range of Allied, Soviet, British, and US diplomatic maneuvering in regard to rescue. Here, on the geographic margins, where the only truly viable rescue efforts could still be undertaken for large numbers of Jews, and especially after the (late) establishment of the American War Refugee Board (which again operated mainly with funds raised by JDC), American Jews could, it seems, rely on support from their diplomatic representatives.[58] The sheer energy and travel schedules of these JDC representatives and the organizations' willingness to commit large sums of money, still in a time of total war and limited communication and transport, is quite breathtaking.

In 1944 and 1945, JDC was working on a macrolevel—moving huge amounts of money and goods around Asia and Africa—from Australia and South Africa and India to Tehran for shipment to Soviet Central Asia and later eventually to Poland, all the while trying to keep accurate accounts for the central offices in Jerusalem and New York of what was going where and how much it cost. At the same time, the New York office responded to individual requests for help with locating loved ones (all too often a vain hope) and help—money, visas—for those who had, remarkably, been found alive (mostly in Romania, Bulgaria, and Hungary).[59]

Not always legible in the bureaucratic correspondence—the tallying of accounts and budgets, the defensive responses to criticism, whether from Orthodox, Zionist, Bundist, or Communist Jews or the plain disgruntled, like the "disappointed Jew from Teheran" who complained to the JDC New York office that the Tehran office was run like a "brodel [*sic*] [brothel]" by a manager ("this stupid, noisy, bad educated and selfish young fellow, who considers himself as the most important person in Teheran") who was having affairs with non-Jewish Polish refugees—was the palpable sense of urgency.[60] Even without knowing the full extent of the calamity, JDC was racing to save the Eastern European Jews who could still be saved—and most of them were struggling in Central Asia or, in much smaller numbers, slowly emerging from the shattered communities in liberated Europe.

Even as the Red Army gradually fought its way through Nazi-occupied Poland and the remnants of Jewish life began to reemerge, Tehran remained the central post from which JDC aid was shipped. Just a few months after the full ramping up of operations in 1944, decisions had to be made about when and how to start diverting aid to survivors in liberated parts of the Soviet Union and then in Poland as well as to other refugees seeking passage to Palestine such as Yemenite Jews. In the first six months of 1944, 44,000 parcels had been shipped to the Soviet Union from Tehran.[61]

As the war in Eastern Europe slowly neared its end in late 1944, a clearer picture of the catastrophe that had enveloped East European Jewry emerged, and JDC ordered supplies from Tehran to be shipped to Poland via Leningrad. Both supplies and funds were redirected to Lublin, where the needs of the survivors were deemed to be even more desperate than

Bales of overcoats at the JDC supply station in Tehran being prepared for shipment to the surviving Jewish community in Poland via the Soviet Union. Tehran, Iran, 1944.

those of the refugees—still minimally estimated in the tens of thousands—trapped in Central Asia. Charles Passman, the JDC official with the most recent experience in Iran, reluctantly agreed to "liquidation of the Teheran service" despite his judgment that "our discontinuation of the parcels service will affect badly the many who are still now in Russia and may remain there."[62] A new phase began in which the most immediate concern was not refugees outside of Europe but the few who had survived under Nazi occupation. The organization now needed to establish cooperative relations with new partners—namely, a victorious Soviet occupation and a pro-Soviet Lublin government in Poland.

In 1946, JDC Chairman Edward M. M. Warburg wrote to Secretary of State Byrnes thanking the US State Department and particularly the "humanitarian sympathy of Lewis G. Dreyfus Jr. your minister [plenipotentiary] and the entire embassy staff" for their "whole-hearted cooperation."[63] Most of the supplies for the parcels had in fact been received from the American Lend-Lease program or from US Army stores at greatly reduced rates. JDC had spent $5.5 million since 1942—apparently more than anywhere else in the world during those momentous years—and had managed to establish contact with 60,000 individuals plus 230 communities in the Soviet Union. Writing to Judah Magnes in Jerusalem in January 1947, Charles Passman, who had been on the ground in the Middle East at regular intervals, took stock of what had been accomplished by the time the operation was fully halted in August 1946. Remarkably, "between 80–90%" of 230,000 parcels shipped from Tehran "reached their destinations"; by January 15, 1947, "130,000 official acknowledgements of receipt," with thousands more waiting to be mailed, had been forwarded from Iran to the Joint's office for the Middle East and Balkans.[64]

The impact of the "Joint Fund Teheran," as it was bureaucratically marked, went, however, well beyond the undeniably vital shipment of packages. The gathering of addresses and receipts ensured that the package operation also served as a kind of invaluable tracing service for locating loved ones in remote areas. And as my audiovisual technician's story indicates, the packages also had enormous symbolic meaning. Even for a young displaced child in an orphanage, it meant that these Jews, stranded in the farthest reaches of the Soviet Union, were indeed not forgotten, neither by relatives nor by the international Jewish community. The JDC Archives contains many letters attesting to that gratitude along with the grumbling ones from donors and sometimes competing Jewish organizations. In July 1946—just as, on July 4, the notorious pogrom in Kielce, Poland, occurred and the repatriates, having endured long and circuitous journeys, were still straggling across the border—the JDC Digest, published in New York, printed a letter that had "recently reached the J.D.C. office in Teheran." Two Polish rabbis "who found haven in Russia during the war years" testified that "[t]hese parcels saved the lives of thousands of refugees in Russia" and added "We wish to express our thanks for the life-saving job done by American Jewry which we and our people will never forget."[65]

"In a world of suffering and need," Joseph C. Hyman, the executive vice chairman of JDC, tried to explain to a Jewish clothing manufacturer in New York who objected to the limitations of the rescue and relief efforts,

> if we can save a remnant of the war-stricken refugees, of the suffering Jews on the continent of Europe, bring about a measurable movement of some of these people to Palestine, to Canada, and to other countries; feed some in the occupied zones, make possible the movement of thousands of others into the neutral countries; and deal with overwhelming new emergencies in the field of rescue—we feel that we shall have discharged our duty to the best of our present ability.[66]

These are all still murky stories, with much archival data as well as press reports, personal collections, and memoirs waiting to be unraveled and pieced together more carefully. Much research remains to be done, including a detailed examination of JDC files that collected receipts and acknowledgments with name and address lists. All this material will tell us much more about the situation of refugee Jews from Poland (as well as the Baltic states) who lived, died, and survived in the Soviet Union. JDC sources illuminate both the Polish Jewish experience after 1941 in Central Asia and, less obviously perhaps, the multinational wartime context in the Persian Gulf in which relief and rescue efforts mobilized. The story of the Joint Fund Teheran, the war's "Jewish Lend-Lease," represents an underresearched and underpublicized piece of JDC's institutional history. It also fills an important gap in our understanding of Holocaust history and the global history of World War II as revealed through the lens of the JDC Archives.

NOTES

1. On JDC activities in, and expulsion from, the Soviet Union, see the chapter by Mikhail Mitsel in this volume.

2. The details of this story have changed in the years since I first heard it, and B cannot precisely remember dates or places; however, what has not changed is the insistent memory about the presence of JDC.

3. See, for example, the important contributions in the issue on Jews in Russia and the Soviet Union in *Holocaust and Genocide Studies* 26, no. 1 (2012); for an older brief survey, see Nora Levin, *The Jews in the Soviet Union since 1917: The Paradox of Survival*, vol. 1 (New York: New York University Press, 1990), 335–97; see also Debórah Dwork and Robert Jan Van Pelt, *Flight from the Reich: Refugee Jews, 1933–1946* (New York: Norton, 2009), 218–30; Markus Nesselrodt, "Der Vernichtung Entkommen: Erfahrungen polnischer Juden in der Sowjet Union, 1939–1945" (diss., Berlin, 2016); Markus Nesselrodt, "'I Bled Like You, Brother, although I Was a Thousand Miles Away': Postwar Yiddish Sources on the Experience of Polish Jews in Soviet Exile during World War II," *East European Jewish Affairs* 46, no. 1 (2016): 47–67; Mark Edele and Wanda Warlik, "Saved by Stalin? Trajectories and Numbers of Polish Jews in the Soviet Second World War," in *Shelter from the Holocaust: Rethinking Jewish Survival in the Soviet Union*, ed. Mark Edele, Sheila Fitzpatrick, and Atina Grossmann (Detroit: Wayne State University Press, 2017), 95–131. My chapter here is specifically focused on JDC in Tehran; for a more general discussion of my research, see, Atina Grossmann, "Jewish Refugees in Soviet Central Asia, Iran, and India: Lost Memories of Displacement, Trauma, and Rescue," in *Shelter from the Holocaust: Rethinking Jewish Survival in the Soviet Union*, ed. Mark Edele, Sheila Fitzpatrick, and Atina Grossmann (Detroit: Wayne State University Press, 2017), 185–218, and "Remapping Survival: Jewish

Refugees and Lost Memories of Displacement, Trauma, and Rescue in Soviet Central Asia, Iran, and India," *Simon Dubnow Institute Yearbook* 15 (2016): 71–97. There are no accurate data and no consensus on the number of Jews who fled Western Poland, how many Poles or specifically Jewish Poles were deported, how many then migrated to Central Asia, how many remained in the Soviet Union, how many survived to be repatriated to postwar Poland, and how many fled again after the war to the displaced persons (DP) camps of US-occupied Europe, where they became the distinct majority—at least 70% of all Jewish DPs and probably up to 85% of all Polish Jewish DPs, the largest group by far among all Jewish DPs.

4. On the general topic of Soviet wartime evacuation to Central Asia, see Rebecca Manley, *To the Tashkent Station: Evacuation and Survival in the Soviet Union at War* (Ithaca, NY: Cornell University Press, 2009). On the Jewish experience of deportation and evacuation in the Soviet Union, see, most recently, Edele, Fitzpatrick, and Grossmann, eds., *Shelter from the Holocaust: Rethinking Jewish Survival in the Soviet Union*. For the term *Asiatics*, see, for example, Yehudah Bauer, *Flight and Rescue: Brichah* (New York: Random House, 1970), 26–31.

5. JDC Archives, Records of the New York Office of the American Jewish Joint Distribution Committee, 1933–1944, Folder 422, Polish Telegraph Agency Report, June 23, 1942; see also Keith Sword, "The Welfare of Polish-Jewish Refugees in the USSR, 1941–43: Relief Supplies and Their Distribution," in *Jews in Eastern Poland and the USSR, 1939–46*, ed. Norman Davies and Antony Polonsky (New York: St. Martin's Press, 1991), 145–60; David Engel, *In the Shadow of Auschwitz: The Polish Government in Exile and the Jews, 1939–1942* (Chapel Hill: University of North Carolina Press, 1978), 114–209.

6. The Polish Government in Exile demanded an investigation after Nazi Germany publicized the discovery of graves of Polish officers killed by the NKVD in a series of massacres in and around the Katyn forest in April and May 1940. The Soviet denial of the charges and rejection of an inquiry by the International Red Cross led to the rupture of all diplomatic relations in 1943.

7. Reports on the numbers, composition, and timing of the Anders Army as it evacuated the Soviet Union into Iran vary. According to the archival

sources cited by Edele and Warlik in Table 4 of their chapter in *Shelter from the Holocaust*, between 6,000 and 7,000 Jews left with the Anders Army. The gender division among the Anders civilian evacuees is unclear; there were Polish nurses, including some Jewish women, serving directly with the army. Despite efforts—confirmed in the US diplomatic files that I have so far examined—to evacuate at least 50,000 more children, Jan T. Gross and Irena G. Gross reported that only 15,000 to 20,000 were transported to Iran. This figure highlights the even smaller number of Jewish children who have nonetheless been given the name "Teheran children." See, among multiple sources, *The Children of Teheran*, directed by Yehuda Cave, David Tour, and Dalia Guttmann, 2007.

8. Maurice Barber to Hon Norman Davis, Chairman, American Red Cross Headquarters, Washington, DC. Tehran, April 5, 1942. Transmitted with despatch no. 247, April 12, 1942, from the American Legation at Tehran, Iran. Earlier—and frequently repeated—reference to "greatest civilian emergency" from telegram sent to American Legation, Cairo, Egypt, from Maurice Barber, American Red Cross representative in Tehran to Ralph Bain, Director, American Red Cross, Middle East, Cairo, Egypt. Transmitted with despatch no. 239, April 2, 1942, American Legation, Tehran to Bain, Cairo. NARA, State Department Refugee Files 840.48, Microfilm Box 1284, Reel 31.

9. JDC Archives, Records of the American Jewish Joint Distribution Committee, Jerusalem, Istanbul Collection, Harry Viteles, Confidential Report on Visit to Bagdad (2.XI to 9.XI 1942) and to Teheran (11.XI to 2.XII 1942), 1. The detailed report is forty-seven pages long and incudes excerpts from much JDC correspondence in regard to the Polish refugees in the Soviet Union and the situation in Tehran up until the date of his tour. Interestingly, I have (so far) found no mention of Viteles's visit in the US diplomatic files, which deal extensively with the crisis of the Polish refugees in Iran, nor in the detailed documentation of the British mission, *Iran Political Diaries 1881–1965, Volume II: 1939–1942*, ed. R. M. Burrell, Crown Copyright Material from the Public Record Office and the British Library, Oriental and India Office Collections (London: Archive Editions, 1997), 371–662.

10. JDC Archives, Records of the New York Office of the American Jewish Joint Distribution Committee, 1933–1944, Correspondence from Moses A. Leavitt to Dr. Judah L. Magnes, October 1, 1942.

11. See the chapter by Mikhail Mitsel in this volume.

12. See JDC Archives, Records of the American Jewish Joint Distribution Committee, Jerusalem, Istanbul Collection, Harry Viteles, Confidential Report on Visit to Bagdad (2.XI to 9.XI 1942) and to Teheran (11.XI to 2.XII 1942), 21, and the string of cables from the New York Office to Tehran in April 1942 regarding money transfers.

13. JDC Archives, Records of the New York Office of the American Jewish Joint Distribution Committee, 1933–1944, "Report concerning the Refugees Arriving in Teheran," marked "Strictly Confidential," sent to the World Jewish Congress by Dr. Dobkin, delegate of the Jewish Agency to Teheran, September 24, 1942, with first part subtitled, "The Human Element in Teheran." For the full three-part report, see Yad Vashem Archives, RG M2 File no. 335.

14. Ibid., 1.

15. Ibid., 2.

16. Ibid., 3.

17. Ibid., 3–4. Strikingly, both Dobkin, 4, and the American Red Cross representative use the term *holocaust*, with a small *h*, in their 1942 reports.

18. Correspondence from Magnes to JDC, April 23, 1942; May 7, 1942; June 1, 1942 (three separate letters).

19. Cable, October 1942, correspondence from the JDC New York Office to Magnes, Jerusalem, received October 21, 1942.

20. The JDC files do contain reports discussing negotiations with the Soviets, particularly after the spring of 1943 when the Polish Government in Exile could no longer function in Central Asia.

21. JDC Archives, Records of the American Jewish Joint Distribution Committee, Jerusalem, Istanbul Collection, Harry Viteles, Confidential Report on Visit to Bagdad (2.XI to 9.XI 1942) and to Teheran (11.XI to 2.XII 1942), 19, 20.

22. JDC Archives, Records of the American Jewish Joint Distribution Committee, Jerusalem, Istanbul Collection, Harry Viteles, Confidential

Report on Visit to Bagdad (2.XI to 9.XI 1942) and to Teheran (11.XI to 2.XII 1942), 28: "On the one hand Poles were inclined to exaggerate their estimates about the total number of Jews for 'propaganda' purposes" while "on the other hand" minimizing estimates in order to reduce their share of supplies and eligibility for evacuation to Iran.

23. JDC Archives, Records of the New York Office of the American Jewish Joint Distribution Committee, 1933–1944, Henrietta Buchmann of JDC writing to C. G., Queen City Bakery, Glen Falls, NY, December 24, 1942. For Viteles's estimate, see JDC Archives, Records of the American Jewish Joint Distribution Committee, Jerusalem, Istanbul Collection, Harry Viteles, Confidential Report on Visit to Bagdad (2.XI to 9.XI 1942) and to Teheran (11.XI to 2.XII 1942), 28. His total refugee numbers for Iran are also very low; some sources have estimated that there were as many as 450,000 refugees altogether in Iran during the war, most of them from the Soviet Union. See Lior B. Sternfeld, "Reclaiming Their Past: Writing Jewish History in Iran during the Mohammad Reza Pahlavi and Early Revolutionary Periods (1941–1989)" (PhD diss., University of Texas, Austin, 2014); Lior Sternfeld, *Between Iran and Zion: Jewish Histories of Twentieth-Century Iran* (Palo Alto, CA: Stanford University Press, 2018). A highly suggestive report (Ishaan Tharoor, "The Forgotten Story of the European Refugee Camps in the Middle East," *The Washington Post*, June 2, 2016) estimates that there were between 114,000 and 300,000 Polish refugees in wartime Iran, part of a larger landscape of refugee camps throughout the Middle East, including Egypt, Syria, Palestine, Iran, and India.

24. See, for example, cables between Chase National Bank and the Imperial Bank of Iran as well as other banks with JDC officials and other communications about the most effective ways to transmit funds to Tehran without violating US Treasury Department rules, 1942.

25. See Parisa Damandan, *The Children of Esfahan: Polish Refugees in Iran 1942–1945, Portrait Photographs of Alboqahasem Jala* (Tehran: Nazar Research and Cultural Institute, 2010), which contains a long list of children's names (as well as portrait photographs), stating, on p. 275, that over 2,400 Polish children were cared for in Isfahan before being transported to locations as varied as Mexico, India, and Kenya. A 2017 Iranian Polish

photo documentation—as well as numerous references, including film material, on the internet—details the experience of the Polish refugee children in the Isfahan orphanage. It is unclear whether any of those children
might have been Jewish, but certainly the shelter was specifically set up for
non-Jewish Polish youngsters.

26. JDC Archives, Records of the American Jewish Joint Distribution Committee, Jerusalem, Istanbul Collection, Harry Viteles, Confidential Report
on Visit to Bagdad (2.XI to 9.XI 1942) and to Teheran (11.XI to 2.XII
1942), 5.

27. Ibid., 8.

28. Ibid., 9.

29. Ibid., 11.

30. See, for example, Joel Sayre, *Persian Gulf Command: Some Marvels on
the Road to Kazvin* (New York: Random House, 1945), a collection of
Sayre's *New Yorker* reportage, and United States Army, *Instructions for
American Servicemen in Iran during World War II* (North Charleston, SC:
CreateSpace, 2012). The history of the US wartime military presence in
Iran and the massive efforts, undertaken under difficult conditions, by the
Persian Gulf Command to aid the Soviet Union and the US role within
an Allied mission encompassing about half a million Soviet, British, and
American troops seem to be remarkably understudied.

31. Barber to Bain, July 13, 1942, NARA 840.48, Film 1284, Reel 32.

32. Draft for Letter to ARC in Tehran, May 27, 1942, Department of
State, Division of Near Eastern Affairs, Signed by Paul Alling. On July
18, 1942, Undersecretary of State Breckinridge Long noted that the US
State Department "believes that it would be particularly unfortunate if the
Iranians were given cause to feel that they were being imposed upon and
were receiving unfair treatment." NARA 840.48, Film 1284, Reel 32.

33. Sternfeld, "Reclaiming Their Past," chap. 2 on wartime Iran. According
to JDC Archives, Records of the American Jewish Joint Distribution
Committee, Jerusalem, Istanbul Collection, Harry Viteles, Confidential
Report on Visit to Bagdad (2.XI to 9.XI 1942) and to Teheran (11.XI
to 2.XII 1942), 12, Iraqi Jews constituted about 10% of the Jews living in
Tehran.

34. JDC Archives, Records of the American Jewish Joint Distribution Committee, Jerusalem, Istanbul Collection, Harry Viteles, Confidential Report on Visit to Bagdad (2.XI to 9.XI 1942) and to Teheran (11.XI to 2.XII 1942), 22.

35. Ibid., 25.

36. Flagging the conflicts with Zionists, Rudolf G. Sonneborn, chair of the National Council of the United Palestine Appeal, wrote to Sidney Hollander, president of the Council of Jewish Federation and Welfare Fund, complaining that "[t]he insistence by the JDC that Palestine in 1945 remain in a subordinate position reflected an unyielding refusal to understand the importance of Palestine, even in terms of pure saving of life, to say nothing of the dynamics of rehabilitation in Palestine, which has given security to over 300,000 refugees since 1933—virtually as many as the rest of the world combined," JDC Istanbul, Box 2, File 22.

37. JDC Archives, Records of the American Jewish Joint Distribution Committee, Jerusalem, Istanbul Collection, Harry Viteles, Confidential Report on Visit to Bagdad (2.XI to 9.XI 1942) and to Teheran (11.XI to 2.XII 1942), 26–27. Interestingly, Viteles also noted on the same page (26) that the Americans advised JDC not to appoint a permanent representative in Tehran, whereas the British seemed to favor such an arrangement, provided that the person in question "not use his position to promote 'Zionism.'"

38. Ibid., 27.

39. JDC Archives, Records of the New York Office of the American Jewish Joint Distribution Committee, 1933–1944, Henrietta Buchmann to C. G., Queen City Bakery, Glen Falls, NY, December 24, 1942.

40. JDC Archives, Records of the American Jewish Joint Distribution Committee, Jerusalem, Istanbul Collection, Harry Viteles, Confidential Report on Visit to Bagdad (2.XI to 9.XI 1942) and to Teheran (11.XI to 2.XII 1942), 23–24.

41. Ibid., 11.

42. Correspondence from Maurice Barber to Hon Norman Davis, Chairman, American Red Cross Headquarters, Washington, DC. Tehran, April 5, 1942. Transmitted with despatch no. 247, April 12, 1942, from the American Legation at Tehran, Iran.

43. Henrietta Szold quoted in JDC Archives, Records of the American Jewish Joint Distribution Committee, Jerusalem, Istanbul Collection, Harry Viteles, Confidential Report on Visit to Bagdad (2.XI to 9.XI 1942) and to Teheran (11.XI to 2.XII 1942), 23–24.

44. David Laor (originally Lautenburg), cited in Devora Omer, *The Teheran Operation: The Rescue of Jewish Children from the Nazis: Based on the Biographical Sketches of David and Rachel Laor* (Washington, DC: B'nai Brith Books, 1991), quotes on 144, 146ff.

45. JDC Archives, Records of the American Jewish Joint Distribution Committee, Jerusalem, Istanbul Collection, Harry Viteles, Confidential Report on Visit to Bagdad (2.XI to 9.XI 1942) and to Teheran (11.XI to 2.XII 1942), 24.

46. Ibid., 7.

47. Ibid., 12–13.

48. Ibid., 17. Viteles noted in frustration on p. 19 that privately, "A number of important official and unofficial members of the British community in Baghdad and Teheran were very outspoken in their criticism of what they called the 'Munich' policy which refused to put pressure on Iraq to permit passage to Palestine for the children."

49. See, for example, JDC Archives, Records of the New York Office of the American Jewish Joint Distribution Committee, 1933–1944, Folder 711, Correspondence from Buchmann to Executive Director, Richmond Jewish Community Council, March 8, 1943.

50. See the chapter by Mikhail Mitsel in this volume.

51. See Annual Report, Bombay Jewish Relief Association, 1944, Personal Collection, Hans S. Grossmann. The India link requires much more investigation. See also JDC Archives, Records of the New York Office of the American Jewish Joint Distribution Committee, 1943–1947, File 1960, Statement on Relief Activities of the JDC for Refugees in the USSR by Charles Passman, May 31, 1944, 4–5.

52. See for example, JDC Archives, Records of the New York Office of the American Jewish Joint Distribution Committee, 1943–1947, File 1960, Statement on Relief Activities of the JDC for Refugees in the USSR by Charles Passman, May 31, 1944. Quote from Passman's report, 5. Aside

from the Viteles Report, this summary statement is the most complete report on JDC in Tehran. Responding to repeated complaints, Passman claimed a remarkably fast turnaround time of about three weeks from the moment an order with an address reached the JDC office in Jerusalem until the packages were shipped from Tehran. The precise routes within the Soviet Union, usually after having been delivered by truck to the border at Ashkabad, still remain unclear to me. See, for example, a postcard in the USHMM Archives, dated April 1944, from (in Russian spelling) "Worker—Peasant Street" in Eniseisk (or Yeniseysk) addressed to Joint Distribution Committee, Teheran, thanking (in pencil-scrawled Yiddish) JDC for a shipment of Matzoh (and surely more); judging by the stamps, the card actually arrived in Tehran (USHMM Archives 1999-A-10016).

53. For example, *Canadian Jewish Weekly*, September 29, 1944, referencing cables from the Jewish Anti-Fascist Committee, September 23, 1944, and letters from Rosen to Joseph C. Hyman. For more detail on Rosen's positions and his disagreements with Rosenberg, a stauncher defender of the Soviet Union, see the chapter by Mikhail Mitsel in this volume. Notably, Jewish Agency Representative Dobkin's detailed September 24, 1942, report from Tehran to the World Jewish Congress in New York had also been decidedly more sympathetic to the Soviet Union, even suggesting that in view of the "virulent anti-Semitism as now holds sway in Polish military circles," it might have been "perhaps our original error that we approached the Polish authorities instead of the Soviet government directly with this problem" of attempting to move Jewish refugees out of Central Asia to Iran. The extensive red-penciled question and exclamation marks, as well as the skeptical comments adorning his text, suggest that this view was not shared by the report's recipients in New York (Dobkin, Part II: "Evacuation of the Polish Jewish Refugees from the USSR," 4, 5, Confidential Report to the World Jewish Congress, Yad Vashem Archives, RG M2 File no. 335).

54. JDC Archives, Records of the New York Office of the American Jewish Joint Distribution Committee, 1943–1947, Folder 426, Charles Passman, Memorandum from Jerusalem to NY Office in Response to Letters Forwarded by HIAS, September 23, 1945.

55. JDC Archives, Records of the New York Office of the American Jewish Joint Distribution Committee, 1943–1947, Correspondence from JDC Accountant Fred Grubel, JDC New York Office, to HIAS, February 23, 1946. The dating can be misleading because some of these communications refer to past events.

56. JDC Archives, Records of the New York Office of the American Jewish Joint Distribution Committee, 1943–1947, Memorandum from Charles Passman to Moses A. Leavitt, November 20, 1945. The dating can be misleading because some of these communications refer to past events. See, for example, JDC Archives, Records of the New York Office of the American Jewish Joint Distribution Committee, 1943–1947, Minutes, JDC New York Office, September 20, 1944.

57. Dobkin, Part II: "Evacuation of the Polish Jewish Refugees from the USSR," 4, 5, Confidential Report to the World Jewish Congress, September 24, 1942, Yad Vashem Archives, RG M2 File 335, states on the first page that he had "called on the American Ambassador in Teheran, who is a Jew" after being urged in a meeting (the previous day in Tehran) with the Polish (Government in Exile) Ambassador to Kuibyshev, Kot, to ask for American and British intervention with the Soviets to help forestall forced citizenship for Polish refugees. He was presumably referring to the US plenipotentiary Lewis G. Dreyfus Jr. (who noted that he "doubted information issuing from Polish sources" and that it "did not form a sufficient basis for his intervention in Washington"). I have found no further mention or verification of Dreyfus's religious affiliation. The detailed description of Neuwirth is in Dr. Marianne Leppmann (Hempel)'s unpublished memoir of refugee life in Tehran. Cited with permission of her family.

58. See the important new book by Rebecca Erbelding, *Rescue Board: The Untold Story of America's Efforts to Save the Jews of Europe* (New York: Doubleday, 2018). On JDC cooperation with US government authorities, see also Glaser's chapter in this volume, particularly in regard to Shanghai.

59. The JDC Archives, Records of the New York Office of the American Jewish Joint Distribution Committee, 1933–1944, contain a large swath of letters and cables documenting this entire process, starting in 1941 and (despite the title) extending through 1947.

60. Letter to Passman, Middle East Director, AJJDC, 19 Ibn Gabriel Street, Jerusalem. Teheran, February 20, 1946. One can well imagine that given JDC's constantly exposed position, this is not the only such missive to be found in the archives.

61. For this figure and a succinct summary of JDC efforts, see JDC Archives, Records of the New York Office of the American Jewish Joint Distribution Committee, 1933–1944, Joint Cable News, August 3, 1944. See also, for example, the report prepared by Charles Passman, Jerusalem, Palestine, Brief Outline of Relief Work among the Jewish Refugees in the USSR, through the Parcel Service, February 10, 1944, and Statement on Relief Activities of the JDC for Refugees in the USSR by Charles Passman, May 31, 1944.

62. JDC Archives, Records of the New York Office of the American Jewish Joint Distribution Committee, 1943–1947, Memoranda from Charles Passman, Jerusalem, to Moses A. Leavitt, New York, March 26, 1946; March 27, 1946.

63. JDC Archives, Records of the New York Office of the American Jewish Joint Distribution Committee, 1943–1947, Correspondence from Edward M. M. Warburg to James F. Byrnes, October 30, 1946.

64. For postwar inventory, see JDC Archives, Records of the New York Office of the American Jewish Joint Distribution Committee, 1943–1947, File 1960, Letter from Charles Passman to J. L. Magnes, January 15, 1947.

65. *JDC Digest* 5, no. 5 (1946): 1.

66. JDC Archives, Records of the New York Office of the American Jewish Joint Distribution Committee, 1943–1947, Letter from Joseph C. Hyman, Executive Vice Chairman, to S. Z., Internal Dress Company, 1400 Broadway, March 23, 1944.

8

Destination Australia

The Roles of Charles Jordan and Walter Brand

SUZANNE D. RUTLAND

"I think we have woefully neglected this wonderfully rich and resourceful country both as a source of funds as well as a future and inexhaustible place of settlement for new populations. The Zionists have been smarter again: they are sending emissaries all the time, their appeals never end—they are carrying the money out of here in boatloads. Either because we have no time or we are trying to save travelling expenses we neglect to educate a small but financially powerful community of truly good Jews to an understanding of the broader aspects of the Jewish tragedy—beyond what the Zionists are prepared to admit."

Charles H. Jordan, JDC Archives, Records of the New York Office of the American Jewish Joint Distribution Committee, 1945–1954, Folder 90, Letter from Charles H. Jordan (Charlie) to Moses A. Leavitt (Moe), August 29, 1947

INTRODUCTION: AUSTRALIAN JEWRY AND EARLY JDC CONTACTS

IN 1933, AUSTRALIAN JEWRY was a small, isolated community of a mere 23,000 Jews. Between 1933 and 1960, the community almost tripled in size to 61,000 Jews, largely resulting from postwar survivor migration. Indeed, Australia has the highest percentage of Holocaust survivors on a pro rata population basis of any other country outside of Israel. However, due to the anti-Jewish refugee outcry from the Australian media and other public bodies such as the Returned and Services League, the government was not prepared to extend funds to enable the resettlement of Jewish refugees before the war and survivors after the war in Australia.[1] Finding funds to assist in the resettlement of these refugees and survivors was a challenging task that the small Jewish community could not manage on its own. The American Jewish Joint Distribution Committee (JDC) stepped into this breach, and JDC professionals, including Charles Jordan and Gertrude van Tijn, along with Emery Komlos of the Refugee Economic Corporation (REC), an offshoot of JDC, played roles in these efforts. They were directly involved, visiting Australia and making recommendations. Jordan, a JDC director, in particular became a major facilitator of the migration process, first from Shanghai (1945–1948) and later from Paris (1948–1955). For seventeen years, in a close if sometimes contentious partnership, he worked with Walter Brand, the general secretary of the Australian Jewish Welfare Society (AJWS), enabling the community to absorb 17,000 survivors from 1946 to 1954 and another 10,000, including Hungarian escapees, until 1961.

Through this particular case study, this chapter will highlight the seminal role that JDC played in the reception of survivors in Australia. It will focus on the nature of Australian Jewry, divisions in the community, its lack of fundraising traditions, and national antisemitism. Indeed, JDC assistance was required due to antisemitism and a small and isolated Australian Jewish community, which needed assistance with the challenges it was facing in bringing survivors to Australia and integrating the newcomers. The global nature of this collaboration, reflected in the correspondence, created a "transnational social space" that can be defined as social welfare networks that stretch across national borders. This operated at both the personal level, through the social relations among the relatively small and overlapping group of globe-trotting JDC activist officials, and the institutional level through JDC's relief work.[2] This story illustrates how JDC history depended on the personal relationships nurtured between dedicated professionals who were able to influence the local and global impact of JDC, enabling these individuals to negotiate complex local political divisions. In this way, critical players, local politics, and global forces influenced JDC's work as it developed a transnational profile assisting Jewish communities worldwide. Although migration literature has tended to focus on "dispersed networks of family, compatriots or persons who share a religious and ethnic identity,"[3] this case study illustrates that such networks can be institutional as well as personal. In the postwar era, the Jewish world worked together despite tensions to assist Jewish survivors of the tragic destruction of European Jewry during the Holocaust in rebuilding their lives, as seen in the collaboration between JDC and the AJWS.

From 1933 onward, in response to the worsening crisis, Australia was seen as a possible place of refuge for Jews wishing to escape from Nazism. In 1936, the recently formed British Council for German Jewry, located at Woburn House in London, requested assistance from Australian Jewry in fundraising for German Jewry. Led by Sir Samuel Cohen, the scion of Sydney Jewry, the German Jewish Relief Fund was established and a major appeal held across Australia. Also in 1936, the Australian government liberalized its "alien migration" policies, reducing the landing permit charge from 500 Australian pounds to 50 Australian pounds for family-sponsored migrants (this constitutes a reduction from 43,350 US dollars to 4,335 US dollars in 2016) (Form 40) and also permitting an organization to sponsor migrants. In response to these changes, Woburn House requested that the funds raised be used to sponsor Jewish refugee migration to Australia. The AJWS was formed in 1937, with Cohen as its Sydney president, to meet this need.

The government insisted that all dealings with the Jewish community be carried out through the AJWS, and its president, Sir Samuel Cohen, personally signed all applications through Form 40, assuring that sponsored migrants would not become a charge on the state for five years. This involved a significant financial undertaking that Australian Jewry believed it could not sustain on its own. In 1939, Gerald de Vahl Davis and Paul Cullen (Sir Samuel's son) visited New York to discuss possible American funding assistance. They met with Charles J. Liebman, who had taken over the chairmanship in 1937 of the REC, formed in 1934 to aid in the resettlement and rehabilitation of refugees from Nazi Germany and, subsequently, from other parts of German-occupied Europe. The prime mover of the REC was JDC founder Felix M. Warburg, who led the organization until his death in 1937, when Charles J. Liebman succeeded him. It aimed to support long-term resettlement projects through interest-free loans that were "self-liquidating." In 1953, by which time most of the survivors had been resettled, it was amalgamated within JDC.

Liebman supported their request, and a total of 140,000 Australian pounds was allocated before the war to the AJWS in Sydney for the creation of Mutual Farms and Mutual Enterprises. (This would be almost 1.214 million US dollars in 2016.) Mutual Farms aimed to settle refugees on the land, and a training farm was established at Chelsea Park, Baulkham Hills, on the outskirts of Sydney. A number of Jewish refugees settled on the land, mainly as chicken farmers. However, most of these efforts did not last very long, and the refugees eventually moved back to the city. A group settlement at Cowra also proved to be a disaster due to the effects of draught, flood, inexperience, and the fact that most of the younger men enlisted in the army after their change of status to "friendly aliens." This failure of Jewish farming projects reflected Jewish experiences elsewhere, such as the farming projects assisted by Baron de Hirsch funds in New Jersey, Connecticut, and Argentina. Most were also one-generation farmers before returning to the city. Mutual Enterprises, a voluntary aid society providing assistance to the refugees, granted interest-free loans to refugees to help establish them in business. This was a great success, and a number of refugees were able to re-create their lives in Sydney because of the assistance they received from the AJWS.

In these early years, administration of the AJWS lacked both professionalism and compassion. The Welfare Society assumed a snobbish, patronizing attitude to the refugees and tended to treat them as charges to be managed rather than people in need. Frank Silverman, the general secretary, spoke only English and was very officious in his manner. The local Sydney Jewish paper, the *Hebrew Standard of Australasia*, acted as the official organ of the AJWS and published a weekly page titled "The New Australian," but the paper's editor, Alfred Harris, was not sympathetic to the problems facing the refugees. For example, he instructed the migrants to speak only English and criticized them for "congregating in

Kings Cross and Bondi, perhaps not realizing that they are looked upon as forming colonies which is positively undesirable." He repeatedly exhorted them to settle on the land in order not to undermine the economic position of the established community.[4]

In 1940, Walter Brand was appointed general secretary of the AJWS. He was to work closely with JDC official Charles Jordan, first when Jordan was in Shanghai and later when he transferred to Paris, a relationship based largely on correspondence, although the two men came to know each other personally when Jordan visited Australia in 1947. In 1948, Jordan wrote in a letter to Brand: "It is always difficult to talk about really important matters through letters,"[5] but due to the distance to Australia, there was often no choice. Through an analysis of the correspondences among Brand, Jordan, and other central actors, including Gertrude van Tijn and Emery Komlos, this chapter seeks to analyze the attitude and the actions of JDC in regard to what they called "The Australian Immigration Project." In so doing, it provides insight into the global activities, the tensions and successes, and especially the transnational networks created by JDC in the immediate postwar period, bringing together diverse personalities dispersed across the world, from Europe to America and Asia to Australia, at both the personal and the institutional levels.

THE FIRST AUSTRALIAN JEWISH PROFESSIONAL WELFARE OFFICER: WALTER BRAND

In 1940, Jewish welfare worker Walter Levi Brand took over the running of the AJWS Sydney office from Frank Silverman, serving as the society's general secretary for twenty-three years until his death in 1964. He was born June 3, 1893, in Hackney, London, son of David Brand, a horsehair merchant, and his wife Rose, née Harris.[6] Educated at the Haberdashers' Aske's Hampstead School (1905–1908), Walter visited Australia in 1911 on a business trip and then returned to London, planning to migrate to Australia. During World War I, he enlisted and served in the Royal Army Medical Corps on the Western Front, when he was promoted to lieutenant. Migrating to Sydney in 1920, Brand worked as a manager in his uncle's fur and hide business. On September 14, 1921, at the city's Great Synagogue, he married Vera Rosetta Davis; they were to remain childless. With the onset of the Depression, his business collapsed. Vera, a fashion designer, opened a successful shop on Elizabeth Street while Walter hawked vacuum cleaners.

In Sydney, Brand quickly became involved in local Jewish affairs. He served as a council member (1922–1946) of the Sir Moses Montefiore Jewish Home for the Aged and was an active participant in the Sydney Jewish Aid Society; the War Memorial's Employment Bureau; the Returned Soldiers and Sailors and Airmen's League, Jewish Division; and the New South Wales Jewish War Memorial, serving as its president from 1949 to 1952.[7] With all these activities, he represented a typical profile of the Anglo Jewish establishment in Sydney, with its conservative approach of being "more British than the British."

Lacking in formal social work training, Brand essentially operated as a professional welfare administrator. He served under three presidents: Sir Samuel Cohen, Saul Symonds, and Sydney David Einfeld, who assumed the presidency of the Federation of Australian Jewish Welfare Societies (FAJWS) after Saul Symonds's sudden death in 1952 and remained in this position for twenty-five years. Maintaining a scrupulously apolitical stance, Brand tried to deal as effectively as he could with government authorities.[8] From 1940 to 1949, the Australian Labor Party was in government, but in December 1949, it was defeated by the more conservative Liberal Party, which remained in power for twenty-three years. During World War II, he helped persuade the authorities to change the status of refugees from "enemy aliens" to "refugee aliens." He supported programs to bring out orphaned children who had survived the Holocaust and sponsored three himself, among them William Markovicz (later Bill Marr), who became his welfare "guardian boy." He wrote that when the first group of Jewish orphans arrived in Australia, it would be "the happiest day of my life."[9] At the same time, he maintained the necessity of rules "to govern . . . inmates" in the Jewish migrant hostels that had been established with JDC funding and could be condescending in his attitude toward the Jewish refugees. Despite health problems, he dedicated himself to his welfare work. He often met refugees at their ship's first Australian port of call, whether this was in Perth, Western Australia, or Darwin, coming from Shanghai, in Northern Australia. However, like his predecessor, he only spoke English, and he was hampered by his officious manner and his lack of Yiddish or any other European language and so found it difficult to reassure the newcomers. In the late 1950s, his role involved more administrative work when subcommittees were created to represent different national groups. In 1956–1957, he traveled with Jewish Welfare Society president Sydney David Einfeld to Europe and, at the request of JDC, to Morocco.

Despite his obvious limitations due to his condescending Anglo Jewish attitude, Brand was compassionate and cared deeply about his "distressed brethren overseas." In 1947, he wrote: "If I can be successful in bringing a large number of people from there I would feel that I have accomplished something."[10] He certainly achieved this aim.

A strong believer in the importance of newcomers assimilating into Australian culture, Brand supported the government's postwar policy of "Anglo-Saxon conformity."[11] He expected the newcomers to acculturate quickly by adapting Australian cultural norms and values, learning English quickly, and Anglicizing their names. He regularly attended annual citizenship conventions convened in Canberra by the Liberal government in the 1950s to facilitate migrant integration and was an executive member of the state branch of the New Settlers' League of Australia (later the Good Neighbour Council of New South Wales). In addition, he was secretary of the Australian Federation of Jewish Welfare Societies and a member of the New South Wales Board of Jewish Deputies. Survived by his wife, Brand died of a cerebral hemorrhage on March 31, 1964, in Surfers Paradise, Queensland, and was buried in Rookwood Cemetery, Sydney.

Brand's contribution to Jewish social welfare aroused controversy because his clients often saw him as being insensitive to their needs due to his officious, condescending manner and strict observance of government regulations. He came into conflict with the Association of Refugees (later the Association of New Citizens) over conditions in internment camps established for former citizens of Germany and Austria who were classified in the British Commonwealth as "enemy aliens." Initially no differentiation was made between Jewish refugees and German expatriates who were members of the Nazi Party, resulting in the Jewish refugees forming their own association to campaign for recognition of their refugee status. However, Brand warned the secretary of the Department of the Interior in 1942 and Australian intelligence in 1945 against the association's campaign on behalf of internees. He considered the association to be problematic because it was intervening in the AJWS's role as the official body representing the Jewish community vis-à-vis the government.

In the long term, Brand's inadequacy in handling the new arrivals created a sense of bitterness and resentment among many of them. Yet, as his ongoing correspondence with JDC representatives clearly shows, he cared deeply about his clients and was a dedicated, if at times very misguided, Jewish public servant. This dichotomy between Brand's behavior, which appeared to be uncaring despite his compassion for his suffering brethren, reflected the significant cultural gulf between the established Anglo Jewish community in Australia and the European Jewish survivors. It also represented differences between the monolingual Australian culture and the multilingual European culture. In addition, his lack of social work training was a major factor because he did not have the necessary perspective and skills of a professional social worker. He meant well but did not have the skills or methodology to understand the needs of his survivor clients to intervene in a professional way.

Postwar Jewish Survivor Migration to Australia

In 1933, Australian Jewry was a small, isolated community, consisting of a population of 23,000 located mainly in Sydney and Melbourne. By 1945, a further 8,000–9,000 Jewish refugees had been absorbed so that only about half of the Jewish population was native born, with the rest being divided between Eastern European Jews who had migrated just before and after World War I and Central European Jews from Western Europe, most of whom had arrived in the period between 1937 and 1941 as refugees from Nazi Germany. However, there was a clear ethnic divide in the settlement patterns of the Europeans between Sydney and Melbourne, with most of the Central European Jews settling in Sydney and the Polish Jews settling in Melbourne. Analyzing the results of a study undertaken by two social scientists in Melbourne in 1948, Oeser and Hammond explained the differences between the two European groups as follows:

> The Eastern European group is drawn from Jewish communities which were extremely closely knit, self-contained and strongly religious. . . . The Western European Jews, on the other hand, came from groups which had been at least partly assimilated to the national culture and their Jewish ties were correspondingly attenuated.[12]

As a result of these ethnic differences, the Western European nature of Sydney Jewry and the Eastern European nature of Melbourne Jewry were reinforced through chain migration, with 60% of survivors going to Melbourne and fewer than 40% going to Sydney. The Polish Jews were much stronger in their support of Zionism. Under the leadership of Samuel Wynn (Shlomo Weintraub), who arrived in Melbourne in 1913 from Ushiman near Lodz in the Russian Pale and had become a successful wine merchant, the Melbourne Jewish community was very effective in their organization and Zionist fundraising.

In August 1945, in response to the request to resettle Jewish refugees from Europe through family reunification by the newly formed Australian Jewish roof body, the Executive Council of Australian Jewry (ECAJ), Arthur Calwell, the newly appointed immigration minister, announced that 2,000 close relatives (excluding uncles, aunts, nephews, and nieces) of Jewish residents in Australia would be granted landing permits (LPs) on a humanitarian basis. All applications had to be processed through the AJWS with a guarantee that they would not become a charge on the state for five years.[13] Calwell's announcement led to an outcry against Jewish refugee migration, reflecting the strong antisemitic views, which manifested themselves throughout the free world both before and after the Holocaust, as well as the xenophobic attitudes of Australians. Indeed, in their study, Oeser and Hammond found that Jews were seen as "undesirable immigrants," ranking just above the blacks in their study of eight-race nation groups.[14] These attitudes had a direct impact on Australian migration policies because Calwell often bore the brunt of these criticisms, highlighted in negative cartoons in the press.

With the end of the war, JDC and the AJWS resumed their collaborative efforts and sought ways to resettle refugees from Europe, including refugees who were stranded in Shanghai. In order to assist with the facilitation of the migration process, JDC professionals visited Australia, meeting with Brand and other communal leaders as well as key government ministers and officials. The deep involvement of the different JDC-affiliated social workers, including Gertrude van Tijn, Charles Jordan, and Emery Komlos, in facilitating the migration of Jewish Holocaust survivors from Europe and Shanghai to Australia illustrated the transnational social space that JDC projects created.

Following Calwell's announcement in August 1945, Gertrude van Tijn, the first JDC representative to visit, arrived in Australia to visit her brother Ernst en route from Shanghai to New York, thereby bridging the transnational social space between her personal family connections with her brother and her institutional world working for JDC. As an example of the multiple and complex paths of some JDC postwar relief workers, she was a German Jew who had been living in Amsterdam since before the war. She was actively involved in refugee work there, and after her release from Bergen-Belsen in a prisoner exchange program came to the United States, working after the war for the United Nations Relief and Rehabilitation Administration (UNRRA) in Shanghai and then for JDC.[15] She spent two months in Australia from December 1946 to January 1947 with the aim of building a cooperative endeavor with the AJWS and the government. During this time, she met with Calwell to discuss the plight of Jewish refugees in Shanghai and Europe as well as with various AJWS officials. As the JDC representative, van Tijn was quick to recognize and negotiate the complex local political divisions, which were affected by the anti-Jewish migration hysteria, and she kept her overseas colleagues fully informed of the situation in detailed correspondence. She noted that when she arrived, Calwell had officially ceased issuing LPs for Jewish refugees in Europe and that they were being held up for Jewish refugees from Shanghai.[16] Despite the anti-Jewish refugee feelings expressed in Parliament and the media, she reported positively to Jordan about her meeting with Calwell but noted that she learned that in the future, LPs would be granted on the basis of occupations and economic priorities rather than family reunification. She realized that the Department of Immigration was still not facilitating Jewish LPs, and before her departure, she met with Tasman Heyes, the department's chief secretary. She also reported to Jordan that Australian LPs were being traded for money in Shanghai and that even Walter Brand was accused of being involved with this.[17] In addition, the community was raising funds to support the Labor Party in order to foster more pro-Jewish policies in terms of both immigration and Zionism.

In her report, van Tijn also noted that the picture of Jewish leadership was "confused and unhappy," largely because of "jealousies, incompatabilities [*sic*] of personalities" and that "competition between Melbourne and Sydney is extreme."[18] In December 1946, she attended a meeting in Melbourne of the AJWS and the United Jewish Overseas Relief Fund (UJORF), established during the war to send relief to war-torn Europe and led by Polish-born Leo Fink, at which Brand was also present. They discussed the coordination of reception facilities, and it was decided that rather than establishing a new organization, the activities of the AJWS and the UJORF would be administered jointly. Toward the end of her stay, van Tijn sent Jordan a further report, along with a list of the main Jewish communal organizations. She explained that Brand was the "recognised liaison officer between the Jewish organisations and the Department of Immigration."[19] She also predicted that the AJWS and the UJORF in Melbourne would amalgamate, a prediction that proved to be correct with the formation of the Melbourne-based Australian Jewish Welfare and Relief Society (AJW&RS), with Fink as its president in mid-1947.

In a short, formal report to Moses A. Leavitt, JDC executive vice president, van Tijn managed to cover all the major issues in regard to the general xenophobia and antisemitism in Australian society, the Jewish community's lack of professional structure, and the Melbourne and Sydney tensions. She recommended that an Australian Jew be appointed as a JDC representative, a suggestion that did not eventuate, and that Charles Jordan should visit Australia himself.[20] Brand, for his part, wrote highly of van Tijn, informing

Jordan that she was "one of the few people who have arrived in this country to carry out a mission, who is prepared to listen to the local bodies on matters of approach, and who is willing to see the local point of view."[21] Writing to van Tijn, he promised her that if Jordan did visit Australia, he would "do everything possible to make his trip enjoyable from the social

Charles Jordan, head of the JDC Emigration Department. Paris, France, circa 1949. Photo by Jerome Silberstein.

side and give every moment I can, so that he may be able to do all the work required and achieve his object."[22] Shortly after Brand wrote this letter, Jordan's visit became a reality, further reinforcing the JDC transnational migration networks.

Jordan was eighteen years Brand's junior, born in 1908 in Philadelphia. In contrast to Brand, Jordan was a trained social worker. He began his studies at the University of Berlin and then did graduate studies in Philadelphia and New York, receiving his master's degree from the Columbia University School of Social Work. He married Elizabeth Namela in 1931. Like Vera and Walter Brand, they were childless, with both men devoting themselves to the welfare of the Jewish people. Jordan was reported as saying, "Do I need children of my own when I have many thousands of them throughout the world?"[23] Before joining JDC in 1941, he worked for a number of different social welfare agencies in Philadelphia and New York. He began his JDC career as director for the Caribbean area, which had its headquarters in Havana, assisting German Jewish refugees fleeing to Cuba. In 1943, he enlisted and served for two years in the US Navy, before rejoining JDC after the war, as the JDC director of Far Eastern activities in Shanghai. He took over this position from Laura Margolis, who had worked in Shanghai during the war years and had played a key role in assisting the Jewish refugees. In 1948, Jordan was transferred to Paris, which after the war became the epicenter of JDC's relief and resettlement work, to head the JDC Emigration Department. In 1951, he was appointed assistant director general of JDC, and in 1955 he was promoted to the post of acting director general of overseas operations.[24] In 1965, two years before his death, he became JDC director general, based in the overseas headquarters of JDC, which were in Geneva at the time.[25]

Shanghai and Jordan's Visit, 1947

In October 1945, following further negotiations with the ECAJ, Calwell's humanitarian scheme was extended to include Jewish refugees from Shanghai, Manila, and other Far Eastern countries, including mostly German and Australian Jews as well as the Eastern European Jews who had managed to escape to Shanghai.[26] In November 1945, the classification was widened to include all relatives, with Calwell agreeing to accept a quota of up to 2,000 Jewish refugees from Shanghai.[27] This concession was important, as the 18,000 mostly Austrian and German Jewish refugees who had migrated before the outbreak of war in 1939 to Shanghai had been ordered to leave China by the Nationalist leader Chiang Kai-shek in 1945.[28] In January 1947, at Calwell's request, ECAJ President Alec Masel visited Shanghai to undertake the selection of 2,000 Jewish refugees who could be admitted under the new Australian quota.

As director of JDC in Shanghai, Jordan was desperately exploring all resettlement possibilities in 1946 and 1947. He had followed van Tijn's Australian reports with great interest, the two of them having worked together for a few months in Shanghai. Australia's geographic proximity made it an attractive choice. Calwell's offer of the new Australian quota of 2,000 stateless Jews in Shanghai raised their hopes.

Then, in July 1947, Calwell traveled to Europe to negotiate Australia joining the International Refugee Organization (IRO), which aimed to resettle the remaining displaced persons (DPs) in the camps in Germany, Austria, and Italy who had refused repatriation after the end of the war. Most of these DPs were not Jewish and feared returning to their home countries because of the Communist takeover of Eastern Europe. In addition to the Shanghai quota, it was presumed that a large number of Jewish survivors from Europe would be permitted to settle in Australia under the IRO umbrella, provided that the AJWS sponsored them and guaranteed their accommodation. In order to plan for this influx and to coordinate JDC involvement, Jordan decided to visit Australia. He spent an intensive month from August 20 to September 20, 1947, traveling to all the main possible reception centers in Sydney, Melbourne, Brisbane, and Perth, after which he wrote a detailed report.[29]

During his month in Australia, Jordan was able to develop a nuanced picture of the community as a result of the thoroughness of his approach. He visited the main institutions and interviewed key community members and newcomers, including both prewar refugees and survivors. He was aware that even though in theory the community was organized on a democratic basis, in practice the leadership was limited to a small coterie of people who served on the boards of several different organizations. He correctly identified that there were three main but very different groups—the Polish Jews, the Germans and Austrians, and the Anglo Jews—and that there was a "distinct difference between the Polish Jews on the one hand and the German and Austrian [Jews] on the other hand."[30] This led to conflicting immigration policies: Led by Anglo Jews Saul Symonds and Walter Brand, the Sydney community believed that "immigration should cover all eligible Jewish refugees indiscriminately, without considering their places of origin," whereas the Melbourne Jewish community, led by Bialystoker Leo Fink, "has been interested almost exclusively in the fate of Polish Jews, particularly Bialystokers."[31] Jordan argued that this state-based division made it difficult for the ECAJ to operate effectively.

Another aspect of Australian Jewish life that Jordan observed was the fact that almost all the work of Jewish welfare and other communal activities was carried out on a voluntary basis by lay leaders. There were almost no Jewish professional social workers or clerical staff to carry out the work. He described Brand as "the outstanding welfare administrator in Australia" but commented that "[h]e has great difficulties in finding staff and does a backbreaking job himself."[32]

In addition to these administrative difficulties, Jordan called attention to the anti-Jewish feelings in Australia, again perceptively noting that there was a hierarchy in terms of preferred migrants, with the first preference to Americans, second to Northern Europeans, and third to Eastern Europeans. He noted: "Jews are actually the last line. They are almost as far removed from the thinking of Australians generally as colored people."[33] Moreover, Jordan was aware of media criticism of Calwell, who was the target of antigovernment sentiment, and the enormous pressures on the minister due to his support for the Jewish survivor resettlement/immigration program. In a private letter to Moses A. Leavitt, he stressed the unpopularity of Calwell's immigration policies "with the crowd," particularly with returning soldiers who blamed the newcomers for the housing shortage.[34] Jordan's insight into the difficulties facing the newcomers adjusting to the Australian way of life is clearly demonstrated in the following observations:

. . . Australians are insular in their outlook, super-nationalistic and "against" everybody who isn't Australian, or whatever that may mean, including the British who, to their disgust, are called "pommies," which loosely parallels the terms "dago." The Jews, of course, are in a category of themselves, purely because in addition to everything else, they are Jewish.[35]

Jordan was particularly critical of the Anglo Jews, who did not react positively to the prewar Jewish refugees, whom they described as "bloody refos," accusing them of introducing "black marketing" and "sharp business practices."[36]

Jordan also felt that the local Jewish community had no understanding of what the survivors had gone through or how difficult it was to start a new life, sometimes for the third or fourth time. As he put it:

> Jews in Australia . . . have no sensitivity to the new kind of WELTSCHMERZ, the unhappiness of displaced persons, their trying to hold on to the crown of martyrdom, their last futile attempt to evade the gross reality of normal life, the life of a tenant and wage-earner, the loneliness of the camp-inmate who had dreamed of the luxury of a private room with bath, and finds he misses the canteen and all his fellow-sufferers . . .
>
> Social workers might wish to debate whether or not it is healthier to ignore these feelings, to force people to suppress them. I for one do not think so. I think that what rejection the refugees who have become immigrants experience, will make them into people worse than those who are now rejecting them. In terms of human relations I can think of no greater mess than is made by the Jews of Australia. Instead of contributing Jewish qualities as tolerance, forbearance, etc., they add to the typical Australian difficulties by overemphasizing differences and criticizing those among the newcomers they consider "foreign" to their ways.[37]

Jordan believed that the Australian Jews were "incompetent and amateurish in their fundraising ideas"[38] and that JDC needed to send one of their top professionals for half a year to Australia to teach the local Jews how to run their affairs more professionally, but this suggestion was not implemented. Thus, Jordan was critical of Australian Jewry for its unprofessional management and fundraising, and at the same time he also criticized their parochialism, with the latter revealing his compassion and insight. Both of these understandings were gained from his broader transnational experiences from his social work training and his work as a JDC official. This stood in stark comparison to the parochial Australian Jewish approach.

While Jordan was in Australia, there were two key developments. First, a conference was held in Melbourne, convened by Saul Symonds, to form a FAJWS, combining all the different state organizations, with Brand as its executive general secretary.[39] The second was the amalgamation in 1947 of the Melbourne AJWS with UJORF. In a private letter to Moses (Moe) Levitt, Jordan explained this tension:

> Brand and Symonds . . . want to allocate responsibility for absorbing immigrants on a quota basis. They dare not yet ask for control of finances. But they are opposed by Melbourne; it is primarily a fight between British-non-Zionist Jews (Sydney) versus Polish Zionist Jews (Melbourne). The Sydney group wishes to control the influx and the integration to make sure that the newcomers don't create difficulties for all Jewry. The Melbourne group claims (off the record, of course) that the Sydney group isn't really interested in helping people to come to Australia—or at least will make it as difficult as possible. There is no doubt, they have encouraged the government to take all their time. On the other hand, they were instrumental to secure thousands of permits originally by assuring the government that not all will be used.[40]

As a result of these tensions, despite the formation of the FAJWS, Melbourne and Sydney failed to work cooperatively. In the end, the JDC leadership found it easier to deal with Melbourne separately from the FAJWS, which represented Sydney, Brisbane, and Perth.[41] Under Leo Fink's leadership, in cooperation with the various mostly Polish Jewish *landsmanshaftn* that existed in Melbourne, the community was much more aggressive in sponsoring so-called family members, so that 60% of survivors went to Melbourne, only 40% went to Sydney, and a very small number went to Perth and Brisbane. The smaller state capital cities did not have the facilities or the Jewish communal structure to integrate the newcomers, so Melbourne and Sydney served as the major reception centers.

Australia was not the only Jewish community to suffer from such a dichotomy. Laura Hobson Faure and Veerle Vanden Daelen reveal a similar division in Chapter 11 regarding the tensions between the two major Belgian centers: Flemish-speaking Antwerp and French-speaking Brussels. Indeed, their subheading "A Small Jewish Community Divided between Two Cities" applies equally to Australia. In the end, JDC also found it easier to deal with these two centers separately, with Melbourne mirroring the situation in Antwerp. One key Melbourne Jewish leader in postwar Melbourne was Abraham (Roman) Leibler, a Belgian Antwerp diamond dealer who arrived in Australia in 1939. Other members of his family managed to escape to New York after the outbreak of war, eliciting further parallels between the histories of the JDC operations in these two countries.

In terms of local funding, Jordan was not optimistic about the ability of the local Australian Jewish community to raise sufficient funds for the reception and integration of survivors. The Melbourne conference passed a resolution requesting $100,000 as a capital investment from JDC to help in establishing migrant hostels. Jordan explained the reasoning behind this request in terms of shaming local wealthy Jews into giving. He also stressed that

> . . . such a move on the part of AJDC will have a salutary effect upon the Government, which will be pleased to know that the comparatively small Jewish community is being assisted by the large and wealthy American Jewish Community in its efforts to assume the responsibility for newcomers in Australia so as to save the Government burden and embarrassment.[42]

Jordan strongly supported this request, especially as it would encourage "the few responsible Australian Jewish leaders," particularly "Symonds and his associates," in their fundraising.[43] He explained that most of the funds raised in Australia went to Zionist causes, so it was much more difficult to raise funds for local concerns. He felt that the community needed a united appeal, like the United Jewish Appeal in the United States, but that the leadership was not yet ready to accept such a proposal.[44]

In 1947, Australia signed an agreement with the IRO and accepted a significant number of non-Jewish DPs, including 50,000 in 1949 and 100,000 in 1950. However, the initial hopes that Jewish survivors from both Shanghai and Europe would be included in these numbers were dashed through the introduction of discriminatory policies by the Department of Immigration.[45] This was due to the prevailing antisemitic attitudes in

A group of Jewish refugees boards the bus to Marseille; from there they will then emigrate to Australia aboard the *SS Sagittaire*. Paris, France, circa 1947–1948. Photo by Al Taylor.

Australia, which Jordan had so clearly identified. Very negative reports from Australian officials in Shanghai accused the Jewish refugees of being influenced by the immorality of the city so that "intrigue, sharp practice, crime, espionage and acting as agent provocateurs for foreign governments have . . . reduced the morale of the refugee population to the lowest levels of depravity and despair."[46] As a result, the 1947 quota of 2,000 Jewish refugees from Shanghai was slashed to 300, and the granting of further permits was tightly controlled. In addition, the numbers of Jewish survivors permitted to migrate to Australia from Europe were also restricted, with a quota of 3,000 per annum being agreed to in January 1949.[47] Thus, the optimistic hopes that led to Jordan's 1947 visit were not fulfilled. Despite these restricted numbers, the Australian Jewish community continued to be heavily dependent on JDC funding for buying up properties for hostels (and maintaining them) as well as for their other reception activities required by Australian antisemitic immigration policies.[48]

Jordan's Move to Paris

In 1948, Jordan was appointed to head JDC's Paris office, which was then JDC's overseas headquarters. He remained in close contact with the Australian Jewish communities, particularly with Brand, but continued to be highly critical of Australian Jewry's failure to fundraise successfully and to question whether they should receive further JDC funding. Financial problems continued to beset the FAJWS, and in 1949, the organization requested more assistance.[49] By mid-1949, Symonds decided that no further applications could be made for Federation-sponsored cases because it was impossible to provide the housing Australian Jewry had guaranteed in exchange for refugee admission.[50] The situation was even more acute in Melbourne because many more applications had been put forward on behalf of various *landsmanshaftn*.

In light of the difficult financial situation of the FAJWS, Brand wrote to New York to Emery H. Komlos of the REC, which was headed by Charles Liebman, begging that he or one of his colleagues come to Australia to investigate the situation. Komlos agreed to visit Australia on behalf of JDC, as well as the Hebrew Immigrant Aid Society (HIAS) and the REC, to study the exact needs of the FAJWS. Komlos had been involved with Australian financial problems since early 1949 and had quite detailed knowledge of the situation through his lengthy correspondence with the Sydney president of the AJWS, Symonds.[51] Upon his arrival in September 1949, Komlos held discussions with Welfare Society officials in Sydney and then visited the various Australian states.[52]

After his investigations, Komlos flew on to Paris, where he met with Jordan and wrote a preliminary report, leaving a copy in Paris.[53] Tragically, he died in an Air France disaster on his flight to New York.[54] Komlos's death was felt as a great loss to Australian Jewry where, as Rabbi Rubin-Zacks of Perth wrote, "his quiet, persuasive manner, coupled with singular charm and tact and added to sound knowledge and judgement, made him the centre of admiration."[55] In a confidential letter to Brand, Jordan stressed that he fully supported Komlos's recommendations. On the basis of Komlos's preliminary report as well as a visit to New York by AJW&RS President Leo Fink in November 1949, $200,000 was set aside for Australia in 1950 to be paid in installments.[56]

Subsequently, the Australians requested additional funding. The JDC leadership continued to be highly critical of the local leadership's fundraising failures, noting that they were demanding too much from outside sources. For example, in June 1950, Jordan wrote to New York, stating that although the Australian Jewish leadership was budgeting for an intake of another 4,000 DPs from Europe, he believed that the numbers would be much lower, more in the vicinity of 1,500.[57] In the end, Jordan's estimate was too low, as approximately 2,500 survivors arrived in 1950.[58] Jordan continued to be highly critical of the Australian Jewish leaders, noting in November 1952 that "they are probably asking for double the amount they are willing to accept, and that, in the face of sharply reduced emigration to Australia, we should keep our assistance down to an absolute minimum."[59]

At times there were fairly tense communications between Brand and Jordan about issues other than funding requests. For example, in August 1950, Jordan responded tersely to a number of complaints that Brand had raised. These included Brand's accusation that JDC was "passing the bad cases to Australia," reflecting Brand's concern about the quality of Jewish immigrants due to the antisemitic outcry against Jewish immigrants that had been so prominent after 1945. Jordan strongly rejected this charge. He also referred to an individual complaint Brand had raised about corruption in the allocation of cabins on ships traveling from Genoa. Jordan wrote:

> I thought we had gone beyond this sort of thing where every time a refugee makes a charge we assume that there must be some truth to what he says. Nevertheless, I appreciate that you should be concerned about this matter in the interest of the good name of the Joint.[60]

Other issues raised by Brand were JDC sponsorship of non-Jewish partners in mixed marriages, which JDC officials tried to police by checking the Jewish background of each applicant for assistance. However, there was always a margin of error by JDC officials in Europe, especially regarding married couples. In addition, there was the question of IRO funding for Jewish refugees, which Australia had insisted be dropped.[61]

Repayment of outstanding transportation costs was another point of ongoing contention in the correspondence between Brand and Jordan. They debated whether legal action could be taken on the basis of the promissory notes that the refugees had signed in terms of their repayment obligations. Brand consistently complained that those who were struggling financially tried to keep up their repayment while those who had benefited financially in Australia failed to do so or that they lied about the amount of money they had when they arrived in Australia.[62]

In 1954, Sydney President Einfeld again requested funds from JDC. He defended the community's record and need for more funds, writing to JDC Executive Vice President Leavitt:

> Yet, I do not think Australia has anything of which to be ashamed. Large amounts of money have been given by the Jewish residents of this country to Appeals generally, and I think I ought to remind you again that our intake of migrants is far in excess of our proportion per capita share

of those who have gone from Europe to receiving countries
all over the world, except Israel.[63]

From December 1953 to January 1954, Leslie B. Prince visited Australia,
representing the Jewish Colonization Association (ICA) and JDC to further examine the situation. He produced a detailed report,[64] and in a letter
to Jordan he was very complimentary about the welfare work undertaken by
both Brand and Einfeld.[65] But Prince also observed that the local dynamics
had not changed since 1947. On his return, he discussed restructuring the
whole Australian welfare scene with Jordan. However, these proposals were
not adopted, largely because the Conference on Jewish Material Claims
Against Germany (Claims Conference)[66] began to function in Australia
in 1954 and assumed an important role in the funding of Australian
Jewry's welfare and relief needs. JDC continued to be involved, serving
in an oversight role on behalf of the Claims Conference and visiting
Australia annually to assess the Jewish communities' requests for financial
support. However, JDC was no longer the direct funder of Jewish welfare
in Australia. When it became known that the Claims Conference funding
would end in 1964, Jordan made it clear to the Australian Jewish community that there were other parts of the Jewish world that were much more
in need than Australian Jewry.[67]

An Ambivalent Relationship

For seventeen years, from their first meeting in 1947 until Brand's sudden passing in April 1964, Jordan and Brand maintained close contact.
Although they rarely met during the intervening period, they wrote to each
other regularly. Jordan had ambivalent feelings about Brand. On one hand,
he was grateful to Brand for "the wonderful collaboration JDC has always
had from JWS [Jewish Welfare Society] in Australia."[68] When Brand
completed fifteen years of service to the AJWS in 1955, he praised Brand,
describing him as a "partner," a man "filled with compassion" and "executive ability and stature."[69] On the other hand, as previously discussed,
Jordan could be highly critical of the Australians, including Brand, when
writing to JDC officials in New York. When Brand was finally able to

visit Europe in 1956, Jordan asked Herbert Katzki, then head of the Paris office, in a confidential letter to ensure that Brand "be given as much attention as possible" during Brand's Paris visit in order to facilitate Katzki's Claims Conference visit to Australia later that year, implying that Brand was vain and self-centered. Jordan also noted that Brand was not "the most important man," referring to AJWS President Sydney Einfeld, who was also the president of the roof body of Australian Jewry, but that "his stamp of approval was needed" for all decisions made in regard to survivors in Australia.[70]

Brand often included personal comments in his missives to Jordan, providing a window of understanding into his life at both the personal and professional levels. For example, in 1951, he wrote to Jordan and his wife, Ellie, about his weekend retreat at Avalon Beach, a relaxing, beautiful spot with its own gardens, where he grew his own bananas, fruit, and vegetables. He stressed: "Just fancy getting away to a spot like that where there are no Jewish refugees and no one knows your telephone number." He then described the chaotic financial situation in Australia, with problems of inflation, due to the unstable nature of the Australian economy in the 1950s.[71] Occasionally, he also requested favors not related to JDC work—for example, to assist a Sydney friend in Europe or on one occasion in 1954 for help in retrieving from a Paris bank some diamond clips left by his late sister-in-law for his wife, Vera, and sending them to Sydney. In this letter, he described Vera as still being "the same dynamic, pint-sized motor."[72] He noted that not a week would go by without the mention of Jordan's and Komlos's names in their home.[73] He also expressed his frustrations to Jordan when Australian requests were not met. When Jordan defended the JDC record, Brand responded that he understood the financial challenges, but his complaint was more against Moses Leavitt who, he claimed, "sees red whenever Australia comes into question."[74]

Despite Brand's hard work, he did not visit Europe in person until 1956 because of lack of funding. In 1954, Brand wrote to Jordan expressing his disappointment that despite his dedicated service, there were no funds available for his travel and hoping that Jordan would visit instead.[75] This hope was not fulfilled until a decade later. A planned visit in 1962 had to be canceled because Jordan was suffering from severe arthritis in his neck.[76] When Jordan was able to travel again in 1964, Brand, who had suffered from a heart condition for years, suddenly passed away. Upon hearing this news, Jordan expressed sorrow that Brand would not be there to greet him because "he has always meant a great deal to me."[77]

Jordan continued to dedicate himself to JDC work and contributed to international refugee work in an honorary capacity. However, while in Prague on holidays in 1967, his life ended tragically, when at age fifty-nine his body was found floating down the Vltava River.[78] The Czechoslovak government claimed it was suicide, but JDC leaders believed he was murdered.[79] In its obituary, the *New York Times* outlined his outstanding service record and wrote:

> A tall, husky man, he was a popular figure at the annual United Jewish Appeal conventions. He was quick to supply figures of how much aid money was needed, without the benefit of a prepared chart, and time and again was sought out for advice on how to cope with assistance programs by both Jewish and non-Jewish welfare agencies.[80]

Despite extensive investigations over time, no hard evidence about the cause of Jordan's death has emerged.[81] His had been a lifetime of service to the Jewish people and the broader public, a dedication and devotion that is clearly revealed in his ongoing and extensive correspondence with Walter Brand and other Australian Jewish leaders.

Conclusion

The official and personal correspondence between Walter Brand and other American emissaries, including Jordan, Komlos, and, for a brief period, van Tijn, provides important insights into the life and welfare work of these professionals and the challenges they faced in working for the resettlement of Jewish survivors after the Holocaust. In addition, the correspondence between the JDC officials revealed tensions and dissatisfaction with the Australian leadership. The collaboration between Brand and Jordan reflected the "transnational social space"[82] at both the relationship level (through their personal contacts) and the institutional level (through the global connections of JDC). Inspired by humanitarian concerns to assist their Jewish brethren, the American German-educated professional social worker Jordan worked with British-born Australian welfare administrator Brand. Their correspondence traversed the globe, including Shanghai, Australia, Paris, and New York, indicating the transnational nature of JDC's work on behalf of the Jewish Holocaust survivors who were desperately seeking final resettlement options—an approach that has remained a key aspect of JDC's work, reaching out to Jews wherever they are in need. They facilitated the migration of the survivors, most of whom wished to leave Europe, which for them was a graveyard. Some wished to go as far away as possible—distant Australia was very attractive—but their migration was only made possible by the transnational personal and institutional networks created by JDC.

Thus, through reading this correspondence, the historian can gain a deeper insight into the global nature of JDC's mission and its efforts to rescue Jews both before and after the Holocaust and to bring them to the distant shores of Australia. The Americans persevered despite their frustrations with the Australian Jewish community, which suffered from internal divisions and limited fundraising traditions—features present in other Jewish communities, as will be discussed in the next chapter dealing with Belgium divisions. In this way, the refugees and survivors could find a safe sanctuary where they could rebuild their lives. This story reveals the critical role JDC played in assisting survivors of the Holocaust as well as the global and local political forces that influenced this relief work. It helps shine a light onto the global work of JDC and its pre- and post-Shoah efforts on the part of its suffering Jewish brethren.

NOTES

1. For a detailed discussion, see Suzanne Rutland, "Postwar Anti-Jewish Refugee Hysteria: A Case of Racial or Religious Bigotry?" in "Sojourners and Strangers," special issue, *Journal of Australian Studies* 7 (2003): 69–79; Suzanne D. Rutland and Sol Encel, "No Room in the Inn: American

Responses to Australian Immigration Policies, 1946–1954," *Patterns of Prejudice* 43, no. 5 (2009): 497–518.

2. Peggy Levitt and Nina Glick Schiller, "Conceptualizing Simultaneity: A Transnational Social Field of Society," *International Migration Review* 38, no. 2 (2004): 1006. For a detailed discussion of the *concept of transnational social space*, see Thomas Faist, "Transnationalization in International Migration: Implications for the Study of Citizenship and Culture," *Ethnic and Racial Studies* 23, no. 2 (2000): 189–222, https://doi .org/10.1080/014198700329024.

3. Levitt and Schiller, "Conceptualizing Simultaneity," 1006.

4. See, for example, "Editorial," *Hebrew Standard of Australasia*, July 27, 1939; Suzanne D. Rutland, *Pages of History: A Century of the Australian Jewish Press* (Sydney: Australian Jewish Press, 1995), 99.

5. JDC Archives, Records of the New York Office of the American Jewish Joint Distribution Committee, 1945–1954, Folder 96, Letter from Charles H. Jordan to Saul Symonds and Walter Brand, December 1, 1948.

6. Suzanne D. Rutland, "Brand, Walter Levi (1893–1964)," Australian Dictionary of Biography, National Centre of Biography, Australian National University, accessed June 29, 2014, http://adb.anu.edu.au/biography/brand -walter-levi-9572/text16865. This article was first published in hard copy in *Australian Dictionary of Biography*, vol. 13 (MUP, 1993). See also Anne Andgel, *Fifty Years of Caring: A History of the Australian Jewish Welfare Society, 1936–1986* (Sydney: Australian Jewish Welfare Society and Australian Jewish Historical Society, 1988), 221–22.

7. Ernest J. Burger, "They Serve the Community: Portraits of Jewish Officials—Walter L. Brand," *Young Men's Hebrew Association News*, November 13, 1947, 15–16.

8. "Walter Levi Brand (1893–1964)," Annual Report, AJWS, 1965, 17.

9. JDC Archives, Records of the New York Office of the American Jewish Joint Distribution Committee, 1945–1954, Folder 97, Letter from Walter Brand to Gertrude van Tijn, July 7, 1947. For details about the "Save the Children" and the "Jewish Welfare Guardian" schemes, see Suzanne D. Rutland, "A Distant Sanctuary: Australia and Child Holocaust Survivors," in *The Young Victims of the Nazi Regime: Migration, the Holocaust and*

Postwar Displacement, ed. Simone Gigliotti and Monica Tempian (London: Bloomsbury Academic, 2016), 71–90.

10. JDC Archives, Records of the New York Office of the American Jewish Joint Distribution Committee, 1945–1954, Folder 97, Letter from Walter Brand to Gertrude van Tijn, July 7, 1947.

11. Burger, "They Serve the Community," 16.

12. O. A. Oeser and S. B. Hammond, eds., *Social Structure and Personality in a City* (London: Routledge, 1954), 78–79.

13. For details of this scheme, see Michael Blakeney, *Australia and the Jewish Refugees, 1933–1948* (Sydney: Croom Helm Australia, 1985), 291–92; Andrew Markus, "Jewish Migration to Australia," *Journal of Australian Studies* 13 (November 1983): 25; Peter Y. Medding, *From Assimilation to Group Survival: A Political and Sociological Study of an Australian Jewish Community* (Melbourne: Cheshire, 1968), 151; Suzanne D. Rutland, "Australian Responses to Jewish Refugee Migration before and after World War II," in "On Being a German-Jewish Refugee in Australia," ed. Konrad Kwiet and John A. Moses, special issue, *Australian Journal of Politics and History* 31, no. 1 (1985): 42–45; Suzanne D. Rutland, *Edge of the Diaspora: Two Centuries of Jewish Settlement in Australia* (New York: Holmes & Meier, 2001), 225–29.

14. Oeser and Hammond, *Social Structure and Personality in a City*, 55.

15. For full consideration of her career and the controversies surrounding her work in Amsterdam, see Bernard Wasserstein, *The Ambiguity of Virtue: Gertrude van Tijn and the Fate of the Dutch Jews* (Boston: Harvard University Press, 2014), 234–37, as well as the transcript of the brief interview with her by Yehudah Bauer, 1968.

16. JDC Archives, Records of the New York Office of the American Jewish Joint Distribution Committee, 1945–1954, Folder 97, Letter from Gertrude van Tijn to Moses A. Leavitt, Subject: Short Report on Visit to Australia, March 22, 1947.

17. Ibid., Folder 97, Memorandum from Charles H. Jordan to Moses A. Leavitt, January 6, 1947.

18. Ibid., Folder 97, Letter from Gertrude van Tijn to Moses A. Leavitt, Subject: Short Report on Visit to Australia, March 22, 1947.

19. Ibid., Folder 90, Letter from Gertrude van Tijn to Charles H. Jordan, January 17, 1947.

20. Ibid.

21. JDC Archives, Records of the Geneva Office of the American Jewish Joint Distribution Committee, 1945–1954, Folder AT.9, Letter from Walter Brand to Charles Jordan, January 22, 1947.

22. Ibid., Folder 97, Letter from Walter Brand to Gertrude van Tijn, July 7, 1947.

23. See JDC Archives website exhibit, "In Memoriam: Charles Jordan, 1908–1967, Extended Profile," http://archives.jdc.org/exhibits/in-memoriam/charles-jordan/.

24. See JDC Archives, Records of the New York Office of the American Jewish Joint Distribution Committee, 1955–1964, File 1505, Press Release: Charles H. Jordan Appointed Acting JDC Director-General, December 22, 1955. Titles as per JDC press release.

25. Ibid.

26. Archive of Australian Judaica, University of Sydney (AAJ), NSW Jewish Board of Deputies, correspondence files, Box B40.

27. *Australian Jewish Herald*, November 16, 1945.

28. Suzanne D. Rutland, "'Waiting Room Shanghai': Australian Reactions to the Plight of Jews in Shanghai after the Second World War," *Leo Baeck Institute Year Book* (1987): 407–33.

29. JDC Archives, Records of the New York Office of the American Jewish Joint Distribution Committee, 1933–1944, Folder 438, Report No. 410, Report of Trip to Australia of Charles H. Jordan (Arrived August 20—Left September 20), October 4, 1947.

30. Ibid.

31. Ibid.

32. Ibid.

33. Ibid.

34. JDC Archives, Records of the New York Office of the American Jewish Joint Distribution Committee, 1945–1954, Folder 90, Letter from Charles H. Jordan (Charlie) to Moses A. Leavitt (Moe), August 29, 1947.

35. JDC Archives, Records of the New York Office of the American Jewish Joint Distribution Committee, 1933–1944, Folder 438, Report No. 410, Report of Trip to Australia of Charles H. Jordan (Arrived August 20—Left September 20), 12, October 4, 1947.

36. Ibid.

37. Ibid.

38. JDC Archives, Records of the New York Office of the American Jewish Joint Distribution Committee, 1945–1954, Folder 90, Letter from Charles H. Jordan (Charlie) to Moses A. Leavitt (Moe), August 31, 1947.

39. JDC Archives, Records of the New York Office of the American Jewish Joint Distribution Committee, 1933–1944, Folder 438, Report No. 410, Report of Trip to Australia of Charles H. Jordan (Arrived August 20—Left September 20), 17–24, October 4, 1947. Jordan provides a detailed summary and analysis of the discussions at this conference.

40. JDC Archives, Records of the New York Office of the American Jewish Joint Distribution Committee, 1945–1954, Folder 90, Letter from Charles H. Jordan (Charlie) to Moses A. Leavitt (Moe), August 31, 1947.

41. Ibid., Folder 95, Letter from Saul Symonds to Moses A. Leavitt, May 29, 1950. This was an ongoing issue.

42. JDC Archives, Records of the New York Office of the American Jewish Joint Distribution Committee, 1933–1944, Folder 438, Report No. 410, Report of Trip to Australia of Charles H. Jordan (Arrived August 20—Left September 20), 19, October 4, 1947.

43. Ibid.

44. Ibid.

45. Suzanne D. Rutland, "Subtle Exclusions: Postwar Jewish Emigration to Australia and the Impact of the IRO Scheme," *Journal of Holocaust Education* 10, no. 1 (2001): 50–66.

46. National Archives of Australia (NAA): A1068, IC47/3/15, Memorandum for the Department of Immigration Marked "TOP SECRET," Legal and Consular Immigration: Migration from Shanghai, July 22, 1947 (Note 82), 1.

47. Rutland, "'Waiting Room Shanghai,'" 407–33.

48. For more detail, see Suzanne D. Rutland and Sol Encel, "Three 'Rich Uncles in America': The Australian Immigration Project and American Jewry," *American Jewish History* 95, no. 1 (2009): 451–87.

49. AJWS Executive Council Minutes, Sydney, March 7, 1949.

50. AAJ, ECAJ correspondence files, Box E14, Brand to E. H. Komlos, July 18, 1949.

51. See, for example, AJWS, Sydney, correspondence files, Symonds to Komlos, nine pages of detailed replies to questions, April 5, 1949.

52. AJWS Executive Council Minutes, Sydney, September 6, 1949.

53. JDC Archives, Records of the New York Office of the American Jewish Joint Distribution Committee, 1945–1954, Folder 96, Emery H. Komlos, Survey of Jewish Migration and Settlement in Australia with Budget for 1950, October 26, 1949. Komlos dictated his draft report in Jordan's Paris office so that they had a copy of it.

54. Minutes, AJWS, Sydney, General Secretary's Report, December 12, 1949; *Sydney Jewish News*, November 4, 1949.

55. AAJ, Rubin-Zacks, Subject: Komlos to ECAJ, Standing Committees, ECAJ correspondence files, Box E45, June 1949 to June 1950.

56. AJWS Executive Council Minutes, Sydney, October 18, 1949; June 5, 1950; August 7, 1950.

57. JDC Archives, Records of the New York Office of the American Jewish Joint Distribution Committee, 1945–1954, Folder 95, Letter from Charles H. Jordan to Robert Pilpel (Bob), June 1, 1950.

58. Ibid., Folder 95, Letter from Robert Pilpel to Saul Symonds, June 16, 1950; ibid., Folder 95, Letter from Charles Jordan to Moses Leavitt, July 7, 1950. The final figure was 2,478. See Rutland, *Edge of the Diaspora*, 405, Appendix I.

59. JDC Archives, Records of the New York Office of the American Jewish Joint Distribution Committee, 1945–1954, Folder 91, Letter from Charles H. Jordan to Moses A. Leavitt, November 24, 1952.

60. Ibid., Letter from Charles H. Jordan to Walter Brand, August 11, 1950.

61. For a detailed discussion, see Rutland and Encel, "No Room in the Inn," 511–15. The issue of IRO funding is a major and complex story because Calwell refused to permit the IRO to continue to refund JDC for its

sponsorship of Jewish survivors to Australia, costing JDC over $1 million between December 1948 and October 1949. The Australian Jewish leadership was worried about antagonizing the Australian government over this issue, and indeed the JDC leadership was as well.

62. See, for example, JDC Archives, Records of the New York Office of the American Jewish Joint Distribution Committee, 1945–1954, Folder 92, Letter from Walter Brand to Robert Pilpel, May 17, 1951; ibid., Folder 92, Letter from Walter Brand to Henry L. Levy, September 25, 1951.

63. Ibid., Folder 95, Letter from Sydney D. Einfeld to Moses A. Leavitt, January 22, 1954.

64. Ibid., Folder 91, Report by Leslie B. Prince, August 2, 1954.

65. JDC Archives, Records of the Geneva Office of the American Jewish Joint Distribution Committee, 1945–1954, Folder AT.15, Letter from Leslie B. Prince to Charles Jordan, December 23, 1953.

66. For the Australian side of the story, see Suzanne D. Rutland, "Debates and Conflicts: Australian Jewry, the Claims Conference and Restitution, 1945–1965," *Dapim: Studies on the Holocaust* 28, no. 3 (2014): 155–72, https://doi.org/10.1080/23256249.2014.944023. In 1952, the West German government proposed that both moral and material reparations should be made for the destruction of European Jewry by allocating funds to the various Jewish communities throughout the world. In October 1951, representatives from those countries that had received survivors, including Australia, met in New York for the first meeting of what became known as the "Claims Conference."

67. JDC Archives, Records of the New York Office of the American Jewish Joint Distribution Committee, 1955–1964, Folder 115, Letter from Charles Jordan to Walter Lippmann, July 14, 1964.

68. JDC Archives, Records of the Geneva Office of the American Jewish Joint Distribution Committee, 1945–1954, Folder ADM.291, Letter from Charles Jordan to Walter Brand, August 30, 1954.

69. JDC Archives, Records of the Geneva Office of the American Jewish Joint Distribution Committee, 1955–1964, Folder AT.71, Letter from Charles Jordan to Walter Brand, April 4, 1955.

70. Ibid., Folder AT.71, Letter from Charles Jordan to Herbert Katzki, March 14, 1956.

71. JDC Archives, Records of the Geneva Office of the American Jewish Joint Distribution Committee, 1945–1954, Folder AT.7, Letter from Walter Brand to Charles Jordan, January 25, 1951.

72. Ibid., Folder AT.7, Letter from Walter Brand to Charles Jordan, January 13, 1954.

73. Ibid.

74. JDC Archives, Records of the Geneva Office of the American Jewish Joint Distribution Committee, 1945–1954, Folder AT.7, Letters between Walter Brand and Charles Jordan, May 19, 1954; June 2, 1954; June 25, 1954.

75. Ibid., Folder AT.7, Letter from Walter Brand to Charles Jordan, March 4, 1954.

76. JDC Archives, Records of the Geneva Office of the American Jewish Joint Distribution Committee, 1955–1964, Folder AT.13, Letter from Charles Jordan to Walter Brand, March 30, 1962; ibid., Folder AT.13, Letter from Walter Brand to Charles Jordan, April 5, 1962.

77. Ibid., Folder AT.13, Letter from Charles Jordan to David Einfeld and Walter Lippmann in Response to Einfeld's Cable with the News, April 2, 1964.

78. "Body of American Missing in Prague Is Found in River," *New York Times*, August 21, 1967; Irving Spiegel, "Investigation Is Pressed," *New York Times*, August 21, 1967; "Body of Charles Jordan, J.D.C. Executive Vice-Chairman, Found in Prague River," *JTA Daily News Bulletin* XXXIV, no. 161, August 21, 1967, 1.

79. "Czech Govt. Attributes Jordan's Death to Drowning; Claims Autopsy Showed No Violence," *JTA Daily News Bulletin* XXXIV, no. 162, August 22, 1967, 1.

80. Irving Spiegel, "Investigation Is Pressed," *New York Times*, August 21, 1967.

81. Dinah Spritzer, "Unresolved JDC Death Invites Speculation," *JTA*, August 30, 2007, accessed June 29, 2014, http://www.jta.org/2007/08/30/news -opinion/israel-middle-east/unsolved-jdc-death-invites-speculation. Various theories have been proposed, including that he was murdered by the Egyptian Intelligence or by Arab students after the 1967 Arab-Israeli War.

82. For discussion of the concept of *transnational social space*, see Peter Kivisto and Thomas Faist, *Beyond a Border: The Causes and Consequences of Contemporary Immigration* (Los Angeles: Pine Forge Press, 2010), 138.

9

Imported from the United States? The Centralization of Private Jewish Welfare after the Holocaust

The Cases of Belgium and France

Laura Hobson Faure and Veerle Vanden Daelen

INTRODUCTION

AFTER WORLD WAR II, the heavily damaged and decimated Jewish communities struggled to rebuild Jewish life in Europe. In France, 25.2% of the Jewish population of approximately 300,000 persons had been deported. In Belgium, this percentage was almost double: 46% of the approximately 65,000 Jewish inhabitants had been deported. Belgian numbers stood in the middle between those of France and the Netherlands. Antwerp, the most northern Belgian city with a large Jewish population, had lost 65% of its Jewish population (as registered in 1942), approaching the extremely high deportation rate in the Netherlands, where 83.6% of the prewar Jewish population of 140,000 was deported.[1] In Antwerp, all Jewish life was officially demolished, and the city was left behind by the Nazis as *judenrein*. In both France and Belgium, Jewish property had been looted. As Europe was liberated, people returned from hiding or safe havens abroad and, for a small minority, from concentration and death camps. Thus, each individual began the task of rebuilding his or her life with the aid of welfare organizations that had survived the war or were created in its aftermath.

As we know from the growing body of research on post-Holocaust European Jewry, American Jewish welfare organizations supported reconstruction, not only giving considerable financial support but also sending staff and experts to Europe. Yehuda Bauer's *Out of the Ashes* (1989)[2] demonstrates how the American Jewish Joint Distribution Committee (JDC) led these efforts in the name of American Jewry. The historiography has grown in more recent decades, especially after the 1996 publication of Bernard Wasserstein's *Vanishing Diaspora: The Jews in Europe since 1945*,[3] not least because of disagreement with Wasserstein's picture of demographic and cultural decline. Maud S. Mandel, for example, in *In the Aftermath of Genocide: Armenians and Jews in Twentieth-Century France* (2003),[4] counters Wasserstein's pessimistic portrait, showing that French Jews fought to "maintain a visible presence" as Jews in post–World War II France in order to rebuild a multifaceted Jewish community. In her book and more significantly in a 2002 article, Mandel analyzed the important influence of JDC on French Jewish reconstruction. The title of Mandel's article, "Philanthropy or Cultural Imperialism? The Impact of American Jewish Aid in Post-Holocaust France," suggests the dominance of overseas welfare organizations over local reconstruction initiatives.[5]

Indeed, theoretically, there were three candidates for the "lead role" in the reconstruction of Jewish life in postwar Europe: (1) local Jewish survivors and/or newcomers who organized reconstruction efforts on their own, (2) overseas Jewish welfare organizations, and (3) national or local governments. The last scenario never occurred to our knowledge, even though governments did play a role in the sense that they could facilitate or subsidize these endeavors (or remain neutral or even hinder such projects). Each of the first two scenarios came with tensions and challenges as multiple ideas and convictions clashed. Divergent ideas on how to organize Jewish life abounded, not only between "local" Jews and overseas Jewish welfare organizations but also within the local Jewish populations themselves.[6] Here, we seek to question these local versus overseas tensions and respond to Mandel's assertion that "No matter how resistant native organizations were to Joint intervention, however, their dependence on its funds rendered them essentially powerless. By using money as a prod, Joint [JDC] officials were able to induce local organizations to follow their rules."[7] Although we agree with the larger argument that European Jewish life was strongly influenced by American Jewish philanthropy, we also argue that the Americanization of postwar Jewish life in Europe was not the sole result of the financial dependency of the receiving party but rather a negotiated process in which local Jews played a lead role. This is not to say that power relations were symmetrical. By focusing on local responses to JDC aid in comparative perspective, new understandings of JDC's "Americanization" of French Jewish life can be obtained. Mandel based her conclusions on JDC in France, yet Yehuda Bauer's work demonstrates how the practical implementation of aid from JDC differed greatly from country to country and even in different cities within the same country. A comparative case study of JDC in postwar France and Belgium provides the opportunity, then, to build on that research to show that JDC was not always successful in its Americanization efforts even while providing needed funds.

This chapter focuses on the Americanization of European Jewish life by examining JDC's attempt to establish a centralized welfare structure for each country in which it operated, modeled after the United Jewish Appeal (UJA) and federation system in the United States. Before turning to the case studies, it is thus necessary to provide some background on the structure of American Jewish philanthropy in the United States and JDC.

Exporting American Jewish Welfare: JDC in Comparative Perspective

American Jewish life can be characterized by its highly developed network of private philanthropy dating back to the colonial period. At the end of the nineteenth century, Jewish aid societies flourished with the massive immigration of Jews from Eastern Europe. Seeking greater coordination, Jewish communities introduced the practice of financial federation (the unification of fundraising campaigns and the distribution of funds) at the citywide level.[8] In the interwar period, a nationwide federation struggled to emerge amid divisions and was finally established as the UJA in 1939.[9] The UJA united fundraising for domestic welfare needs in the Yishuv and overseas.

After World War II, as the foremost American Jewish welfare organization and main beneficiary of the UJA, JDC came to the aid of European Jews by organizing large-scale welfare operations in the displaced persons camps and helping local Jewish communities reconstruct Jewish life.[10]

Two policies, inspired by the precepts of American welfare, guided the work of JDC in postwar Europe. With the goal of rendering local Jewish populations self-sufficient, JDC policy stipulated that it would support local initiatives only. This policy, inspired by community organization techniques that had become one of the established skills of American social work, sought to build consensus and develop local leadership within the European Jewish communities in order to create sustainable change. This policy was often evoked in internal policy discussions, and it was used to persuade eager-to-help American Jewish organizations and individuals that they should support the UJA but remain in the United States. The case study of Belgium shows how in some cases, such as Antwerp, local leadership and self-organization were easily achieved, whereas other cities were highly dependent on JDC's input and know-how.

Centralization was a second policy to foster a coordinated approach to welfare guiding the work of JDC in Europe. The duplication of services was perceived by JDC as the first barrier to efficient welfare. JDC offices in all countries worked toward greater coordination. For example, in 1945–1946, the JDC office in France established a file card system on every individual who had received services from a Jewish social service agency. Although this was an effective tool for family relocation, its main purpose was to curtail the strategy of the *schnorer ambulant* (wandering beggar)—that is, individuals who sought aid from multiple sources—and to enable greater coordination among welfare organizations. With the goal of long-term reconstruction, JDC sought to establish a centralized welfare organization in each country based on the UJA model. Although these efforts proved to be successful in France, JDC did not achieve the same results in Belgium.

JDC in France and Belgium: Shared Policies

The comparison of France and Belgium is bolstered by the fact that both countries had diverse Jewish communities and held considerable hope for the rebirth of European Judaism after the Holocaust (even if the Jewish population of France was considerably larger than Belgium's). Other similarities, such as a shared JDC staff, reinforce the comparison. Indeed, as JDC social workers circulated in Europe, JDC policy remained relatively constant, even though local differences conditioned its application. For example, in both France and Belgium, JDC had three objectives: (1) emergency relief for survivors (e.g., cash relief, food, clothing, accommodations), (2) care for Jewish children, and (3) economic rehabilitation.[11] During the first two years after the liberation, approximately 95% of all funding of the centralized organization for Jewish aid in Brussels (the Aide aux Israélites Victimes de la Guerre [AIVG]) came from JDC. In France, JDC supported 72% of the expenses of Jewish welfare agencies in 1946 and 54.5% of these costs in 1949.[12] Without this extended help, it is safe to assume that the reconstruction and relief aid to Jewish survivors in these countries would have been greatly hindered.[13]

Between 1945 and 1948, the highest amounts of JDC aid were spent for relief in the displaced persons camps in Austria and Germany as well as in Hungary and Poland.[14] Yet Belgium and France also received a considerable part of this European aid. Compared to the size of their Jewish communities, Belgium received proportionally even more money than France, whose Jewish population was six times larger than that of Belgium.[15]

In the 1950s, JDC assistance to Belgium and France remained at a high level when compared with that of other countries. For JDC, France and Belgium held the future of European Jewry due to the size of their Jewish populations and the tenacious determination of the survivors to rebuild

Table 9.1. Annual JDC Aid to Europe, 1945–1948

Country	1945		1946		1947		1948	
	US$	%	US$	%	US$	%	US$	%
Belgium	1,917,000	10.83	1,801,000	5.38	1,354,000	2.94	1,024,000	3.31
France	1,998,000	11.29	2,831,000	8.46	5,906,000	12.82	3,583,000	11.58
Total Europe	17,698,000	100.00	33,473,500	100.00	46,054,000	100.00	30,945,000	100.00

Source: Bauer, *Out of the Ashes*, xviii, table 3.

their communities. The permanent presence of JDC representatives in France, including the European headquarters located in Paris until July 1958 (then moved to Geneva), as well as the presence of a local JDC office in Brussels from 1945 until 1950 and then again from 1959 onward, also played a role in JDC's hope to rebuild flourishing Jewish communities in these countries.[16]

These observations on JDC in France and Belgium point out the strong role of JDC funding in the countries' respective reconstruction processes and provide the needed background to explore the question of who took the lead in reconstruction by looking at the case of France and then Belgium.

FRANCE: REVISITING THE CENTRALIZATION OF FRENCH JEWISH WELFARE

As a result of postwar migrations, France was one of the rare places in Europe where the Jewish population was actually growing.[17] New immigrants encountered a diverse Jewish population in which divisions among French and foreign Jews persisted. On the collective level, ideological diversity manifested itself in a rich network of Jewish aid organizations that had survived the Occupation or had emerged in the immediate aftermath of the war. These organizations helped Jews as they sought to rebuild their lives and communities and provided an infrastructure into which American Jewish aid could be infused. Indeed, as discussed previously, JDC played a central role in France not only by funding welfare services but also by encouraging their centralization.

When Zionist leader Marc Jarblum returned to France from exile in Switzerland in the fall of 1944, he immediately began trying to alleviate the conditions of French Jews as president of the Fédération des Sociétés Juives de France (the Federation or the FSJF) and the French representative of the World Jewish Congress (WJC). His observations provide an idea of the challenges the Jews of France faced:

> Things here are in a complete mess, in incomprehensible disorder. Organizations and agencies are growing like mushrooms. This competition creates a duplication of services,

A visit during mealtime to Rueil-Malmaison, a home in the western suburbs of Paris for the orphaned children of French deportees. Visitors included JDC Representative for France Abbott Kaplan (in uniform), officials from the Oeuvre de Protection des Enfants Juifs (OPEJ), and an American guest. The home was supported by JDC and maintained by the OPEJ. Paris, France, 1946. Photo by Alexander Taylor.

and the results are pretty meager. The situation for Jews is far from good. Vichy law has been abolished, but from a material point of view, the return of Jews to their belongings and to their homes will not happen quickly. Everything is slow and while we wait, thousands of Jews remain in the same situation as before. . . . While we wait for governmental decisions, we need to do something about this ourselves.[18]

Jarblum thus criticized and justified the rapid development of the private Jewish welfare network that was helping Jews meet their basic needs. Jews of foreign descent who had their French nationality revoked during the Vichy regime or who had never obtained French citizenship were in a particularly difficult situation after the war, as they often could not qualify for governmental aid.[19] Children represented a distinct group: Beyond their inherent vulnerability, they required stable care and guidance that their missing parents could not provide.[20]

The FSJF provides an example of how one French Jewish welfare organization developed in a "cradle to grave" approach. Established in 1926, this organization had unified the *landsmanshaftn* of the Jewish immigrant populations in the interwar period and had provided extensive assistance to its members during the war. At the end of 1945, eleven cultural associations, forty-eight aid societies in Paris, and thirty-five aid societies outside the capital were affiliated with the FSJF. Funded by JDC, the WJC, the *Vaad Hatzala* of Palestine (not to be confused with its Orthodox homologue; see later in the Belgian case), the Intergovernmental Committee on Refugees (IGCR), and an Argentine aid committee, the FSJF and its affiliated aid societies were able to offer an extensive care network in addition to a program for children run primarily by the Oeuvre de Protection des Enfants Juifs (OPEJ), including fourteen homes. The total cost of these services in 1945 was $1.7 million.[21] In addition to its monthly newspaper, *Quand Même!*, FSJF board members and close affiliates ran two important publications, the Yiddish daily *Unzer Wort* (*Our Word*) and *La Terre Retrouvée*, both of a Zionist slant. This vast social service network was therefore connected to a clearly articulated political ideology.[22] Fiercely opposed to the FSJF, the

Communist-affiliated Union des Juifs pour la Resistance et de l'Entraide (UJRE) also ran a network of services, including medical dispensaries and legal assistance for recovering stolen property. Its Commission Centrale de l'Enfance operated six children's homes in 1945.[23] The Communist Yiddish newspaper, *Naye Presse*, represented this faction of the Jewish population. Smaller in number, the Bundists (the General Jewish Workers' Union of Lithuania, Poland, and Russia) also maintained a network of children's homes run by the Cercle Amical and a newspaper, *Unzer Stimme* (*Our Voice*).[24]

Because Jewish relief was organized along ideological lines, expanding one's social service network was a means of increasing one's political clout. This led to a strong expansionist tendency in Jewish welfare. A brochure published by the Paris Consistory in 1946 listed thirty-eight Jewish welfare organizations in Paris alone, without counting the numerous mutual aid societies and cultural associations.[25] The Oeuvre de Secours aux Enfants (OSE), which was the largest Jewish children's organization in France, was running seventeen children's homes in March 1945 and had over 3,000 children under its care.[26] By January 1, 1946, this organization had twenty-four children's homes and offices in fourteen French cities, where it provided medical care for adults and children, professional orientation services, and recreational activities.[27] The Éclaireurs Israélites, the national Jewish scouting movement that began in the 1920s, had developed a resistance network during the war known as La Sixième. In March 1945, this organization still had 500 children in its care. After the war, it also ran the Service Social des Jeunes to aid unattached adolescents and created a Jewish studies institute (École des Cadres Gilbert Bloch) in 1946, all while expanding its scouting programs in France and North Africa.[28]

Funding from American sources, particularly JDC, fueled this expansion of private Jewish welfare. Yet at the same time, as we will see, the American organization attempted to centralize and streamline aid according to an American model.

JDC in France

As they liberated France, Jewish chaplains and soldiers from the US Armed Forces actively sought to help surviving Jews, providing blankets, rebuilding synagogues, and organizing seders. These individual efforts helped bridge the gap between the end of hostilities and the reestablishment of JDC, which constituted the largest American program for French Jews: Between 1944 and 1954, JDC contributed $26.9 million to French Jewish life.[29] In 1945, JDC aided 50,000 individuals in France through its subsidized agencies, which represented between 25% and 28% of the estimated Jewish population at this time.[30]

Staffed primarily by US-trained social workers, JDC employees were especially shocked by the state of welfare services in France, which they found disorganized and overtly political. Arthur Greenleigh, a social worker who had previously served as the executive director of the National Refugee Service, was in charge of setting up the French program. Upon his arrival in December 1944, he criticized French Jewish organizations'

> tendency to "empire building" as we used to say in public administration. Each agency is continually reaching out for new fields of activity even though there may be three or four already in that field and no need existing for any additional agencies. There has been in many cases a political motive, either communist [*sic*] or Zionist or bundist [*sic*], etc. And we are expected to foot the bill.[31]

As Maud Mandel has analyzed, JDC worked progressively to impose a more centralized, efficient welfare system in France. Arthur Greenleigh first distributed JDC funding widely and then slowly began to increase demands on the agencies. In March 1945, JDC facilitated the merger of the three major relief organizations to create one centralized family agency, the Comité Juif d'Action Sociale et de Reconstruction (COJASOR). As early as March 1946, Greenleigh mentioned the need to create a "central committee representing all subventioned agencies, for purposes of planning and discussion of matters of mutual interest."[32] As discussed previously, in 1945–1946, JDC established the Social Service Exchange, the file card system on every individual who had received services from a Jewish social service agency. To encourage greater accountability, JDC set up the requirement that agencies submit monthly and annual reports and then began performing audits of their financial records. Laura Margolis, who arrived in June 1946 to direct JDC's office for France, continued Greenleigh's overhaul, adding budget cuts as a means of "shocking the agencies into facing reality."[33] Finally, in 1949, in collaboration with French Jewish leaders, JDC established the Fonds Social Juif Unifié, a centralized fundraising organization based on the UJA that was seen as the structure that could replace JDC as it gradually reduced its program in France.

THE CREATION OF THE FONDS SOCIAL JUIF UNIFIÉ: NEW PERSPECTIVES

JDC's successful importation of the UJA and other American structures in France has been attributed to two factors: (1) the financial dependence of French Jewish organizations on JDC funding and (2) the gradual process by which JDC sought to centralize Jewish welfare, allowing French Jewish organizations ample leeway in their programming.[34] Mandel has emphasized the power of its financial weight, pointing out that JDC used money as a "prod," leaving French Jews essentially powerless.[35] If this research on the French case largely supports Mandel's overall conclusions on JDC's fundamental influence on the structure of postwar French Jewish life, greater attention to French sources shows that French Jews were not "powerless": They did not passively accept JDC's ideas simply because they needed its money. Although JDC funding motivated French leadership, it was never in simple "carrot/stick" fashion.

Indeed, although French Jewish leaders initially accepted JDC aid with gratitude, they increasingly questioned JDC's role in the management of their institutions. This situation became especially evident in 1947, when JDC began to scale back its program in France. JDC budget cuts sparked protest from all corners of French Jewish life. One official from the main childcare organization (the OSE), for example, declared in the spring of 1947 that JDC was attempting to "transform the OSE into its own agency" and announced that "the moment had come to strongly oppose this tendency."[36]

Yet even before the budget cuts, some French Jews had expressed concern over JDC's decision-making powers. In December 1946, Léon Meiss, president of the Conseil Répresentatif des Israélites de France (CRIF),[37] voiced his concern that JDC was making decisions on behalf of French Jews without consulting them and incited the CRIF to form a three-person committee on JDC.[38] In February 1947, he spoke out again:

> The JDC, while providing a considerable amount of aid for France, does so in "splendid isolation" and is accomplishing its mission without consulting French Jewry [judaïsme de France]. Yet the moral responsibility of the Jews of France is still being engaged, and not just their moral responsibility: the current JDC budget for France is 50 million [francs], yet it cannot carry out this effort in the long run. It will be French Jews who will have to shoulder this responsibility.[39]

Evoking the dysfunctional nature of French Jewish welfare and injustices in JDC's distribution of funding, Meiss suggested in February 1947 that the CRIF expand its three-person committee into a twelve- to fourteen-person advisory commission on JDC that would represent the major French Jewish welfare organizations.[40] Meiss's suggestion provoked debate among the members of the CRIF and French Jewish welfare organizations.

The OSE, for example, voiced its concern over the implications of housing such a committee within a political organization (the CRIF) in an August 1947 memo, yet nonetheless supported the creation of a centralized structure to coordinate French Jewish welfare. Acknowledging the political divisions among the welfare organizations, the OSE stressed two important commonalities that could serve to unite them: (1) the common nature of their work and (2) their shared financial dependence on JDC. According to the OSE, JDC budget cuts made coordinating French Jewish welfare organizations more important than ever:

> As long as this [JDC] aid was meeting the needs of each organization, the welfare organizations could be contented with a direct relationship with this structure [JDC] and not

require an examination of the total needs and a planned distribution policy. But difficult times are approaching. Already, the funds made available to some have proven insufficient, and the prognosis for American aid is pessimistic. What will the thousands of children under the responsibility of the Jewish collective become under these circumstances . . . ?[41]

Parallel to the OSE's federative efforts, the CRIF voted to establish the Advisory Commission on the JDC in September 1947.[42] Far from being powerless, French Jewish leaders had chosen unification as a means of counterbalancing the power of JDC.

French Jews had thus already decided to unite in a commission when Laura Margolis, director of the JDC office for France, put into action JDC's long-term plan of importing the American fundraising model to France. In her accounts, she reports meeting with leaders such as Baron Guy de Rothschild[43] and then convening a larger meeting in the fall of 1947 that was attended by the leadership of the primary Jewish institutions of France: the CRIF, the Central Consistory, the FSJF, and possibly the Communist Union des Juifs pour la Resistance et de l'Entraide and the recently formed Fédération Sioniste de France.[44] An ad hoc committee led by Léon Meiss was established, and in March 1948 it took on the name Fonds Social Juif Unifié (the United Jewish Social Fund [FSJU]).[45] In October 1949, it held its constitutive assembly, gathering about 250 representatives from Jewish welfare organizations.

JDC's successful centralization efforts have been attributed to its financial weight and its gradualist approach.[46] However, a third factor deserves consideration: Some at JDC operated with a keen awareness of "American imperialism." Indeed, JDC employees had differing levels of experience in France and different approaches to working with this population. When Margolis approached Dr. Schwartz, the director of JDC's European operations, with her idea to import this structure, he reportedly responded, "Laura, are you going to try to make good Americans out of the French?"[47] Margolis's response, later recalled in an oral history interview, indicates a similar sensitivity to this issue: "I never expected them to take over the American total pattern. But I was convinced I could sell them the idea of building something more permanent."[48]

If Margolis and Schwartz benefited from a close relationship to French Jewish leadership and, in the case of Margolis, a strong mastery of French, this was not true of all JDC employees. Harry Rosen, a social worker specializing in community organization, was brought in from New York in May 1948 to assist French Jews in the task of establishing the FSJU.[49] His letters to JDC officials in New York demonstrate an attitude that was most likely interpreted by the French as chauvinistic, on one occasion calling French Jewish leaders "fickle, unstable"[50] and complaining about "the blessed French temperament which our French Jews have absorbed. It isn't exactly a '*mañana*' attitude. It isn't even one of not being concerned. I can't pin it down. Suffice it to say that the situation needs constant supervision and follow-up."[51] At one point in 1950, Guy de Rothschild sent a delegation to Margolis to announce the refusal of the FSJU to work with "the person" Margolis had brought from New York. According to Margolis, the delegation provided her with an ultimatum: "Either you get him out or we break up; we're not going to work with this man."[52] Guy de Rothschild reportedly told Margolis: "We're going to have our own man. You can teach him, you can work with him. We'll work with you and we'll work with him, but we don't want another American here."[53] Margolis respected the refusal of the FSJU, sent Rosen back to the United States, and took over his responsibilities. Contrary to Rothschild's wishes, Margolis was also American, and she certainly wasn't a man. The fact that the FJSU leadership found Margolis's solution acceptable testifies to her local acceptance. JDC's attention to the opinions of French Jewish leaders and awareness of "American imperialism" shows its concern over gaining French support for the FSJU, a key factor in the adoption of this structure by the French.

What we see here is that JDC capitalized on the desire of French Jewish leaders to influence JDC's policy: The CRIF's Advisory Commission on the JDC—a project designed to curtail JDC's influence—essentially became the ad hoc committee of the FSJU, a project envisioned by JDC. This scenario is thus more complex than JDC "flexing its financial muscle," threatening to withdraw funding if local groups did not centralize. French

Jewish leaders were not powerless, nor were they passive actors in the JDC centralization process. The case of Belgium shows an altogether different portrait of JDC's interaction with local Jewish communities.

BELGIUM: A SMALL JEWISH COMMUNITY DIVIDED BETWEEN TWO CITIES

The Belgian case study provides another account of the practical implementation of JDC's overseas aid. It not only brings a different perspective of JDC's activities when compared with France or other European countries but also testifies to JDC's diversified and pragmatic approach to dealing with local communities within the same country. Indeed, Brussels and Antwerp had strikingly different interwar and wartime experiences, which translated to distinctly different postwar developments. Whereas before the outbreak of World War II, Antwerp had counted the largest number of Jewish inhabitants in Belgium (estimated at 35,000 on the eve of World War II), the high deportation rates and the bombings on that city made Brussels home to the largest Jewish community. In 1945, Brussels counted an estimated 12,000 Jewish inhabitants and Antwerp only 2,000. By 1947, returning Jews and newcomers

Children living in a JDC-sponsored home take a ride in a JDC jeep. Belgium, circa 1946. Two thousand children were cared for in the JDC-supported homes and institutions in Belgium.

had made the overall Jewish population rise to about 40,000, a number that would remain more or less stable over the next decades. Antwerp's numbers rose to 10,000 to 15,000 but would not surpass those of Brussels.[54]

The unmistakable differences in the outlook of Jewish Antwerp and Brussels in the postwar period had already been noticeable before the war. Antwerp's Jewish population had a more Orthodox religious profile and was concentrated within the diamond sector, whereas Brussels' Jewish population was more diverse, from both a religious and economic point of view. Furthermore, unlike Antwerp, Brussels lacked a distinctive "Jewish neighborhood." The cities also differed from one another with regard to their welfare traditions. Since the end of the nineteenth century, Antwerp had had a continuously growing Orthodox Jewish community that organized its own Jewish welfare institutions, just as it had for religious needs and education. State welfare systems did not take the specific needs of religious Jews into account, which provided them with a need to organize their own system. In Brussels, the Jewish population was, in comparison, considerably less Orthodox and therefore felt less of a need to organize Jewish-specific umbrella organizations. Certainly not every Jew in Antwerp was Orthodox, but the biggest Jewish institutions in the city were Orthodox in orientation, and the rest of the religious and even nonreligious Jewish population adapted to these norms. The religious duty of every Jew to give *tzedakah* (charity) was pointed out more explicitly in Antwerp than in Brussels, for example. The close quarters in which the Jews in Antwerp lived and worked made for a sort of "social control system." It is thanks to this social control that a welfare system based on voluntary contributions could work (as compared to state-organized welfare, for example).[55] Different social welfare initiatives in the city had unified into the Centraal Beheer van Joodse Weldadigheid en Maatschappelijk Hulpbetoon (the Central Jewish Charity and Social Aid Administration or Centrale for short), a central social welfare organization, in 1920.[56] As a Jew in Antwerp before the war, one either gave money to the Centrale or was supported by it. Brussels, however, did not have this kind of centralized organization before the war.

Another factor—albeit not a decisive one—fueling the organization of Jewish welfare after World War II was nationality: Most Jews in Belgium did not possess Belgian nationality. Before World War II, only 5% held Belgian citizenship. (In France, in contrast, about 56% of Jews were French citizens.[57]) Noncitizens could receive money from the state, but Jewish newcomers feared that becoming a "burden" on the state system would reduce their chances of receiving Belgian nationality. And perhaps this sentiment was stronger in Antwerp, with its distinct religious, economic, and geographic characteristics.[58]

JDC in Belgium

Just as in France, JDC sought to organize its help in Belgium according to the principles agreed upon at its headquarters in New York and Paris. Even though the nature of JDC management was similar to that of France (with, for example, Laura Margolis in the Brussels office from 1945 until early 1946, followed by Beatrice Vulcan from early 1946 to 1947, and from 1948 until 1950, when JDC closed its Brussels office until 1959, Kate Mendel), the outcome in Belgium was quite different. Unlike in France and the Netherlands, where JDC had been able to establish and then work through one central national organization (the Joodse Coördinatie Commissie in the Netherlands and the FSJU in France), this goal could not be reached in Belgium despite JDC's efforts.

JDC initially chose to centralize its aid through the Brussels Aide aux Israélites Victimes de la Guerre (Aid to Jewish War Victims [AIVG], founded on October 11, 1944) because the largest Jewish population was situated in this city. Local committees of the AIVG were established to take care of Jews outside the Belgian capital.[59] This also meant that the Antwerp social welfare committee, the de facto continuation of the Centrale, became a local committee of the Brussels AIVG. The Antwerp committee, which after liberation was composed mostly of Jewish resistance fighters, changed its name in April 1945 from the Committee for the Defense of Jewish Interests to Hulp aan Israëlieten Slachtoffers van de Oorlog (Aid to Jewish War Victims [HISO]), the Dutch translation of the French name of the central committee, the AIVG.

The Antwerp-Brussels cooperation was very difficult. Nonetheless, considering the huge amounts of JDC funds that were only available via the AIVG, the Antwerp committee initially accepted the situation. Yet the fact that Antwerp Jewry, which could fall back on a well-functioning prewar unified welfare tradition, was forced to depend on Brussels played a very important role in JDC's failure to centralize welfare in Belgium.

The Antwerp-Brussels cooperation was not only difficult because of differences in tradition and know-how—it also had to do with major differences in the characteristics of Jewish life in both cities. Part of the leadership of the AIVG in Brussels originated from the wartime Communist resistance. These individuals had fought in divisions of the largest umbrella organization of the Communist-inspired resistance and had continued their rescue work after the liberation. Brussels also had members who sympathized with Communist ideology but who were not necessarily members of the Communist Party. This did not mesh well with the Antwerp Orthodox leadership.[60] In Antwerp, the left-wing resistance fighters were initially tolerated, but the return and growth of Orthodox and more central and Conservative political forces led the former to leave the organization in Antwerp in 1949, "not finding a possibility to work in such an unhealthy atmosphere."[61] This left few members of leftist orientation in the Antwerp committee, the most extreme of whom were now socialist Zionists. These differences made for numerous conflicts. For example, whereas the Brussels committee served kosher meals only to those who had specifically requested them—and then only by allotting the same budget as for non-kosher meals (thereby, due to the higher cost of kosher food, leaving less food for individuals who kept kosher)—the Antwerp committee served kosher meals to everybody from early 1945 on.[62]

Antwerp's Orthodoxy did not go unnoticed. A Jewish officer of the Allied troops added, when describing the dire situation in the Antwerp shelter for returning Jews in June 1945: "But, Gentlemen of J.I.R. [Jewish Institute of Religion], you should have seen the richness of a Jewish Sabbath here. You should have seen these people, some of whom kept Kashrut throughout their captivity, praying. There is more Hebrew spoken here than in any of our seminaries. There is more pride in their Jewishness locked up in this shelter than in all of New York City."[63]

The Orthodox character of Antwerp's Jewish leadership came to the forefront in the most pronounced way in discussions on the situation of Jewish children who were living in a non-Jewish environment after the liberation, either with Catholic families or in convents where they had survived the war. Brussels reacted in a pragmatic manner, placing basic needs before religion: The needs of survivors without a home, people returning from the camps and hiding places, were enormous. The Brussels committee did not see why they should hurry to take the children out of the environment in which they were being cared for, an act that would have added more stress for all parties. The Antwerp committee, on the other hand, reasoned more from a religious-cultural point of view: The children had to be brought back into a Jewish environment as soon as possible because their being Jewish was more important than their living conditions. They reproached the Brussels committee for doing too little to relocate the children. In these discussions, the Antwerp committee even alerted the JDC office in New York and other American Jewish welfare organizations in the United States about the fact that the central committee in Brussels knowingly left Jewish children in a non-Jewish environment.[64]

JDC had to recognize that the idea of working through one national Jewish welfare organization posed many problems in Belgium, especially because it had to deal with a very self-aware and independent community in Antwerp that did not need or want advice, particularly not from the Brussels committee. Furthermore, quarrels between Antwerp and Brussels occasionally gave rise to negative reports in New York on JDC's work. The local Antwerp Jewish community stayed closely connected to the Orthodox Antwerp diamond dealers who had remained in the United States after World War II. The latter were potentially major donors to the UJA—and therefore JDC—but equally to Orthodox organizations who collected funds outside the UJA. When Antwerp Jews complained to Antwerp New Yorkers, it was feared that such complaints could diminish contributions of the latter to the UJA. The JDC office in New York wrote to the local JDC representative in Brussels in July 1945: "[T]hey [the Relief for Belgian Jews based in New York] complain that the Antwerp community is receiving a very minor part of the relief which is being sent into Belgium by the JDC."[65]

At the end of March 1947, this specific situation forced JDC to adapt their working methods to the local situation, keeping Brussels the responsible central welfare organization for all of Belgium, except for Antwerp, which would receive its allocations directly from JDC.[66] To this end, JDC opened an Antwerp office in April 1947, but with little to do to improve local welfare services, JDC had closed its Antwerp office by the end of 1947, practically giving the Antwerp committee carte blanche. JDC gave the Antwerp committee a working budget, for which the committee was required to give detailed reports (although the JDC bookkeepers were never too sure they had gotten the full information).[67] The independent position of Antwerp worked against the JDC policy of establishing nationalized central committees; Belgium no longer had a unified or even centralized welfare system. JDC considered it most regrettable that there was not more solidarity between the Jews in Antwerp and Brussels who lived within such close proximity to each other: As one JDC official noted in 1959, "our UJA representatives in Chicago, Los Angeles or New York can go and run to collect money for problems in Brussels, for example. But the same appeal addressed by a Belgian collector in a Belgian city for problems of Jews in another Belgian city is rejected most of the time as being 'chutzpehdik.'"[68]

One can ask, then, why JDC gave Antwerp so much liberty.[69] The answer may lie in the working methods of JDC itself, which stressed work through the local community. The Antwerp welfare system, including fundraising, was effectively and independently organized, which was, in fact, the most important thing to JDC.[70] JDC representative Kate Mendel wrote to Dr. Joseph Schwartz in 1948: "I feel Antwerp has taken much more responsibility toward needy Jews than Brussels. While the committee in Brussels considered as their main objective to allocate the JDC funds given to them, Antwerp started at an early date to organize its own fund raising activities."[71] However, JDC representatives continued to use their own methods to ensure that every needy person was effectively registered in a common file in order to avoid the duplication of services, although in Antwerp the Jewish community had already set up such measures through its own initiative.

JDC was concerned about the level of social work expertise of the local organizations it funded. In 1954, it sent a social worker to review the effectiveness of the welfare services in Belgium. In Brussels, JDC determined that local social workers could clearly use more training to reduce the number of dependent cases in the shortest time possible. In Antwerp, however, the JDC representative disagreed with the Antwerp social workers' decisions to maintain receiving relief in only 12 cases out of a total of 245.[72] Antwerp had built up enough know-how and did not need the introduction of the specific American welfare structures, whereas Brussels was very interested in obtaining JDC's assistance, especially since it had a difficult time collecting its own funds within the local community. This explains as well why JDC had much more liberty to organize its welfare according to its own principles in Brussels: "The AIVG in Brussels looked forward eagerly not only to getting outside financial help, but also to receiving advice and guidance from the JDC wherever possible. . . . The HISO in Antwerp showed very early that they were eager to stand on their own feet and that they desired as little interference from the outside as possible."[73] A JDC field report on Antwerp from 1960 states: "What they need from the outside world is money, not advice."[74]

MAINTAINING JDC's ROLE AS THE PRIMARY AMERICAN OVERSEAS WELFARE ORGANIZATION

Antwerp's fight for independence from Brussels also challenged JDC's monopoly on overseas welfare, as seen in the case of two of Antwerp's Jewish orphanages, the Manaster and the Tiefenbrunner Homes. In 1945, JDC's condition for financial support was that the recipient organization operate under the umbrella of the AIVG, JDC's chosen central Jewish welfare organization in Brussels. However, as both Antwerp-based orphanages considered the AIVG insufficiently supportive of Orthodoxy, they challenged this requirement by seeking funding from overseas Jewish welfare organizations other than JDC.

When the AIVG opposed the Manaster orphanage's idea to send the children to Jewish day school in 1945 (the AIVG wanted the children to attend public schools), the local community looked for financial support elsewhere.[75] Late in 1945, the Antwerp orphanage—which would open a few months later in February 1946—received the necessary funding via the WJC, which could donate this money thanks to a gift from the Belgian Jewish Representative Committee/Relief for Belgian Jews.[76] Even though the funding came from Antwerp diamond dealers in exile in New York, the fact that it was provided via the WJC challenged JDC's goal of centralizing overseas Jewish welfare organization in Europe.[77] Probably in an effort to exclude WJC from its sphere of influence, JDC therefore agreed to fund the Manaster Home directly, releasing it from AIVG control.[78] The local Antwerp committee therefore brought about an early fissure in JDC policy to work via one centralized welfare organization per country.[79] In addition to the children's homes, the WJC's Foster Parents Plan was also taken over by JDC—albeit not without trouble.[80] Such negotiations with the WJC clarified the role of JDC as the principal organization of overseas Jewish welfare and most definitely played a role in the accommodating attitude of JDC toward what was now the largest Orthodox community of Europe.[81]

A second Antwerp orphanage, the Tiefenbrunner Home, was an Orthodox institution, organized by the Comité Central Israélite pour la Réorganisation de la Vie Religieuse. The Comité Central considered the AIVG anti- or areligious (distrust and conflicts were clearly present) and therefore sought funding elsewhere.[82] It found the necessary financial support thanks to the American Orthodox *Vaad Hatzala* (founded by the Union of Orthodox Rabbis).[83] However, a separate overseas welfare organization for Orthodox Jews was yet again an infringement on JDC's desire to establish a monopoly on overseas Jewish welfare.[84] JDC therefore began negotiations with the Union of Orthodox Rabbis in the United States, which resulted in a victory of the unification/centralization idea. On January 1, 1948, JDC came to an agreement with Rescue Children Inc., the Orthodox fundraising organization of the *Vaad Hatzala*.[85] This agreement stipulated that the Orthodox groups would entrust JDC with all the overseas welfare tasks, including aid for Orthodox communities and individuals. In return, the Orthodox groups would stop their separate fundraising campaigns in the United States and join the campaign of the UJA, which provided JDC with its operating funds.[86]

In Belgium, JDC was therefore to take over the Tiefenbrunner Home.[87] It had been agreed that the orphanages would remain strictly kosher and

Orthodox. For reasons of efficiency, JDC wanted to incorporate the orphanage into its Belgian structure, the AIVG, leaving the religious supervision nonfunded but in the hands of the Comité Central Israélite.[88] These plans led to such heavy resistance from the Comité Central Israélite—which had alerted the US Orthodox leadership—that JDC decided to leave the Comité Central Israélite in place as its local representative, directly financed by JDC.[89]

Orthodoxy was the key motor behind the Antwerp story. By firmly holding their ground and seeking financial support elsewhere, representatives of the Antwerp community made JDC support projects it would normally not have considered "relief." After refusing to support Jewish day schools in Antwerp for many years, JDC began to do this in 1954 (when the Claims Conference could cosponsor) and provided aid to Hassidic schools in Antwerp from 1958 onward.[90] A JDC report on Antwerp from 1959 illustrates this new attitude at JDC: "[I]f we really and truly believe in our purpose of wanting to reconstruct Jewish life in Europe, we must support rather the indigenous source and strengthen the core than those many streams and currents which have branched off from this core and which ultimately get their impulses and strength from that core."[91]

DISCUSSION

This research shows the strong response of local and transnational Jewish organizations in the aftermath of the Shoah to help meet the needs of fellow Jews. The reconstruction of Jewish community life in Europe was dependent on who took the lead in reconstruction efforts, who could rely on networks to bring in the necessary funding to support welfare needs, and which political and religious needs or priorities were covered as such. It is a story of spheres of influence in very harsh and dire circumstances throughout the Jewish world embedded in different national systems.

As the Belgium case demonstrates, it is also a story of official policies and exceptions to the rules taken in order to achieve the overall goal. JDC representatives struggled to balance the policies of the JDC headquarters in New York, the needs of donors in the United States, and the dominance of the UJA with the task of establishing efficient measures that fit into the local communities it funded, which also asserted their visions of reconstruction. All had their own objectives and communication; decision making among these different levels did not necessarily follow the same track. The JDC headquarters in New York were contacted directly by local communities instead of by representatives in the field, and JDC negotiations with other American Jewish organizations were not only determined by the leaders of these organizations but also by pressure from foreign local communities and their contacts in the United States.

At the same time, the case of France shows that sometimes European Jews and their American funders sought out the same goals, albeit for different reasons. For JDC, centralization was a necessary step for the long-term survival of French Jewish welfare. For French Jews, it was a means of counterbalancing JDC's power over French Jewish life. The decision of French Jews to adopt the UJA structure can therefore be understood as the outcome of a complex process and not simply the result of JDC's financial weight. Furthermore, JDC's attempt to import American Jewish welfare was characterized, at least in Paris, by a high level of self-awareness among JDC staff. "Cultural imperialism" may explain why JDC sought to import an American structure to France, yet it cannot explain how the structure was implemented and why it was adopted by the French.

Finally, when seen in comparative perspective, it becomes obvious that the success or failures of JDC did not only depend on the strength of local Jews to mobilize networks or the sensitivity of JDC staff. Important structural factors tempered JDC's ability to impose centralized welfare in Belgium (where the mentality of *shabes far zikh* [working in isolation] in Antwerp and Brussels made JDC representatives talk about Belgium as if it were two different countries).[92] In France, however, one sees structural factors that supported a centralized welfare system. Like French structures in general, since the end of the nineteenth century, French Jewish life had been fairly centralized in Paris.[93] Even if a vibrant Jewish community with its own distinct culture and structure had reestablished itself in Alsace-Lorraine after the war, the Paris-centric bias, present in French society in general, may have allowed both JDC and Parisian Jews to easily forget their brethren in the East. Although Strasbourg could have been "France's Antwerp," this clearly did not occur, although future research should explore why. Finally, the Jews of postwar France, while a politically and nationally diverse group, did prove to be more homogeneous from a religious point of view. These structural factors can help explain why JDC and French Jewish leaders were able to find support for the FSJU, whereas efforts to do this failed in Belgium.

It is clear that the postwar reconstruction of Jewish life in Europe is not an easy-to-generalize story. Even though the international key players were largely the same, local circumstances and structural differences within Jewish communities made for variations. However, by and large, the general view is one of JDC as the primary provider of overseas Jewish aid in Europe, becoming the largest sponsor (from merging forces with the Claims Conference in 1954) and provider of know-how and aid for the European communities. Nonetheless, local communities determined the variations in the story and explain the differences in Jewish life that again came into being in a Europe that the Nazis had tried to annihilate. The rebirth of European Jewish life was thus not only a story of "cultural imperialism." European Jewish communities mobilized strategies to assert their own visions, proving that they, too, were actors in their reconstruction.

NOTES

1. Serge Klarsfeld, *Vichy Auschwitz. Le Rôle De Vichy Dans La Solution Finale De La Question Juive En France. 1943–1944* (Paris: Fayard, 1985), 179; Klarsfeld, *De bezittingen van de slachtoffers van de jodenvervolging in België: spoliatie—rechtsherstel—bevindingen van de Studiecommissie. Eindverslag van de Studiecommissie betreffende het lot van de bezittingen van de leden van de joodse gemeenschap van België, geplunderd of achtergelaten tijdens de oorlog 1940–1945* (Brussel: Diensten van de Eerste Minister, 2001), 36.

2. Yehuda Bauer, *Out of the Ashes: The Impact of American Jews on Post-Holocaust European Jewry* (Oxford: Pergamon Press, 1989).

3. Bernard Wasserstein, *Vanishing Diaspora: The Jews in Europe since 1945* (Cambridge, MA: Harvard University Press, 1996).

4. Maud S. Mandel, *In the Aftermath of Genocide: Armenians and Jews in Twentieth-Century France* (Durham, NC: Duke University Press, 2003).

5. Maud S. Mandel, "Philanthropy or Cultural Imperialism? The Impact of American Jewish Aid in Post-Holocaust France," *Jewish Social Studies* 9, no. 1 (2002): 53–94.

6. As such, our analysis connects with Rakevet Zalashik's contribution in this book, which also seeks to analyze how JDC sought to transfer its structure and management to OZE in interwar Europe.

7. Mandel, "Philanthropy or Cultural Imperialism?" 64; Mandel, *In the Aftermath of Genocide*, 162–77.

8. Roy Lubove, *The Professional Altruist: The Emergence of Social Work as a Career* (Cambridge, MA: Harvard University Press, 1965), 186; Herman D. Stein, "Jewish Social Work in the United States, 1654–1954," *American Jewish Yearbook* 57 (1956): 2–98. By 1917, Jewish communities in forty-five cities had established federations.

9. Abraham J. Karp, *To Give Life: The UJA in the Shaping of the American Jewish Community* (New York: Schocken Books, 1981), 71.

10. Yehuda Bauer, *American Jewry and the Holocaust: The American Jewish Joint Distribution Committee, 1939–1945* (Detroit: Wayne State University Press, 1981); Yehuda Bauer, *Out of the Ashes: The Impact of American Jews on Post-Holocaust European Jewry* (Oxford: Pergamon Press, 1989).

11. Isabelle Goldsztejn, "Le Rôle De L'American Joint Dans La Reconstruction De La Communauté," *Archives Juives* 28, no. 1 (1995): 23–37, cited in Mandel, "Philanthropy or Cultural Imperialism?" 56, for the case of France. We join in this observation for Belgium.

12. JDC Archives, Records of the Geneva Office of the American Jewish Joint Distribution Committee, 1945–1954, Folder ADM 15, Appendix: Statistical Material, October 1, 1952.

13. Veerle Vanden Daelen, *Laten we hun lied verder zingen. De heropbouw van de joodse gemeenschap in Antwerpen na de Tweede Wereldoorlog (1944–1960)* (Amsterdam: Aksant, 2008), 96–97; "American Joint Distribution Committee," in *Neues Lexikon des Judentums*, ed. Julius H. Schoeps (Gütersloh: Güthersloher Verlagshaus, 2000), 46–47; Hanne Hellemans, *'Zij die verloren zijn, zullen niet vergeten worden' (II Samuel 14:14). Pogingen tot herintegratie van de kinderen in de joodse gemeenschap na de Tweede Wereldoorlog. Een ideologisch debat* (unpublished thesis, University of Ghent,

2002), 63–64; Laura Hobson Faure, *Un "Plan Marshall Juif": La présence juive américaine en France après la Shoah, 1944–1954* (Paris: Editions Armand Colin, 2013); Bauer, *Out of the Ashes*, xviii, Table 2.

14. Bauer, *Out of the Ashes*, xviii, Table 3.

15. Maurice J. Goldbloom, "5706 (1945–1946): France/Belgium," *American Jewish Year Book* 47 (5707): 289–95; Maurice J. Goldbloom, "5709 (1948–1949): France/Belgium," *American Jewish Year Book* 51 (1950), 300–306. In 1945–1946, these populations were estimated at 30,000 and 180,000 for Belgium and France, respectively. By 1948–1949, these populations had grown to an estimated 42,000 and 250,000, respectively.

16. Vanden Daelen, *Laten we hun lied verder zingen*, 97–98, 103–7.

17. Anne Grynberg, "Après la tourmente," in *Les Juifs de France. De la Révolution française à nos jours*, ed. Jean-Jacques Becker et Annette Wieviorka (Paris: Liana Levi, 1998), 267.

18. American Jewish Archives, World Jewish Congress (Collection 361), H 115/7, Letter from Marc Jarblum to Nahum Goldmann, November 21, 1944. This citation and all further citations from French have been translated by the authors.

19. Mandel, *In the Aftermath of Genocide*, 62–64. Mandel has pointed out that aid and services provided by the French government were often inadequate for French Jews, who had lost their support networks. A one-time payment of 5,000 francs (later raised to 8,000 francs), along with a ration book for clothing, transportation, and medical care for nine months, was technically provided to all returning deportees, regardless of the reason for deportation. Yet unnaturalized, foreign-born Jews often didn't qualify for governmental aid, and others had difficulties accessing it. Other times, funds were simply not available for those who did qualify.

20. On the central place of children in French Jewish reconstruction, see Daniella Doron, *Jewish Youth and Identity in Postwar France* (Bloomington: Indiana University Press, 2015), 31–73.

21. Archives Nationales (AN), AJ/43, File 1252, Fédération des Sociétés Juives de France, Rapport général d'activité, 1945.

22. Marc Jarblum began publishing *Unzer Wort* in 1944. Joseph Fisher and Israël and Jules Jefroykin were involved in the publication of *La Terre*

Retrouvée, which was affiliated with the National Fund (KKL) and had been published since 1928.

23. Katy Hazan, *Les Orphelins de la Shoah: Les maisons de l'espoir, 1944–1960* (Paris: Les Belles Lettres, 2003), 399. For a fictional account of the Communist Jewish children's homes, see Robert Bober, *Berg et Beck* (Paris: Gallimard, 1999).

24. YIVO, American Jewish Committee RG-347.7.1, FAD 1, Box 20, File: France Jews 1943–1961, Non-titled Report on the Jewish Community in France, 1954. In 1954, the American Jewish Committee estimated the circulation of the *Naye Presse* to be at 4,500; that of *Unzer Wort* to be at 4,000 in France and 1,800 elsewhere in Europe; and that of *Unzer Stimme*, the Bundist newspaper, to be at 500 to 700.

25. Consistoire Israélite de Paris, *La communauté de Paris après la Libération* (Paris: Consistoire Israélite de Paris, 1946).

26. JDC Archives, Records of the New York Office of the American Jewish Joint Distribution Committee, 1945–1954, Folder 249, Letter from Louis H. Sobel to Edward O'Conner, July 13, 1945. On the OSE, see Laura Hobson Faure, Mathias Gardet, Katy Hazan, and Catherine Nicault, eds., *L'Œuvre de Secours aux enfants et les populations juives au xxe siècle, Prévenir et guérir dans un siècle de violence* (Paris: Armand Colin, 2014).

27. AN, AJ 43/1252, Role de l'Œuvre de Secours aux Enfants OSE en tant qu'agent bénévole du Comité Intergouvernemental pour les réfugiés, Extrait du rapport general d'activité de 1945, January 1946.

28. JDC Archives, Records of the New York Office of the American Jewish Joint Distribution Committee, 1945–1954, Folder 249, Letter from Louis H. Sobel to Edward O'Conner, Subject: Child Care in France under the Auspices of the American Jewish Joint Distribution Committee, July 13, 1945; JDC Archives, Records of the Geneva Office of the American Jewish Joint Distribution Committee, 1945–1954, Folder FR.407, Memorandum from Laura L. Margolis to M. W. Beckelman, December 18, 1948.

29. JDC Archives, Reference folder: France, Report by Loeb and Troper, October 1914 through December 31, 1973.

30. JDC Archives, *JDC Primer*, p. France-8. This range is based on a Jewish population of 180,000 and 200,000, as estimated by A. Wieviorka, "Les

Juifs en France au lendemain de la guerre: état des lieux," *Archives Juives* 28, no. 1 (1995): 4–22.

31. JDC Archives, Records of the New York Office of the American Jewish Joint Distribution Committee, 1945–1954, Folder 247, Letter from Arthur Greenleigh to Moses Leavitt, April 7, 1945.

32. Ibid., Folder 247, Arthur D. Greenleigh, Monthly Report for November and December 1945, March 5, 1946.

33. Ibid., Folder 249, Report of Child Care Department, Office for France from October 1946 to October 1948, April 1, 1949.

34. Mandel, "Philanthropy or Cultural Imperialism?" 63. "Centralization worked precisely because the Joint did not immediately impose its own social agenda on the agencies it supported." On the creation of the FSJU and similar structures in the Netherlands and Belgium, see also David Weinberg, *Recovering a Voice: Western European Jewish Communities after the Holocaust* (Oxford: The Littman Library of Jewish Civilization, 2015), 115–23.

35. Mandel, "Philanthropy or Cultural Imperialism?" 64.

36. OSE Headquarters Archives, Archives de direction 1948–1952 (uncatalogued), Procès-verbal de la réunion du conseil de la direction, May 16, 1947.

37. This organization was formed in 1943 by French Jews to politically represent the different factions of French Jewish life. On its activities in the postwar period, see Samuel Ghiles-Meilhac, "Centralizing the Political Jewish Voice in Post-Holocaust France," in *Post-Holocaust France and the Jews, 1945–1955*, ed. Sean Hand and Steven Katz (New York: New York University Press, 2015), 58–70.

38. Centre de Documentation Juive Contemporaine (CDJC), Archives CRIF, Fonds MDI, Carton 1, Procès-Verbal, December 1946.

39. Centre de Documentation Juive Contemporaine (CDJC), Archives CRIF, Fonds MDI, Carton 1, Procès-Verbal, February 4, 1947.

40. Centre de Documentation Juive Contemporaine (CDJC), Archives CRIF, Fonds MDI, Boîte 1, Procès-Verbal, February 4, 1947.

41. Centre de Documentation Juive Contemporaine (CDJC), Fonds OSE, OSE (1–191), Projet de création d'un Comité de coordination des œuvres sociales juives de France, August 5, 1947.

42. Centre de Documentation Juive Contemporaine (CDJC), Archives CRIF, Fonds MDI, Boîte 1, Procès-Verbal, September 22, 1947. Potential members included Meiss, Adam, Fisher, Kelman or Jarblum, Braunschvig, Guy de Rothschild, Racine, E. Dreyfus, A. Kahn, Katlin, Halter, F. Schrager, E. Lévy, A. Meyer, and several others.

43. JDC Archives, Records of the New York Office of the American Jewish Joint Distribution Committee, 1945–1954, Folder 258, Letter from AJDC Paris to B. M. Joffe, Subject: Your Letter #3013—Survey of Relief Rolls in France, October 2, 1947.

44. JDC Archives, Individual Files, Laura Margolis Jarblum, Reflections on the Creation of the Fond [*sic*] Social Juif Unifié and Excerpts from the JDC Office for France Report to the Joint Distribution Committee Headquarters in Paris and New York, May 17, 1981; Raphaël Elmaleh, *1950–2000 Fonds Social Juif Unifié. L'espoir en mouvement* (Paris: Fonds Social Juif Unifié, 2000), 13. According to Elmaleh, this meeting took place on October 12, 1947.

45. Elmaleh, *1950–2000 Fonds Social Juif Unifié*, 13.

46. Mandel, "Philanthropy or Cultural Imperialism?" 63–64.

47. Oral History Division of the Avraham Harman Institute for Contemporary Jewry, Israel (128) 56, Laura Margolis Jarblum Interview, 34.

48. Oral History Division of the Avraham Harman Institute for Contemporary Jewry, Israel (128) 56, Laura Margolis Jarblum Interview, 34.

49. Mandel bases some of her conclusions on JDC on statements made by Harry Rosen, yet he was a prime example of an American expert who blindly applied American theory to the French context.

50. JDC Archives, Records of the New York Office of the American Jewish Joint Distribution Committee, 1945–1954, Folder 287, Memorandum from Harry Rosen to Mr. Philip Skorneck, Subject: Progress Report on United Campaign for France, June 22, 1948.

51. Ibid., Folder 287, Memorandum from Harry Rosen to Mr. Philip Skorneck, Subject: Progress Report on United Campaign for France, June 22, 1948.

52. Oral History Division of the Avraham Harman Institute for Contemporary Jewry, Israel (128) 56, Laura Margolis Jarblum Interview, 34.

53. Ibid. Margolis does not date this event, which most likely occurred in November 1950. Rosen's departure was discussed by his JDC colleagues

and was attributed to the poor FSJU campaign results and conflict with the "French Jewish community" (JDC Archives, Records of the New York Office of the American Jewish Joint Distribution Committee, 1945–1954, Herman Stein Papers, Box 1, Letter from H. Selver to H. Stein, November 21, 1950).

54. Vanden Daelen, *Laten we hun lied verder zingen*, 27–43.

55. Ibid., 111–12; Derek J. Penslar, "The Origins of Modern Jewish Philanthropy," in *Philanthropy in the World's Traditions*, ed. Warren F. Ilchman, Stanley N. Katz, and Edward L. Queen II (Bloomington: Indiana University Press, 1998), 197–209.

56. Roger Van Ransbeek, *50 jaar Centraal Beheer van Joodse Weldadigheid en Maatschappelijk Hulpbetoon (1920–1970)* (Antwerpen: Centrale, 1970), 71; Andrée Katz, *75 jaar Centrale. Armoede en Uitsluiting . . . een uitdaging!* (Antwerpen: De Vries-Brouwers, 1995), 42.

57. *De bezittingen van de slachtoffers van de jodenvervolging in België*, 36.

58. Vanden Daelen, *Laten we hun lied verder zingen*, 39–41, 107–18, 264–68.

59. Vanden Daelen, *Laten we hun lied verder zingen*, 44, 107–9; Archives Service Social Juif, Brussels, "Appel à la population juive de Belgique," *L'Appel (Bulletin mensuel d'informations de l'asbl Aide aux Israélites Victimes de la Guerre)* 2 (May 1947), 3–4; Cathérine Massange, *Bâtir le lendemain. L'Aide aux Israélites victimes de la Guerre et le Service Social Juif de 1944 à nos jours* (Bruxelles: Didier Devillez Editeur, 2002), 220.

60. Vanden Daelen, *Laten we hun lied verder zingen*, 109–10; American Jewish Archives, World Jewish Congress (Collection 361), H60/1, Wolkowicz aan Tartakower, January 14, 1946; ALR from SWD, January 23, 1946, "Rapport sur la situation des Juifs en Belgique et sur l'activité du Conseil," March 11, 1946, plus handwritten notes in the same file.

61. S.n., "Fun yidishn lebn in Belgye. Fun Antverpn: Algemeyne farzamlung fun 'Hiso,'" *Unzer Vort (Brisl)* (March 11, 1949), 2. Yiddish translations by the authors.

62. Vanden Daelen, *Laten we hun lied verder zingen*, 119. Immediately after the liberation, the Antwerp committee had been serving non-kosher meals but changed this pretty quickly—at the beginning of 1945—into strictly kosher meals only.

63. American Jewish Archives, World Jewish Congress (Collection 361), D 78/15, Belgium, Children, January to September 1945, A Letter from Warrant Officer Herbert Weiner to Mr. Jacobs at the Jewish Institute of Religion, June 17, 1945.

64. Vanden Daelen, *Laten we hun lied verder zingen*, 271–79.

65. JDC Archives, Records of the New York Office of the American Jewish Joint Distribution Committee, 1945–1954, Folder 149, Letter from Moses A. Leavitt to Laura Margolis, July 27, 1945.

66. Ibid., Folder 149, Report of JDC, Belgium, Activities—1947, 2, May 15, 1948; Felixarchief Antwerp, MA 26.344, Doss XV e 3, Doc. 28: S. Turksma, "Ledenvergadering HISO," *Nieuw Israëlietisch Weekblad (Belgische Editie)* 78, no. 20 (May 2, 1947—12 Ijar 5707), 3.

67. JDC Archives, Records of the New York Office of the American Jewish Joint Distribution Committee, 1945–1954, Folder 149, Report of JDC, Belgium, Activities—1947, 2, May 15, 1948; Vanden Daelen, *Laten we hun lied verder zingen*, 113.

68. Translated from French: s.n., "M. L. Seidenman parle de 'l'American Joint Distribution Committee' en Belgique," *Centrale* VI, no. 24 (June 1959): 13.

69. Archival evidence on the split between Brussels and Antwerp and the closure of the JDC office in Antwerp is scarce.

70. Fully nationwide centralized funding campaigns did not develop in Belgium (as opposed to what is stated in Weinberg, *Recovering a Voice*, 117–18).

71. JDC Archives, Records of the Geneva Office of the American Jewish Joint Distribution Committee, 1945–1954, Folder BG.86, Letter from Kate Mendel to Dr. Joseph J. Schwartz, Subject: HISO Antwerp, August 17, 1948.

72. S.n., "Jaarverslag en werkzaamheden der Centrale 1954. Algemene vergadering 8 januari 1955," *Centrale* II, no. 7 (April 1955): 3. In eleven of these twelve cases, the JDC representative was indeed successful in making the recipients self-sufficient. S.n., "Martin Greenberg gaat weg," *Centrale* VII, no. 28 (June 1960): 15–16. Martin Greenberg of JDC came to help modernize the *Centrale*'s membership recruitment system.

73. JDC Archives, Records of the New York Office of the American Jewish Joint Distribution Committee, 1945–1954, Folder 149, Report of JDC, Belgium, Activities—1947, 1, May 15, 1948.

74. JDC Archives, Records of the New York Office of the American Jewish Joint Distribution Committee, 1955–1964, Folder 138, Field Report on Antwerp, June 7, 1960, June 7, 1960.

75. American Jewish Archives, World Jewish Congress (Collection 361), D78/15, Report to Dr. A. Leon Kubowitzki, Headquarters, New York, from Sophie Perelman, Secretary, WJC Office, Brussels, July 6, 1945.

76. American Jewish Archives, World Jewish Congress (Collection 361), D78/16, Correspondence from A. Leon Kubowitzki (New York) to Joseph Brandes (Brussels), December 24, 1945.

77. On the WJC and its complex relationship to JDC during World War II, see Haïm Avni, "The Zionist Underground in Holland and France and the Escape to Spain," in *Rescue Attempts during the Holocaust: Proceedings of the Second Yad Vashem International Historical Conference. Jerusalem, April 8–11, 1974*, ed. Yisrael Gutman and Efraim Zuroff (Jerusalem: Yad Vashem, 1977), 555–90; Zohar Segev, *The World Jewish Congress during the Holocaust: Between Activism and Restraint* (Berlin: Walter de Gruyter, 2014), 134–57. On their relations in France and Belgium in the postwar period, see Hobson Faure, *Un Plan Marshall Juif*, 186–93; Vanden Daelen, *Laten we hun lied verder zingen*, 288–312.

78. The JDC funding was channeled through the AIVG, but the latter had no say over how the home was run.

79. Archives of the Centraal Israëlitisch Consistorie van België, 3.4.242, Jaarverslag AIVG, 1948, 21.

80. American Jewish Archives, World Jewish Congress (Collection 361), H60/1, Correspondence from C. Varshaver (Child Care Division) to Sophie Perelman (RJVB), January 29, 1946; Vanden Daelen, *Laten we hun lied verder zingen*, 308–12.

81. Vanden Daelen, *Laten we hun lied verder zingen*, 295–98, 312; American Jewish Archives, World Jewish Congress (Collection 361), C247/5; D78/15, 16, and 17; G69/3; H57/1, 2, and 7; H58/13 and 15; H59/7; H60/1 and 3; J11/5; JDC Archives, Records of the Geneva Office of the American Jewish Joint Distribution Committee, 1945–1954, Folder BG.69, Agreement between American and World Jewish Congress and JDC, December 26, 1947; ibid., BG.146, Letter from S. Perl to Mademoiselle Vulcan, October 17, 1947;

ibid., Memorandum from Beatrice Vulcan to Amelia Igel, Subject: Paris Letter 1024—Child Care Divisions of the Conseils des Associations Juivres, December 2, 1947; ibid., ADM.187, Letter from World Jewish Congress to M. W. Beckelman, January 5, 1948.

82. Yeshiva University Archives, Vaad Hatzala, 22/9, Vaad Hahatzalah, Belgian Section an die Hijefs, Montreux, Brussel, July 31, 1945. See also Veerle Vanden Daelen, "De houding van de Amerikaanse Joint ten opzichte van de orthodoxie," *Les Cahiers de la Mémoire Contemporaine/Bijdragen tot de Eigentijdse Herinnering* 6 (2005): 214–21; Vanden Daelen, *Laten we hun lied verder zingen*, 289–305.

83. Their full names were Vaad Hahatzala (Emergency Committee for War-Torn Yeshivot) and Agudas Harabonim (Union of Orthodox Rabbis of the USA and Canada); Bauer, *American Jewry and the Holocaust*, 127.

84. Alex Grobman, *Battling for Souls: The Vaad Hatzala Rescue Committee in Post-Holocaust Europe* (Jersey City, NJ: Ktav, 2004), 103.

85. JDC Archives, Records of the New York Office of the American Jewish Joint Distribution Committee, 1945–1954, Folder 1742, Agreement between the American Jewish Joint Distribution Committee and the Union of Orthodox Rabbis of the USA and Canada, July 29, 1947; Yeshiva University Archives, Collection Maurice Enright, Box 1, Folder 3, Agreement between American Jewish Joint Distribution Committee, Inc., and Rescue Children, Inc., January 1, 1948; Efraim Zuroff, *The Response of Orthodox Jewry in the United States to the Holocaust: The Activities of the Vaad Ha-Hatzala Rescue Committee, 1939–1945* (New York: Yeshiva University Press, 2000), 35; Grobman, *Battling for Souls*, 99–100, 103, 289; Bauer, *American Jewry and the Holocaust*, 127.

86. JDC Archives, Records of the New York Office of the American Jewish Joint Distribution Committee, 1945–1954, Folder 1742, Agreement between the American Jewish Joint Distribution Committee and the Union of Orthodox Rabbis of the USA and Canada, July 29, 1947. To assure the Orthodox organizations of the seriousness of the JDC intent to take into account Orthodox needs, a Jewish Central Orthodox Committee was founded on July 29, 1947; its task was to form a consultative voice for JDC.

87. JDC Archives, Records of the Geneva Office of the American Jewish Joint Distribution Committee, 1945–1954, Folder BG.60, Agreement between American Jewish Joint Distribution Committee, Inc., and Rescue Children, Inc., May 4, 1948. Two Comité Central Israélite homes, as well as seven Orthodox orphanages in France and one in Sweden, were taken over by JDC.

88. Ibid., Folder BG.60, Letter from Kate Mendel to David Goldberg, May 18, 1948; ibid., Folder BG.60, Agreement between American Jewish Joint Distribution Committee, Inc., and Rescue Children, Inc.; ibid., Folder BG.60, Letter to Kate Mendel, May 24, 1948.

89. Ibid., Folder BG.60, Letter from M. Diamant, S. Miller, et al. to Herbert Tenzer, May 23, 1948; ibid., Folder BG.60, Letter to Kate Mendel, May 24, 1948; ibid., Folder BG.60, Letter from Moses A. Leavitt to Herbert Tenzer, May 11, 1948.

90. Vanden Daelen, *Laten we hun lied verder zingen*, 339–43.

91. JDC Archives, Records of the Geneva office of the American Jewish Joint Distribution Committee, 1955–1964, Folder BG.226, Letter from the Education Department to Mark Uveeler, Subject: My Visit to Belgium and Luxemburg, September 15, 1959.

92. S.n., "Di tsienistishe landes-konferents in Antverpn. 2. Brisl un Antverpn," *Unzer Vort (Brisl)* (December 22, 1948), 2; Interview, V. Vanden Daelen with S. Kagan, New York, November 6, 2003. We read the expression *Shabes far zikh* in an article describing the differences in the Zionist Federation between Antwerp and Brussels, so it was clear to JDC that there were noticeable differences between both cities.

93. Wladimir Rabinovitch provides estimates that for the period preceding 1956, 200,000 Jews lived in the Paris region, 40,000 in the eastern regions, 50,000 in other cities, and 30,000 in small towns in the provinces. See Wladimir Rabinovitch, *Anatomie du Judaïsme français* (Paris: Editions du Minuit, 1962), 150. Renée Poznanski also confirms the rebirth of Paris as the center of French Jewish organizational life. See Renée Poznanski, "L'Heritage de la guerre: Zionisme en France dans les années 1944–1947," in *Les Juifs de France, Le Sionisme et L'Etat d'Israël, Actes Du Colloque International 1987, Langues Orientales,* ed. Doris Bensimon and Benjamin Pinkus (Paris: Publications Langues'O, 1987), 241.

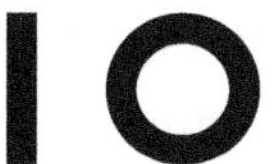

Behind the Iron Curtain

The Communist Government in Poland and Its Attitude toward the Joint's Activities, 1944–1989

Anna Sommer Schneider

The American Jewish Joint Distribution Committee (hereafter the Joint), arguably the most important global American Jewish relief organization, started operations in Poland shortly after its inception in the United States in 1914. The organization assisted the Jewish community in Poland in the interwar period and later, after the Holocaust, played a crucial role in helping survivors in post–World War II Communist-era Poland.

Although the work of the organization is well documented, it has never received fundamental and comprehensive attention by historians of post-Holocaust Jewish history in Poland.[1] Furthermore, the Joint's work was equally important in the decades that followed, sustaining Jewish cultural, intellectual, and sociopolitical life in the new Communist reality. Although this New York City–based organization became an ideological enemy of the postwar Polish government, which constantly accused the organization of committing espionage for the West, the Joint carried out operations, both legal (officially endorsed and launched by the government) and semi-legal (namely, with government approval but without any official agreements being signed) throughout the Communist rule in Poland. One of the key questions addressed by this chapter is *What was the rationale of the Communist authorities for allowing this American organization to operate actively in Poland?* Did the Communist authorities in the Union of Soviet Socialist Republics (USSR)—and later Poland—attempt to use humanitarian assistance to gain credibility in the Western world and legitimize their power through their work with such American Jewish organizations? Moreover, what was the scope and form of the assistance provided by the Joint in post–World War II Poland?

In order to better contextualize the importance of the Joint for both the Jewish community in Poland and the Communist authorities, this chapter provides a brief history of the prewar Joint operations followed by analysis of three major periods covering the years 1944 and 1945 to 1949, 1957 to 1967, and 1981 to 1989—the periods when the Joint was authorized to work in Poland. These periods represent major turning points in the Polish postwar history of Communist rule. It is hardly a coincidence, then, that the Joint was both welcomed and also forced to cease operations at these pivotal moments of Polish postwar history.

Throughout almost five decades when the Joint was authorized to work in Poland, the government's policy toward this organization was inconsistent. Any help provided by the Joint was destined for Holocaust survivors, yet the state benefited from this assistance indirectly. Because the currency coming from the Joint was transferred and exchanged in the Polish National Bank, the government could count on a significant influx of foreign funds. The Joint also supplied Jewish cooperatives and individual enterprises with high-quality machinery, raw material, and other supplies. Thus, the Polish economy also benefited from the revenue generated by Jewish cooperatives, artisans, and other productive ventures.

At various intervals when the Joint was present in Poland, the organization's employees developed very good and at times excellent working relations with the country's authorities. Although the Joint did not have a direct impact on the course of actions and the decision making of the Polish government, the organization did have a significant impact helping shape the postwar Jewish community. But the Joint's influence on the community was not always transparent. Although the Joint was the donor of record for much of the community's early support, the public decision making on where and how to spend these funds rested with the leadership of the Jewish community. Despite such arrangements, it was nevertheless understood that the Joint's wishes and intentions for where and how these funds should be used were to be recognized and followed.

This triangular working relationship among the Joint, the Jewish community leadership, and the government satisfied all three parties for various reasons—the government's willingness to open doors to outside and foreign entities while helping the Jewish community "legitimized" the regime in the eyes of many in the international community. The Joint was able not only to advance its humanitarian mission by helping rebuild and assist the Jewish community but also to do so according to its vision and view of how the postwar community should emerge. And, finally, the Jewish community was able to successfully straddle the immense needs of a distraught and depleted community, balancing multiple socioeconomic and political interests, including the Communist regime and overseas Jewish communal leaders.

HISTORICAL BACKGROUND

The Joint, although created and based in the United States over a century ago, continues to actively support brethren in various parts of the world. The Joint was established in 1914 in response to Jewish suffering in Palestine and Eastern Europe during World War I. In the aftermath of wars, pogroms, and the destitution that affected the Jewish communities of Eastern Europe, the Joint focused on the rescue, relief, and rehabilitation of Jews in different parts of Europe. The Joint's approach to social welfare work was comprehensive; in the face of desperate poverty, it helped Polish Jews devise new solutions to economic needs.

In Poland, the Joint started resident operations in February 1920 following the visit of Dr. Boris Bogen in June 1919, who at that time represented both the American Relief Administration and the Joint. Upon his return to the United States, Dr. Bogen helped organize the first group of social and administrative workers, physicians, and teachers who later began welfare work in Poland. Some 126 professional staff provided necessary assistance to the needy Jews, particularly children who often lived under the poverty line across the country. Since its creation, the Joint has focused primarily on childcare, health care, and support for the economic development of impoverished Eastern European Jews. In the interwar period, following both World War I and the Polish-Soviet War in 1920, and after the pogroms that swept through Eastern Europe at that time, the assistance provided by the Joint to a suffering Jewish community was indispensable and no doubt saved thousands of lives in the Jewish community.

In the interwar years, the Joint created models of constructive assistance that proved to be extremely successful in future decades, including vocational training programs for Jewish youth and adults alike. Thanks to cooperation with the Organization for Rehabilitation through Training (ORT), a number of vocational training programs that included workshops for Jewish craftspeople, were launched across the country. Vocational schools, along with *loan kassas* (interest-free loan banks), inaugurated by the Joint's country director, Yitzhak Gitterman, a local Polish Jew, helped create Jewish entrepreneurship for small businesses.

Initially, the outbreak of World War II did not stop the Joint from providing assistance to needy Jews. The main work focused on food and medical supplies as well as facilitating emigration from Poland. But after the United States declared war on Germany in December 1941, the Joint was compelled to cease its work in Poland. In the following years, the Joint's local leadership nonetheless continued to work underground, trying to provide relief to the starving Jews in the General Government throughout the war. During World War I and the interwar period through 1941, the Joint provided an estimated $30 million in aid in Poland (today's equivalent of nearly $450 million).

During World War II, the Jewish community suffered unprecedented losses. Less than 10% of the prewar Jewish population in Poland survived the Holocaust. The *She'erit Hapletah* could rely on the Joint and its workers from the first days of the liberation of the Eastern part of Poland by the Red Army. Although it was not until July 18, 1945, that the Joint started authorized work in Poland, already in the preceding year, New York–based officials had provided assistance to individuals, mostly by sending food packages, clothing, and medications.

Immediately after World War II, apart from providing welfare and medical aid, the organization's representatives were intent on mobilizing the community of Polish Jews to seek work or a suitable trade leading to paid employment. Hence, the Joint focused its efforts on setting up professional training, creating loan organizations, and helping people acquire and import modern equipment for their professions. Thanks to the models set up long before the outbreak of World War II, immediately after the end of hostilities in Poland, it was possible to begin rebuilding the foundations of life for the small handful of surviving Jews. The work begun by the Joint after World War II, including investments in the development of the Jewish economy, as well as schooling, educational, and cultural work, had an enormous impact on the development of Jewish life in later years.

The loan banks, for example, greatly contributed to the rebuilding of Jewish life in the postwar context. The support for Jewish craftspeople helped not only to develop their workplaces but also to *renew* Jewish morale and the spirit of self-help. Within several months, numerous Jewish institutions, all of them dependent on the Joint, began operations throughout the country, including orphanages and sanatoria for children, Jewish schools, hospitals and soup kitchens, vocational training programs, and other vital services. These initiatives, however, did not stop the surviving Jews from emigrating from Poland. For many of those who survived the horrors of the war, it was virtually impossible to rebuild their lives in a country that was perceived by the majority of survivors as a large Jewish cemetery and where everything constantly reminded them of their tragic losses. As has now been well documented, postwar antisemitism and pogroms additionally contributed to the mass emigration of Jews in the immediate postwar years. Although emigration had not traditionally been within the Joint's domain, this changed after World War II. For those who wished to leave the country, the Joint used all possible means to facilitate emigration from Poland. As Joseph Hyman, executive vice chairman of the Joint, argued: "We have recognized for some time that we cannot impose our own individual or group views, whatever they may be, upon any of our fellow Jews who have undergone such horror, deprivation, and decimation. Ours remains the task of enabling such of our fellow Jews as wish in the first instance, to migrate to Palestine, which has become to them not merely a hope for refuge but a symbol of a new and renewed Jewish dignity."[2]

IN THE NEW POST–WORLD WAR II REALITY

The end of World War II revealed unprecedented loss and destruction caused by the German occupation throughout Poland. Nearly 6 million

Polish citizens were murdered during the war, among them almost 3 million Polish Jews—90% of the prewar Jewish population. This tragedy constituted the destruction of a centuries-long Jewish civilization. The majority of a tiny group of Holocaust survivors initially decided either to return or to stay in Poland in the hope of finding their relatives. Among them were primarily people who survived Nazi concentration camps located in occupied Poland and Germany; some were also in hiding and on the so-called Aryan side, usually under false identities. This group soon expanded after Jewish repatriates started arriving from the Soviet Union. Their hopes were soon dashed, as the majority of those who were still alive after the liberation were the only survivors from their families, many of them in very poor physical and mental condition. Various diseases, exhaustion, and disability did not allow them to undertake any work, and it was difficult to find food, medication, and clothing. As one of the survivors described it:

> The most difficult moment in our lives . . . was the liberation. . . . Shock to find the reality. You . . . have [nowhere] to go. You couldn't find [anybody] you [knew]. . . . You [couldn't] stay in a place where you [lived]. . . . I realized it was a hostile village. They were not sympathetic to Jewish survivors. . . . How to go and where to go? . . . That was the most terrible time in all [that we went through] . . . the so-called liberation was the terrible hit of . . . reality.[3]

It is not clear how many Polish Jews survived the Nazi and Soviet occupation because the statistical data are not complete and are very confusing. According to data compiled by the Centralny Komitet Żydów w Polsce (the Central Committee of Polish Jews [CKŻP]), as of July 1, 1946, 243,926 Jews lived in Poland, which constituted the largest number of Jews ever counted after the war in Poland. It is very likely that at least 10% to 15% of those enumerated in this count were registered in more than one local committee. This would then put the figure at 205,000, with 210,000 perhaps being a more accurate number.[4] The Joint's archival sources show that in the years between mid-1944 and the summer of 1946, between

266,000 and 280,000 Jews were present in Poland; however, these numbers seem to be exaggerated, and we don't know exactly on what grounds these numbers were determined.[5] Barely a handful of children had survived the Nazi occupation—no more than 5,000 of the youngest members of the prewar Jewish community, most of them orphans or semi-orphans. In July 1946, this figure increased to 25,000[6] as a result of the repatriation of Polish citizens from the USSR, only to shrink to 15,000 a couple months later after the Kielce pogrom in July of that year.[7]

All the Holocaust survivors were in immediate need of food, clothing, and other supplies. Almost all of them had no place to go; thus, the majority of the survivors sought shelter in homes organized and supervised by Jewish leaders in Lublin, which had become the provisional capital of Poland in July 1944. In one of the reports presented by a division of the Polish Committee of National Liberation (Polski Komitet Wyzwolenia Narodowego [PKWN]), we read about "the most awful picture of poverty and helplessness" and about how the survivors were "living in horrendous material circumstances. Literally without a roof over their heads, naked, barefoot, lacking everything."[8]

The first institution to help Jewish survivors, the Office for Assistance to the Jewish Population, headed by Szlomo Herszenhorn from the Bund, was created as early as August 8, 1944, when a large area of Poland was still under Nazi occupation, and it was subordinated directly to PKWN. A few months later, on November 4, 1944, PKWN authorized another Jewish institution headed by Emil Sommerstein: the Temporary Central Committee of the Jews in Poland (CKŻP).[9]

The committee was a government-funded institution, and it soon became the most important body representing the remaining Jews in Poland. It served as an intermediary body between the state bureaucracy and the Jewish community. Until the end of 1949, when the CKŻP was disbanded, it operated under the immediate supervision of the Polish Ministry of Public Administration (Ministerstwo Administracji Publicznej [MAP]) as an umbrella institution for all legally operating Jewish organizations. Its primary task was to provide economic assistance to the small community of Jews who survived. In order to facilitate welfare assistance to surviving

Jews, Emil Sommerstein, a prewar Zionist who didn't affiliate with any political party after the war; Adolf Berman representing the Poalei Zion Party; and Michał Szuldenfrei from the Polish Bund were included in the State National Council (Krajowa Rada Narodowa [KRN]). Sommerstein, the most prominent of the three men and who had served as a prewar deputy in the Sejm, was soon appointed head of the PKWN Department of War Reparations at a rank equivalent to that of government minister. The appointment of Sommerstein and two other prominent Jews as PKWN department heads—Bolesław Drobner in the Department of Labor, Social Welfare, and Health and Jan Stefan Haneman in the Department of National Economy and Finance—allowed them to more immediately respond to urgent Jewish material needs.[10]

All these actions undertaken by the Communist authorities created the impression among leaders of Jewish organizations abroad and in the political establishment in the United States that the Communist authorities in Poland were benevolent and supportive of the Jewish community. Because the new Communist authorities did not have the appropriate resources to support all those in need, the goal was to reach out to potential funding institutions abroad. Emil Sommerstein was entrusted with the task of contacting foreign Jewish organizations capable of providing material and monetary assistance to the needy Jews. In August 1944, he sent a telegram to the Joint and the Jewish Agency urging them to organize immediate aid for the Jews in Poland.[11]

The representatives of the Communist authorities in Lublin were guided by similar considerations. It was important for them to obtain foreign aid, but without inviting those considered foreign political agitators into Poland. Furthermore, no other Jewish organization had greater experience than the Joint in working in that part of Europe, nor did any other Jewish organization have more employees on the ground in Europe than the Joint.[12]

The discussion about extending assistance to Polish Jews in the area of Eastern Poland that was soon to be liberated by the Red Army started in the Joint's New York headquarters a few months before the Soviet Army entered Polish territory. Moses Leavitt, the Joint executive vice chairman, began negotiations with the US State Department in May 1944. This conversation focused on providing supplies from the Lend-Lease program for Polish Jews who were still living in Soviet territory. The argument prevailed among American decision makers that Jews should receive assistance and support from the supplies designated for refugees in the Soviet Union (particularly the Asiatic part of the country).[13]

Initial discussions with the head of the Office of East European Affairs, US Department of State, Elbridge Dubrow centered on the permission to send food and other supplies from Tehran to the USSR within the contours of the Lend-Lease program.[14] Although it was still too early to start negotiations with the state department about future work in the liberated territory of Eastern Europe, American government officials used this opportunity to discourage American Jewish leaders from establishing any relationship or cooperation with Soviet and Polish Communists due to the complex political situation emerging at the end of the war. Ultimately, the US government agreed to send packages worth $100,000 from the Lend-Lease program to Polish Jews who still resided in the Soviet Union through Tehran.

Global geopolitics and the developing Cold War played an outsized role in the Joint's ability to operate in the aftermath of the war. British, American, and Soviet interests were complicated and, at least from the American perspective, there was little trust in Stalin. Therefore, the US State Department appealed to American humanitarian organizations, both Jewish and non-Jewish, to abstain from any work overseas, particularly in the territory controlled by the Red Army, as long as the political situation in the region was not clear. At this point, it was obvious that a new era in international politics had begun.

The US administration decided to wait until the end of the war and until the peace settlement was finalized before clarifying this position with groups such as the Joint. As it related to Poland, the American objective was to prevent any actions leading to the development of any form of relationship with the Polish Committee of National Liberation, a new Communist leadership that had been operating since July 1944 in the liberated part of Eastern Poland. These actions indicate that international political leaders still had no clear plan for addressing the region's political tensions; in fact, the Joint's leadership had tried, since liberation, to find a way to reach out to people in need. As early as August 3, 1944, Joseph Hyman, in a letter to Andrei Gromyko, ambassador of the USSR to the United States, asked to convene a conference to discuss the question of assistance for Polish Jews from the liberated territories.[15] A few days later, on August 16, Emil Sommerstein, a well-known Zionist leader of the prewar Jewish community who had survived the Holocaust in the Soviet Union, sent a cable to the Joint's headquarters in New York requesting immediate assistance for the surviving remnant.[16] He also suggested that representatives of the Joint come to Poland to evaluate the extent of destruction and needs among the surviving Polish Jews. The Joint's leaders criticized Sommerstein at the Executive Committee meeting.[17] James Rosenberg argued that Sommerstein's actions were premature because the international politics were too volatile. The question of delivering humanitarian aid in the liberated territories was still being discussed by both the American and Soviet governments. Thus, it was irresponsible, Rosenberg suggested, to raise this issue before decisions about delivery of aid were made by representatives of the Soviet, US, and Polish governments.

The prevailing argument was that any actions and cooperation by the foreign agencies with newly created authorities could lead to legitimization of Communist power in Poland. Therefore, President Truman's administration strove to prevent any actions that could be used by the Communist authorities in Poland for propaganda purposes.[18] It was not until July 1945 that the American government officially recognized the new Communist government: the Provisional Government of National Unity (Tymczasowy Rząd Jedności Narodowej). The same month, on July 18, 1945, the Joint began authorized operations in Poland.

Despite these governmental and political restrictions on humanitarian aid, Joint activities in the region had commenced earlier. According to Stefan Grajek, a member of and an activist in the pioneering Zionist He-Halutz movement (and wartime member of the Jewish Fighting Organization in Warsaw):

> [T]he Joint resumed activities in Poland as early as July 18, 1945, but even before that, the organization was transferring

money to the Central Committee of the Jews in Poland. All Jewish institutions, including institutions affiliated with Zionist parties—mostly kibbutzim—benefited from the Joint's assistance, which also supervised the activities of the CCJ[P]. However, members of PPR [Polish People's Party] in the Central Committee of the Jews in Poland objected to this supervision. The Joint also supported legal emigration of the Jews from Poland and aided TOZ[19] [Society for Safeguarding the Health of the Jewish Population, an organization that provided for health needs] and ORT.[20]

The Kremlin authorities decided to turn over the decision on the subject to PKWN. The Soviets believed that this strategy would help strengthen the position of the Communist authorities in Poland by building the foundations and structures for the future Communist government while also legitimizing the new regime, which was rejected by the majority of Polish society. These administrative, logistical, and cooperative steps with US organizations were important measures to help gain confidence among Poles and strengthen the international position of the new authorities.

In May 1945, David Guzik, the only survivor of the Joint's prewar leadership in Poland, initiated work aiming to help the few Jewish survivors of the Holocaust. To carry out this process efficiently, Guzik started rebuilding structures of the Joint in Lublin, which became a temporary capital and residential town for the new government. The same month, in a cable to the Joint's office in New York, Guzik reported that "we are ready to continue work, 40 thousand Jews need immediate assistance. I am waiting for instructions."[21] For the Joint's leaders in the United States, Guzik was a natural candidate for the position of new Joint country director given his experience and work for the organization before and during the war.

In the 1940s, the question of the nature and scope of the Joint's assistance was continuously discussed by the leadership of CKŻP, which soon tried to assume complete control of funds provided by the Joint, leading to endless conflict with the Zionists, the religious community, and the Joint. The government still controlled operation of the CKŻP yet permitted it considerable latitude in determining the nature and scope of its work. For the CKŻP leadership, which in mid-1946 was taken over by progovernment Jewish activists, the control over all the funds would have granted the CKŻP the sole decision-making power over the future of Jewish life in Poland, including the character of Jewish institutions and Jewish education. This issue, similar to the question of funds allocation, was debated, inter alia, at the meeting of the CKŻP Executive Committee on July 8, 1945.[22] Paweł Zelicki, from the Jewish Faction of the Polish Workers' Party, emphasized the importance of the cooperation between CKŻP and the Joint for the future of Polish Jews, calling the Joint "the only institution which cared about assistance for the remaining Jews in Poland."[23] Szlomo Herszenhorn (the Bund) drew attention to the differences resulting from changes that had occurred after the war in Poland.

In pre–World War II Poland, the Joint cooperated with various Jewish institutions trying to reach out only to the needy Jews, whereas after the war, every surviving Jew was in the same position and desperately needed assistance. Therefore, among the CKŻP leaders the argument prevailed that centralized funds allocation would enable just distribution of funds. In fact, such a move would have given the CKŻP leadership a free hand and arbitrary authority in decision making in matters related to the distribution of social aid. As a result, the CKŻP, dominated by the Communists, could have had unlimited control of the cultural and ideological shape of the postwar Jewish community. Nonetheless, although the Communists sought to entirely eradicate religious life and their ultimate goal was to discontinue operations of religious institutions, at this same July 1945 CKŻP meeting, Professor Józef Sack (from the socialist Zionist Hitachdut-Poale Zion) emphasized the need to support religious institutions that were authorized by the government to officially operate in Poland—namely, the Union of Jewish Religious Congregations (Związek Gmin Wyznaniowych Żydowskich), which was renamed in 1949 as the Religious Association of the Mosaic Faith (Związek Religijny Wyznania Mojżeszowego [ZRWM]).

One of the Joint's operating principles from its very beginnings had been involving local leaders in its work. As a result, local bodies were made responsible for the distribution of funds and other supplies. William Bein,

Director of the Joint in Poland (1946–1949), describing relations with the CKŻP and how the program on the ground developed, said that

> our relations with the organizations are such that we are presenting the problem, inspiring them and controlling them and we are checking them, we are scolding them, we are petting them. But we do not actually handle the program. We work on the principle of turning as much responsibility as possible over to local organizations so that we would rather make a mistake than be compelled as JDC to handle the program. We have to take care of emigration and *Landsmannschaften* organizations, but we don't handle any program as such, directly.[24]

The Joint supervised programs through a number of inspectors who monitored Joint Distribution Committee–assisted programs in different parts of the country and were responsible for implementing the Joint's programs and initiatives.

The local organizations did not like this construct because it interfered with their internal affairs and did not leave any space for autonomous decision making in regard to ideological assumptions or disbursement of subsidies. Although Bein made it clear that the Joint did not take direct responsibility for the programs implemented in Poland, it was the organization's priority to give special attention to all matters concerning religious groups. Bein argued that because 70% of the Jews throughout the world came from Poland and the religious community had lost its spiritual leadership during the war, it was the Joint's duty to provide necessary attention in order to secure traditional Jewish life[25]—given the fact that the subsidies received by the ZRWM were insufficient for the survival of this institution and its branches.

In addition to subventions, which covered costs for the development and running of Jewish communal institutions, the Joint's direct postwar budget included special funds dedicated to searching for and recovering children who had survived the war years in hiding in the care of ethnic Poles or in religious communities, mainly in Catholic monasteries and convents.[26] In many cases, children who had survived the Nazi occupation in hiding were too young to remember their origins. Therefore, one of the goals of workers on the "Jewish street" was to search for and recover children who had lost their parents during the war.

Between January and September 1946, the Joint allocated 603,000 złoty (just over 6,000 US dollars), out of an overall budget of over 743 million złoty (7.43 million US dollars), for this endeavor.[27] The CKŻP and Zionist organizations both worked independently to recover children and provide essential assistance for the youngest survivors. A Zionist Coordinating Committee (Koordynacja Syjonistyczna) was formed that set up shelters for children, independent of the CKŻP. Children discovered by Zionists usually ended up in kibbutzim in Poland, which soon became their new homes.[28]

Another important factor that shaped the Joint's priorities and marked its lines of action was the need for housing for Jews who had lost their possessions, property, and businesses due to the war; the shifting of Polish borders; and the confiscation of their property by Germans, Poles, or new Communist authorities. Many were forced to look for new shelter in the so-called Recovered or Regained Territories,[29] which soon became a new destination for survivors, particularly Lower Silesia. The existing infrastructure and households that belonged to those Germans evicted from this territory after the war allowed many relocated Jews to start rebuilding foundations for their new lives soon after the war. Adapting to this new reality was not easy.

Detached from their prewar communities, in territory that had been part of a different nation-state, so different culturally from the environment in which they had lived and grown up, survivors found it difficult to adapt to the new situation. Because few survivors could rely on their relatives who had perished, their only hope was aid from foreign humanitarian organizations, particularly the Joint. At the same time, there were some advantages to being resettled in this part of the new Polish territory, especially the ease in finding housing and an open labor market providing better chances to find employment in abandoned former German factories and workshops. Moreover, in this newly acquired part of Poland, there was less antisemitism

Transportation of supplies labeled *Joint* to a warehouse. Warsaw, Poland, circa 1946–1947.

compared with other parts of the country because the majority of the population constituted new settlers, who, like the Jews, were relocated from different parts of Poland or the Soviet Union. This served as a significant factor in limiting antisemitic violence provoked by Jewish property claims, something seen on a wide basis in other parts of the country.

The official decision to authorize the Joint's work by the Polish government was preceded by negotiations among Jewish community leaders from CKŻP, the Ministry of Public Administration (Ministerstwo Administracji

Publicznej [MAP]), and the Joint. In April 1945, the first letter sent by the CKŻP Presidium to the Ministry of Public Administration stated that due to the very difficult position of the Jewish population in Poland, representatives requested the government's support to establish official cooperation between the Joint, the Polish government, and the CKŻP. Based on this appeal, the director of the political department of the Ministry of Public Administration wrote to the minister of foreign affairs, requesting support for the Jewish community. The minister of public administration noted, among other things, that

> after the horrible experience of the Jewish population under Hitlerites' occupation of Poland and the extermination of over 3 million Jews, only shreds of the Jewish Nation remained alive. This handful, after surviving in bunkers, woods and concentration camps, is currently in a very difficult financial situation, without clothing, barefoot, completely exhausted, homeless, without basic existential conditions.
>
> The Provisional Government of Poland provided both material and moral assistance to the Jewish population. The capabilities of the Provisional Government, however, are very limited and insufficient considering the enormity of needs of the Jewish population.
>
> With the above in mind, it is necessary to ask for assistance abroad. The most efficient foreign aid can be provided by the "Joint" organization in America. The Political Department of the MPA [Ministry of Public Administration] is asking to remove any obstacles and difficulties, to expedite the arrival of the "Joint" representative to Poland.[30]

It was equally important for the Joint to develop a good working relationship with both the Polish government and the surviving leadership of the Jewish community. Because the goals and vision regarding the future of the Jewish community in Poland varied considerably among members of the Central Committee, it was not clear what form of assistance they were expecting to receive from the American organization. Different political agendas and ideological diversity characterized the leadership of the Central Committee, which greatly influenced the shape of the postwar Jewish community.

Various religious and political organizations, particularly the Zionists and the communal institutions that they represented, were challenged by many obstacles. They had to contend with the hostility of the Communist authorities while at the same time being confronted by opposition from Jewish leaders involved with newly created secular institutions. Here, a dichotomy existed: Although the centralization of power within one institution representing all authorized and legally operating Jewish political parties in postwar Poland facilitated contact with the authorities and the distribution of funds and other supplies, finding common ground among people representing so many different political views and ideologies became difficult and often led to continual misunderstanding and conflicts. The Zionists strove to organize and facilitate the emigration of Jews, continually urging those living across the country to emigrate from Poland, ideally to Palestine, and later, after proclamation of the state, to Israel. The Communists in the CKŻP, along with the Bundists, argued that survivors should stay in Poland, which, under the new Communist government, offered previously unimaginable promising conditions based on equality and freedom for all citizens.

Although it may seem that the Joint was trapped in these conflicts or among opposing camps on the "Jewish street," in fact the organization did everything possible to remain nonpartisan and to work toward meeting the needs of all surviving Jews. The Joint's staff did not support any particular political orientation among Polish Jews, nor did they advocate any specific solution. The organization's work focused on actions that could make life easier for the remaining Jews. Thus, the Joint's subsidies were indispensable to building a solid foundation for the future life of Jews who wished to stay in Poland while the Joint helped facilitate emigration of those who decided to leave Poland and start their new life elsewhere. Ironically, the Zionist organizations sometimes were in opposition to the Joint, arguing that the assistance provided by the organization improved Jewish life in Poland, making emigration less tempting. The Communists from the CKŻP, however, accused the Joint of supporting and financing emigration of Jews from Poland instead of encouraging people to remain in their home country.

Jewish Communists and Bundists openly declared their opposition to the creation of Jewish communal institutions based on prewar models. They maintained that traditional religious communities (*kahal*) had led to the isolation of Jews from the rest of the Polish population before the war, arousing hostility among Poles toward Jews and ultimately contributing to anti-Jewish violence in the country. The Jewish Communists and Bundists did not necessarily speak with one voice. Unlike the Bundists, the Communists, according to historian Jaff Schatz, "did not regard Jewish culture as a value in itself but merely as a means in political work among Jews. In essence, they embodied the absolute primacy of political ideology over ethnicity."[31] Because the Central Committee was responsible for distribution of funds among Jewish organizations—both government subsidies and donations provided by foreign organizations such as the Joint—religious institutions were in serious danger of losing their funding. David Guzik emphasized that the Joint would be working through the Central Committee as long as no other Jewish organizations and institutions emerged. Because the Central Committee did not endorse religious and Zionist organizations, including kibbutzim, the Joint allocated additional funds to support those organizations. In a letter to JDC Director General Joseph Schwartz from November 1, 1946, Bein expressed his concern regarding the number of institutions supported by the Joint and the allocation of funds in Poland. He stated:

> Now, as we are approaching the new year, we are again faced with the problem of how to provide the necessary zlotys for the budgets of the Jewish organizations supported by JDC in Poland. . . . While considering budgetary needs we must remember the fact that despite the exodus which took place, the over 25 organizations (in this number Central Committee is considered as one organization) which received regular subsidies from JDC during the last few months were

enabled to organize themselves and establish institutions for their own needs. The Central Committee established regional, district and local committees with numerous children homes, homes for the aged, day nurseries, schools, day schools, kitchens, cultural and economic institutions, loan kassas, and cooperatives. The Jewish Congregation simultaneously established 80 kihiloths [congregations] with synagogues, schoichtem [shochetim], rabbis, moilim, kitchens, talmud torahs, some children homes, mikvahs etc. The Zionist organizations established themselves as official party factions and every one of them established adult and children kibbutzim, workshops, kitchens. They are carrying on seminaries, preparing their activities, publishing newspapers. Practically all parties maintain parallel organizations. The Bund maintains, similar to Zionists, apprentice homes, kitchens, children homes, cooperatives etc.[32]

Soon after the Joint was authorized to begin work in Poland, the director of the Political Department of the Ministry of Public Administration agreed to allow the Joint to acquire suitable quarters for its office due to "the extremely important work of this representation."[33] In October 1945, Joseph Schwartz arrived in Poland. In just a few days, Schwartz visited Jewish schools, orphanages, kibbutzim, and other Jewish institutions across the country. He was surprised to see that Jewish life, despite the extent of destruction and suffering from the ravages of the war, was slowly resuming in Poland. The visit also gave him an opportunity to discuss important questions such as budget issues and further cooperation with local Jewish leaders and Polish authorities. One of the key questions related to the budget was the actual costs for welfare services, estimated at about 87 million złoty. This amount did not include additional funds needed for investment in infrastructure, medical supplies, and CKŻP staff salaries. The budget did not include any funding for the Productivization Bank (interest-free loans) either, which helped reduce unemployment and helped Holocaust survivors attain self-sufficiency. In 1947, Jewish cooperatives comprised 95% of all cooperatives in the Wrocław district and 81% in the Szczecin district, both in the so-called formerly German Recovered Territories. William Bein, the director of the Joint in Poland (1946–1949), emphasized that the Joint contributed not only to Jewish economic development but also to the development of the western region known as the Polish Recovered Territories.[34]

The Joint's work did not last long in the immediate postwar period. Due to increasing Stalinization[35] and the impact of the Cold War, at the end of 1949, the Joint was compelled to officially cease operations. However, local staff members, working underground, continued their efforts to aid Jews remaining in Poland.

Shortly before the Joint was forced to terminate its mission in Poland in December 1949 and in anticipation of the upcoming events, William Bein expressed both his concerns and his hope about the future of the Jewish community in Poland:

At a Jewish school, children are escorted by a guard. Kłodzko, Poland, circa 1946. Photo by John Vachon.

JDC worked in Poland for over 20 years and became not only the helper, but the symbol of the Jewish population. We may be compelled, with developments, to conclude JDC's work sooner or later—rather sooner than later—but we cannot know exactly when. The work of the many subsidized organizations will be integrated into the economy and social care of the country. But, nevertheless, there is the hard core of which I spoke. There is that spiritual hard core. . . . I would like to say that the time will soon come when we should think of what will happen if JDC pulls out. How will we be able to help those organizations, and those institutions, and those people who need our care?[36]

The Joint was only able to operate in immediate post–World War II Poland from 1945 to 1949. Nevertheless, the organization played a major and significant role in rebuilding Jewish life—making it almost impossible to imagine what Jewish life would have been like if not for this organization. Efforts focused either on sustaining and improving the lives of those Holocaust survivors who wished to stay in the country or on facilitating the emigration of thousands of Jews who could not imagine rebuilding their lives in a place seen by many Jews who survived the horrors of the war as a vast Jewish graveyard.

In the immediate postwar period, the Communist authorities were benevolent toward the Jewish community to the point that they permitted the creation of Jewish autonomy within the Polish state. Would this have been possible without the Joint? Certainly yes, because the Joint and its local employees had no direct impact on Polish government decision making. But would this unprecedented autonomy have thrived, as it did, without the Joint's support? Probably not. The country, plunged into economic ruin, could not afford to support and had no interest in supporting any of the ethnic or religious minorities in the country, given the fact that within five years of imposing Communist rule on Polish society, the authorities sought to create a state free of national minorities. Although it was impossible for the government to entirely eliminate ethnic or religious minorities, its larger project sought to integrate all segments of Polish society. Such perspectives also prevailed in the discussion about emigration.

It was not clear to William Bein why the authorities permitted Jewish emigration from Poland to Israel, provided they wished to settle there permanently. In one of his last reports submitted in October 1949 shortly before the government announced the decision to terminate the Joint's work in Poland, he stated:

> I cannot get rid of the feeling that there is a certain logic in the action taken by the Polish government. I watch it careful-ly. They want to eliminate the Jewish problem as such. They don't want to have a Jewish problem. Poland has no minori-ties. Why[?] The Ukrainians were sent back to Ukraine, the Germans were sent back to Germany, the Jews to a certain extent went via Germany or otherwise to Israel. There is a small Jewish population of about 75 or 80 thousand. The government has taken steps which show that they have decided to stop treating Jews as a special group.[37]

At the same time, the cultural and intellectual diversity of Jewish life, embodied in the work of various Jewish organizations, political move-ments, and strands of Judaism, was suppressed or even terminated. Thus, the following decades were much more challenging for the remaining Jews, especially those who tried to maintain a relationship with the Jewish community and preserve Jewish religious or traditional life.

THE 1950S AND THE JOINT'S RETURN IN 1957: ACTIVITIES IN A NEW POLITICAL REALM

The political changes of the late 1940s initiated the creation of a new Jewish institution in lieu of the CKŻP, which closed down at the end of 1949. The impetus to replace the CKŻP with a new Jewish organization came from Grzegorz (Hersz) Smolar, president of the CKŻP. His goal was to create an organization representing Jews in Poland and allowing them to maintain contacts with Jewish communities throughout the world. As a result, in 1950, the government endorsed the Jewish Social and Cultural Association in Poland (Towarzystwo Społeczno-Kulturalne Żydów w Polsce [TSKŻ]). The TSKŻ fulfilled these roles and at the same time became a "conveyor belt" or conduit for the party's policies. The TSKŻ, headed by the aforementioned Smolar, was run by Jewish Communists. The non-Communist Jewish political organizations were disbanded by the end of 1949, and their leaders, particularly Zionists, left Poland. The Jewish Labor Bund dissolved itself at the beginning of 1949, and its members either merged with the Polish United Workers' Party or emigrated. In addition to the TSKŻ, the Jewish community in Poland was also affiliated with the ZRWM, which set up twenty-three congregations throughout the country.[38]

The period of Stalinization in the early 1950s came to an end soon after Stalin's death in 1953. With his death, a number of positive changes were initiated but ultimately led to the notable political crisis in postwar Poland, which is discussed later in this chapter.

The beginning of the 1950s and the changes associated with the liquidation of the CKŻP and the establishment of the TSKŻ set a new direction for the Jewish community in Poland. In fact, the TSKŻ served as a convenient tool to move the structures of the Communist state and its ideology and worldview directly to the "Jewish street" (i.e., the Jewish community). In this newly created secular world, represented by the activists doctrinally associated with the Communist regime, there was no place for either religion or Jewish nationalism. Therefore, any initiative referring to Jewish tradition was associated with a prewar "ghettoization" of the Jewish community, which the TSKŻ leadership tried to destroy as standing in opposition to the internationalism represented by the leadership of the TSKŻ.

It is hard to determine how many people joined the TSKŻ because they believed in its ideology and how many actually hoped to benefit from this relationship. In times of crisis such as that which affected Poland and particularly the Jewish community in the 1950s, the TSKŻ was the only institution distributing subsidies provided by the Joint after its return to Poland in 1957. Thus, it was the only authorized Jewish organization capable of securing material assistance and also helping to find employment for Jews who lost their jobs mostly due to the increased antisemitism of the 1950s. Therefore, in a relatively short period of time, this secular institution created a monopoly, setting the agenda for Jewish existence and activities in Poland. The ZRWM, bereft of appropriate funding, was relegated to the margins of Jewish life, later attracting barely a handful of Jews faithful to Jewish tradition.

The Joint resumed work in Poland soon after the government of Poland extended an invitation to reestablish relations and renew the organization's work in the country. Formal discussions about a possible return of the Joint to Poland began in August 1957 in the Polish Embassy in Washington, DC. Two months later, in October 1957, the Joint's representatives, Charles Jordan and Moses Levine, visited Poland. Based on conversations with Polish officials the same month, the Central Jewish Committee for Public Welfare in Poland, also called the Central Jewish Relief Committee (Centralna Żydowska Komisja Pomocy Społecznej [CŻKPS]), headed by Salo Fiszgrund, was created to run the Joint's operations in Poland. The following month, Charles Jordan officially announced the Joint's return.

As smooth as it may seem in retrospect, the Joint's return to Poland was preceded by numerous events that permanently influenced Polish post–World War II history. The year 1956 was a pivotal moment for Poland when the government was struggling with major political and economic crises. Deteriorating living conditions led to public demonstrations and riots, mostly in Western Poland, leading to major governmental changes in October of that year. Władysław Gomułka, the Communist leader of postwar Poland who was arrested in 1951, was restored to power and soon became the first secretary of the Central Committee of the Polish United Workers' Party—the most important political position in Communist Poland. The same man was later responsible for implementing the government-controlled antisemitic campaign known as March '68.

In the 1950s, the dominant argument within political circles was that Gomułka would help rebuild public confidence toward the Communist regime. Gomułka, on the other hand, was aware that public unrest was a direct consequence of the economic crises. As a result, it was his priority to adopt new economic policies and improve international trade cooperation while also changing the existing agreements with the Soviet Union and possibly expanding cooperation with the United States.

The liberalization of the country's politics became an opportune moment for American charity organizations, such as the Cooperative for Assistance and Relief Everywhere, American Relief for Poland, and JDC, to resume their work in Poland. Despite being invited back, however, the Joint, like all American (and not only American) humanitarian agencies, was under steady surveillance by the security services. Indeed, such surveillance had begun in the 1940s, when the Joint and other organizations carried out authorized work and continued in the following decades. For example, data collected in the 1940s were used against the Jewish community in Poland in the early 1950s. In 1951, the security service known as UB (Office of Public Security) started an organized campaign directed against "the hostile Jewish community." It is hard to define precisely against whom this campaign was directed, but we know that among those targeted were the Joint's former employees. This was the period when the Joint was not present in Poland and the organization had lost the right to work in the country. Nevertheless, even then, the Communists considered the Joint to be an espionage agency.

According to security service primary sources, in the 1940s, the Joint allegedly controlled the work of all Jewish organizations and institutions operating in post–World War II Poland—including Zionist organizations, the Central Committee of the Jews in Poland, and religious congregations, thanks to the funds transferred from the United States. The security service also believed that through contacts and good relationships with employees of the state apparatus, the Joint aimed to control Polish state institutions, economy, and cultural life. In 1953, as a result of an ongoing investigation, the former secretary general of the Joint in Poland, Józef Gitler-Barski, was arrested for espionage. Security service documents stated that "his work for the 'Joint,' [an] institution which was financed and controlled by Americans, [his] extensive contacts with American and Israeli citizens, and also robbery and diversionary activity for the 'Joint,' finally his frequent travels abroad indicate, that he has been still used by foreign intelligence."[39]

This state action ironically coincided with the so-called Doctors' Plot and the campaign directed against the "criminal organization Joint" that was unleashed in the Soviet Union.[40] In light of these events, it is surprising that only four years later, the Polish authorities extended an invitation to the Joint to resume its work in Poland. It is not clear precisely what motivated Polish authorities to invite the Joint to reactivate its work, although the return of thousands of Jews from the Soviet Union to Poland in the late 1950s may have provided the impetus. Given estimates that 18,000–19,000 Jews would be arriving in Poland from the Soviet Union, the impoverished government, which was incapable of handling the burden and providing assistance to so many people, sought outside help.

In the 1950s, based on a new agreement with the Soviet authorities, more than 250,000 Polish citizens were repatriated from the Soviet Union, with Jews representing about 7% of this group. The agreement signed between the Polish and Soviet governments at the end of 1956 was the basis for further repatriation of Polish nationals who still resided in Soviet territory.[41] The decision to resume the repatriation process was motivated by the separation of families ten years earlier and was facilitated by Stalin's death and the ensuing political changes in Poland. Ultimately, out of nearly 1.6 million ethnic Poles still residing beyond the eastern Polish border, nearly 250,000 arrived in Poland by the end of 1959, mostly people who had not taken advantage of the repatriation process a decade earlier.[42]

Based on information supported by the Joint's reports, between January and July 1957, about 90,000 Poles were repatriated to Poland, with 9,000–10,000 Jews among them. By October of the same year, about 3,000 more Jews arrived in the country.[43] Although the repatriation agreement expired by the end of 1958, those who registered for repatriation within the allotted time could leave the country until the beginning of the 1960s. It was estimated that at least 19,000 Jews arrived in Poland at that time, 6,000 of whom immediately left for Israel.[44] Many years later, in a conversation with Prime Minister Cyrankiewicz, Charles Jordan asked why for 20,000 people (a relatively small group of repatriates) the Joint was invited to cooperate with the Polish government. Prime Minister Cyrankiewicz responded that while Polish repatriates had families either in Poland or elsewhere, for the Jews he wanted the Joint to become their family.[45]

Yet if assistance to repatriating Jews played a critical motivating role in Poland's decision to bring the Joint back, other causes cannot be ignored—namely, that cooperation with the American-based organization ensured an influx of foreign currency to Poland. Also, work with an American charity helped create legitimacy and gave Poland credibility in the Western world. Certainly, these factors helped legitimize Communist power on the ground. In other words, thanks to closer cooperation with American-based charity organizations, the post–October 1956 authorities strived to prove that Poland actually could become a country open to cooperation with the Western world, especially with the United States. It was clear to the Communist authorities in Poland that the Soviet government was not able to provide sufficient assistance to their country. Surprisingly, high-ranking Polish officials believed that the only government capable of fulfilling Polish needs was that of the United States.

During negotiations with representatives of the US government, Polish Deputy Minister of Foreign Affairs Józef Winiewicz stressed that what Poland really needed were long-term loans from the Import-Export Bank; the waiving of restrictions with regard to Public Law 480 (supply of surplus food from the United States); and obtaining Most Favored Nation status, allowing possible trade between the two countries. Poland refused to accept charitable assistance from the US government because, as was argued, this form of help would allow Americans to interfere in internal Polish affairs. The Polish government was willing, however, to accept assistance provided by American humanitarian organizations (which were easily controlled by the Polish authorities). In October 1957, Minister of Foreign Affairs Adam Rapacki continued negotiations with US government officials. In a conversation with Secretary of State John Foster Dulles, Rapacki argued that organizations such as JDC had already started working in Poland, thereby giving credence to the notion of enhanced US-Polish ties.[46]

The discussion about the possible return of the Joint to Poland began in the US State Department in January 1957, a few months before the first Polish delegation set foot on American soil. Later that year, in August 1957, the Polish ambassador to the United States, Romuald Spasowski, attended a meeting with representatives of the American Jewish Committee, at which many issues were discussed, the most important being the growth of antisemitism in Poland and the financial situation of Polish Jews. Ambassador Spasowski stated that Poland was addressing the country's antisemitism. He also pointed out that the Jewish community needed financial assistance from the American Jewish community. This was a pivotal moment that changed the dynamics in the working relationship between the Poles and American Jewish leadership. The course of these conversations indicates that Spasowski's invitation for the resumption of the Joint operations in Poland had already been discussed by Polish decision makers. The Polish ambassador, without the slightest hesitation, also agreed to issue a visa to any representative of the Joint who wished to visit Poland.[47]

The question of the revival of the Joint's work in Poland did not depend only on the Polish authorities. Indeed, any project run by an American charity behind the Iron Curtain had to be first endorsed by the US government. Because almost all of the requirements of the US government were fulfilled (including duty-free shipping of supplies to Poland), eventually the Joint was authorized to develop closer working relations with the Polish authorities and particularly Jewish organizations on the ground. Polish authorities, however, did not allow a Joint representative to establish permanent residence in Poland. Ultimately, the Joint operated through the Warsaw-based Polish Jewish organization, the CŻKPS, which ran fourteen local branches; however, as previously mentioned, the TSKŻ was responsible for the distribution of funds and other goods. A permanent presence of the Joint's representative in the country, although important, was not mandatory, as long as the organization's representative was allowed to supervise work on the ground. However, engaging with indigenous Jewish communities and leaders had been the Joint's policy since its inception in the early twentieth century. As Charles Jordan explained: "In this matter we learn to understand community needs better and, by drawing local leadership into our work we make them jointly responsible for the carrying out of the program."[48]

Although both the US and Polish governments reached an agreement, for the Joint's leadership it was more challenging to handle the TSKŻ because its leadership believed that Polish Jews did not need American money and refused to cooperate with any organization representing "Western imperialism." Ironically, it soon turned out that the Joint's cooperation with the Communist government was much better than with the Polish Jewish leadership. Akiva Kohane, the Joint's country director, born and educated in Poland, who held a doctorate degree in law from the prestigious Jagiellonian University, was well acquainted with Polish political and sociological culture. His personality and undeniable erudition allowed him to develop a very good working relationship with the staff of the Ministry of Labor and Social Welfare (the latter was in charge of Jewish affairs in Poland). Kohane usually traveled to Poland once a month, staying from three to fourteen days. His frequent visits allowed for an in-depth understanding of the situation in the country, both within the Jewish community and at the governmental level. Although his skills and knowledge proved to be useful in his contacts with the country's authorities, this was not the case when it came to local Jewish leaders.

The TSKŻ was dominated by the Communist doctrinaires who perceived the Joint as an ideologically hostile organization, and the fact that it was a Jewish charity institution, created to provide help for Jews in need, did not change much in their attitude toward the Joint's staff and their work. The TSKŻ was created by the Jews and for the Jews, yet it remained a creature of state initiative alone and there was an expectation for this institution to correspond with the party's ideological line. Because Polish Jews did not pay much attention to the TSKŻ after its inception in 1950, nor appreciate its work, the TSKŻ leadership used all possible means to win favor within the remaining Jewish community.

Inasmuch as it rejected the presence of the Joint in Poland, the TSKŻ was willing to accept any funds and other supplies provided by the organization, under one condition: Its Executive Committee wanted to take overall control over the expenditure of subsidies transferred by the Joint to Poland. On one hand, the control over finances and their distribution would allow the TSKŻ to freely carry out ideological indoctrination in

Jewish educational institutions and summer camps. On the other hand, as in the 1940s, the machinery, raw materials, and other supplies provided by the Joint would facilitate the establishment and development of Jewish cooperatives, potentially generating sympathy for the TSKŻ among Polish Jews. Apparently, the TSKŻ leaders achieved, at least partially, their goal because many beneficiaries of the Joint's aid did not realize that help was coming from this New York–based organization. Similarly, people who in the past had participated in the summer camps funded or subsidized by the Joint truly believed that the funding was coming from the TSKŻ.

In February 1959, an article appeared under Grzegorz (Hersz) Smolar's name in an issue of the Jewish weekly *Fołks Sztyme*, titled "Assistance Yes, but to Whom and How," in which he questioned the need for the Joint's work in Poland.[49] Samuel Haber, who had been tasked by JDC with helping improve the situation of Jews in Poland, recalled that in his article Smolar criticized "the individual demoralization resulting from welfare activities. And while recognizing that certain elements of the population need assistance, this program must be carefully executed."[50] Smolar admitted that welfare was important for orphans, children, and the sick, as were soup kitchens for the poor. But his goal was to develop mechanisms for constructive aid that could help people find jobs instead of providing welfare, especially after the arrival of thousands of Jews repatriated from the Soviet Union, among them many young and strong people capable of work. He further stated that the program should be divided into three types—the establishment of cooperatives, support of people's own enterprises, and assistance to individual artisans—while insisting on more effective administrative measures. Smolar probably hoped that his arguments would provide a rationale for the Communist-dominated TSKŻ to take control of the funds transferred by the Joint through the local structures of the CŻKPS.

Just a few months earlier, the TSKŻ Executive Committee had allocated 250,000 złoty, coming from the Joint, for "productivization" without the Joint's approval. Thus, Smolar's article implied that the TSKŻ was looking to legitimize its position in the Jewish community by providing assistance in various areas of Jewish social, cultural, educational, and professional life with the Joint's funds but without the Joint's direct involvement in the program.

Although the Joint provided funding for a broad spectrum of assistance to needy Jews who remained in Poland, it was the Communist government–approved TSKŻ that was responsible for implementing programs on the ground. Therefore, technically the TSKŻ activists had a decisive voice, but because JDC was funding the TSKŻ, it could refuse to allocate funding to programs that did not correspond with its expectations. The arrangement led to constant tensions between the TSKŻ and the Joint leadership. Despite these disagreements, the Joint fought to support both the repatriation and the emigration processes. According to various sources, in mid-1957, 65,000–70,000 Jews lived in Poland, but that number dropped significantly to 18,000 by the end of the 1950s because of the opening of borders for Polish Jews, which resulted in mass emigration, mostly to Israel.[51]

Nonetheless, by the late 1950s, feeding programs at schools for Jewish children, the creation of kindergartens, and providing welfare for needy Jews were as important as supporting repatriation and emigration. Interestingly enough, school food programs funded by the Joint encouraged Jewish parents, particularly those who cut themselves off from Jewish life, to register their children in Jewish schools, where they could receive a daily hot meal. Welfare assistance and medical aid to the disabled, the chronically ill, Jewish senior citizens, and Jewish students were also priorities.[52]

Available primary sources indicate that the Joint sought to create appropriate conditions for educating Jewish children in the spirit of *Yiddishkeit* (Jewish heritage and identity) and to support Jewish religious and traditional life. *Yiddishkeit* was strengthened through Joint-supported cultural and educational activities and sports clubs for Jewish youth. In the 1950s, no program had a more profound impact on Jewish youth than the summer camps where children were able to embrace the richness of their heritage and traditions. These programs were particularly important for children who arrived from the USSR because many found it very difficult to adapt to the new conditions. After visiting one of the Jewish summer camps, operated by the TSKŻ, in the summer of 1959, Akiva Kohane recalled in one of his reports that he was "most favorably impressed by the summer camp program, which I consider may be the most important part of our work in Poland. Three thousand Jewish children attended the summer camps, living in a Jewish environment, many of them for the first time being among fellow Jews."[53]

Developed after the World War II model of "productivization," the Joint aimed to help Jews adapt to the economic realities of Communist-era Poland. This model proved to be vital in the 1950s, when impoverished Jews were looking for new employment after losing their jobs due to economic crises but also after a new wave of antisemitism swept through Poland. The Joint, along with its longtime partner the ORT, developed vocational schools that afforded Jews the ability to learn new occupational skills. New training schools along with cooperatives for different trades provided livelihoods for Jews already living in Poland and newly arrived repatriates. These programs enabled families to achieve self-sufficiency in the immediate post–World War II period and in the late 1950s through the 1960s.

Jewish workshops and larger enterprises not only provided employment for thousands of Jews living in Poland but also reinforced the concept of Jewish self-help in social welfare efforts and contributed to the development of Jewish social, educational, and cultural life. This was all possible thanks to subsidies allotted by the cooperatives from their revenue (a fixed percentage of the cooperatives' income was transferred to Jewish institutions through the TSKŻ). As a result, in the late 1950s–1960s, the Socio-Cultural Association of the Jews in Poland, the central institution representing the Jewish community, was considered the most prosperous and successful minority institution in the country.[54]

Deteriorating Political Conditions

The situation with regard to the Joint and the Jewish community deteriorated as early as 1960. The changes were marked by the return to power of General Kazimierz Witaszewski, the Polish Army's political chief. In April of that year, Akiva Kohane, the Joint's country director, wrote: "The political changes—some of which may have a strong impact on our work in

Poland, and to a larger degree on the future existence and development of the Kulturverband, are generally ascribed to General Witaszewski's return to power."[55] Minister of Labor and Social Affairs Stanisław Zawadzki—government representative to Jewish affairs and the Joint's work in Poland—was dismissed. His successor, Jerzy Licki, according to Kohane, was "an anti-Semite in spite, or because, of the fact that he is a Jew who tries hard to conceal this fact."[56]

The work of the Joint was once again abruptly interrupted in August 1967 following the Six-Day War in the Middle East.[57] After being accused of espionage, of working for Western imperialism, and of Zionism, the Joint was forced to wind down its activities in Poland. The termination of the Joint's work in August 1967 can be seen today as a prelude to the government-sponsored antisemitic campaign that began only a few months later. The events known in history as March '68 led to the expulsion of almost 13,000 Polish nationals of Jewish origin from Poland.[58]

After the wave of emigration following the 1968 events in Poland, only a handful of Jews remained in the country.[59] Those who decided to stay in Poland cut themselves off from Jewish affairs and descended to the "underground." As a result, abandoned Jewish institutions entirely lost their vitality and resilience. As Kohane recalled:

> The building at Nowogrodzka 5 (Socio-Cultural Association of the Jews in Poland, TSKŻ) with its four floors of office space is completely deserted. . . . The buffet on the second floor exists and even serves cholent on Saturday . . . and on that day more people are coming to Nowogrodzka 5 than usual. Consequently, the TSKŻ is now being called among the Jews "the cemetery with cholent."[60]

In 1968, approximately 6,000 people received the Joint's aid, a total of $116,780, which was extended to 2,584 family case units, including residents of a home for the elderly in Warsaw and those awaiting emigration. The

Joint's family caseload declined to 1,148 in the following year.[61] It became a major challenge for the organization to continue to provide its indispensable help, particularly for impoverished and ill Holocaust survivors. But once again, the Joint found ways to reach those in need. In December 1967, Samuel Haber, in his letter to Alexander Easterman, wrote:

> For your confidential information I can tell you that we are able to continue to send money directly to the Religious Congregations, and of course we shall continue to do this as long as we are permitted to do so.[62]

Martial Law and Another Return of the Joint to Poland, 1981

It took twelve long years until another opportunity to resume work in Poland emerged. In 1981, when Polish government officials once more extended an invitation to the Joint, merely 5,000 Jews remained in the country (including apparently only twenty-five children with two Jewish parents).[63] Most were elderly Holocaust survivors, the sick and disabled, and those families who most needed support and assistance. Further complicating matters was the younger generation, represented by people raised outside Judaism who did not identify with the culture, tradition, and legacy of their ancestors. Many of them did not know about their Jewish heritage at all.

Technically, negotiations with Polish officials started as early as 1967, but it was not until the summer of 1981 that the decision was finalized at the time of a visit of a Joint delegation to Poland headed by Henry Taub, the Joint's president, and Ralph Goldman, executive vice president. A few months later, on December 14, 1981—coincidentally a day after martial law was declared—the Polish government, represented by Jerzy Kuberski, head of the Office of Religious Affairs, and Ralph Goldman signed an agreement allowing the Joint to return to Poland. From that moment on, the Joint has been continuously providing assistance to the Polish Jewish community based on the Joint's mission of "rescue, relief, and renewal."

The return of the organization in January 1982 helped strengthen the remnants of Jewish life in Poland and assist the community in awakening from hibernation, a process that took root in the late 1970s prior to the Joint's direct involvement. As recommended by the Office of Religious Affairs, at that time the Joint was operating through the Warsaw-based Coordinating Committee of Jewish Organizations and Institutions in Poland (Komisja Koordynacyjna Organizacji i Instytucji Żydowskich w Polsce). It was composed of the following institutions: the TSKŻ, the ZRWM, the Jewish Historical Institute (Żydowski Instytut Historyczny), the Jewish State Theatre (Państwowy Teatr Żydowski), and the editorial board of the Jewish weekly *Fołks Sztyme*.[64]

In the 1980s, Polish Jewish activities were limited, for the most part, to membership in the fourteen secular clubs of the Socio-Cultural Association of the Jews in Poland across the country. In fact, these were the only places providing an alternative for Jewish cultural life while also attempting to create a link to Jewish tradition. The remaining Jews rarely observed religious practices at this time, but many were looking for connection to Jewish tradition and culture. With the Joint's assistance, clubs run by the TSKŻ received hundreds of films and recordings of Jewish music.

Akiva Kohane, who once again supervised the Joint's operations in Poland, recounted with satisfaction that during lunch programs, one could listen to songs in Yiddish in every Jewish canteen. Funds were also allocated for actors from the Jewish Theatre to go on tour and to perform across Poland. For Kohane, who was born and raised in Poland, his work undoubtedly had sentimental significance, but it was often a challenging task. The fact that he was born, raised, and educated in Poland definitely helped him better understand the situation of those Jews who remained in his native country. His emotional involvement in what he was doing also shines through documents describing the Joint's work in Poland. The hardest part was always associated with his visits to his hometown, Kraków, which despite the passage of time since the war evoked the most painful memories. In an interview in the 1980s, he recalled that every such visit was "always emotionally draining."[65] For him, "Poland is a vast cemetery of Jewish history. . . . for over 1,000 years [the Jews] shared with [the Poles] a splendid history, which no longer existed after the Second World War." Kohane felt that "within a few years there will be no Jewish community in

Poland because there are no young people." As he recalled, "Every week there are several funerals." Furthermore, from his perspective, rebuilding the Jewish community in Poland was a lost cause: "We won't be able to make this community self-sufficient."[66] Regardless, Kohane believed that both the Joint and the Jewish community worldwide shared the responsibility to provide a decent life for the remaining Holocaust survivors so that they could live out their final days in dignity.[67]

This grim scenario, expressed in the aforementioned interview, soon began to fade and was clearly at variance with what Kohane wrote in his reports in the second half of the 1980s. For example, in March 1987 he wrote about a meeting of sixty young people organized by various TSKŻ branches that had taken place in December 1986 at the center in Śródborów. Although a small minority of the participants had grown up in Jewish homes, they demonstrated a growing interest in the culture and history of their ancestors.[68] Kohane recalled:

> [The participants] expressed an interest in continuing these meetings and learning more about *Yiddishkeit*. Therefore, smaller youth groups are meeting in Wrocław, Katowice, Wałbrzych and Warsaw. They attend lectures on Jewish history, holidays and literature. . . . What is astonishing is that this group is making it a priority to do something about the phenomenon of marrying outside the faith. Consequently, *Folks Sztyme* is soon to begin publishing matrimonial advertisements for this group. . . . The future will show if this is a real and serious attempt on the part of some of these young people to identify themselves as Jews and whether they will become involved in Jewish life, or whether it will be a short-lived enthusiasm, partly the result of free vacations at Śródborów, and some of them will lose interest in seeking their "roots." It is to be hoped that this interest will develop into a deeper involvement, to becoming a Jew. Whatever the future might bring, I believe that we must definitely support these activities. They can still bring results.[69]

As Kohane described, this was undoubtedly the start of a new era in the postwar history of the Jews in Poland. Young people discovering their Jewish ancestry were key to the rebuilding of Jewish life. For many, this was the start of a struggle with their own identity. As a result, interest in Jewishness began to grow in popularity.

Upon the Joint's return to Poland in the 1980s, the organization did not follow the pattern of activities developed in the previous decades. Following the events of the 1960s and mass emigration, there was no need to create the same institutions, such as Jewish cooperatives or vocational schools. The Jewish community was now composed of older and, in many cases, ill Holocaust survivors who needed palliative rather than constructive assistance. Young people who discovered their Jewish origin mostly struggled with their new identity. Kohane, for his part, was not convinced that people who had grown up outside the Jewish community, especially in Catholic families, would be able to continue the heritage of the Polish Jews. From his perspective, the Joint's responsibility was to provide financial assistance to the needy Jews who survived the Holocaust. Over time, Kohane also recognized a need to subsidize programs for younger Jews often entering the Jewish community that focused on education in the spirit of *Yiddishkeit*. He thus distinguished between those who were seriously involved with Jewish community life and had integrated into it (and who were even considering conversion) and those who, motivated by curiosity, continued to be practicing, mainly Catholic, Christians.[70] Kohane wrote in one of his reports: "We are ready to support these groups as long as *Yiddishkeit*, the history of the Jewish people, Jewish literature, Jewish religion and so on remain the focus of their attention. However, young people declaring Christianity [as their religion] and/or going to mass should be excluded, unless they wish to return to Judaism."[71]

Soon, the focus of reviving Jewish life again became the well-known center of Śródborów, located 30 km southeast of Warsaw, which over the years had become a historical as well as a symbolic site. For a number of years after the war, it had served as a children's home and a sanatorium for Jewish children. Toward the end of the 1950s, its last owner had proposed selling the site. Because the suggested price for the whole complex was not excessive, the Joint allocated special funds to purchase it, given that the owner was keen to be paid in US dollars in installments over ten years. The building was eventually restored thanks to Joint funds, with substantial support from the Polish government. The site has been continuously serving the Jewish community since World War II for both recreational and educational purposes.[72] It is there that meetings of Jewish youth have been continually held.

Conclusion

Throughout the five decades of the Polish People's Republic, the Joint successfully continued its mission of rescue, relief, and renewal. Although its work was certainly not always easy or free of controversy, the Joint significantly contributed to the rebuilding and sustaining of Jewish life in Poland. Challenged by the Communist authorities' requirements and frequent animosity from the Jewish leadership on the ground, the Joint, to a large degree, leveraged and shaped Jewish communal life in the new realm of Communist Poland. In different periods, the Joint's staff worked hard to meet the changing needs of Poland's Jewish community while at the same time maintaining its commitment to help meet the welfare needs of impoverished Holocaust survivors. Community development programs, welfare, and constructive assistance were key aspects of the Joint's work in Poland throughout the Communist era.

Notes

1. Most of the publications devoted to the Joint's work merely recall work of the organization in Poland. Aside from the general sources referenced in the introduction to this volume, see specifically on Poland, Tom Shachtman, *I Seek My Brethren: Ralph Goldman and "The Joint": The Work of the American Jewish Joint Distribution Committee* (New York: Newmarket Press, 2001); Yosef Litvak, "The American Joint Distribution Committee and Polish Jewry, 1944–1949," in *Organizing Rescue: Jewish National Solidarity in the Modern Period*, ed. Selwyn Ilan Troen and Benjamin Pinkus (London: Routledge, 1992), 269–312.
2. JDC Archives, Records of the New York Office of the American Jewish Joint Distribution Committee, 1945–1954, Folder 2183, Memorandum from Overseas Trip of Joseph C. Hyman, September 17, 1947.

3. USHMM Archive, Oral history interview, Oscar Haber, Holocaust survivor, May 17, 2000.

4. See David Engel, "The Reconstruction of Jewish Communal Institutions in Postwar Poland: The Origins of the Central Committee of Polish Jews, 1944–1945," *East European Politics and Societies* 10, no. 1 (1996): 88; JDC Archives, Records of the New York Office of the American Jewish Joint Distribution Committee, 1945–1954, Folder 734, Statistical Data of the Emigration Department of JDC, February 7, 1947. According to the Joint's archival documents, no more than 50,000 Jews lived in Poland in May 1945. This number was soon increased by 20,000 Jewish soldiers serving in the Polish army and 160,000 Jews who in 1946 were repatriated from the USSR.

5. JDC Archives, Records of the New York Office of the American Jewish Joint Distribution Committee, 1945–1954, Folder 734, Statistical Data of the Emigration Department of JDC, February 7, 1947; see also Mark Edele and Wanda Warlik, "Saved by Stalin? Trajectories and Numbers of Polish Jews in the Soviet Second World War," in *Shelter from the Holocaust: Rethinking Jewish Survival in the Soviet Union*, ed. Mark Edele, Sheila Fitzpatrick, and Atina Grossmann (Detroit: Wayne State University Press, 2017), 95–131. According to the Joint's archival documents in May 1945, no more than 50,000 Jews lived in Poland. To this, one can add 20,000 Jewish soldiers serving in the Polish army and some 160,000 Jews who in 1946 were repatriated from the USSR. Research on these numbers is ongoing.

6. Józef Adelson, *W Polsce zwanej Ludową in Najnowsze dzieje Żydów w Polsce w zarysie* (do 1950 roku), ed. Jerzy Tomaszewski (Warszawa: Wydawnictwo Naukowe PWN, 1993), 398.

7. JDC Archives, Records of the New York Office of the American Jewish Joint Distribution Committee, 1945–1954, Folder 734, Report on Poland, September 30, 1946.

8. Engel, "Reconstruction of Jewish Communal Institutions," 93.

9. Ibid., 85–107.

10. Ibid., 94.

11. Telegram from Emil Sommerstein to the office of the Joint Distribution Committee in New York and the Jewish Agency in Palestine on August 24,

1944, requesting immediate assistance for the surviving Jews in Poland, in Yehuda Bauer, *Out of the Ashes: The Impact of American Jews on Post-Holocaust European Jewry* (Oxford: Pergamon Press, 1989), 2.

12. Alex Grobman, *Battling for Souls: The Vaad Hatzala Rescue Committee in Post-War Europe* (Jersey City, NJ: Ktav, 2004), 22. In the first months after the liberation, the Joint had 266 employees in Europe; the Jewish Agency, 92; HIAS, 34; and the Vaad Hatzala Rescue Committee, 12.

13. See Grossmann's chapter in this volume for a discussion of redirecting aid sent from Tehran to liberated Poland rather than Central Asia.

14. National Archives and Records Administration, College Park, MD, 59/1173C Box 4, Memorandum from Conversation of Moses A. Leavitt with Elbridge Durbrow, May 4, 1944.

15. Yosef Litvak, "The American Joint Distribution Committee and Polish Jewry 1944–1949," in *Organizing Rescue: Jewish National Solidarity in the Modern Period*, ed. Selwyn Ilan Troen and Benjamin Pinkus (London: Routledge, 1992), 270.

16. Litvak, "American Joint Distribution Committee and Polish Jewry," 270.

17. JDC Archives, Records of the New York Office of the American Jewish Joint Distribution Committee, 1933–1944, Folder 24, Minutes of the Meeting of the Executive Committee, September 13, 1944.

18. The government of the United States attached enormous importance to controlling the operations of American nongovernmental organizations (NGOs) operating in different parts of the world. Starting in May 1946, all US humanitarian NGOs, irrespective of where they were operating, were brought under the auspices of the Advisory Committee on Voluntary Foreign Aid and were thus obliged to follow the regulations of this government body, set up by President Truman. The committee continues to be the central organization regulating relations between the government of the United States and charitable organizations, and it defines areas of competence in providing aid and rebuilding various communities and ethnic groups outside the United States.

19. In 1921, the Joint initiated the Society for Safeguarding of Jewish Health (known as TOZ), and it went on to support the establishment of Jewish hospitals, childcare institutions, and food distribution stations throughout

the country in cooperation with local Jewish institutions, saving thousands of lives. Over sixty such institutions were being run by the Joint in 1929.

20. Stefan Grajek, *Po wojnie i co dalej. Żydzi w Polsce, w latach 1945–1949* (Warszawa: 2003), 213–14. For a discussion of TOZ in interwar Poland, see the chapter in this volume by Rakefet Zalashik.

21. Yehuda Bauer, *Out of the Ashes: The Impact of American Jews on Post-Holocaust European Jewry* (Oxford: Pergamon Press, 1989), 76.

22. August Grabski, *Działalność komunistów wśród Żydów w Polsce, 1944–1949* (Warszawa: 2004), 126–30. Distribution of funds led to exacerbated arguments among CKŻP Executive Committee members until termination of the Joint activities in Poland in 1949.

23. Jewish Historical Institute, Folder 303/I/1b, 95, Memorandum from a Meeting of CKŻP, July 8, 1945.

24. JDC Archives, Records of the New York Office of the American Jewish Joint Distribution Committee, 1945–1954, Folder 730, Letter from William Bein, March 6, 1948.

25. Ibid.

26. JDC Archives, Records of the New York Office of the American Jewish Joint Distribution Committee, 1945–1954, Folder 734, Report January to September 1946, AJDC Poland, October 7, 1946.

27. Ibid.; Bauer, *Out of the Ashes*, 78. According to Bauer's estimates, JDC calculated the value of the złoty at 100 to the dollar. In March 1946, the Central Committee of Polish Jews requested a total monthly budget of $1 million per month, but Schwartz and JDC could approve only $475,000 per month—nearly $6 million at today's value. According to JDC's own publication *1946: Year of Survival*, JDC sent $8.4 million in cash grants and supplies to Poland in 1946. See G45–54_ADM_051_0672 YEAR OF SURVIVAL 1946, 7.

28. See David Engel, *Bein Shichrur Li-Verichah: Nitzulei HaShoah Be-Polin Ve-Hamavak al Hanhagatam, 1944–1946* (Tel Aviv: Am Oved, 1996), 203. According to the calculations of historian David Engel, in the spring of 1945, 7.5% of the total Jewish youth in Poland had joined the kibbutzim of Zionist youth movements, and by the fall of 1945, this number had grown to 17%. Between June and November 1945, the number of Jewish

youth living in the kibbutzim of youth movements grew by at least 500%. Among the youth movements that emphasized "pioneer" training (*Hashomer Hatzair*, *Dror*, and *Gordoniah*), the number had increased to 7,167 members by the spring and summer of 1946 from as few as 800 the winter before.

29. The term *Regained Territories* was invented by the Communist propaganda to describe the German territory of Western Poland that was incorporated into Poland based on the decision of the major powers during the Potsdam Conference in July 1945. Before the outbreak of World War II, this territory was inhabited by approximately 7 million Germans. At least 50% of the German population left this area before the end of the war. After expelling the remaining 3.5 million Germans, the so-called Regained Territories became home to almost 5 million people, including 90,000 Jews. It soon became the largest center of Jewish life in post–World War II Poland.

30. Ministry of Foreign Affairs in Poland Archive, Folder 6/105/1685, Letter from Director of Political Department of the Ministry of Public Administration A. Grabowski to the Minister of Foreign Affairs, April 28, 1945.

31. Jaff Schatz, *The Generation: The Rise and Fall of the Jewish Communists of Poland* (Berkeley: University of California Press, 1991), 235.

32. JDC Archives, Records of the New York Office of the American Jewish Joint Distribution Committee, 1945–1954, Folder 756, Letter from AJDC Warsaw to Dr. Joseph J. Schwartz, November 1, 1946.

33. Central Archives of Modern Records, Warsaw, Poland, AAN MAP Folder 795, 81, Letter from A. Grabowski to the Board of the Department of Housing Management in Warsaw, July 18, 1945.

34. JDC Archives, Records of the New York Office of the American Jewish Joint Distribution Committee, 1945–1954, Folder 729, Poland General—1948.

35. The period of Stalinization was marked by increased terror; elimination of political opposition; unification of all social and educational institutions, which were subordinated to the Communist ideology; and introduction of the economic system modeled on the Soviet system.

36. JDC Archives, Records of the New York Office of the American Jewish Joint Distribution Committee, 1945–1954, Folder 728, Memorandum from the Meeting of the Executive Committee, October 11, 1949.

37. Ibid.

38. JDC Archives, Records of the New York Office of the American Jewish Joint Distribution Committee, 1955–1964, Folder 658, Memorandum from Zachariah Shuster to Foreign Affairs Department, Subject: The Situation in Poland, August 14, 1957.

39. Institute of the National Remembrance Archive, Folder 192/433/6, vol. 4, 35–36, Decision to Turn Over Józef Gitler-Barski Case, March 27, 1951. At the time, Barski was the director of the General Department in the PKO Bank; therefore, his case was investigated in 1951 by the 5th Department of the Ministry of Public Security.

40. For more on this topic, see the chapter in this volume by Mikhail Mitsel.

41. Mikołaj Latuch, *Repatriacja ludności polskiej w latach 1955–1960 na tle zewnętrznych ruchów wędrówkowych* (Warszawa: 1994), 78.

42. Ibid., 81. Repatriation agreements from the years 1956 to 1959 referred to the agreements signed in the 1940s, as evidenced by the record of the agreement concluded in 1957 with the government of the Polish People's Republic and the Soviet government on the timing and mode of further repatriation:

> Given that the majority of people of Polish nationality, have expressed a desire to repatriate . . . based on the previous Polish-Soviet agreements, given the fact, that many people of the Polish nationality have not exercised the right to repatriation, and guided by the desire to further strengthen Polish-Soviet friendship it was decided, in accordance with the Joint Polish-Soviet Declaration, signed in Moscow on November 13th 1956 to conclude the following agreement.

Although in the 1940s everybody who was a Polish citizen before September 17, 1939, could return to the country, in the 1950s every request for repatriation had to be approved by the authorities of both countries (including those released under the amnesty of June 27, 1956).

43. National Archives and Records Administration, College Park, MD, 59 848.46/2–855, Box 4550, Memorandum from Conversation Sent by the US Ambassador to Poland Jacob Beam to the US State Department after the Meeting with the Representatives of the Joint, October 1, 1957.

44. JDC Archives, Records of the New York Office of the American Jewish Joint Distribution Committee, 1955–1964, Folder 1251, Report of the Executive Vice Chairman to the Executive Committee, October 6, 1959.

45. Central Archives of Modern Records, Warsaw, Poland, AAN MZiOS Folder 13/31, 262, Memorandum from a Meeting of Charles Jordan and Akiva Kohane of JDC with Jan Rutkiewicz, Undersecretary of State in the Ministry of Health and Social Welfare, October 12, 1966.

46. "Memorandum of a Conversation, Department of State, Washington, October 16, 1957," in *Foreign Relations of the United States, 1955–1957*, vol. XXV, *Eastern Europe*, ed. John P. Glennon, Edward C. Keefer, Ronald O. Landa, and Stanley Shaloff (Washington, DC: US Government Printing Office, 1990), 676.

47. National Archives and Records Administration, College Park, MD, 59 848.20/6–255, Box 4548, Memorandum from Conversation of Seymour Rubin with Valdemar Johnson, August 27, 1957.

48. JDC Archives, Records of the New York Office of the American Jewish Joint Distribution Committee, 1955–1964, Folder 658, Press Release Issued by Samuel Jaffe, Public Relations Director of JDC, December 2, 1957.

49. Grzegorz Smolar, "Pomoc tak, ale dla kogo i w jaki sposób," *Fołks-Sztyme*, February 5, 1959.

50. JDC Archives, Records of the New York Office of the American Jewish Joint Distribution Committee, 1955–1964, Folder 656, Memorandum from Samuel L. Haber to Charles H. Jordan, Subject: Field Trip Poland—February 4–14, 1959, February 16, 1959.

51. Ewa Węgrzyn, "Emigracja ludności żydowskiej z Polski do Izraela w latach 1956–1959. Przyczyny, przebieg wyjazdu i proces adaptacji w Erec Israel" (PhD diss., Jagiellonian Univeristy, Kraków, 2012), 72.

52. Central Archives of Modern Records, Warsaw, Poland, AAN MZiOS Folder 13/31, 41, Memorandum from an Inspection in the CKŻP Office, October 1961.

53. JDC Archives, Records of the New York Office of the American Jewish Joint Distribution Committee, 1955–1964, Folder 931, Report by Akiva Kohane, August 11, 1959.

54. Eugeniusz Mironowicz, *Polityka narodowościowa PRL* (Białystok: 2000), 201.

55. JDC Archives, Records of the New York Office of the American Jewish Joint Distribution Committee, 1955–1964, Folder 990, Report by Akiva Kohane, April 26, 1960.

56. Ibid.

57. The Six-Day War in the Middle East triggered the so-called anti-Zionist campaign sponsored by the government of Poland. According to Polish scholar Dariusz Stola, it is misleading and inappropriate to refer to the campaign as "anti-Zionist" because the campaign initially directed against the State of Israel soon became anti-Jewish and affected the majority of Polish Jews. The terms *Zionism* and *Zionist*, used by the Polish propaganda in numerous publications and public speeches, became a substitute for the words *Jew* and *Jewish*.

58. Dariusz Stola, *Kraj bez wyjścia? Migracje z Polski 1949–1989* (Warszawa: 2010), 221. For further reference, see also Dariusz Stola, "Anti-Zionism as a Multipurpose Policy Instrument: The Anti-Zionist Campaign in Poland, 1967–1968," *Journal of Israeli History* 25, no. 1 (2006).

59. JDC Archives, Records of the New York Office of the American Jewish Joint Distribution Committee, 1965–1974, Folder 319, Memorandum: Polish Refugee Movement since Six-Day War until December 31, 1969, January 23, 1970. Kohane indicates three stages of emigration triggered by the "anti-Zionist campaign." The first was marked by the Gomułka's speech in 1967; 380 people left the country prior to the March events. In the immediate post-March period (between March 1968 and June 1969), approximately 5,700 people left Poland. Of this number, 4,693 people emigrated via Vienna in Austria to various countries and about 1,000 emigrated to Scandinavian countries, mostly Denmark. The last stage began in July 1969 after the government revised emigration regulations and lasted until the end of this year. It was estimated that 4,800 people left Poland at that time. Kohane believes that the emigration was halted because of a very negative response in the Western media, condemning the Polish government's actions. The data provided by Kohane indicate that in the years between 1967 and 1969, about 10,900 people (mostly Jews and their non-Jewish spouses and children) left Poland. This is a much lower number than the estimates provided by Stola, who believes that 12,927 people emigrated in this time span.

60. JDC Archives, Records of the New York Office of the American Jewish Joint Distribution Committee, 1965–1974, Folder 319, Memorandum to File from Akiva Kohane, March 18, 1969.

61. JDC Archives, Records of the New York Office of the American Jewish Joint Distribution Committee, 1965–1974, Folder 319, Memorandum from Akiva Kohane, JDC–Geneva, to Samuel L. Haber, JDC–New York, Subject: Transfers to Poland, January 10, 1969.

62. JDC Archives, Records of the New York Office of the American Jewish Joint Distribution Committee, 1965–1974, Folder 321, Letter from Samuel L. Haber to Alexander L. Easterman, December 20, 1967.

63. JDC Archives, Records of the New York Office of the American Jewish Joint Distribution Committee, 1975–1989, Folder PL1, Situational Analysis for Poland, April 18, 1985.

64. Institute of the National Remembrance Archive, Folder 1585/7151, p. 4, May 17, 1982.

65. K. Friedman, "Kohane—Custodian of Polish Jewry's 'Lost Cause,'" *Palm Beach Jewish World* 1, no. 16 (1987).

66. Ibid.

67. Ibid.

68. JDC Archives, Records of the New York Office of the American Jewish Joint Distribution Committee, 1975–1989, Folder PL5, Report by Akiva Kohane, March 10, 1987.

69. Ibid., Folder PL5, Report by Akiva Kohane, March 10, 1987.

70. Kohane referred to young Poles who were raised Catholic in often intermarried families or who at some point in their lives learned about having Jewish ancestors in their families. It is a widely known Polish phenomenon in today's Poland—the so-called deathbed confessions—when parents or grandparents share information about their Jewish origin.

71. JDC Archives, Records of the New York Office of the American Jewish Joint Distribution Committee, 1975–1989, Folder PL5, Report by Akiva Kohane, May 6, 1987.

72. Ibid.

11

Years of Survival

JDC in Postwar Germany, 1945–1957

Avinoam Patt and Kierra Crago-Schneider

The work of the American Jewish Joint Distribution Committee (JDC) with the survivors of the Holocaust in postwar Germany is a tale of remarkable achievement and incredible resilience framed against a backdrop of frustration and disappointment. Although JDC succeeded in raising enormous sums to aid the survivors living in Europe after liberation (approximately $194 million between 1945 and 1948) and helped support a vibrant, albeit temporary, community of survivors in the displaced persons (DPs) camps, even these vast sums proved to be wildly insufficient. For the survivors, who despaired during the war over lack of contact from world Jewry and then felt betrayed and abandoned at the moment of liberation when it seemed no one came to their aid, JDC was, in the words of Yehuda Bauer, "the agency that came too late."[1] Despite this, JDC in postwar Germany worked with the US Army, the United Nations Relief and Rehabilitation Administration (UNRRA), and its successor, the International Refugee Organization (IRO), as well as the Central Committee of Liberated Jews (CCLJ or Zentral Komitet [ZK]) to rehabilitate the surviving population in postwar Germany while respecting the DPs' desire for autonomy and control over their own destiny.

The vocal independence of the DPs and the lingering sense of abandonment manifested in a perceived sense of entitlement among the survivors, who demanded the right to dictate their own futures on account of the immense suffering they had endured. Throughout the postwar period, JDC struggled to bridge the immense gaps that existed in understanding and communicating with the surviving population while responding to the immediate and long-term needs of a population in flux. Throughout the postwar period, the nature of the surviving population shifted as the number of Jewish DPs increased with the arrival of infiltrees from Eastern Europe, many of them funneled to Germany by the Bricha, and as the number of camp inhabitants decreased with the mass emigrations between 1948 and 1952. The transformation of the surviving population from individual survivors, often unattached and without family, to young families with children, many of whom had survived in the Soviet Union, also posed a challenge to JDC in organizing relief and aiding resettlement. Striving to help the Jewish DPs rebuild their lives, JDC fostered a robust educational, cultural, and religious life in the DP camps and assisted in the development of vocational training opportunities to facilitate emigration from Germany (presumably to countries of the DPs' choosing) as soon as possible.

Although it was an established international aid agency, JDC had never faced a challenge such as the one it encountered in its daily work with the Jewish DPs under its care in camps throughout West Germany. The demands, convictions, and goals of the DPs challenged the core fundamental principles dictating the operational goals of JDC. Working with the Holocaust survivors who made up the *She'erit Hapletah* (or surviving remnant, as these Jewish DPs in Germany referred to themselves) convinced JDC that the model it had previously employed in caring for Jews in need would not work for the Jewish DPs. Perhaps the greatest illustration of this change in JDC policy can be found in its approach to the problem of statelessness among the DPs. Although JDC had historically striven to remain "apolitical," in this circumstance, it gradually came to support Zionist efforts for a political solution, hoping that the creation of the Jewish state would end the Jewish DP problem. The DP situation also challenged JDC's guiding principles when it came to the organization's philanthropic model, which traditionally mandated that the relief agency maintain control over the distribution of resources. Interactions between JDC and the survivors in postwar Germany would be marked by struggles over control of funding and supplies, with the latter demonstrating a fierce independence that reflected a self-reliance forged during the war, which also complicated JDC's work.

Although Zionism and Israel had emerged as the consensus solution to the statelessness of the surviving remnant, after the creation of the State of Israel in May 1948 and the conclusion of hostilities there in 1949, JDC struggled to tend to the needs of a small but "hard-core" population of survivors in Germany who either could not or would not leave the temporary "waiting life" in the DP camps, oftentimes perceived by the DPs to be the safest haven for them in Germany.

This chapter will trace the work of JDC in postwar Germany (with a specific focus on the American zone of liberated Germany) between the years 1945 and 1957. The first part of the chapter will examine the work of JDC in the American zone between 1945 and 1948; the second part of the chapter will examine JDC's work with the "hard-core" DPs who remained in Germany even after the creation of the State of Israel and changes in American immigration laws had allowed some 200,000 former DPs to resettle abroad. The work of JDC in postwar Germany, that unlikely but crucial haven for survivors after the Holocaust, can arguably be pointed to as one of JDC's greatest challenges, and greatest accomplishments, in its century of relief work.

THE JEWS IN GERMANY AFTER LIBERATION

As Allied forces conquered Nazi Germany in the spring of 1945, they began to discover atrocities "beyond belief" in camp after liberated camp. The freeing of prisoners in Buchenwald, Dora-Mittelbau, Flossenbürg, Dachau, and Mauthausen, as well as those in northern Germany, including Neuengamme and Bergen-Belsen, brought relief, salvation, and tremendous uncertainty for the Jewish prisoners who had survived. Although most of the 10 million DPs, prisoners of war (POWs), and forced laborers liberated in Germany were quickly repatriated after the war, the 50,000 or so Jewish DPs faced a much more challenging set of choices. Unsure of what awaited them at home and often fairly certain that their families had been murdered, those who decided to stay in hastily erected DP camps found themselves living among collaborators who had also refused to return home.[2] Jewish DPs who decided to remain in Germany thus faced a choice: They could remain in the DP camps (established at highly diverse sites, such as German military barracks, former POW and slave labor camps, tent cities, industrial housing, or even in the midst of cities) or they could leave the DP camps if they chose to settle in Germany permanently, a choice that some 15,000 German Jewish survivors, not generally classified as DPs, made in the summer of 1945.[3] Of the approximately 50,000–60,000 Jewish survivors, most of whom were not German Jews, liberated in Germany, many thousands perished from complications arising from disease, starvation, and the camp experience within the first weeks following liberation.[4]

Jewish chaplains serving with the American military were among the first Jews to encounter the survivors in the camps (along with the occasional Jewish Brigade soldier—the Brigade was a division from Palestine serving with the British Army).[5] Although JDC sought to gain access to the camps as early as May 1945 (Joseph Schwartz and Saly Mayer, who was the JDC honorary representative in Switzerland, were the first JDC representatives to enter Germany that spring), JDC's first organized group did not enter the American zone of occupation until August 1945, some three months later.[6] This meant that in the earliest stages after liberation, the survivors depended on the US Army and UNRRA for relief and on a small group of Jewish chaplains who played an especially significant role in tending to the needs of the survivors. One particularly active chaplain, Rabbi Abraham Klausner, who aided in the early political organization of *She'erit Hapletah*, reported to his superiors in the United States on the situation facing Jews in postwar Germany. Klausner found deplorable conditions, poor accommodations, no plumbing, no clothing, rampant disease, continuing malnourishment, and a lack of any plan on the part of the American military. "Liberated but not free, that is the paradox of the Jew," Klausner concluded: "[S]uffering continues to be [their] badge." As Klausner summarized in his June 24, 1945, report to Philip Bernstein, executive director of the National Jewish Welfare Board Committee on Army-Navy Religious Activities:

> There seems to be no policy, no responsibility, no plan for these . . . stateless Jews. . . . Twelve hours a day I tell my lies.

"They will come," I say. "When will they come?" they ask me. UNRRA, JDC, Red Cross—can it be that they are not aware of the problem? It is impossible. . . . Of what use is all my complaining; I cannot stop their tears. America was their hope and all America has given them is a new camp with guards in khaki. Freedom, hell no! They are behind walls without hope.[7]

Organizing among themselves, Jewish DPs voiced their frustration in letters to military authorities and world Jewish organizations (such as the World Jewish Congress and JDC), pleading for assistance from the US military government and UNRRA to rectify their miserable situation.[8] Expecting to be welcomed by the world with open arms, liberation was a rude awakening, as Jewish DPs continued to struggle to obtain bearable living conditions and yearned for contact from the rest of the Jewish world, which had still largely been denied access to the DP camps by military authorities seeking to establish order in the chaotic postwar situation. As Saly Mayer, former head of the Swiss Jewish community prior to the war and JDC honorary representative in Switzerland, noted in a cable to the JDC New York office following a visit to Germany in May 1945, moral support to alleviate the feeling of "being left to oneself and forgotten" was as important as material concerns to the survivors and the urgent questions about whether any family had survived.[9]

With JDC denied access to the military zone of occupation, survivors worked together with GIs and Jewish chaplains to organize help for themselves. Klausner met Zalman Grinberg, a doctor and a survivor from Kovno, who commandeered part of a Benedictine monastery at St. Ottilien for use as a Jewish DP hospital and would become a close colleague in the rebuilding of Jewish life in postwar Germany during his early work in Bavaria.[10] As Grinberg wrote to the World Jewish Congress in May 1945, disappointment with the slow arrival of relief was evident:

It has been four weeks since our liberation and no representative of the Jewish world, no representative from any Jewish organization has come to be with us after the worst tragedy of all time, to speak with us, to give us help, and to lighten our burden. We must, ourselves, with our own diminished strength, help ourselves.[11]

Chastened by the absence of any assistance from world Jewry, Grinberg and Klausner, with the assistance of other survivors and representatives from the Jewish Brigade, decided to take matters into their own hands, establishing the CCLJ (or ZK) in the US Zone of Germany on July 1, 1945, as the official representative body of the Jewish DPs.[12] The purpose of the Central Committee was to champion the interests of the Jewish DPs and to draw attention to their plight before the US Army and UNRRA just as other national groups of DPs had done (the ZK would eventually gain official US Army recognition as "the legal and democratic representation of the liberated Jews in the American zone" in September 1946). The Central Committee focused its work on the survivors' immediate needs, including food, shelter, medicine, and security, and addressed the question of emigration, soon reaching a consensus that the surviving population should be encouraged to prepare themselves for immigration to Palestine at the earliest point possible.[13] The ZK appointed the American chaplain Abraham Klausner honorary president and elected Dr. Grinberg as chairman of the Executive Committee. At subsequent early meetings of the CCLJ in Germany and Bavaria (on July 25, 1945, and August 8, 1945), Klausner reminded the survivors that "we must help ourselves"[14] while initiating an "effort to stir the conscience of the world in view of our endless sufferings."[15]

At the August 8, 1945, meeting, the first meeting attended by representatives of JDC, the ZK summarized its accomplishments—all done "unofficially" and without outside assistance, including aiding Jews in Landsberg, Feldafing, St. Ottilien, and elsewhere; compiling lists of Jews throughout Bavaria; surveying conditions; and detailing the most pressing needs.[16] Eli Rock, who would become the first US zone director of JDC, apologized for the organization's late arrival, explaining that the US Army had not authorized its presence until July 30.[17] "I know that the Jews (here) feel bitterness towards the international organizations . . . and I apologize in the name of the JDC. . . . We have been here four days and do not know yet what we will be able to do. . . ." Rock went on to list the areas where JDC would focus its energies: emigration, clothing, supplies, economic work, and self-help work. In response, Yitzhak Ratner captured the bitterness felt by the survivors over the absence of JDC thus far:

> The representatives of the JDC claim that it is too soon to give a report. However, what did the JDC do during the six years that we were being burnt in the crematoria? And why did the JDC not come before today, even if it had to be illegally? Things have happened from the side of our brothers which cannot be forgotten, that is, the fact that during the war they never got directly involved [in our fate]. [Also] much could have been spared us if the JDC had come earlier. They must know that we do not want rations, the only thing we want is to be able to return to a normal life. The only place we want to go is Palestine.[18]

Over time, reports from survivors, Jewish chaplains, and American Jewish soldiers about continuing deprivation in the liberated camps and poorly organized recovery efforts prompted American officials to take a greater interest in the problem of the DPs, leading President Truman to dispatch Earl Harrison, dean of the University of Pennsylvania Law School, to Germany to investigate conditions there.[19] Once Harrison arrived in Germany, accompanied by Dr. Joseph J. Schwartz, director of JDC's overseas operations, the Jewish DPs, along with Abraham Klausner and soldiers from the Jewish Brigade, worked to make sure that he was aware of the miserable conditions facing the Jews.[20] Harrison visited Jewish DPs in thirty separate camps following his July 22, 1945, arrival and witnessed firsthand the deplorable conditions they continued to face three months after liberation.[21]

Harrison's scathing report prompted American authorities to ameliorate conditions for Jewish DPs, moving Jews to separate camps and establishing an adviser for Jewish affairs. Harrison's proposal that the Jewish DPs immediately be granted 100,000 immigration certificates to Palestine as well as his suggestions for separate all-Jewish camps and improved conditions served to link the resolution of the Jewish DPs' statelessness with the situation in Palestine, thereby elevating the diplomatic implications of the DP question. The Harrison report also smoothed the way for the formal entry of JDC workers into the DP camps. The US Army was most comfortable working with a trusted and respectable Jewish welfare agency that could serve as an interpreter between the Jewish DPs and the military.[22]

After the Harrison report, JDC joined four other Jewish organizations—the American Jewish Conference, the Jewish Agency for Palestine, the World Jewish Congress, and the American Jewish Committee—to represent DP questions to the US government.[23] Rabbi Judah Nadich, the first adviser for Jewish affairs, also advocated for the US Army to invite JDC to send teams to the DP camps, and in August, Eli Rock and his group obtained a building at Siebertstrasse 3 in Munich, adjacent to the ZK offices, which would headquarter JDC for the next few years. These moves helped support the development of a more robust and organized JDC campaign to assist the Jewish DPs in the American zone of postwar Germany.

Nonetheless, the failure of JDC to organize relief until September 1945 would prove to be a point of bitterness for Klausner and the Jewish DPs. In a September 1945 letter sent to JDC on behalf of the Central Committee, Klausner voiced this frustration with JDC's slow arrival and with what seemed like a policy of misleading publicity about its aid efforts:

> Perhaps we can understand why [the] Joint was delayed in coming to our aid. Perhaps we can understand why the JDC could not help us after they arrived but understanding is not ours with regard to JDC publicity. Is it wise to lead the world to believe that the wounds of our people are being healed when their sores fester daily?[24]

JDC work in the US zone would indeed be defined by initial confusion over its mission as well as by constant reorganization and rotating leadership (the first four zone directors between October 1945 and January 1947 were Eli Rock, Lavy Becker, Leo Schwarz, and Samuel Haber).[25] Even so, reporting on JDC work in an October 21, 1945, report, Rock noted that over the six weeks since General Eisenhower had implemented Harrison's suggestions, "the situation of the Jews had improved considerably," with physical, housing, clothing, and food needs gradually being met.[26] Thirteen regular JDC representatives were now in the US zone, and "all of the large Jewish installations are now covered by JDC personnel."[27]

In the fall of 1945, just as the Joint began to organize its operations in the US zone, its field operatives grew increasingly concerned with the growth of the Jewish population, which was swelling due to the Bricha from Eastern Europe. The Bricha (literally "flight") was the semi-organized movement of Jews from Poland shortly after the liberation of the eastern part of the country.[28] As JDC's Joseph Levine reported to Eli Rock in late October, Jews continued to stream in from Poland, swelling the DP population: "Jews are arriving daily from Poland who were never here but who somehow managed to survive elsewhere. On the other hand, many Jews are arriving who went to Poland immediately after liberation and who are returning either alone or with relatives."[29] In his October 21, 1945, report, Rock noted that in the six weeks since mid-September, some 10,000 Polish Jews had entered Bavaria following anti-Jewish outbreaks in Poland (including incidents in Kraków, Rzeszow, Kielce, Lublin, and Warsaw). Many of them lacked food and clothing, and the vast majority required immediate medical attention.[30] These "infiltrees," as they were known (many of whom had been repatriated from the Soviet Union where they had survived the war), lacked the legal status of DPs and were denied necessary support, exacerbating the situation.[31] Additional JDC reports confirmed Rock's account, documenting a lack of sufficient camps in the eastern US zone to accommodate arrivals from Poland; homeless Jewish refugees wandering the streets of Munich without food; and a pressing need for clothing and medicine for the new arrivals.[32] The American military authorities created new camps to reduce overcrowding and improve sanitary conditions, including establishing Föhrenwald as an alternative to Landsberg and Feldafing at the end of October.

The arrival of large numbers of Jews from Eastern Europe and the expansion of JDC relief coincided with a growing awareness on the part of the Jewish Agency for Palestine that the DP population could be mobilized in support of the Zionist cause. In this, the Jewish Agency, Bricha operatives in Poland, and American Jewish chaplains—most notably Herbert Friedman, chief military aide to Adviser on Jewish Affairs Philip Bernstein—collaborated to promote the Eastern European Jewish migration to the American zone of Germany so as to force the Jewish DP issue onto the American and international postwar agenda.[33] A January 1946 report from Jay Krane (JDC chief, reports and analysis branch) detailed the American military's growing concern with the new arrivals:

> Infiltration of Jewish people from Poland to Bavaria in early November became so critical and resulted in such overcrowding of the already established Jewish Centers, that General Truscott cabled USFET [United States Forces European Theater] for instructions. He was ordered to establish special centers for these infiltrees, but to reject non-Jewish infiltrees and all persons, whether Jewish or non-Jewish, who had already been repatriated.[34]

As Krane noted, General Truscott, working with UNRRA director Jack Whiting, agreed to provide the same rights to the infiltrees (as other DPs), who already numbered close to 25,000. The critical situation would require high-level government solutions to accommodate what was expected to be a growing wave of refugees from Eastern Europe. While offering no definitive proof that the flow was part of an organized movement (i.e., the Bricha), Krane seemed to agree with the assessment of US Army and UNRRA officials who felt that "the current deliberations of the Anglo-American Commission on Palestine—would seem to indicate that the infiltration movement is part and parcel of a plan to force the issue."[35] JDC, which assured the US government that it was not involved in organizing this mass movement, was nevertheless committed to assisting Jews in distress.[36]

Lavy Becker, a Canadian Jew from Montreal, replaced Eli Rock as the next JDC US zone director in late 1945, and it seems that his willingness to work with the Bricha movement and recognize the Zionist imperative for the DPs earned him the trust of the survivors.[37] Moreover, Becker developed a good working relationship with the Central Committee and avoided overly stringent administrative supervision of ZK activities. However, in April 1946 he was replaced as JDC zone director by Leo Schwarz, who would impose closer scrutiny over ZK expenditures. Relations between the ZK and JDC again seemed to decline with the arrival of Schwarz, even as JDC noted a growing efficacy around its efforts in the camps.[38] Indeed, by that spring, JDC had achieved greater organization of supply distribution and greater success working with UNRRA and the Central Committee. JDC teams worked throughout the DP camps under its jurisdiction as well as in kibbutzim and other communities to provide supplies and support educational, cultural, and religious activities (and both UNRRA and the US military government were quite happy to have JDC take on so much responsibility for the populations of Jewish DPs while bearing the burden of funding for supplemental aid). Still, as the DP population continued to increase, growing struggles over the control and distribution of these goods reflected questions of DP independence, self-esteem, efficiency, equity, and distribution, as well as the role of supplies in DP politics.[39] For his part, Leo Schwarz also quickly began to tire of the constant interference by Chaplain Klausner in his work and the regular complaints over the lack of adequate aid and soon made it his mission to have the troublesome Klausner removed from the American zone altogether. He also saw Klausner's criticism of JDC, such as in the GI letter-writing campaign that the young chaplain had called for at the High Holiday services in the fall of 1945, as hampering the organization's fundraising efforts in the United States. After convincing military and UNRRA authorities that Klausner had arranged unauthorized travel orders and was less than meticulous in his bookkeeping procedures, the military agreed to have Klausner returned to the United States in July 1946.[40] In a report that month to Jack Whiting, Schwarz noted "the only efficient thing JDC has done was to have him [Klausner] removed from the zone."[41]

Not surprisingly, Klausner's dismissal coincided with a continuing dispute between JDC and the Central Committee over the latter's independence. In a letter to Edward Warburg, chairman of JDC in New York, Zalman Grinberg described the Central Committee leadership as "an agency representing the political and material needs of the people."[42] He maintained that "the American Joint, if it so desires, can supply the budgetary needs of the Central Committee [but] it [should] not be granted the right to determine whether or not we shall support a newspaper, purchase a clarinet, or manufacture *talethim*."[43] The Joint would have the right to supply rations but not to determine how they were distributed. Following Klausner's dismissal, Grinberg wrote to Warburg:

> The Central Committee of Liberated Jews in the American occupied zone in Germany is compelled at the present time to call to the attention of the JDC that after July 15, 1946 it will cease to operate as an organization dependent on the resources of the Joint. This decision was reached after a series of discussions involving the Joint Directors of the American Zone and of Germany respectively. The various members of the Central Committee participated in these discussions . . .[44]

Grinberg reminded Warburg that by the time the Joint had arrived in the American zone, the Central Committee was already fully functioning but "put its resources at the disposal of the Joint." Illuminating the divide that existed between the *She'erit Hapletah* and the American Jewish leadership, Grinberg noted:

> [I]t is our feeling that the Directors of the American Joint look upon us as DPs. The use of the term DP in this sense connotes an individual not only displaced in terms of home but also in terms of vision and responsibility. Those Americans who have met our leadership or who have examined their work will testify to the absurdity of this attitude.[45]

Grinberg and the leadership of the CCLJ resented the patronizing attitude of American Jewish leaders who did not truly understand the needs of the survivors and felt they could dictate terms to them. For his part,

Leo Schwarz suspected that growing political factionalism among various Zionist political parties within the Central Committee would make the sharing of supplies unequal and therefore struggled to enforce equal representation on the Central Committee. Following Klausner's dismissal and the dispute between the ZK and JDC, Joseph Schwartz intervened, and a compromise was reached on August 3, 1946, that would leave the distribution and control of supplies to joint management by JDC and the Central Committee.[46]

Although some of the dispute between JDC and the Central Committee focused on the division, control, and allocation of resources, the ZK also resented what it saw as JDC's failure to recognize the role of the ZK in caring for the DPs, taking credit for achievements made by the ZK.[47] For JDC, relations with the ZK were not the only complicating factor in postwar Germany, as the Joint also had to negotiate relationships with other Jewish organizations representing various constituencies in the DP camps, including the Jewish Agency; myriad Zionist political parties and youth groups; religious groups focused on rebuilding Torah Judaism and Hasidic groups after the war, including *Vaad Hatzala* and Agudath Israel; and other aid organizations such as the Hebrew Immigrant Aid Society (HIAS), the Organization for Rehabilitation through Training (ORT), and the World Jewish Congress, which all sought to share credit for relief work in the camps.[48]

CHANGING DEMOGRAPHY, CHANGING NEEDS

As 1946 continued, the influx of Jews arriving from Eastern Europe, many in groups organized by the Bricha, had markedly transformed the demography of the *She'erit Hapletah*. By the end of the year, JDC estimated that the Jewish DP population in the American zone of Germany numbered over 145,000. This constituted a nearly 300% increase over the nearly 50,000 Jews in the zone at the beginning of the year.[49] With this tremendous growth came a transformation in the age structure of the population as well as shifts in their material, educational, and cultural needs. As JDC employee Georg Muentz noted in his JDC population survey for 1946, the arrival of large numbers of "repatriated" Jews who had been repatriated to

Poland from the Soviet Union and then fled again from postwar antisemitism shifted the demography of the *She'erit Hapletah*, which was now composed of 20.3% children under the age of 17 (8.5% were infants and children up to the age of 6) and 79.7% adults.[50] The percentage of babies had skyrocketed, as the Jewish DP population had undergone a veritable baby boom. Twenty-two percent of all children under the age of 17 were babies under 1 year old (5,349 out of 23,989).[51] Atina Grossmann has argued that such births reflected a "conscious affirmation of Jewish life" after the Holocaust.[52]

The much-celebrated DP baby boom also had practical implications. While immediately following liberation, unattached and orphaned young adults gravitated to Zionist frameworks promising speedy migration to Palestine, new families were less mobile and shifted how JDC worked to provide resources and how it imagined future resettlement.

In light of these difficulties, JDC struggled to keep up with growing needs and spiraling costs. The organization's 1946 annual report *Year of Survival* highlighted these challenges while celebrating JDC's remarkable accomplishments in delivering relief supplies to Jews in postwar Europe:

- Despite "chaotic European transportation conditions," JDC
  delivered some $14,000,000 in supplies on the basis of
  its 1946 program, including 41,500,000 pounds of foodstuffs; 6,800,000 pounds of wearing apparel and shoes,
  and 6,500,000 pounds of other necessities—medicines and
  surgical equipment, school books and educational materials,
  blankets and other commodities.

- "To relieve hunger in Germany and Austria, the JDC in
  1946 furnished 15,000,000 pounds of food, or better than
  one-third of the total foodstuffs shipped into all countries.
  These supplies, consisting principally of high-energy food,
  such as fish, meat, butter, fats and sugar, were augmented by
  local purchases. Distribution of food during the first half of
  the year was on a per capita basis, but later in the year after
  large numbers of infiltrees arrived destitute and hungry,
  allocations were based on the degree of need."[53]

The Year of Survival: 1946 JDC Annual Report, American Jewish Joint Distribution Committee, 1947.

Nevertheless, the challenges continued to mount. For example, on December 15, 1946, the United Nations passed a resolution dissolving UNRRA and replacing it with the successor organization, the IRO. Funding was greatly reduced, meaning that JDC had to provide even greater support for the DPs than it had previously. As Joseph Hyman noted in *Year of Survival,* "UNRRA is fading out of the picture and the shape of post-UNRRA relief is uncertain," meaning that JDC would be expected to carry the burden for supplies once they were provided by UNRRA:

> How does this affect the JDC? In Poland, Czechoslovakia and other countries where UNRRA was engaged in relief and rehabilitation programs, there will be an inevitable increase in general relief needs. Large scale supplies of scarce materials, formerly brought in by UNRRA and distributed at low prices, will no longer help to stabilize the economies of these countries as they have done in the past. Moreover, in the camps of Germany and Austria there are indications that the JDC will be expected to carry on much of the UNRRA program for displaced Jews.[54]

"BETWEEN HOPE AND DISAPPOINTMENT," 1947

By early 1947, outside observers had begun documenting a growing demoralization among Jewish DPs in Germany, fed up with overcrowding and impatient to leave the temporary existence of the DP camp. Abraham Klausner, who managed to orchestrate his own return to the US zone of Germany in the beginning of 1947, drafted a report in March that captured what he saw as the growing demoralization of the DPs in Germany:

> Spirit: The spirit of the people reflects a radical change. There is no longer an air of excitement, a darting of the eyes, a flood of questions—there is a feeling of resignation. Many leaders speak of the "demoralization" of the people. The use of the term should be qualified. Children housed in centers and organized into "kibbutzim" trained for a new life in Palestine are fiery in spirit, full of hope and faith.[55]

Klausner lamented the growing involvement of the DPs in the black market in Germany. As he noted, "typical of the prevailing spirit is the Dachau survivor who says 'The strong survive. Steal! That's it! Steal all you can, get what you need, there is no end to it all, there is no justice!'"[56] He also feared that the Central Committee no longer represented the will of the people and was now merely an institutionalized apparatus that "tries to assert authority on the people."[57]

In a letter to his friend and confidant, JDC welfare worker Ann Liepah, Klausner described the growing corruption of the political party system, which he suggested had hijacked the Central Committee's original mission. He also bemoaned the creation of an employment and rationing system that encouraged the Central Committee and camp committees to inflate the number of workers reported to JDC in order to increase rations and dole out favors.

> . . . I have been compelled to take a stand against the Committees. The organization grew rapidly after I left. It was taken over by various Zionist factions and is used in the interest of petty political differences rather than as an instrument for the good of the people. Munich alone has 1400 "employees" of which perhaps 100 work. The 1400 (1.5% of the people) consume 21% of the District 5 food. Similarly, the Regional Committees have grown up as political entities that serve no purpose other than providing a slush fund for the party in power. Munich, beside the Central Committee has a Munich committee and <u>two</u> Regional Committees. There is much to be said about the disease of party politics . . . one party will not give way to another. The tragedy is great when it is realized that the basic problem confronting the people is common to all factions.[58]

In conclusion, Klausner noted that although the leadership of the Central Committee agreed with his critique, they felt that "the system is overwhelming and little can be done." JDC was well aware of the problem of double-counting by camp committees (and thus inflating rations' distributions) and the abuse of rationing as a means of ensuring political power but found it equally difficult to deny rations to DPs and DP camps in need.[59] Even so, from the perspective of individual DPs, JDC, while celebrated for offering relief, was still a target for a bitter and impatient population. Henny Durmashkin, who sang in the Vilna ghetto and performed extensively with the St. Ottilien Orchestra in DP centers across Germany, lamented the policies of UNRRA and the Joint in her song "Joint'l": "What good are all these speeches / From Joint and Uncle Sam to me? / You either drop with hunger / Or take what you see. / These overflowing pledges / These promises to be / Have left us still in tatters / Nothing have we!"[60]

Jewish DPs in Germany thus faced 1947 with a declining sense of hope, particularly as options for immediate *aliyah* continued to decrease due to the continuing British policy of blockading migration to Palestine.[61] There was also reason to fear that DPs would fall into a pattern of idleness and demoralization: Whereas in February 1946, 25% of Jewish DPs were employed (vs. 36.25% of Germans working at the time), by the beginning of 1947, Georg Muentz of JDC estimated that no more than 15% of the over 50,000 infiltrees who had arrived between August 1946 and January 1947 had managed to find employment.[62]

Furthermore, American policy had shifted in an effort to limit the number of "infiltrees" into the American zone. General Lucius D. Clay (American commander as of March 1947) published an order stating that any Jews who arrived in the zone after April 21, 1947, would no longer be accepted in the DP camps and would be denied food from American sources. While the borders of the zone would never actually be closed to Jewish refugees, the housing shortages intensified as American efforts came to focus increasingly on German reconstruction.[63] To address these concerns, JDC began emphasizing existing vocational training programs (along with groups like ORT) to turn DPs into better emigrants while also developing programming for DP children, including summer camps.[64] As detailed in the *1946 Year of Survival*:

> It is . . . urgent for the JDC in 1947 to develop in Germany
> work programs on a scale so large that employment will

be provided for some 32,000 displaced Jews. One such
program calls for the establishment of a clothing factory
capable of turning out 1,000 suits and 300 overcoats weekly,
to serve the double purpose of supplying urgently needed
clothing and creating work opportunities for displaced Jews.
This clothing factory is but one of the many work projects
planned for 1947. Others include shoe factories and carpen-
ters' shops.[65]

As the *ha'apalah* (underground immigration to Palestine via ship) campaign intensified, particularly with the drama of the Exodus Affair in July 1947 and the disappointment following the passengers' return to Germany, it seemed to the DPs that they would have to settle in for another long winter without any break on the diplomatic front.[66] And then on November 29, 1947, following the recommendations of the United Nations Special Committee on Palestine, the United Nations voted to adopt the Palestine Partition plan, sending the Jewish DP camps into frenzied celebration. The *Jidiscze Cajtung* (formerly the *Landsberger Lager Cajtung*), the largest DP newspaper in circulation, tried to capture the excitement of the moment. The top headline read "The Yishuv Greets the UN Decision with Joy" and just under that, "Spontaneous Demonstrations by the *She'erit Hapletah*."[67] Spontaneous marches and demonstrations took place in all of the DP camps, and the Berlin Jewish community decided to hold special evening services in all of the synagogues to commemorate the occasion.[68]

Furthermore, it seemed that a massive immigration to the new state was imminent. Ben-Gurion announced a plan to bring 1.5 million Jews to the state in the next 10 years. The US special adviser for Jewish affairs in the zone, Judge Louis E. Levinthal, suggested that immigration would begin from the DP camps of Germany to Israel as early as February 1948. He estimated that as many as 600,000 Jews could be absorbed by Israel over six years.[69] The moment for which the Jewish DPs had waited for so long had arrived.

Even so, on March 15, 1948, at the first meeting of Jewish DP leadership with the new US adviser on Jewish affairs to the American zone, William

Haber (the brother of Samuel Haber, JDC US zone director), noted that there was still considerable concern over the morale of the DPs after over two and a half years in the camps, with the possibility of at least another year.[70] Although there was general consensus among the parties at the meeting that emigration to Palestine would be the best solution, the Central Committee was most consistent in its firm belief in the need for immediate departure. At the meeting with Haber, David Traeger, head of the ZK, argued that now was the time that "the Camps must be shaken up and the people must be reminded of their mission with respect to Palestine."[71]

From the leadership's perspective, emigration solved two major problems: black market participation and the fear that vocational training would immerse DPs in the German economy, making departure from the camps even less likely.[72] And yet, just as emigration to Palestine/Israel became a real possibility, American Jewish observers began to lament what they saw as the decreasing willingness of the DPs to leave. Observers such as Abraham Klausner suggested that, ironically, JDC might have made life in postwar Germany too comfortable for the survivors. In a confidential May 1948 report submitted to the American Jewish Conference, Klausner warned that because other immigration options were largely nonexistent (and especially given America's restrictive policy), most Jewish DPs would attempt to remain in Germany, isolated in separate camps, as wards of the US Army but also increasingly integrated into the German economy. The collective inertia of the Jewish DP population, he argued, had to be reversed by force. As Klausner suggested, "there is no social force in the world today as capable as that of Palestine to mold the mass now in Germany into positive members of a Jewish society. I am convinced that the people must be forced to go to Palestine."[73] With the unanimous consent of world Jewry, Klausner believed, such a program could be implemented, removing all of the comforts of life in the DP camps for Jews in Germany and withdrawing JDC supplies—those very comforts that Klausner had struggled to implement three years earlier!—making life so uncomfortable that Jews would choose to leave for Palestine.

Following Klausner's report, on May 4, 1948, a group of thirteen American Jewish leaders came together for a "Meeting of the Jewish

Co-operating Organizations on Rabbi Abraham Klausner's Suggestions Respecting the Jewish DP Situation." Among them were former Jewish advisers Rabbi Philip Bernstein and Judge Louis Levinthal; Nachum Goldmann of the Jewish Agency; Moses Leavitt and Boris Joffee from JDC; Kurt Grossmann, Stephen Wise, and Ignacy Schwartzbart of the World Jewish Congress; Herman Gray, Eugene Hevesi, and Simon Segal from the American Jewish Committee; and Meir Grossman and Arthur Liverhant from the American Jewish Conference, as well as Klausner himself. Klausner's characteristically dramatic presentation certainly alarmed the American Jewish leadership, although they drew differing conclusions. While some rejected Klausner's alarmist figures and generalizations out of hand, others took them as a warning of the dangers of demoralization and complacency among the survivors should nothing be done to remedy their situation. Philip Bernstein pointed to the irony of the present situation—while in the early stages of Jewish life in postwar Germany administrators had resisted any attempt to incorporate the DPs into the German economy in order to facilitate their speedy departure for Palestine when the time came, "today we face the fact of steady, catastrophic demoralization."[74] Morris (Moe) Leavitt of JDC downplayed what he saw as exaggerated statistics regarding DP involvement in the black market, arguing that on the contrary, Jewish DPs would need to engage in black market activity to a greater extent if supplies from JDC were reduced. William Haber noted Jewish Agency estimates that over 70% of Jewish DPs would seize the opportunity to immigrate to Palestine (still a decline from the 95% in earlier surveys but more in line with actual postwar migration patterns).

Klausner's anxiety pointed to a deeper concern—how many Holocaust survivors would actually choose to immigrate to the Promised Land given the outbreak of another war (with open armed confrontations between Arabs and Jews already a reality in Palestine)? When the time came for departure, would the DPs reject the Zionist solution to the DP problem? From JDC's perspective, the question was how to get Jewish DPs to leave Germany in a timely manner while maintaining supplies and making sure that they did not turn to black market activity in Germany. Clearly, a speedy emigration to Palestine would lessen the burden on JDC in postwar

Germany and solve the problem of statelessness. But what of those DPs who did not desire migration to Israel? Or who did not want to travel to a new war zone? Or preferred to wait for migration to the United States or elsewhere? How would JDC continue to care for them?

The creation of the State of Israel in May 1948 and the cessation of hostilities there at the end of 1949 saw between one-half and two-thirds of the Jewish DP population immigrate to Israel by 1952. Other DPs journeyed to the United States, Canada, Australia, Argentina, South Africa, and elsewhere. As much as JDC had hoped that mass migration would lead to the closing of the DP camps, the establishment of Israel and the resettlement of the vast majority of survivors in the rest of the Jewish Diaspora did not entirely conclude the DP chapter in JDC history.

From Separate "Safe" Space to German Control

Authorities in the different *Länder* in West Germany had started to request control over the remaining DPs in the late 1940s, arguing that they could not have a separate society within Germany if they were to ever regain control over the country. However, the Allied authorities rejected these requests, stating that they wanted to ensure that DPs would receive fair treatment under the new democratic government in West Germany. The Office of the US High Commissioner to Germany (USHCG) worked with the Federal Republic to formulate a new law on the legal status of stateless foreigners in Federal territory (*Gesetz über die Rechtsstellung Heimatloser Ausländer im Bundesgebiet*), which guaranteed them many of the same rights as German citizens and placed them under the same legal system as the Germans.[75] Even though the new law was introduced in the spring of 1951, the USHCG waited until December of that year before handing over control of the last DPs.

Although 1948 had been a critical year for both world Jewry and West Germany, it had not solved the Jewish DP problem. Certainly, the declaration of the Jewish State of Israel symbolized an end to Jewish wandering for healthy DPs who had spent three years waiting in limbo for their emigration. It was also in 1948 that the Federal Republic was formed and started gradually assuming control over many of the offices that had formerly been operated by the American occupation forces. This shift in power and the fact that Germany, the former enemy of the Allies, had become a partner with the democratic West signified to many DPs the coming change in their administration, care, and control and led many Jews, as well as the Jewish organizations working with them in Germany, to push for their immediate immigration and resettlement in Israel. Yet for many ill, elderly, or infirm DPs, immediate departure proved to be elusive and illusory. Resettlement for these Jews was a long, drawn-out struggle for JDC, one for which there was no easy solution; in many cases, the only available option was integration in Germany, a plan that had initially been firmly rejected by both the Jewish DPs and their Jewish caregivers.

Realizing that the Jewish DPs living throughout West Germany would meet the transfer of camp control to German authorities with fear, hesitancy, and anger, JDC officials met with the land commissioner for Bavaria, whose offices would be assigned part of the managerial and monetary responsibility for running the DP centers. They also met with authorities from the medical and welfare offices in the West German government to ensure that these parties understood how best to deal with the needs of the DPs.[76] Finally, JDC met with representatives of the camp community to keep them apprised of the ongoing negotiations and agreements.

Outraged by the proposed transfer of their control, Jewish DPs began to vocally object to the impending change in the months preceding the handover. The Föhrenwald "camp population" called a meeting in October 1951 and unanimously voted for a resolution condemning the transfer of power to West Germany. The camp population

> [d]eclare[d] publically the intention of all of the residents
> of the Fohrenwald camp, the sick and the disabled, not to
> submit themselves to German administration. We have no
> desire to be under either the political or legal protection
> of those who murdered our parents, children, sisters and
> brothers.[77]

Tempers flared when these DPs learned that the Federal Republic had scheduled a mandatory registration of all camp inhabitants who would soon fall under its care for October 31, 1951. For many of the DPs who had survived the Shoah, the idea of Germans entering the camp, which they considered the only truly safe place in Germany, and conducting a census was reminiscent of similar *aktionen* under the Nazis that led to the arrest and murder of so many of their brethren. Fearing the imminent German takeover and feeling powerless to change the coming events, the Föhrenwald DPs took to the streets to protest on October 28, 1951, and threatened to go on a hunger strike if the registration was not canceled.[78]

Jewish DPs correctly argued that JDC was actively working with the West German government to accelerate the transfer. JDC Director for the US Zone of Germany Samuel Haber was unapologetic when he wrote to his colleague Morris Laub saying, "[W]e have taken steps to actually pressure the IRO people to begin an orderly transfer of the camp."[79] The motivation behind JDC's actions did not stem from its strong desire to see the Jewish DPs under German control but rather from an understanding that the IRO was leaving and there was no one else who was willing to take on the cost and responsibilities associated with the operation of the remaining DP centers. Although the DPs felt betrayed, JDC did continue to work on their behalf, stressing the need for the Germans "to recognize the special character of camp Föhrenwald" with its vulnerable population, composed mainly of the elderly, the tubercular, and their families.[80]

Haber stated that JDC's central role throughout this process was to secure as many concessions from the Germans on behalf of the DPs as possible. In this, JDC was successful. The Germans agreed to keep Föhrenwald a Jewish-only center regardless of the number of inhabitants living in the camp and to ensure that the German administrators would be free from any Nazi past.[81]

These concessions did little to set the minds of the DPs at ease, especially after the Germans sent armed police with loudspeakers and dogs into Föhrenwald to carry out the scheduled registration. The German actions led many Föhrenwalders to refuse to register, saying that they would "'never live under the Germans.'"[82] Anticipating the conflicts that could arise from the continuation of these protests, JDC officials called a special meeting for the Camp Committee, JDC camp representatives, the IRO, members

A family of Jewish refugees in their apartment in the Föhrenwald displaced persons camp. The housing was originally built for IG Farben employees and during the war was used to house forced laborers. Föhrenwald, Germany, 1953. Photo by Jerome Silberstein.

of the *Zentralrat der Juden in Deutschland*, and the German representatives from the local *Länder* at which the DPs were told that if they were not registered by October 31, 1951, they would lose their JDC aid. The DPs continued to search for an alternative solution to German control, stating,

> . . . it is bad enough to have to live in the bloody land of
> Germany, but it is intolerable to have to remain here under
> the protection of the Germans. After the expiration of IRO,
> we propose that a representative Jewish organization—such
> as the Jewish World Congress—take over the camp and that
> the inmates actually run it themselves.[83]

Realizing that they had no chance of preventing the German takeover, the DPs instead demanded that the final camps be closed and the inhabitants be resettled abroad. They believed it was "world Jewry's" responsibility to help the ill and infirm DPs and their families leave Germany. In reality, even healthy DPs with valid visas to the United States were unable to immigrate because of the continual postponement of their departures by US immigration. If these DPs could not leave Europe, what did that mean for the remaining displaced Jews who were too sick or infirm to qualify for a visa?

Despite the protests over the handover of power, the few remaining DP centers were transferred to German authority on December 1, 1951, just as scheduled.[84] At that point, the status of the remaining Jewish DPs changed to *Heimatloser Ausländer* (HA; stateless foreigners). For their part, the German authorities met the calls and demands set forth for them by the office of the US High Commissioner for Germany and JDC, and camp life was no worse under German control than it had been under that of the IRO. The Bavarian government, which was responsible for the operation of Föhrenwald, worked hard to keep the stateless Jews in clean, well-kept facilities with adequate rations, and they provided emigration and integration grants for those who qualified. Although the German federal government wanted to close the remaining centers for HAs as quickly as possible, it was willing to work with JDC and the Central Council of Jews in Germany to try to resettle as many Jews abroad as possible. However, nearly six years after securing power from the USHCG, the West German government still found itself caring for more than 1,000 Jewish HAs who either did not qualify for emigration or refused to resettle outside the camps. The fact that many HAs were ineligible for emigration meant that the situation in Germany remained at a standstill occasionally punctuated by conflict. The interactions between German authorities and the displaced Jews were generally amicable. However, when conflicts arose, they erupted in violence, and JDC was forced to mediate in order to help ease the tension.

"FOR THEM THERE EXISTS NO FUTURE—ONLY A TRAGIC PAST": THE CASE OF JEWISH "HARD-CORE" DPS IN GERMANY

The responsibility for resettlement and the cost for this endeavor fell almost entirely to JDC after December 1951 when the IRO transferred its control over all remaining DPs in Germany to the Federal Republic.[85] In addition to resettlement activities, JDC also continued to care for the needs of the last Jewish DPs, provide them with medical aid, and act as their advocates in negotiations with the West German government and the various *Bundesländer* (West German Federal States).[86] Despite JDC efforts on behalf of the Jewish DPs, the relationship between the two groups continued to be rife with tension and to deteriorate over the course of the later DP era as depression and fear set in among the remaining Jewish DPs. By the time the final Jewish DP was settled outside of Föhrenwald, the last remaining Jewish DP camp, in 1957, relations between JDC and the Jewish DPs were hostile at best and were often near the point of breaking off completely.

Although the number of Jewish DPs had dropped drastically by 1952, there were still 2,000 displaced Jews living in centers in Germany who had not been able to secure visas and leave the camps during the "great post war migrations (1948–1952)."[87] While there are few exact emigration statistics from this period, scholars generally agree that around 136,000 Jewish DPs had immigrated to Palestine/Israel (both legally and illegally) by 1952. The Displaced Persons Act of 1948 and its subsequent amendment in 1950 allowed an estimated 80,000 Jewish DPs to finally immigrate to the United States; Canada accepted between 16,000 and 20,000. Within Europe, Belgium took in about 8,000 Jewish DPs, and France admitted a further 2,000. Finally, an estimated 5,000 Jewish DPs settled in South Africa and Latin America.[88] Along with these departing DPs went their former leadership, resulting in the dismantling of several DP organizations.

Unlike the majority of their brethren who had been resettled abroad, the remaining DPs, also known as the "hard-core" DPs by the authorities charged with their care, were considered extremely unattractive candidates by immigration boards confronted with a population identified as elderly, infirm, mentally ill, physically disabled, and occasionally criminal.[89] These Jewish DPs continued to live in the few remaining camps in postwar West Germany as the country worked to regain control over its government, rebuild its economy, and ally itself with its Western occupiers.

THE 1952 FÖHRENWALD RAID

While the Federal Republic had ultimate control over the Jewish HAs, the remaining inhabitants in Föhrenwald continued to think of the center as a separate and safe space protected from the rest of Germany. Although many aspects of the lives of Föhrenwald's HAs remained the same after the transfer of control, the introduction of German authority destroyed the sense of safety to which these stateless Jews had become accustomed. Although the residents had been left largely to their own devices by the German government, the center had become a frequent target of customs raids beginning in early 1952.[90] These had been conducted in an orderly manner without any violence until May 28, 1952, when many HAs sunbathing by the camp entrance became embroiled in a violent clash with German authorities.[91]

These events illustrate the complex relationship among the Federal Republic of Germany, the Jewish HAs living in Föhrenwald, and JDC. Unlike preceding raids on Föhrenwald, this customs search did not target a few shops alleged to be selling black market goods. Instead, a large German force, including 33 armed German police, 115 officials from the State Revenue offices, and officers of the Bavarian customs police, attempted to enter Föhrenwald.[92] As Samuel Haber reported later, the raid seemed reminiscent to those of the Nazis, with Haber stating that the "raid was conducted in the style of the Einsatz gruppen [*sic*]."[93] He argued that for many HAs, the behavior of the German authorities had reminded them of "similar actions by Germans under the Nazis in liquidations of Ghettos [and] Concentration camps."[94] The police were "met by a vociferous expression of derision" as Föhrenwald residents grabbed what they could throw and rained rocks and chunks of wood down upon the police cars as they made their way toward the camp. The chaos of shattered windshields and dented trucks finally came to a halt as one officer discharged his weapon, leading to mayhem among the gathered Jewish HAs. JDC workers in the camp called Haber requesting help. Using his connections, Haber was able to get the police removed from the camp.[95] However, the police officers did not withdraw before allegedly hurling antisemitic insults at the HAs, yelling the "gas chambers are waiting for you and are still warm" and "the crematorium are still there."[96] Other police shouted, "The accursed Jew, the oven is not yet closed, it stands open for you. This is only the beginning."[97]

Recognizing the threat of continued violence between the Jewish HAs and German authorities, JDC officials immediately sent Akiva Kohane and Jerry Kolieb, JDC director for Germany, to the camp in an effort to calm the crowd. They arrived at the center just as German authorities were leaving and were almost attacked by the crowd of DPs who were incited to violence. Haber reported that general feelings of resentment were inflamed by "underworld characters in the camp," who pushed the crowd to physically assault the newly arrived JDC officials.[98] Realizing the level of emotional distress among the crowd, Dr. Kohane called an immediate meeting to discuss the events and how best to proceed. Over 1,000 residents attended, and in the end Dr. Kohane was able to calm the crowd and convince them to disperse. The threat of violence against JDC officials created new tensions. In order to immediately address this matter, Haber met with the Camp Committee and stressed that if even one JDC member was harmed, JDC would fully withdraw all assistance.[99] The fear and helplessness these events inspired among the HAs led JDC officials to move even more quickly with their attempts to resettle camp inhabitants.

Heartened by the more than 200,000 former Jewish DPs and HAs that JDC had aided in emigrating, JDC officials set forth to finish the job. JDC was able to settle more than 500 old and infirm HAs, as well as their families, over the course of 1952 to 1955, including 17 patients who had been diagnosed as chronically ill with diseases other than tuberculosis (TB) who were sent to Israel and the United States.[100] The majority of these HAs left in the second half of 1955 when the Israeli government agreed to a special dispensation waiving the health regulations, thereby allowing elderly and sick HAs to make *aliyah*. This agreement was made possible by JDC's willingness to take full responsibility for all of the medical costs associated with these new immigrants and to open special health facilities under its Israeli Malben division for the ill and disabled. JDC enlisted the help of the United Nations High Commissioner for Refugees and the Intergovernmental Committee for European Migration to find hospitable countries willing to take the HAs who rejected immigration to Israel. It also received a grant from the Ford Foundation to help cover the costs of resettlement.[101] By 1955, Argentina, Uruguay, Brazil, Australia,

Norway, and Sweden, as well as Israel, had agreed to accept some of the most ill residents of Föhrenwald.[102] Nevertheless, many of Föhrenwald's remaining stateless Jews were frustrated with the resettlement process, a frustration that finally reached a boiling point in 1954 when Föhrenwald HAs hired minibuses for the day and left the camp to protest everything that they believed JDC was doing wrong in terms of the care it provided in Föhrenwald, the compensation the Jews would receive upon emigration, and resettlement.

THE FÖHRENWALD DEMONSTRATION

By 1953, the process of closing the camp was well under way. However, 1,300 of the remaining 1,750 inhabitants who had come directly to the center after the war were still unable to emigrate because their war experiences had left them with so many mental and physical ailments that immigration boards deemed them "unattractive candidates."[103] Despite this, JDC officials, camp representatives, and members of the Central Council of Jews in Germany met regularly to discuss how best to proceed toward the resettlement, emigration, or absorption of these last Jewish HAs.[104] While the German government pushed to close the camp as quickly as possible, JDC argued for more time, explaining that the closure had to be done in a manner that would allow for the largest number of Jewish HAs to be resettled abroad, thereby leaving only a handful of HAs to be integrated into German society.

Although relations between Jewish HAs and their caregivers were strained after the 1952 attempted raid, some advances had been made in resettling some of the hardest of Föhrenwald's "hard-core" cases. To this end, JDC secured $650,000 from the Conference on Jewish Material Claims Against Germany (the Claims Conference) to help pay for the emigration of those HAs left in Germany, Italy, and Austria who were able to emigrate as well as those for whom emigration was not an option and who had to settle in the countries where they resided. The West German government agreed to provide an additional $714,000 for these efforts as "recognition of the harm done the Jewish people by the Nazis."[105] Those emigrating would receive travel expenses and a cash grant from JDC for incidentals associated with their departure. JDC also paid for furniture and short-term living expenses for those remaining in the country. Despite all of this, the actual problem of finding a place to resettle these Jews continued to bedevil JDC workers.

The HAs remaining in Föhrenwald in 1954 feared that the closure of the center would lead to their forced resettlement in Germany. Fearful about how they would survive among their "enemies," many HAs wanted to build up their resources to ensure that they could get by when the camp closed. This led them to demand grants and funding from both the German government and the global Jewish organizations tasked with caring for them.

This was the case in January 1954 when the Föhrenwald Camp Committee requested a $5,000,000 restitution and resettlement grant from the Claims Conference. This request was denied. The Claims Conference explained that the funds it had received from the West German government were for all of the Jews who had suffered under the Nazis, not just those who remained in Föhrenwald.[106] The Camp Committee asked JDC to intervene, but when given the same response the committee claimed that JDC was actively blocking their restitution efforts. Relations between the Jewish HAs and JDC deteriorated into shouting matches and threatened violence.[107] A small group of Föhrenwalders even demanded that JDC close its "Joint Fund" office in the camp on Friday, February 12, as, they argued, it had failed to do its job.[108] The Joint Fund staff heeded the Föhrenwalders' call and withdrew from the camp. Within a matter of days, the Camp Committee and JDC were embroiled in a struggle that would soon turn violent.

The Camp Committee called a meeting of all inhabitants in Föhrenwald the following weekend. Outraged over the rejected grant proposal and frustrated over rationing changes that led to reductions in the goods provided for the HAs, residents demanded immediate action.[109] Rumors soon spread throughout the camp, reaching as far as James Rice, JDC director for the US zone of Germany, claiming that buses had been hired to take 700 camp residents into Munich to occupy JDC headquarters. Rice argued that while interfering with JDC offices in Föhrenwald was a local matter that happened quite regularly, the invasion of JDC offices in Munich was intolerable and would not be permitted. He thus notified the German police of the planned occupation, asking them to prevent the demonstrators from entering JDC offices and to protect JDC workers.[110] Camp inhabitants' dissatisfaction with JDC finally boiled over on February 17, 1954, when several hired buses carried over 200 protesters from Föhrenwald to Munich. These HAs set out to occupy JDC offices until their demands were met. They rushed JDC buildings only to meet 250 riot police with water cannons. The streets surrounding JDC offices were closed in anticipation of the sit-in, and the police were armed with clubs that they had been instructed to use on the protesters if necessary. The presence of the police officers shocked many of the HAs, and panic gripped the crowd. In the ensuing clashes, several HAs were wounded, and three needed hospitalization.[111]

Camp inhabitants started contacting Jewish leaders at several different Jewish organizations, claiming that sixty-five people had been injured, fifteen of them seriously. The remaining Jewish protesters who had not fled or been injured mostly sought sanctuary in the Möhlstraße synagogue. More than 100 remained in the synagogue overnight despite police objections, demanding that JDC address and resolve their grievances.[112] JDC offices were under siege, surrounded by police for two days, while another seventy-five officers hid within the building to protect the staff in case any protesters managed to get inside the building.

Throughout the crisis, JDC officials sought to calm the HAs. Moses Beckelman, JDC director general, described the demonstration in a statement, saying:

> The attempted forcible entry and occupation of 200 residents of camp Föhrenwald of the Munich offices of the American Joint Distribution Committee, reflects a desperate and exasperated action on the part of a group of unfortunates whose efforts to leave Germany have been thwarted again and again by circumstances outside their or our control.[113]

Beckelman explained that JDC was more than willing to meet with organized committees for orderly discussions but could not permit disruptions and occupation.[114]

JDC officials met with camp representatives over the course of the following days, but negotiations stalled. Finally, Rice proposed to JDC officials and the camp representatives what he argued was the only possible solution: moving the JDC offices from Munich. He reiterated Haber's statements from 1952 explaining that JDC staff would not work under siege. Rice explained that the choice of Munich as the location for JDC headquarters had originally been made because of the organization's desire to work with the Jewish DPs who settled in camps in Bavaria at the close of the war.[115] However, JDC did not work exclusively for or with the HAs and helped communities throughout Germany. If it became impossible to work with the Föhrenwalders, as the recent actions of the HAs had proven, JDC would have no choice but to move. The demonstration was finally called off after two days of protests and negotiations, with the assurance that the Camp Committee would come to Munich to discuss the matter with JDC officials. The two parties finally reached an agreement on March 9, which stipulated that the Camp Committee would not stage another demonstration and that JDC would reopen its liaison office and resume medical care in the camp.[116]

Despite all of the trouble, frustration, and exasperation associated with aiding these Jewish Shoah survivors, JDC continued with its nearly impossible task of resettlement. Relations between the two parties returned to their prior strained but functional status, and the JDC threat to close its offices in Munich was withdrawn. While the number of employees in the office was reduced, the office itself remained open until 1957. The former camp offices were combined into one office located in Munich. Exceptions were made for "direct services" such as medical aid, consultation with social workers, and emigration registration, which continued in the camp through liaisons who regularly visited.[117] As the actual closing date for Föhrenwald neared, JDC moved its offices to Frankfurt, which was emerging as the new center of Jewish life in the Federal Republic, to be closer to the other Jewish aid organizations.[118] It became clear to everyone that the last remaining HA camp would soon cease to exist. However, JDC staff in Germany continued to work for the eventual resettlement of all of Föhrenwald's Jews in adequate housing with welfare services for those who needed it and for emigration and integration grants for all.

Although the creation of the State of Israel had reignited hope for their future resettlement among many Shoah survivors who remained in DP centers in Germany, it took less than a year before a new, unexpected wave of Jews began to trickle into the country and settle in the American-run DP camps, mainly Föhrenwald. These individuals had formerly been DPs but had been resettled abroad in North and South America, Australia, and especially Israel. In a painfully ironic turn, they now left their new homelands to cross illegally into Germany, demanding the return of their status as stateless people and their resettlement in a more "favorable" country than the one from where they had come.

The returnees cited several reasons for leaving Israel, including the climate, war, ill health, separation from family members, and their inability to adapt to the "pioneer" lifestyle.[119] The prospect of restitution also drew a significant number back to Germany as the compensation negotiations between the Adenauer government and the Claims Conference in 1952 made it easier for those seeking restitution to secure these funds if they were present in Germany.[120] While the Israeli returnees gave several different reasons for their return, they all agreed that they had come back to Europe to find what they could not get in Israel: medical care, viable business opportunities, and a chance to emigrate elsewhere.[121]

The status of the first Israeli returnees to Germany fell into a "gray zone" as they arrived in the country on passports marked invalid for travel in Germany but with valid visas to enter Germany issued at German embassies in Rome and Paris. Additionally, the illegal returnees who had emigrated after 1949 and entered Germany after the spring of 1951 did so under the provisions specified in the 1951 law on the legal status of stateless foreigners, which allowed stateless individuals who had formerly lived in Germany to return to the country within two years of their departure.[122]

The small group of illegal returnees initially caused very little concern. However, the quick surge in their number began to cause problems in southern Bavaria, especially in Föhrenwald. There were an estimated 418 illegal returnees living in the camp in June 1952, despite the official closure of the center to newcomers.[123] This number grew to around 800 by August

1953 and continued to climb.[124] By the end of 1953, some 3,500 illegal returnees had come through Föhrenwald, sparking a sense of urgency among both JDC and authorities from the Bavarian government anxious to prevent a further influx.[125]

The flow of illegal returnees increased so rapidly in the early 1950s that more entered Camp Föhrenwald every month than the number of Jews emigrating out. Föhrenwald's population was 1,800 in October 1952, of which an estimated 50% were believed to have been illegal returnees, making them the single largest group in the camp.[126]

There was no existing protocol in place in Germany to deal with this embarrassing population because no one had ever anticipated that any of the resettled Jewish DPs would return to the country of their former oppressors. The IRO—and later the West German government as well as the Jewish aid organizations—considered these returnees nationals of the countries they had left, but the returnees insisted on their statelessness.[127] These Jews returned to Germany demanding the reinstatement of their DP status. In a JDC report from August 2, 1954, the JDC country director for Germany noted that the illegal returnees with whom he had met emphasized that they "did not recognize that they were Israeli Nationals."[128] Instead, these *chozrim* (returnees), as they called themselves, demanded the return of their papers that had identified them as stateless.[129]

Discussions over the care of the returnee population took place among every group involved in the maintenance of the Jewish HAs. JDC Director of the Reconstruction Department in the JDC Paris office Leonard Seidenman argued in 1952, "What the Germans do for them is their own affair, but I personally feel that it is morally wrong on the part of the JDC to provide any assistance for any of these people."[130] The IRO and the West German government seconded this position. Their ineligibility to receive aid meant that hundreds (and later thousands) of Jewish returnees were left without supplies, proper clothing, or food. Many of these undocumented returnees squatted in the parts of Föhrenwald that had been abandoned as camp inhabitants emigrated, surviving initially with the help of their friends and relatives legally living in the camp who provided care and housing for many returnees. JDC was finally able to convince the German government to provide the undocumented returnees in Föhrenwald with emergency relief, thereby ensuring that these people received some limited support despite their highly irregular status.[131]

While the issue of the undocumented returnees was especially difficult for the authorities overseeing the care and control of the Jewish HAs, the remaining camp inmates were also affected. They were torn between their desire to aid their brethren and their concerns about this new competition for resources and emigration visas. In the early 1950s, when the number of returnees was highest, the HAs who remained in Föhrenwald consisted mainly of survivors who had little chance of emigrating anywhere but Israel. These DPs resented the undocumented population who had already been resettled and now wanted the authorities to find them another new home. Indeed, it was the insistence of the Camp Committee that pushed Federal Minister for Displaced Persons, Refugees, and War Victims Dr. Theodor Oberländer to call for the closing of Föhrenwald to all newcomers in 1952.[132] In a meeting to discuss how to combat the returnee population, Ludwig Erhard, the German minister of economics, stated that "the Jews themselves demanded protection against the illegals."[133] In several reports from August through October of 1952, the HA Camp Committee of Föhrenwald asked JDC and the Bavarian government to seal the center, illustrating the HAs' desire to remain separated from the returnee community.

The HAs noted increased resentment from Jewish aid workers as well as Germans, which they attributed to the undocumented returnees. H. Leivick, the Yiddish poet, gave voice to these concerns when he asked his readers to try to distinguish between the legal residents and the returnees in Föhrenwald. He said, "I believe, however, that the shade of disdain that we have towards the 'Chozrim' should not fall on the sick D.P.s."[134] The presence of these returnees in Jewish centers made resettling the legal HAs more difficult and caused many aid workers and immigration officials to mistakenly lump all HAs into one category of refugees who could not be satisfied with resettlement and were willing to do whatever they must to get what they wanted.

Although JDC's initial response to the returnee problem had started as a total disavowal of any responsibility, it begrudgingly admitted that it would help "hard-core" cases on an individual basis, and over the course of the 1950s JDC became involved in several aspects of the returnee issue. Charles Jordan explained JDC's position in July 1952:

> Obviously, we have decided that the returnees from Israel are not our problem and that as a matter of principle we will not assist them. Nevertheless, we cannot close our eyes to the fact that in any number of cases of returnees, welfare and medical problems arise which must be dealt with, regardless of our policy and that to an extent they are as much of a problem to us as are the others [legal HAs].[135]

Driven by the desire to help Jews in need, JDC went against its own official position to ensure that returnees who qualified would have access to medical help, winter clothing, and legal assistance.[136] JDC was assured "that the German government accepts this problem [returnees] as its responsibility." Nonetheless, it was JDC that found itself supplying returnees with limited rations as the 1950s wore on. Hoping to end the issue of continued illegal return to Germany, the members of the Bavarian government decided that any returnee caught crossing into Germany illegally "will be deported back across the border from whence they came."[137] With this declaration, the Bavarian government began actively seeking out new returnees to deport. Nevertheless, returnees continued to arrive in Föhrenwald.

Motivated by the preceding events, Dr. Nahum Goldmann of the World Jewish Congress and Samuel Haber of JDC met in Geneva with Dr. Chaim Yahil, an emissary from the Israeli Mission, Cologne, and Dr. Frohwein, the German foreign minister, in early August 1953 to discuss the problem of returnees in Föhrenwald.[138] Members of JDC were informed that on June 12, 1953, the Bavarian government had offered to allow the returnees to remain in Germany for an additional six months while they secured emigration visas if they would voluntarily register for resettlement in Funk Kaserne, the largest non-Jewish camp for HAs in southern Germany.[139] All unregistered Jews would be deported. The various German ministries and international aid organizations hoped that by transferring the returnee population from their base in Föhrenwald, it would illustrate to other potential returnees that there was no possibility for their resettlement in the center. The returnees rejected the proposal, instead demanding that their stay in Föhrenwald be legalized.

Regardless of their position on the returnees, JDC became the main organization to which the illegal returnees turned when in need. Refusing to register, but fearing deportation, 150 returnees staged a sit-in at the JDC offices on August 12–13, 1953, demanding asylum in the Federal Republic until they were able to migrate overseas. JDC officials met with the Bavarian government and convinced them to delay the deportation. In the end, it was decided that all returnees living in Föhrenwald who registered with the Bavarian administration would be allowed the six-month reprieve in Föhrenwald while they arranged their emigration.[140] While the Bavarian government agreed not to deport the returnees immediately, it pushed JDC to develop a plan to address the problem.

Official registration took place in Föhrenwald between August 14 and August 17, 1953, with the willing participation of 687 returnees.[141] Although those who registered were allowed to remain in the camp and receive care, unlike the fully legal residents, they were denied supplemental rations and had no voting rights for Föhrenwald elections. They were also denied residents' permits, which prevented their settlement in Germany; employment; passports; and marriage.[142] Those who had not registered by August 17 faced deportation.

Although a handful of deportations did take place, returnees continued to enter Germany. Those who were turned away from Camp Föhrenwald settled in the Munich synagogue where 150 people slept in October 1953, "living under the most wretched physical conditions."[143] The synagogue squatters posed a special problem, as they had arrived in Germany too late to qualify for assistance. However, negotiations between JDC, HIAS, and the West German government ended in an agreement that the returnees who continued to live in the Möhlstraße synagogue, in the heart of what had been Munich's lively DP district, would be given a few months' reprieve, during which JDC and HIAS would work to secure their emigration. JDC and the Central Welfare Agency of Jews in Germany, which had been established by the Central Council of Jews in Germany in 1951, agreed to cover the cost of these returnees while in the country, and HIAS paid for their eventual emigration. On January 4, 1954, the remaining 110 "bedraggled" individuals left the synagogue for Hamburg, where they would remain in an emigrants' hostel until they were moved to countries in South America. Although JDC regularly acted as the mediator between the *chozrim* and the German and Bavarian governments, returnees remained dissatisfied, claiming that JDC, HIAS, and the Israeli Mission, which had opened an office in Munich in 1953, had betrayed them. Their real enemies, they provocatively stated, were not the Germans but the Jewish organizations who acted in a way reminiscent of the "Hitler period when the most diabolical method used against the Jews was to set up a 'Judenrat' to aid in liquidation!"[144]

German policy relaxed a bit by 1954, and officials worked with JDC and other Jewish aid organizations to find a place for the returnees without deporting them. Although the Bavarian government was willing to work with JDC and the already existing returnee population in Föhrenwald, it was staunchly against the admission of any new returnees into the center. In August 1954, Bavarian officials replaced the HA police with German officers who oversaw the entrance of all individuals into the camp and ensured that everyone who entered did so legally. This finally led to the stabilization of the number of camp inhabitants in Föhrenwald. While the German authorities set deportation dates, these departure deadlines came and went without much follow-through. JDC negotiations continued to convince the Bavarian and West German governments to delay deportation while JDC worked to resettle the returnees abroad.

By March 1954, only about 150 returnees remained in Föhrenwald. The rest had resettled abroad or returned to their former countries of emigration. Realizing that deportation was an option with few real benefits, the Bavarian Ministry of Work and Social Welfare mandated that eighty-four of the remaining returners in Föhrenwald be transferred to the Ludwigsfeld center near Munich. Ludwigsfeld was a non-Jewish center mainly inhabited by Eastern European HAs, and the eighty-four returnees who resettled there had valid emigration visas but were not scheduled for immediate departure. Another fifty-four returnees in Föhrenwald were booked to depart Germany within weeks. The remaining returnees in Camp Föhrenwald had no chance of emigrating and were ineligible for integration in Germany or the resettlement grants offered there. It was finally decided that these returnees would be given the same legal status as the HAs, thereby making them eligible for integration into German society. Some returnees remained in the camp hidden in the homes of legal inhabitants of the center, but the vast majority had been resettled by the end of 1956, bringing their illegal stay in Föhrenwald to a close.[145]

The End of Camp Föhrenwald

The West German government worked with JDC officials and the Central Council of Jews in Germany to develop a plausible plan to resettle the HAs in Föhrenwald who could not emigrate and would remain in Germany. For their part, German authorities pledged to match the funding provided by JDC and the Claims Conference in an effort to resettle the last of the "hard-core" Jews.[146] Additionally, the German government stated that it would secure housing and employment opportunities for those who decided to remain in the country while also providing institutional assistance for those too sick to live without constant care.[147] Unfortunately, the German housing and economic crisis—a postwar carryover—made it impossible to keep these promises. While the German economy began to recover in the 1950s, cities such as Munich, which took the majority of Föhrenwald's DPs, could not rebuild housing fast enough to replace those destroyed during the war. The severity of the situation was illustrated in late 1953 when the West German government agreed to pay for housing units for 500 camp residents at a time when 1,300 legal HAs still needed to be resettled because no additional housing could be spared.[148]

Housing shortages, combined with the fact that the Jews in Föhrenwald were so hesitant to leave the camp, meant that the resettlement process was slow at best. The number of residents was in constant flux over the course of the next two years as camp inhabitants were resettled and *chozrim* continued to arrive illegally. Just under 1,000 Jewish HAs remained in Föhrenwald in early 1954, but this number dropped to 416 residents by

April of that year. The majority of the last remaining HAs had begrudging-ly agreed to settle in West Germany. The Jews who had signed up for reset-tlement in Germany clamored to move to their new homes—not because they wanted to leave Föhrenwald, which continued to be considered a safe community, but because they did not want to be left with nowhere to go.[149] The continued housing shortages meant that more Jews were signed up to leave Föhrenwald than there was available housing, causing fear and ten-sion among the HAs. This situation further worsened when the Catholic Settlement Work and the Archdiocese of Munich and Freising, the center's owner since 1955, began to take over some of the buildings for renovations.[150] ORT ended its operations in Föhrenwald at this time, signaling the center's impending closure, at which point the remaining HAs started to panic about their resettlement.[151]

Although 150 HAs were resettled in Munich, Frankfurt, Hamburg, and Wiesbaden in February 1956, resettlement slowed down in the spring.[152] In April 1956, JDC had estimated that it would be able to resettle the major-ity of the remaining camp residents over the following two months, but in actuality there was almost no movement out of the center during that period. In total, 24 people were "resettled in German cities in April and May with 11 settling in Munich, 12 in Düsseldorf and 1 in Stuttgart."[153] While not all of the apartments were ready for the HAs, 174 residences in Munich, Frankfurt, Düsseldorf, Cologne, Hamburg, and Wiesbaden remained empty in April 1956 awaiting the arrival of their new tenants.[154]

The liquidation of Camp Föhrenwald happened quickly once integration began again in the fall of 1956. In the days leading up to the closing of Föhrenwald, seventy-five Jews who had called the camp home for twelve years exited its gates, bringing with them the "end of the post-Hitler epoch."[155] On February 28, 1957, Alter Haimowitz and eleven other HAs, the last residents of Föhrenwald, left the center. Haimowitz had spent sev-enteen years in camps both during the Shoah and after the end of World War II. His departure was accompanied by speeches from West German officials, JDC, and the HIAS, all marking the monumental nature of the day. There would be no big victory celebration by JDC or the Ministry of the Interior for, as Theodore Feder noted, this would not "make a good impression on the Föhrenwalders who still have to remain and live in Germany."[156] Instead, a small private dinner was planned, and a twenty-word internal note stating "Congratulations to all on the job well done in liquidating one of the most difficult problems JDC has ever had" circulated through JDC offices.[157] In his final report on Föhrenwald, Charles Jordan noted that "[w]hen human dignity and self-respect have been so thoroughly destroyed as was theirs [the HAs'], it takes many years of normal and independent living to restore them."[158] JDC believed that the closing of Föhrenwald would bring with it the chance for these displaced Jews to begin their lives anew.[159]

Although they only made up just over 3% of the original 50,000 Jews who had settled in Jewish-only DP camps in Germany in the spring and summer of 1945, the Jewish HAs who remained in Föhrenwald after 1952 and the even smaller group who were "forced" to settle in Germany after the camp's closure continued to grapple with the same issues they had faced upon liberation: fear, uncertainty, a sense of abandonment, a deep-seated need to emigrate, a desire to secure restitution, and a longing for family. For the last remnant of Jewish survivors living in Föhrenwald, the daily interactions with international Jewry in the form of organizations such as JDC did not alleviate their sense of having been forsaken by their brethren worldwide, nor did these interactions satisfy their beliefs that world Jewry owed them more. While a significant portion of these Jews had been among the first residents of the DP camp system in Germany in early 1945 and 1946, their way of thinking no longer resembled that of the DPs who had lived in the camps before 1952. Seventeen years of camp life, both as prisoners under the Nazis and their allies and as survivors in postwar Germany, had transformed these Jews. A number of these HAs had just entered adulthood when the war broke out. Few beyond the elderly had been self-sufficient members of society before World War II, and the children often did not know a life outside of the camps. Instead, camp inhabitants who had lived separated from "normal" society experienced constant fear, demoralization, unemployment, and almost total reliance on outside aid for survival. This, combined with years spent waiting for emigration without any control over whether they would get a coveted visa and the crushing realization that their only chance to leave Germany was through immigration to Israel, an option deemed unacceptable for many Jewish HAs because of the hardships of life there as well as the threat of war, affected every aspect of these Jews' lives. This reality, along with a steadily growing sense of entitlement shared by the final remnant of the HAs, resulted in a group of people who could not fathom that their demands would not be met and who could no longer imagine a future beyond dependency. Health issues and age barred many of these Jews from reaching their desired destinations, but so too did the size of their families, which in many cases had grown over the course of their confinement in DP centers. The group of an estimated 250 children of "hard-core" HAs had no idea what life was like outside of Föhrenwald. Their parents had never worked, they thought that supplies such as food and clothing came in large boxes with *JDC* marked on the side, and they only really knew the small community that had lived within the gates of their center. Although these children were not expected to leave without their parents, it was understood that they added to the unit's inability to secure emigration abroad.

Despite all of the hardships it had encountered with the "hard-core" population in Föhrenwald, JDC continued to act as the number one organization working to better the lives of survivors. It was willing to adjust many of its central principles in order to ensure that the Jewish DPs were able to rebuild their lives after the Shoah. This meant two fundamental policy changes for JDC: (1) political involvement in the debates over a Jewish homeland in Palestine and (2) allowing Jewish DP leadership to have a say in the dispersal of resources. However, these changes were temporary, and while many JDC workers continued to support Israel, JDC policy changed as it became clear that not all Jewish DPs would make *aliyah*. Additionally, JDC again claimed sovereignty over the supplies and work done by the organization in the later postwar period as the population decreased, Jewish leadership emigrated, and DP demands for increased aid and grants became ever more unrealizable. While the resettlement of the last Jewish DPs in Germany brought an end to Jewish displacement in the country, it did not signal an end to JDC aid, which continued to help finance the care of many former DPs who were too ill or elderly to support themselves. Finally, JDC worked with the Jewish communities throughout West Germany who had absorbed the Föhrenwald Jews in order to ensure that the social, medical, and institutional needs of these Jews continued to be met. Although Föhrenwald had closed, JDC's task in aiding Jewish Shoah survivors throughout Europe continued as it worked to ensure that resettled Jews continued to receive the care they needed to begin living "normal and independent" lives.

Notes

1. See Yehuda Bauer, *Out of the Ashes: The Impact of American Jews on Post-Holocaust European Jewry* (Oxford: Pergamon Press, 1989), xviii, 41. For statistics on JDC aid in 1946, see JDC Archives, Records of the Geneva Office of the American Jewish Joint Distribution Committee, 1945–1954, Folder ADM.594, *The Year of Survival*, 1946, Annual Report of the American Jewish Joint Distribution Committee, 26–27, March 2, 1954.

2. See Ze'ev Mankowitz, "The Formation of She'erit Hapletah," *Yad Vashem Studies* 27 (1990); YIVO Archives, Leo Schwarz Papers, Reel 8, 1032–1037. Mankowitz asserts that most Jews of Hungary and Romania sought to return home following liberation, whereas Polish Jews (some 90% of those liberated) were far more divided on the issue. A survey of the Jewish DP population of the 4,976 residents of Landsberg taken on October 1, 1945, indicated that 75.2% (3,740) of residents were Polish, whereas only 5.7% (283) were Hungarian and 3.3% (162) were from Romania. A survey of the residents of Feldafing taken at the same time indicated that a population drop from 600 to 400 from the summer to October 1945 was attributable to the sizable repatriation of Hungarian and Romanian Jews.

3. On the choice to resettle in Germany, see Ruth Schreiber, "The New Organization of the Jewish Community in Germany, 1945–1952" (PhD diss., Tel Aviv University, 1995), 11. More recent volumes on Jewish life in postwar Germany include Kierra Crago-Schneider, "Jewish 'Shtetls' in Postwar Germany: An Analysis of Interactions among Jewish Displaced Persons, Germans, and Americans between 1945 and 1957 in Bavaria" (PhD diss., Los Angeles: University of California, Los Angeles, 2013); Atina Grossmann, *Jews, Germans, and Allies: Close Encounters in Occupied*

Germany (Princeton, NJ: Princeton University Press, 2009); and Avinoam Patt, *Finding Home and Homeland: Jewish Youth and Zionism in Postwar Germany* (Detroit: Wayne State University Press, 2009). Although some 36% of Jews from Eastern Europe did try to live in German cities in January 1946, the continuing housing shortage and reluctance of some newly formed German Jewish communities (such as Gemeinden) to represent Jews of non-German descent made this option difficult. While not the rule, this was the case in Frankfurt, for example (see Schreiber, "The New Organization of the Jewish Community in Germany, 1945–1952," 33).

4. See Leonard Dinnerstein, *America and the Survivors of the Holocaust* (New York: Columbia University Press, 1982), 28; slightly different statistics can be found in Bauer, *Out of the Ashes*, 45, and Malcolm Proudfoot, *European Refugees, 1939–1952* (Evanston, IL: Northwestern University Press, 1956), 238.

5. For more on the Brigade, see Yoav Gelber, "The Meeting between the Jewish Soldiers from Palestine Serving in the British Army and *She'erit Hapletah*," in *She'erit Hapletah, 1944–1948*, ed. Yisrael Gutman and Avrtal Saf, eds. (Jerusalem: Yad Vashem, 1990), 60–79.

6. Yehuda Bauer, *American Jewry and the Holocaust: The American Jewish Joint Distribution Committee, 1939–1945* (Detroit: Wayne State University Press, 1981), 291. On the rescue work of Joseph Schwartz, see Ruth Baki Kolodny, *Ani Yosef Achichem* [I am Joseph your brother: The life and work of Joe Schwartz] (Israel: Modan Publishing, 2010).

7. June 24, 1945, report of Chaplain Abraham Klausner, "A Detailed Report on the Liberated Jew as He Now Suffers His Period of Liberation under the Discipline of the Armed Forces of the United States," CJH, AJHS, Abraham Klausner Papers, Box 3, Folder 11; Alexander Grobman, *Rekindling the Flame: American Jewish Chaplains and the Survivors of European Jewry, 1944–1948* (Detroit: Wayne State University Press, 1993), 42–43. For a detailed overview of Klausner's role in postwar Germany, see Avinoam Patt, "The People Must Be Forced to Go to Palestine: Rabbi Abraham Klausner and the Surviving Remnant in Postwar Germany," *Holocaust and Genocide Studies* 28, no. 2 (2014): 240–76.

8. See Zalman Grinberg and Puczyc to OMGUS and UNRRA, July 10, 1945, YIVO Archives, DP Germany, MK 483, 340. Noting that many Ukrainians who had collaborated with the SS continued to be well fed, the Jewish prisoners, who had always received the poorest nourishment, continued to be malnourished and were still without proper clothing.

9. JDC Archives, Records of the New York Office of the American Jewish Joint Distribution Committee, 1945–1954, Folder 323, Incoming Cable from Saly Mayer to American Joint Distribution Committee, June 14, 1945. See also Mankowitz, "The Formation of She'erit Hapleita," *Yad Vashem Studies* 27 (1990): 355.

10. Zeev W. Mankowitz, *Life between Memory and Hope: The Survivors of the Holocaust in Occupied Germany* (New York: Cambridge University Press, 2002), 31. For a transcript of the speech given by Zalman Grinberg at St. Ottilien on May 27, 1945, see YIVO Archives, Leo Schwarz Papers, MK 488, Reel 13, Folder 104, 10–14.

11. YIVO Archives, DP Germany, MK 483, Reel 21, Dr. Zalman Grinberg, "Appel an den judischen Weltkongress," St. Ottilien, May 31, 1945. See Abraham J. Klausner, *A Letter to My Children: From the Edge of the Holocaust* (San Francisco: Holocaust Center of Northern California, 2002), 26. Klausner's requests for medical supplies for the newly formed hospital organized by Grinberg were met with replies of "materials unavailable" from JDC, leading Klausner to secure supplies on his own through individual contacts in New Haven, Connecticut.

12. The first CCLJ meeting took place in the Feldafing DP camp, near Dachau. For more on the early and extensive involvement of American Jewish chaplains in the relief efforts and organization of DP institutions, see Grobman, *Rekindling the Flame*. On the Jewish Brigade, see Gelber, "The Meeting between the Jewish Soldiers from Palestine Serving in the British Army and *She'erit Hapletah*," 60–80.

13. See Patt, *Finding Home and Homeland*, chap. 1.

14. YIVO Archives, MK 483, Reel 61, 721–727.

15. CJH, AJHS Archives, Minutes of July 25, 1946, Meeting, from Abraham Klausner Papers, Box 1, Folder 23.

16. YIVO Archives, MK 483, Reel 61, 581.

17. See Protocol of the Meeting of Liberated Jews in Bavaria (August 8, 1945, 15:00), YIVO Archives, MK 488, Leo Schwarz Papers, Reel 15, 135, 581. The JDC representatives at the August 8 meeting were Eli Rock, Leon Holzer, and Dr. Henri Hattman.

18. Protocol no. 6 of ZK (8.8.1945), YIVO Archives, MK 488, Leo Schwarz Papers, Reel 15, 135, 581, see as quoted in Mankowitz, *Life between Memory and Hope*, 115.

19. Grobman, *Rekindling the Flame*, 72. Harrison was also the former US commissioner of immigration and the US representative for the Intergovernmental Committee on Refugees.

20. Protocol, July 14, 1945, Meeting of Executive Committee, YIVO Archives, MK 488, Leo Schwarz Papers, Reel 15, 141.

21. Klausner, *Letter to My Children*, 71. For Klausner's impact on the Harrison Report, see Grobman, *Rekindling the Flame*, 73–75, and Patt, "The People Must Be Forced to Go to Palestine."

22. Bauer, *Out of the Ashes*, 51.

23. The American Jewish Conference was created in August 1943 to unify American Jewish organizations in order to better plan postwar policy. It disbanded in 1949.

24. CJH, AJHS Archives, Minutes of July 25, 1946, Meeting, from Abraham Klausner Papers, Box 1, Folder 2.

25. Klausner, *Letter to My Children*, 114.

26. YIVO Archives, MK 488, Leo Schwarz Papers, Reel 1, 11, 1254.

27. YIVO Archives, MK 488, Leo Schwarz Papers, Reel 1, 11, 1236.

28. For more on its organization and development, see Patt, *Finding Home and Homeland*, chap. 2, and David Engel, *Between Liberation and Flight: Holocaust Survivors in Poland and the Struggle for Leadership, 1944–1946* [in Hebrew] (Tel Aviv: Am Oved Publishers, 1996).

29. See Yosef Litvak, "Trumato shel Irgun Ha-Joint le-shikumah shel She'erit Ha-Pletah be-Polin, 1944–49," in *Yahadut Mizrach Eiropah ben Shoah le-Tekumah, 1944–1948*, ed. Benajmin Pinkus (Sde Boker, Israel: Ben-Gurion University, 1987); Engel, *Between Liberation and Flight*.

30. YIVO Archives, MK 488, Leo Schwarz Papers, Reel 1, 11, 1255.

31. Ibid.

32. See Letter from Rock to Rifkind, November 8, 1945, YIVO Archives, MK 488, Leo Schwarz Papers, Reel, 9, 63; YIVO Archives, Leo Schwarz Papers, Reel 8, 1032. JDC's Jacob Trobe summarized the situation of the Jewish DPs in Germany at the end of 1945, highlighting pro-Zionist enthusiasm but continuing concerns over disillusionment, lack of food and clothing, and idleness that could lead to black market activity.

33. See Jacob Rader Marcus and Abraham J. Peck, eds., *The American Rabbinate: A Century of Continuity and Change* (Hoboken, NJ: Ktav, 1985), 196. Ephraim Dekel, one of the primary organizers of the Bricha from the Yishuv, pointed to Klausner's role: "There was nothing in which the activity of the 'Bricha' was not helped by organizational ability."

34. JDC Archives, Records of the New York Office of the American Jewish Joint Distribution Committee, 1945–1954, Folder 320, Letter from Jay B. Krane to Chief of Operations, Germany, Subject: Observations on the Problem of Jewish Infiltrees, January 18, 1946.

35. Ibid.

36. See discussion in Haim Genizi, "Philip Bernstein: Adviser on Jewish Affairs, May 1946–August 1947," in *Simon Wiesenthal Center Annual, Volume 3, Chapter 6*. Genizi cites correspondence between Edward Warburg and Assistant Secretary of State John Hildring that JDC had "never participated in any organizing of this movement," in JDC Archives, Records of the Geneva Office of the American Jewish Joint Distribution Committee, 1945–1954, File ADM.281, Letter from Edward H. M. Warburg to General J. H. Hildring, August 23, 1946. See http://motlc.wiesenthal.com/site/pp.asp?c=gvKVLcMVIuG&b=395037 (accessed February 23, 2016).

37. Mankowitz, *Life between Memory and Hope*, 115.

38. YIVO Archives, Leo Schwarz Papers, Reel 2, Folder 20, 849. For example, as M. J. Joslow reported to Leo Schwarz (JDC director, US zone) and Herbert Katzki (JDC director, German operations) on the work of the education division in the US zone over the seven months from October 1945 to May 1946, he could characterize the progression of organizing JDC work into three periods: (1) educational chaos, (2) educational relief, and (3) organization and improvement. First came the response to urgent

needs, followed by the arrival of needed relief supplies, only then followed by the creation of a formal system of education.

39. Bauer, *Out of the Ashes*, 120.

40. See YIVO Archives, Leo Schwarz Papers, Reel 14, 221–222, May 1, 1946, Memo from Briansky to Schwarz, Chaplain Klausner's Credit on Central Committee's Books and His Claim to A.J.D.C. On the GI letter-writing campaign, see Grossmann, *Jews, Germans, and Allies*, 146.

41. Letter from Leo Schwarz, JDC zone director, to J. H. Whiting, US zone director, Pasing, July 17, 1946, YIVO Archives, DP Germany, File 161. As Klausner later recorded in his memoirs, "getting rid of me was no simple task. The JDC and the UNRRA did not possess the power. They needed the concurrence of the military. This they accomplished by registering a series of charges with the military."

42. YIVO Archives, MK 483, Reel 3, 37, June 1946 Letter from the Z. K. (Zalman Grinburg and David Traeger) to Edward M. Warburg (English).

43. Ibid. *Talethim* are Jewish prayer shawls.

44. AJHS, Klausner Papers, Box 1, Folder 5; includes letter of July 5, 1946, from Grinberg to Edward Warburg of JDC. On Klausner's remarkable exploits, see Alexander Grobman, "American Jewish Chaplains and She'erit Hapletah," *Simon Wiesenthal Center Annual 1*, chap. 5, 12.

45. Ibid.

46. Bauer, *Out of the Ashes*, 122. See the memorandum signed by three members of the Central Committee on their visit to the United States on January 28, 1947. Also discussed by Leo Schwarz in *The Redeemers: A Saga of the Years 1945–1952* (New York: Farrar, Straus and Giroux, 1953), 364.

47. Bauer, *Out of the Ashes*, 127.

48. See Judith Tydor Baumel, "The Politics of Spiritual Rehabilitation in the DP Camps," http://motlc.wiesenthal.com/site/pp.asp?c=gvKVLcMVIuG&b =395149. Baumel has detailed the complexities of navigating religious life among DPs in postwar Germany for JDC.

49. The Change of Jewish Population in the US Zone of Germany from January 1946 to December 31, 1946, JDC Calculations, YIVO Archives, MK 488, Leo Schwarz Papers, Reel 9, Folder 57, 713. The population rose from 39,902 to 145,735 (a 356% increase).

50. YIVO Archives, MK 488, Leo Schwarz Papers, Reel 9, Folder 57, 715 (December 31, 1946, out of 118,875 investigated); Correspondence from G. H. Muentz, JDC Statistical Office to Dr. Leo Schwarz, JDC zone director, YIVO Archives, MK 488, Leo Schwarz Papers, Reel 9, Folder 56, 525. According to calculations made by JDC at the end of 1946, the population distribution for Germany and Austria was as follows: Germany—179,622 (US zone: 142,084; Berlin: 14,564; Bremen: 885; French zone: 2,089; British zone: 20,000). The Jewish population for Austria as of December 31, 1946, was 35,555.

51. Jewish Population US Zone Germany, November 30, 1946, JDC Report, YIVO Archives, Leo Schwarz Papers, Reel 9, Folder 57, 682; JDC Recapitulation, Jewish Population US Zone Germany, November 30, 1946, YIVO Archives, Leo Schwarz Papers, Reel 9, Folder 57, 692. The Jewish population demonstrated a much higher marriage and birth rate than its German counterparts.

52. Atina Grossmann, "Trauma, Memory, and Motherhood: Germans and Jewish Displaced Persons in Post-Nazi Germany, 1945–1948," in *Life after Death*, ed. Richard Bessel and Dirk Schumann (Cambridge: Cambridge University Press, 2003), 115. See also Grossmann, *Jews, Germans, and Allies*, 184–235.

53. JDC Archives, Records of the Geneva Office of the American Jewish Joint Distribution Committee, 1945–1954, Folder ADM.594, *The Year of Survival*, 1946, Annual Report of the American Jewish Joint Distribution Committee, 8.

54. Ibid., 17.

55. Klausner, *Letter to My Children*, 130–37; Full Text of Klausner Report on Conditions in Bavaria to American Jewish Conference, March 20, 1947.

56. Ibid.

57. Ibid.

58. Ann Liepah Papers (in possession of the author), Letter from Klausner to Liepah, 1947, Bavaria. The author wishes to thank the Slobin family for sharing these materials.

59. See Memorandum from Charles Passman, JDC Munich to Central Committee of Liberated Jews, December 10, 1947, YIVO Archives, Leo

Schwarz Papers, Reel 10, 876–890. According to existing JDC regulations, members of kibbutzim and *hakhsharot* were considered workers and received rations according to these categories. Cigarettes were part of the workers' rations.

60. YIVO Archives, Leo Schwarz Papers, 1214, Henie Durmashkin, Munich, August 1949, *Joint'l*. See Shirli Gilbert, "We Long for a Home: Songs and Survival among Jewish Displaced Persons" in *"We Are Here": New Approaches to Jewish Displaced Persons in Postwar Germany*, ed. Avinoam J. Patt and Michael Berkowitz (Detroit: Wayne State University Press, 2010), 289–307.

61. See Aviva Halamish, *The Exodus Affair: Holocaust Survivors and the Struggle for Palestine* (Syracuse, NY: Syracuse University Press, 1998), 5–7; YIVO Archives, MK 488, Leo Schwarz Papers, Reel 9, Folder 56, 524 (G. H. Muentz, JDC Statistical Office, to Dr. Leo Schwarz, JDC zone director). Had immigration to the United States been a realistic option after the war, it is quite conceivable that a majority of Jewish DPs would have moved there. See also Dinnerstein, *America and the Survivors of the Holocaust*, and Mark Wischnitzer, *To Dwell in Safety* (Philadelphia: Jewish Publication Society of America, 1948) for other calculations.

    JDC also calculated the monthly and annual departure of Jews from Germany for various destinations. The accuracy of the figures, particularly with regard to Palestine, is complicated by the use of forged visas and bogus destinations given to secure exit visas. Nonetheless, as JDC was involved in sponsoring the departure of groups and individuals and assisted with the *aliyah* of some groups, its numbers are noteworthy. According to JDC calculations, the emigration of Jews from the US zone in Germany during 1946 totaled 6,871, with 4,057 sponsored by JDC. Of these, 4,135 went to the United States (2,708 sponsored by the Joint), 793 to Palestine (16 sponsored by the Joint), and 1,430 to South and Central America (850 sponsored by the Joint).

62. Muentz population report for 1946 to Leo Schwarz, YIVO Archives, MK 488, Leo Schwarz Papers, Reel 9, Folder 57, 757.

63. Arieh Kochavi, *Post-Holocaust Politics: Britain, the United States, and Jewish Refugees, 1945–1948* (Chapel Hill: University of North Carolina Press, 2001).

64. See JDC operations in US Zone Germany, 1948, YIVO Archives, Leo Schwarz Papers, 108, Folder 1505, 86. According to JDC, a total of 8,000 Jewish DP children were sent to summer camps supplied by JDC in the US zone during the summer of 1947. The JDC publication presented the summer camps as part of an effort at "building up their health . . . the children spent two-week periods in specially prepared installations, administered by JDC, and were given an opportunity to enjoy a wholesome holiday and much-needed rest during the school vacation."

65. JDC Archives, Records of the Geneva Office of the American Jewish Joint Distribution Committee, 1945–1954, Folder ADM.594, *The Year of Survival*, 1946, Annual Report of the American Jewish Joint Distribution Committee, 19.

66. Halamish, *The Exodus Affair*, 235.

67. *Jidiscze Cajtung*, December 2, 1947, 1, YIVO Archives, Jewish DP Periodicals, Reel 2–1.

68. Ibid., December 16, 1947, volume 93, 161.

69. *Jidiscze Cajtung*, December 5, 1947. Levinthal, aged fifty-five at the time of his posting in Germany, served as a judge on the Court of Common Pleas in Philadelphia. For a profile of Levinthal, see *Weekend: The Magazine of Stars and Stripes* 2, no. 45 (December 6, 1947).

70. "Minutes of a Meeting Held in the Office of the Jewish Adviser on Monday, March 15, 1948," Recorded by Major Abraham S. Hyman, JAGD, YIVO Archives, MK 488, Leo Schwarz Papers, Reel 10, 1378; Bauer, *Out of the Ashes*, 262; see also Yosef Grodzinsky, *Homer Enoshi Tov* (Jerusalem: Hed Artzi, 1998), 153–54.

71. Ibid.

72. Minutes of a Meeting Held in the Office of the Jewish Adviser on Monday, March 15, 1948, YIVO Archives, Leo Schwarz Papers, Reel 10, 1384.

73. Klausner, *Letter to My Children*, 164.

74. JDC Archives, Records of the New York Office of the American Jewish Joint Distribution Committee, 1945–1954, "Meeting of the Jewish Co-operating Organizations on Rabbi Abraham Klausner's Suggestions Respecting the DP Situation," May 4, 1948, American Jewish Archives, online at http://www.ajcarchives.org/AJC_DATA/Files/DP40.PDF.

75. Des Bundesministeriums der Justiz und für Verbraucherschutz, Gesetz über die Rechtsstellung heimatloser Ausländer im Bundesgebiet, April 25, 1952.

76. JDC Archives, Records of the New York Office of the American Jewish Joint Distribution Committee, 1945–1954, Folder 328, Letter from Samuel L. Haber to M. Laub, Subject: Transfer of Föhrenwald, November 2, 1951.

77. JDC Archives, Records of the Geneva Office of the American Jewish Joint Distribution Committee, 1945–1954, Folder GER.796, Translation of an Article in *Unzer Stimme*, Paris, November 14, 1951.

78. Ibid., Folder GER.796, Translation Letter from Föhrenwald Lager Befelkerung, November 14, 1951.

79. JDC Archives, Records of the New York Office of the American Jewish Joint Distribution Committee, 1945–1954, Folder 328, Letter from Samuel L. Haber to M. Laub, Subject: Transfer of Föhrenwald, November 2, 1951.

80. In addition to the aforementioned Jews were a handful of Jewish DPs who had settled into life in Germany, were intermarried, or had prospered on the black market and did not intend to leave the country. JDC considered these DPs especially troublesome, as they were more likely to qualify for visas but often chose to remain in the DP camps.

81. Angelika Königseder and Juliane Wetzel, *Waiting for Hope: Jewish Displaced Persons in Post-World War II Germany* (Evanston, IL: Northwestern University Press, 2001), 149.

82. JDC Archives, Records of the Geneva Office of the American Jewish Joint Distribution Committee, 1945–1954, Folder GER.796, Translation Letter from Föhrenwald Lager Befelkerung, November 14, 1951.

83. Ibid., 2.

84. By that time, the authorities had begun closing the more than thirty major HA centers in the US zone. Most HAs were resettled in Bavaria. The Landsberg DP center closed its gates on November 1, 1950, and Feldafing closed in March 1953, leaving Föhrenwald as the only functioning Jewish HA center in Bavaria.

85. JDC received some aid from HIAS, the Claims Conference, and the Federal Republic of Germany, but this was mostly monetary. The actual negotiations for visas and the arrangements associated with them mainly fell to JDC.

86. The word *Länder* will be used hereafter to denote the West German Bundesländer.

87. JDC Archives, Records of the Geneva Office of the American Jewish Joint Distribution Committee, 1945–1954, Folder GER.803, Report from the American Jewish Joint Distribution Committee (AJJDC), The Föhrenwald Story, February 16, 1954.

88. Grossmann, *Jews, Germans, and Allies*, 252.

89. Many of the Jewish DPs who had a criminal record had either been arrested for carrying false documents or for having traded on the black market. JDC worked to expunge their records in the early 1950s, thereby allowing many of them to finally qualify for a visa.

90. Kierra Crago-Schneider, "Antisemitism or Competing Interests? An Examination of German and American Perceptions of Jewish Displaced Persons Active on the Black Market in Munich's Möhlstrasse," *Yad Vashem Studies* 38, no. 1 (2002). German ideas of Jewish criminality persisted long after the Holocaust had ended.

91. Jewish Telegraphic Agency Jewish News Archive—London, "Germans Indict Seven Jewish DP's for Föhrenwald Riot in 1952," October 14, 1954.

92. StK, Munich: BayHStA, 1952, Freiherr Von Godin, Zollfahndungsaktion im Regierungslager Föhrenwald am 28, May 31, 1952.

93. JDC Archives, Records of the New York Office of the American Jewish Joint Distribution Committee, 1945–1954, Folder 328, Letter from Samuel L. Haber to C. Jordan, Subject: Raid on Föhrenwald, May 29, 1952.

94. Ibid., Folder 328, Letter from Samuel L. Haber to C. Jordan, Subject: Raid on Föhrenwald, May 29, 1952; ibid., Folder 328, Telegram from Haber to Jack Raymond, May 29, 1952.

95. Jewish Telegraphic Agency Jewish News Archive—London, "German Government Charged with Unfairness in Handling Jewish DP's," July 10, 1952.

96. StK, Munich: BayHStA, Dr. Gillitzer, Vormerkung, June 4, 1952.

97. StK, Munich: BayHStA, David Samuel and Jakubowitz Zahler, Memorandum, June 4, 1952.

98. Samuel Haber argued that the Jews who had taken control of the Föhrenwald Camp Committee after the great migrations of 1948–1952 were

only motivated by their own desires and cared little for the other camp inhabitants.

99. JDC Archives, Records of the New York Office of the American Jewish Joint Distribution Committee, 1945–1954, Folder 328, Letter from Samuel L. Haber to C. Jordan, Subject: Raid on Föhrenwald, May 29, 1952.

100. JDC Archives, Records of the Geneva Office of the American Jewish Joint Distribution Committee, 1955–1964, Report from Charles Jordan, The Story of Föhrenwald, 1957.

101. Ibid., Folder GER.482, Press Release Issued by Samuel Jaffe, Mass Movement Out of Camp Föhrenwald Announced by Overseas Director of JDC, March 7, 1956.

102. Ibid., Report from Charles Jordan, The Story of Föhrenwald, 1957.

103. JDC Archives, Records of the New York Office of the American Jewish Joint Distribution Committee, 1945–1954, Folder 327, Letter from George Vida to Dr. Emil Lehman, March 31, 1954.

104. JDC Archives, Records of the Geneva Office of the American Jewish Joint Distribution Committee, 1945–1954, Folder GER.803, Report from the American Jewish Joint Distribution Committee (AJJDC), The Föhrenwald Story, February 16, 1954.

105. Jewish Telegraphic Agency Jewish News Archive—London, "J.D.C. Close Refugee Camps in Germany, Austria and Italy," April 20, 1954.

106. JDC Archives, Records of the New York Office of the American Jewish Joint Distribution Committee, 1945–1954, Folder 381, Telephone Message from Moses W. Beckelman, Paris, to New York, February 17, 1954.

107. Ibid., Folder 381, Report of the Executive Vice Chairman to the Executive Committee, March 23, 1954.

108. Ibid., Folder 381, Telephone Message from Moses W. Beckelman, Paris, to Morris Laub, New York, February 19, 1954.

109. JDC Archives, Records of the Geneva Office of the American Jewish Joint Distribution Committee, 1945–1954, Folder GER.805, *Münchner Merkur*, Translation of the Article "Demonstrationen in Möhlstraßenviertel," February 18, 1954.

110. JDC Archives, Records of the New York Office of the American Jewish Joint Distribution Committee, 1945–1954, Folder 381, Report of the

Executive Vice Chairman to the Executive Committee, March 23, 1954.

111. Ibid., Folder 381, Letter from Arthur T. Jacobs to Moses A. Leavitt, March 2, 1954.

112. Ibid., Folder 381, Incoming Cable from Beckelman to Laub, February 17, 1954.

113. Ibid., Folder 381, Statement by Moses Beckelman, Director General, American Joint Distribution Committee, February 25, 1954.

114. Ibid., Folder 381, Statement by Moses Beckelman, Director General, American Joint Distribution Committee, February 25, 1954.

115. In actuality, JDC chose to rent office space on the Möhlstraße, as most of the organizations working with DPs were located there, and American forces had designated the street for the international aid organizations working in the zone.

116. Jewish Telegraphic Agency Jewish News Archive—New York, "J.D.C. Reaches Agreement with the Jewish DP's: Bars Demonstrations," March 9, 1954.

117. JDC Archives, Records of the New York Office of the American Jewish Joint Distribution Committee, 1945–1954, Report of the Executive Vice Chairman to the Executive Committee, March 23, 1954.

118. Although a number of Jewish organizations were located in Frankfurt, the Zentralrat der Juden in Deutschland—the main representative Jewish organization in Europe—was no longer in the city.

119. JDC Archives, Records of the Geneva Office of the American Jewish Joint Distribution Committee, 1945–1954, Folder GER.803, Report from the American Jewish Joint Distribution Committee (AJJDC), The Föhrenwald Story, 3, February 16, 1954.

120. Ronald Webster, "American Relief and Jews in Germany, 1945–1960," *Leo Baeck Institute Year Book* 38, no. 1 (1993): 306.

121. JDC Archives, Records of the Geneva Office of the American Jewish Joint Distribution Committee, 1945–1954, Folder GER.803, Report from the American Jewish Joint Distribution Committee (AJJDC), The Föhrenwald Story, February 16, 1954.

122. Angelika Königseder and Juliane Wetzel, *Lebensmut im Wartesaal: die jü-dischen DPs (displaced persons) im Nachkriegsdeutschland*, Originalausg. ed., Zeit des Nationalsozialismus (Frankfurt am Main: Fischer Taschenbuch, 1994), 167.

123. JDC Archives, Records of the New York Office of the American Jewish Joint Distribution Committee, 1945–1954, Folder: Germany, Displaced Persons, Returnees, 1950–1954: Letter from Moses A. Leavitt to Louis Lieblich, December 18, 1953.

124. JDC Archives, Records of the Geneva Office of the American Jewish Joint Distribution Committee, 1955–1964, Folder GER.482, Press Release Issued by Samuel Jaffe, Mass Movement Out of Camp Föhrenwald Announced by Overseas Director of JDC, March 7, 1956.

125. Although the responsibility for operating Camp Föhrenwald came under the control of the Bavarian government, the returnee issue was so worrisome that the Bonn government actually involved itself in order to address the problem.

126. JDC Archives, Records of the Geneva Office of the American Jewish Joint Distribution Committee, 1945–1954, Folder GER.796, Memorandum from Leonard Seidenman to Charles Jordan, Subject: Field Trip to Germany concerning Camp Föhrenwald, October 6, 1952. In October 1952, for example, there were thirty-one departures and thirty-eight new arrivals.

127. Jewish Telegraphic Agency Jewish News Archive—New York, "German Government Declines to Waive Visa Requirements for Israelis," March 1, 1956; Webster, "American Relief and Jews in Germany, 1945–1960," 307. Not all of the returnees had been DPs or had been resettled after World War II. A small number of the Jews who came back to Germany after 1949 were German and Eastern European Jews who had immigrated to Palestine or Israel from their respective countries before the war's outbreak or in the first couple of years of fighting.

128. JDC Archives, Records of the New York Office of the American Jewish Joint Distribution Committee, 1945–1954, Folder 327, Report by James P. Rice, Subject: Emigration Grants by the German Government for Legal Residents of Camp Föhrenwald, March 29, 1954.

129. All emigrating DPs had to surrender their papers upon their emigration as they were becoming citizens in their new home countries.

130. JDC Archives, Records of the Geneva Office of the American Jewish Joint Distribution Committee, 1945–1954, Folder GER.796, Memorandum from Leonard Seidenman to Charles Jordan, Subject: Field Trip to Germany concerning Camp Föhrenwald, October 6, 1952.

131. Ibid.

132. JDC Archives, Records of the New York Office of the American Jewish Joint Distribution Committee, 1945–1954, Folder 328, Letter from Charles Jordan, 1952.

133. StK, Munich: BayHStA, 1953, Bavaria Der Ministerrat, Auszug aus dem Protokoll des Ministrrats [Minutes for the Bavarian Ministry Meeting on the Jewish illegal returners], 1953.

134. JDC Archives, Records of the New York Office of the American Jewish Joint Distribution Committee, 1945–1954, Folder 328, Translation from the Yiddish Daily *Unzer Wort*, Föhrenwald—The Last Camp on German Soil, July 8, 1953.

135. JDC Archives, Records of the Geneva Office of the American Jewish Joint Distribution Committee, 1945–1954, Folder GER.814, Notes on a New Approach to Try to Resolve Resident Case Problem in the DP Countries, Speech Notes by Charles H. Jordan, July 10, 1952.

136. JDC Archives, Records of the New York Office of the American Jewish Joint Distribution Committee, 1945–1954, Folder 328, Letter from Morris Laub to Arnold Gurin, February 19, 1953.

137. Ibid.

138. Königseder and Wetzel, *Waiting for Hope*, 162.

139. JDC Archives, Records of the Geneva Office of the American Jewish Joint Distribution Committee, 1945–1954, Report of the Executive Vice Chairman to the Executive Committee, March 23, 1954.

140. Ibid., Folder GER.803, Report from the American Jewish Joint Distribution Committee (AJJDC), The Föhrenwald Story, February 16, 1954; Stadtarchiv München, Folder ZA Ausländer 47, Süddeutsche Zeitung, "Jüdische Rückwanderer streiken in München," 1953.

141. Ibid.

142. Königseder and Wetzel, *Waiting for Hope*, 163.

143. Jewish Telegraphic Agency Jewish News Archive—New York, "110 'Returnees' Moved to Hamburg: Will Immigrate to Latin America," January 4, 1954.

144. Ibid.

145. Jewish Telegraphic Agency Jewish News Archive—New York, "Jewish Refugees Transferred from Föhrenwald to Non-Jewish Camp," April 19, 1956.

146. Jewish Telegraphic Agency, "J.D.C. Close Refugee Camps in Germany, Austria and Italy."

147. Jewish Telegraphic Agency Jewish News Archive—New York, "Föhrenwald Jewish DPs Advance Demands on German Government," May 10, 1954.

148. Jewish Telegraphic Agency, "J.D.C. Close Refugee Camps in Germany, Austria and Italy."

149. JDC Archives, Records of the New York Office of the American Jewish Joint Distribution Committee, Germany, Displaced Persons, Camps: Föhrenwald, 1956–1957, 1962, 1956 Yearly Report, Föhrenwald, 1956.

150. Jewish Telegraphic Agency Jewish News Archive—Munich, "German Catholics Intend to Buy Buildings of Föhrenwald Camp," August 18, 1955.

151. JDC Archives, Records of the Geneva Office of the American Jewish Joint Distribution Committee, 1955–1964, Folder GER.482, Press Release by Samuel Jaffe, Mass Movement Out of Camp Föhrenwald Announced by Overseas Director of JDC, March 7, 1956; ibid., Folder GER.482, Mary Palevsky, Memorandum Concerning the Integration of the Camp Föhrenwald Orthodox Group, February 23, 1956.

152. For more information on life in Föhrenwald and postcamp life, see Beno Salamander, *Kinderjahre im Displaced-Persons-Lager Föhrenwald, München* (Bayerische Landeszentrale für politische Bildungsarbeit: Jüdisches Museum München, 2011). The Föhrenwald Jews who were resettled in Bavaria were often housed together. The individuals in these communities formed a tight-knit group that remained together for decades after they left the camp.

153. JDC Archives, Records of the Geneva Office of the American Jewish Joint Distribution Committee, 1955–1964, Folder GER.482, Memorandum

from Theodore D. Feder, AJDC–Frankfurt, to Charles H. Jordan, AJDC–Paris, Bi-Monthly Report, April 22 to May 5, May 9, 1956.

154. Ibid., Folder GER.482, Translation of Article in *Süddeutsche Zeitung*, "The Liquidation of Camp Föhrenwald," April 9, 1956.

155. JDC Archives, Records of the Geneva Office of the American Jewish Joint Distribution Committee, 1945–1954, Folder GER.803, Report from the American Jewish Joint Distribution Committee (AJJDC), The Föhrenwald Story, February 16, 1954.

156. JDC Archives, Records of the Geneva Office of the American Jewish Joint Distribution Committee, 1955–1964, Folder GER.482, Letter from Theodore D. Feder to S. Jaffe, February 7, 1956.

157. Ibid., Folder GER.483, Cable from Katzki to the JOINTFUND Munich, March 1, 1957.

158. JDC Archives, Records of the Geneva Office of the American Jewish Joint Distribution Committee, 1945–1954, Folder GER.803, Report from the American Jewish Joint Distribution Committee (AJJDC), The Föhrenwald Story, February 16, 1954.

159. For more on the closing of Camp Föhrenwald, see Crago-Schneider, "Jewish 'Shtetls' in Postwar Germany," and Grossmann, *Jews, Germans, and Allies*.

12

JDC Activity in Hungary, 1945-1953

Kinga Frojimovics

Introduction

In Hungary, as in other European countries, counting the survivors of the Shoah and providing them with the barest necessities called for the active participation of international Jewish organizations. The two organizations that primarily took upon themselves the task of assistance to the Hungarian Jewish community were the American Jewish Joint Distribution Committee (JDC) and the World Jewish Congress (WJC). Jean Ancel claims that in Romania, JDC saved the majority of the survivors from certain death by hunger.[1] His claim about the critical importance of postwar aid is also valid for the other countries of Central and Eastern Europe that were in ruins after the war and became part of the Soviet sphere of influence. According to a census that was completed on October 31, 1946, there were about 180,000 Jewish survivors in Hungary, and the overwhelming majority of them were deprived of all of their pre-Shoah possessions.[2]

Preserved among the documents of the Jewish community of Szeged are requests from the returning survivors that document in a shocking manner the survivors' impoverished and needy state.[3] In these letters, survivors returning to Szeged in 1945 turned to the Jewish community of Szeged to ask for basic furniture and clothing because upon their return from the deportation they found their apartments completely empty and looted.

For example, in November 1945, a former deportee asked for knitting yarn from the Jewish community in order to knit warm socks, gloves, and other articles of winter clothing for herself.[4] Another survivor asked for a white medical coat and a sweater as well as an umbrella for the following reason: "My parents disappeared during the deportation and I am alone and without any income, so I cannot buy the required things. However, having a white coat would mean that I could protect my only clothes during my work in the laboratory. The umbrella and the sweater would serve as a transition and winter coat."[5] There were also many people who did not have much-needed medicine or medical instruments. There was, for instance, a survivor who asked for "rags to bandage" her crippled hands that needed constant care.[6]

Relief work immediately after the Shoah focused on two separate but intertwined tasks. One was to recover the human rights and both the communal and individual possessions of the Jews. The other task was to ensure, through a multiphased process, that both communities and individuals could become self-sufficient once again and become part of the social and economic structure of their respective countries.

When we trace the process of getting the Jews of Hungary back on their feet, we can observe a division of labor between the WJC and JDC. Immediately after the Shoah, in 1945–1946, when the creation of the State of Israel was by no means a foregone conclusion, both organizations saw their primary goal as aiding the local Jewish communities in Europe. Whereas JDC held an established position within the network of American Jewish relief organizations, the WJC had only been created a decade earlier. Established in Geneva in 1936, the WJC was created to safeguard Jewish minority rights, which had been embraced by Jewish committees during World War I, at the Versailles Peace Conference in 1919 and within the framework of the League of Nations.[7] In fact, the WJC had much in common with the Jewish Agency, and many of the WJC activists were also Zionist activists. At the beginning of World War II, the WJC viewed its role in political terms as an organization responsible for protecting Jewish interests at a future peace conference. However, with the realities of occupation, it quickly became involved in the business of relief, much to the dismay of JDC leaders, who feared that the WJC, as a political organization, would thwart the Joint's efforts to maintain neutrality and remain apolitical. JDC, for its part, focused its energies on developing local economic and social structures in order to help Jewish communities become self-sufficient.

The achievement of these seemingly reasonable aims proved to be problematic in Hungary. Although all European countries guaranteed the legal security of the Jews and condemned deprivation of civil rights, the issue of returning confiscated properties caused grave disagreements between Jews and non-Jews. Because, in most cases, a significant part of the property confiscated from the Jews fell into the hands of local citizens, the efforts of the Jews to get them back—efforts legally endorsed by the countries concerned—were met with serious resistance. Indeed, the political establishment sought to prevent Jews from retrieving their possessions because of the widespread opinion that non-Jewish citizens had also suffered considerably during the war. Political elites in war-torn countries in both Eastern and Western Europe were not prepared to take away the little that their poverty-stricken masses had acquired.[8]

The aim of integrating the Jews and their communities into the economy and society of their countries rested on the assumption that it would be worthwhile to reintegrate Jews into the democracies that would emerge or reemerge after the war in Europe. It was not until the end of the 1940s, with the establishment of a Stalinist dictatorship in all of these countries but Yugoslavia, that it became obvious that this assumption was unfounded. After the Iron Curtain was drawn, it was very difficult to emigrate from these countries where the Jews had more or less found their places.

In 1949, after the Communist Party takeover in Hungary and the establishment of a totalitarian Communist dictatorship, international Jewish organizations operating in Hungary realized that their strategy concerning the integration of the Jews was increasingly problematic. This is indicated, for example, by the desperate efforts of the European chairman of JDC, Joseph J. Schwartz, to seek ways for Jews to leave the country even though legal emigration from Hungary had been practically impossible since December 1948. The paradox, thus, is apparent: One of the top leaders of JDC, an organization that declared itself to be nonpolitical and was striving to avoid all appearances of "complicity" with Zionism, initiated talks with the leaders of the Hungarian state about permits for Jews to make *aliyah*. Initially, Schwartz offered $2 million to Hungary in exchange for 25,000 *aliyah* permits; over the course of 1949, Hungarian officials, sensing an opportunity to negotiate, would counter with a proposal to allow 5,000 Jews to depart for $1 million.[9] Yehuda Bauer wrote about the final results of the Schwartz talks: "Nothing came of these schemes, but they indicated the line some of the governments in Eastern Europe would take in the future: it was worthwhile, sometimes, to sell Jews for good money."[10]

That the survivors of the Shoah survived its immediate aftermath, while hardly receiving any help from the countries to which they had returned, can be attributed to the enormous efforts of JDC. Following World War II, in 1945, JDC distributed various forms of aid worth $17,508,000 in fifteen European countries. Hungary received 23% of this sum ($3,837,000). In 1948, Hungary received even more—$8,463,000 or 27% of the total sum spent on Europe—at a time when JDC supported the Jewish communities of only nine European countries.[11] Thus, the Jews of Hungary received the largest amount of support from JDC—more than $52 million was spent on Hungary[12] in the postwar period from 1945 until JDC ceased its operations in the country at the beginning of 1953. Furthermore, aiding the Jews of Hungary between 1945 and 1953 was the most expensive project in the history of JDC up to that time. The spending was effective; Hungary proved to be the Eastern bloc country in which JDC was most successful in accomplishing its goal of reintegrating the Jews. The success of JDC can be indirectly measured, for example, by data concerning the intention to emigrate. Immediately following the Shoah, about three-quarters of the Jews of Hungary (as was the case in other Eastern and Central European countries) wanted to leave Hungary.[13] And indeed, a very significant proportion of the Jews from other Communist countries did emigrate. Hungary was an exception in this respect: Although there was large-scale emigration, the greater portion of the Jews remained in the country.

One can argue that JDC's work was (ironically) too successful because it kept many more Jews in Hungary than actually wanted to remain there. At the turn of 1945–1946, almost 80% of the survivors claimed to wish to leave the country for economic, personal, or ideological reasons. But in the end, more than half of the Jews remained in the country, later becoming trapped behind the Iron Curtain. To what extent, this chapter asks, was the choice to remain in Hungary a result of the outstandingly successful reconstruction work carried out by JDC? Studying the situation in postwar Hungary through the lens of JDC work reveals the complexities of postwar Hungarian Jewish community politics and JDC's efforts to navigate them. JDC pursued a dual strategy, supporting those who desired to leave by working with Zionist groups while simultaneously assisting those Jews who sought to rebuild Jewish communities in Hungary. This dual strategy may have had the unintended consequence of encouraging Jews who originally planned to leave Hungary to remain in the country even after the political situation deteriorated, making the possibility of departure become impossible.

THE RECONSTRUCTION OF THE JEWISH COMMUNITY IN HUNGARY

The JDC Committee in Hungary (JDC Magyarországi Bizottsága) began operations in March 1945. JDC activity in Hungary from 1945 to 1953—both its relief policy and its relationship with the regime—can be divided into three phases. Studying the JDC programs in Hungary provides an excellent opportunity to observe the successful reconstruction of a European Jewish community. However, given the eventual political realities in Hungary, with a gradually consolidating Communist dictatorship by 1949, questions arise regarding the (at the time) unclear impact of JDC's initial postwar strategy. Indeed, it was the success of the reconstruction project that enabled the majority of the Jewish community to stay in Hungary even though four-fifths of them had stated their wish to leave the country at the turn of 1945–1946.

Phase I: Frigyes Görög (Spring 1945 to February 1948)

During this early phase, from the spring of 1945 to February 1948, JDC, led by Frigyes Görög, focused on emergency relief: supporting impoverished survivors with housing, medical care, food, clothing, and money.[14] The Department for Individual Relief was one of the first to be established in May 1945.[15] Furthermore, from June 1945, JDC became the sole sponsor of the National Relief Committee for Deportees (Magyarországi Zsidók

Deportáltakat Gondozó Országos Bizottsága), a Hungarian Jewish organization that provided aid for survivors who returned to the country and for those who passed through Hungary in the framework of the Bricha.[16]

In the first few months, the JDC Budapest office operated under the aegis of the JDC Bucharest and Geneva offices, but it began operating as an independent JDC office by June 1945.[17] The leading body of JDC in Hungary, the JDC Committee, consisting of twelve members, including representatives of Neolog (the Hungarian variant of Reform) Jewry, the Orthodox, and the Zionists, was established on June 22.[18]

The National Jewish Relief Committee (NJRC [Országos Zsidó Segítő Bizottság]), the top relief organ in Hungary, was also founded in the summer of 1945 on August 31 by JDC, the Hungarian Zionist Association (Magyar Cionista Szövetség), and the central organs of the Neolog and Orthodox communities.[19] JDC recognized the NJRC as "the central executive organ of the relief project for the Jews of Hungary" and worked with the organization for the distribution of foreign aid.[20] However, JDC reserved the right to also provide financial support directly, independently of the NJRC, to the leading bodies of the Neolog and Orthodox communities, to the local Jewish communities, to the various Zionist associations (*halutzim*) and their *hakhsharot* (agricultural training centers), and to the Office of Statistics and Information (Statisztikai és Tudakozó Hivatal), which operated within the framework of the WJC.[21] Thus, JDC insisted on the freedom to carry out its own reconstruction program. We can also see that JDC had a dual goal from the very beginning. It aimed to support the reintegration of the Jewish community in Hungary but, as we can see from the aid distributed to the various Zionist organizations, it also tried to support those who wanted to emigrate. M. W. Beckelman, the deputy chairman of JDC's European headquarters, explained JDC's dual goal during a visit to Hungary in the summer of 1948. He noted that JDC had not concentrated on emigration issues until the Nazi takeover in Germany in 1933, which then focused JDC efforts on the promotion of emigration and assistance to refugees until the end of the war. After the Shoah, JDC was determined to take on the dual—and dueling—task "of supporting Jews who want to stay in their country by providing relief and helping them to make a living, and of fully recognizing the strivings of others who want to leave Europe, whether for personal reasons or on principle. Therefore, the JDC will do its best to make legal emigration possible for those who want to leave."[22]

At the same time, the Zionist retraining camps (*hakhsharot* and *plugot*), which taught agricultural and industrial skills useful for emigration, sometimes with JDC assistance, also offered useful training for young Jews wishing to remain in Hungary who needed training to adapt to the economic and employment realities in postwar Hungary. Indeed, JDC actually used the aforementioned argument to justify its support of the Zionist organizations to the regime, which was observing JDC's work with increasing animosity. The so-called Work and Workshop Organization Department of JDC (Munka-és Üzemszervező Csoport) had the task of supporting Zionist *hakhsharot* and *plugot*. In May 1946, JDC supported 119 agricultural and 60 industrial ventures with a 5,228-strong workforce.[23]

Support for various Zionist organizations also caused the first open conflict between JDC and the Communist Party. In July 1945, JDC leaders in Hungary met with Zoltán Vas, the Communist mayor of Budapest, who claimed that JDC was promoting the propaganda of the Hungarian Zionist Association. In reaction to this, JDC declared "that the activity of the JDC is completely apolitical. Concerned with social work and charity it does not distinguish between Zionist and non-Zionist persons and goals, since it intends to serve universal Jewish goals by its work."[24] The statement did not stop the attacks against JDC. In March 1946, a ministerial commissioner named Jenő Zeitinger became a member of the JDC Commission on behalf of the Ministry of Welfare, which was already in the hands of the Communist Party. His charge was to supervise the activity of JDC.[25] Two years after the meeting with Zoltán Vas, on July 31, 1947, Zeitinger evaluated the role of JDC in the economic and social life of Hungary in his report for the party:

> It continuously promotes and keeps alive the separation
> of Jews in Hungary from the Hungarians. It keeps several
> thousands of young men and women in 110 retraining camps
> under its control in a reactionary spirit for the purpose of

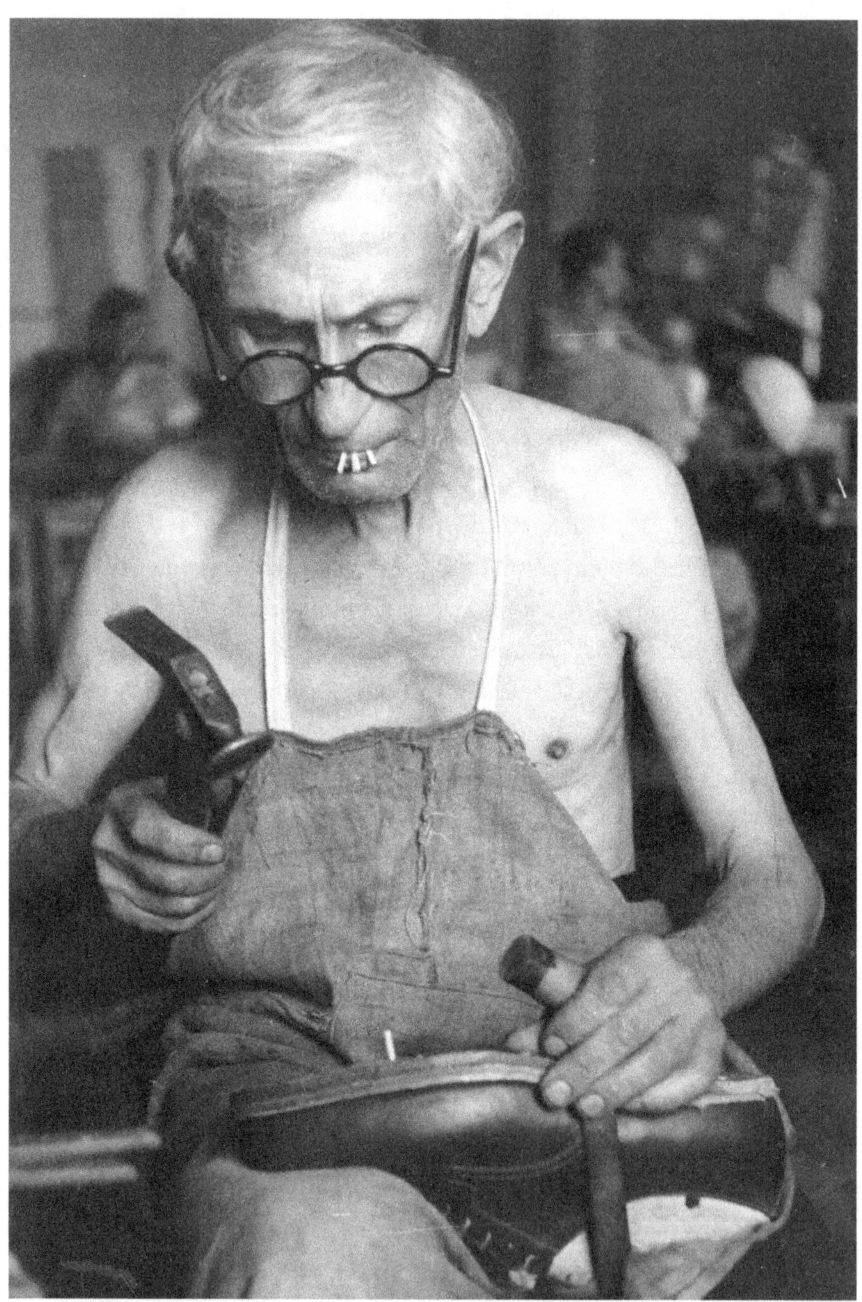

A man at work in the shoemakers' cooperative. Budapest, Hungary, circa 1948.

sending them to Palestine as immigrants. Through its so-called "Work and Workshop Organization Department" it sponsors industrial cooperatives, factories, and agricultural cooperatives, which constitute centers of infection full of pus on the body of the Hungarian Democracy both in Budapest and in the countryside.[26]

Zeitinger would later remark that the work of JDC was still needed in Hungary "because it is by all means advantageous from the economic and social points of view" but urged that Frigyes Görög be removed from his leading position at JDC.[27]

The specific economic and social assistance was indeed of basic importance for both Hungary and the Communist Party because JDC's social work took a significant burden off the shoulders of the government. Moreover, JDC, as the largest foreign organization operating in Hungary after World War II, was Hungary's largest annual provider of foreign currency. In fact, during the preliminary talks regarding JDC's return to Hungary, the representative of the Hungarian state made it clear that the license to operate in Hungary would be granted only if the funds to be used in the country were supplied in the form of foreign currency and changed into Hungarian currency through the Hungarian National Bank.[28]

The Hungarian government also had another way of "taxing" JDC. It insisted that JDC spend 5% of the monthly relief entering the country, whether in money or in kind, on non-Jewish or nonsectarian objectives, mainly on the support of leftist youth groups and social organizations. In May 1946, the JDC Committee, under pressure from Zeitinger, declared that although JDC was an international organization with a primary mission to help Jews, it had always cooperated with non-Jewish relief organizations, helping all needy people in circumstances of crisis, irrespective of race or religion. Consequently, it would be only natural for the organization to provide aid to non-Jewish people in need in war-afflicted Hungary. The statement also pointed out that the majority of JDC's funds for aid to non-Jews had not been distributed by JDC but had been sent to the Ministry of Welfare (Népjóléti Minisztérium) and the Budapest Town Hall (Budapest

Főpolgármesteri Hivatal) for distribution since the beginning of 1946.[29] In short, JDC had been required to pay a kind of tax since 1946.

Surveying the first phase of JDC's operations in Hungary, characterized by emergency relief and providing for the basic needs of the survivors, it can be observed that to a certain extent, JDC had already come into conflict with the Communist Party. By the beginning of 1948, the party managed to ensure that Frigyes Görög, whom it considered unreliable, departed for the United States while JDC continued to operate in Hungary, bringing tens of millions of dollars to the country.

Phase II: Israel Gaynor Jacobson (Early 1948 to December 1949)

Following the departure of Görög, Israel Gaynor Jacobson, an American Jew who had come to Hungary in September 1947, became the chairman of JDC. Prior to his arrival in Hungary, he had worked as a JDC representative in Italy and Greece.[30] While Görög considered the distribution of aid to be the most important task of JDC, Jacobson followed another strategy. According to Jacobson and European Chairman Joseph J. Schwartz, in the first three postwar years JDC had spent most of its money in Hungary in vain because the Jewish community had not become any stronger; rather, masses of Jews had become dependent on JDC relief. Therefore, Jacobson focused on helping those depending on relief to get back on their feet, to become independent and integrated into the Hungarian social and economic structures.

In order to execute his reconstruction project in 1948, Jacobson fundamentally reorganized JDC in Hungary. As a first step, he cut the administrative apparatus of JDC. Then he placed the entire relief policy on new foundations. From that point on, JDC supplied relief only to those who had a very compelling reason for not being able to support themselves and could not expect support from their families. This reduction in the number of people on relief applied to the care of the young and the old alike. Homes for the elderly accepted only totally helpless people who received no support at all from their families. From the beginning of 1948, the children's homes run by JDC accepted only complete orphans. They sent away all children who had any kind of family in the country. In this regard,

A young Romanian refugee with Director of JDC Operations in Hungary Israel Jacobson. Budapest, Hungary, circa 1948. JDC supplied emergency provisions in Hungary to Jewish refugees from Romania and Poland en route to displaced persons camps in Austria. This package was sent from the Canadian Jewish Congress to the JDC office in Hungary.

Jacobson acted according to the principles accepted at the April 1948 JDC Country Directors Conference in Paris at which he asserted that beyond the reconstruction of communities, great emphasis should be placed on strengthening family life.[31] According to the "Standards and Policies for Welfare Programs" accepted in Paris:

> Our general policy is to strengthen family life and therefore to minimize the use of institutions as the solution for child care problems. We feel that institutional care is not only the most expensive, but frequently the least helpful of possible facilities and should be limited to those children

who have no other kind of care available. . . . Admissions to institutions should be limited to full orphans, except for special situations (such as [a] parent's inability to care for the child), where temporary institutional care is required. In such latter cases children should be removed from the Home as soon as the emergency situation is over. The provision of religious, educational or cultural training should not be the basis for admission and care of children in institutions. Such programs should be carried on in the community.[32]

In addition to cuts in JDC's own apparatus and in the number of people receiving relief from JDC, Jacobson established institutions intended to serve as a basis for the reconstruction work. The Reconstruction Credit Cooperative (Önállósító Hitelszövetkezet) and the Reconstruction Department (Rekonstrukciós Osztály) replaced the Work and Workshop Organization Department and the so-called Existential Loans Department (Existenciális Kölcsön Osztály) for providing relief. JDC hoped that these new institutions would aid the economic recovery of those people with professional training who lacked the capital to start an enterprise. Following the example of Poland and Romania, JDC also established Jewish cooperatives through which many Jews could become self-supporting and integrated into the local economic and social structures.[33] The first signs of economic independence soon appeared. On July 1, 1948, the Reconstruction Department was able to report to the JDC Committee that 73.5% of the loans for individual economic recovery had been given to Jews who were previously living on JDC relief.[34]

In the Jacobson era, throughout 1948–1949, the strategy of JDC proved to be successful in Hungary: Contemporaries and present-day historians agree that local Jews became integrated into the economic and social structures of Hungary. Yehuda Bauer evaluates the activity of JDC in Hungary in this period as follows: "[I]n the Hungarian conditions, a mixture of relief, child care, loans and producers' co-ops were the best one could manage, whether it was part of a Communist government's takeover strategy or not."[35] Although this strategy was effective, in hindsight it is, however, more than questionable whether it was the appropriate strategy in the framework of a Communist dictatorship. Doubts about the JDC program could have arisen even at the time, during the Jacobson era, precisely because the Communist Party made it increasingly difficult for the most prominent foreign organization present in Hungary to operate.

Because JDC's new reconstruction strategy accommodated the wishes of the Communist Party, it also facilitated Jewish postwar integration. However, once Jewish reconstruction had been successful by the end of 1949, the actual presence of JDC was no longer needed. Moreover, because it was the largest and most important foreign organization operating in Hungary, limiting its jurisdiction allowed the already strong Stalinist dictatorship a mechanism through which to assert its power at the beginning of the Cold War. The Communist regime succeeded in fundamentally undermining the authority and influence of JDC without giving up access to the funds that it transmitted. From 1948 on, the Communists began to attack foreign citizens working for JDC. The campaign against foreigners reached its peak in December 1949, when Jacobson was arrested, interrogated for twelve days, and finally expelled from Hungary under the charge of spying. In January 1950, Jacobson was already in New York and spoke at a press conference held at JDC's headquarters at 270 Madison Avenue:

> At no time [did] I engage in espionage or in any activity remotely connected with espionage. [. . .] As Director for Hungary of the JDC, which has served distressed Jews throughout the world for thirty-five years as a non-political welfare organization, my one interest in Hungary was to extend relief and medical help to over 100,000 Hungarian Jews in need. My release is, I feel, a clear vindication of the fact that I adhered strictly to a non-political role while in Hungary.[36]

He added a personal comment on his police interrogation as well:

> I was subjected to hardship, but not to physical cruelty. I was searched, and interrogated for about twenty hours a

day about five days. I was questioned about being in touch with our legation in Hungary, and about Jews leaving the country illegally. I stated that it was normal for an American to have contact with his legation, and I said that the Joint Distribution Committee had not engaged in helping Jews to leave illegally.[37]

Phase III: January 1950 to January 1953

Jacobson was the first employee of JDC in Hungary to experience arrest and interrogations. However, after internal discussion, the American and European leaders of JDC decided that the organization would continue sending money to the country in the interests of the Jews of Hungary. It would also keep its offices open, but it would not send a new foreign employee in Jacobson's place.[38] Given that JDC was now declared the symbol of "Western imperialism," which was the archfoe of the Communist regime, JDC had, in fact, lost all opportunity to influence how its money was put to use. In 1950, even the Jewish community's central welfare organization, the NJRC, lost its independence and came under full Communist control. It became a Jewish institution that dealt with only very limited necessary relief work. This final phase of JDC lasted until January 1953, when JDC ceased transferring funds and officially closed down its operations in Hungary.[39]

To summarize, JDC successfully accomplished its goal, working in coordination with the WJC, but failed to understand the developing logic of the Stalinist dictatorship. While JDC focused on relief and reconstruction programs, the WJC focused its efforts on advocacy and in the political realm. By the time JDC realized the consequences of the successful application of its primary objective, which was helping survivors to become integrated into the economic and social life of postwar countries, in the countries of the Eastern Bloc there was no way out. Once the Iron Curtain was drawn, evacuating the Jews from these countries was no longer possible. Paradoxically, JDC's traditional strategy, which also proved to be the most successful after the Shoah, in this case finally became a sort of trap.

1. Jean Ancel, "*She'erit Hapleta* in Romania during the Transition Period to a Communist Regime, August 1944-December 1947," in *She'erit Hapleta, 1944–1948*, ed. Yisrael Gutman and Avital Saf (Jerusalem: Yad Vashem, 1990), 156.

2. *A Zsidó Világkongresszus Magyarországi Képviseletének 2. számú összefoglaló jelentése, 1946. július 1–október 31. 8.* (Hungarian Jewish Archives, WJC XXXIII–3–1). In March 1944, when the German Army occupied Hungary, almost 800,000 Jews lived in the country. On the number of returning survivors and the difficulty of calculating their exact number, see Tamás Stark, *Hungarian Jews during the Holocaust and after the Second World War, 1939–1949: A Statistical Review* (New York: Columbia University Press, 2000), 59–120.

3. *Visszatérő deportáltak kérvényei, A-Z, 1945* [Requests of returning deportees, A-Z, 1945], Archives of the Szeged Jewish Community. See the microfilm copies in Yad Vashem Archives, Jerusalem, JM/31024–31027.

4. Yad Vashem Archives, Jerusalem, JM/31024, 139.

5. Ibid., 346.

6. Ibid., 1295.

7. See Carole Fink, *Defending the Rights of Others: The Great Powers, the Jews, and International Minority Protection, 1878–1938* (New York: Cambridge University Press, 2004). For an early postwar assessment of the WJC's work and its limitations, see Institute of Jewish Affairs, *Unity in Dispersion: A History of the World Jewish Congress* (New York: World Jewish Congress, 1948).

8. David Weinberg, "The Reconstruction of the French Jewish Community after World War II," in *She'erit Hapleta, 1944–1948*, ed. Yisrael Gutman and Avital Saf (Jerusalem: Yad Vashem, 1990), 170–174. See, for example, the not very successful struggle of the Jews of France for the return of their confiscated properties.

9. Yehuda Bauer, *Out of the Ashes: The Impact of American Jews on Post-Holocaust European Jewry* (Oxford: Pergamon Press, 1989), 145.

10. Bauer, *Out of the Ashes*, 146.

11. Bauer, *Out of the Ashes*, xviii.

12. Herbert Agar, *The Saving Remnant: An Account of Jewish Survival since 1914* (London: Rupert Hart-Davis, 1960), 177.

13. See the report written at the beginning of 1946, signed by the leaders of the Neolog and Orthodox top organs as well as by the Hungarian Zionist Association and the leaders of the Hungarian Department of the WJC: "Most Hungarian Jews wish to emigrate due to economic and psychological reasons. They do not want to live in a country which became a graveyard of their families." Quoted in Azriel Carlibach, ed., *The Anglo-American Commission of Inquiry on Palestine: Volume I* (Tel Aviv: Leinman Publishers, 1946), 290.

14. See Randolph L. Braham, *A népirtás politikája. A Holocaust Magyarországon* (Budapest: Belvárosi Könyvkiadó, 1997) 2: 478–79; *Jegyzőkönyv, 1948. február 10.* 1 (Hungarian Jewish Archives, Joint XXXIII–4a–1). Frigyes Görög resigned his post on February 10, 1948. Görög, who led the Joint in Hungary between 1945 and 1948, when there was a coalition government in Hungary, was on friendly terms with the leading power of the coalition, the Independent Party of Small Landowners (Független Kisgazda Földmunkás és Polgári Párt). This connection greatly concerned the Communists, who wanted to get rid of Görög. They succeeded in this by the beginning of 1948. Görög immigrated to the United States, where he established and led the World Association of Hungarian Jews for years.

15. *Jegyzőkönyv, 1945. május 23.* 1 (Hungarian Jewish Archives, Joint XXXIII–4a–1).

16. Concerning the work of the National Relief Committee for Deportees, see Rita Horváth: *A Magyarországi Zsidók Deportáltakat Gondozó Országos Bizottsága (DEGOB) története* (Budapest: MAKOR 1, Magyar Zsidó Levéltár, 1997).

17. Braham, *A népirtás politikája. A Holocaust Magyarországon*, 2: 1251.

18. *Pro Memoria. 1945. június 22.* 1 (Hungarian Jewish Archives, Joint XXXIII–4a–1).

19. *Megállapodás az Országos Zsidó Segítő Bizottság létrehozásáról, 1945. augusztus 31.* 1 (Hungarian Jewish Archives, OZsSB XXXIII–7a–1).

20. *A Zsidó Világkongresszus Magyarországi Képviseletének működésére vonatkozó tervezet, 1945. augusztus 31.* 1 (Hungarian Jewish Archives, OZsSB XXXIII–7a–1).

21. Ibid., 1.

22. *Jegyzőkönyv, 1948. augusztus 23. Melléklete: M. W. Beckelman európai alelnök beszéde a magyarországi Joint munka jelenéről és jövőjéről.* 1 (Hungarian Jewish Archives, Joint XXXIII–4a–1). In reality, the Joint did not support only legal emigration after the Shoah. Concerning, for example, the Bricha, see Yehuda Bauer, *Flight and Rescue: Brichah* (New York: Random House, 1970).

23. *A Munka-és Üzemszervező Csoport jelentése Dr. J. Schwartznak, 1946. június 28.* 1–2 (Hungarian Jewish Archives, Joint XXXIII–4a–8). Concerning the work and Zionist education in the *hakhsharot* and *plugot*, see Attila Novák, *Átmenetben. A cionista mozgalom négy éve Magyarországon* (Budapest: Múlt és Jövő, 2000), 129–44.

24. *Jegyzőkönyv, 1945. július 2.* 1 (Hungarian Jewish Archives, Joint XXXIII–4a–1).

25. *Jegyzőkönyv, 1946. március 29.* 1 (Hungarian Jewish Archives, Joint XXXIII–4a–1).

26. *A népjóléti minisztériumi biztos jelentése az MKP központi tömegszervezeti osztályának a Joint magyarországi kirendeltsége gazdasági, politikai szerepéről, 1947. július 31* (Politikatörténeti Intézet Levéltára, 274. f. 17/11. ő. e.).

27. Ibid.

28. Bauer, *Out of the Ashes*, 134.

29. *Jegyzőkönyv, 1946. május 13.* 1–2 (Hungarian Jewish Archives, Joint XXXIII–4a–1).

30. See Nick Ravo, "Gaynor Jacobson Is Dead at 87; Helped Resettle Jewish Refugees," June 24, 1999, accessed May 9, 2016, http://www.nytimes .com/1999/06/24/world/gaynor-jacobson-is-dead-at-87-helped-resettle -jewish-refugees.html. Jacobson was born in 1912 in Buffalo, New York, in the United States. He received a master's degree in social work in 1941 from the local university. In 1944, Jacobson joined JDC as a country director in Italy and then in Greece and Hungary. In 1949, he returned to the United States, and from 1953 to 1981, he directed programs for the Hebrew Immigrant Aid Society, becoming world director in 1966. He retired in 1981 and died in 1999.

31. *Segélyezési programokra vonatkozó alapszabályok és irányelvek, 1948.* 3–5 (Hungarian Jewish Archives, Joint XXXIII–4a–2).

32. JDC Archives, Records of the Geneva Office of the American Jewish Joint Distribution Committee, 1945–1954, Folder FR.543, Standards and Policies for Welfare Programs, Prepared for JDC Country Directors' Conference, April 5–11, 1948, 3–4, April 11, 1948.

33. Concerning the aims of the institutions for reconstruction and the initial difficulties of their creation, see *Beszámoló a vidéki zsidóság hitelellátásának megszervezéséről, 1948. június 7* and *Aaron Berkowitz jelentése a Joint Committee 1948. június 7–i ülésére* (Hungarian Jewish Archives, Joint XXXIII–4a–1).

34. *Jegyzőkönyv, 1948. július 1.* 1–2 (Hungarian Jewish Archives, Joint XXXIII–4a–1).

35. Bauer, *Out of the Ashes*, 144–45.

36. JDC Archives, Records of the New York Office of the American Jewish Joint Distribution Committee, 1945–1954, Folder 434, Press Release Issued by Raphael Levy, Publicity Director of JDC, "JDC Hungary Job Not Over Says Former Director Israel Jacobson," January 24, 1950.

37. Ibid., 2.

38. Bauer, *Out of the Ashes*, 147.

39. After the expulsion of Jacobson, Aaron Berkowitz headed the Joint in Hungary. He arrived in Hungary in 1947 with Jacobson.

13

JDC and Soviet Jews in Austria and Italy

Inga Veksler

Introduction

Throughout much of its history, the American Jewish Joint Distribution Committee (JDC) supported a vibrant transit migrant program,[1] helping hundreds of thousands of Jewish refugees in the twentieth century. Through this operation, JDC provided care and maintenance (housing, food, local transportation, social service, and medical assistance) as well as educational, cultural, and religious activities to Jews passing a period of time in one or more countries of transit before immigrating elsewhere. This chapter focuses on the organization's biggest, most costly, and most controversial transit migrant group since the postwar migration of Jewish displaced persons (DPs)—Jews from the Union of Soviet Socialist Republics (USSR) who spent anywhere from five weeks to two years in transit in Austria and Italy between 1971 and 1990 when settling in countries other than Israel. Through an enormous outlay of financial and human resources, JDC assisted more than 185,000 Soviet Jews in those two decades; this represented about half of all Soviet Jews allowed to emigrate since the 1960s. Along with the Hebrew Immigrant Aid Society (HIAS), which prepared and processed all visa and legal formalities, JDC offered migrants a safe, supported, and well-organized transit period—a safety net for what for them was an anxiety-ridden period of uncertainty as well as an eye-opening period of discovery.

The emigration of Jews out of the Soviet Union in the last decades of the twentieth century was one of the great mass migrations in Jewish history. It garnered international attention and support from those outside the Soviet Bloc, creating a vibrant social movement and drawing recurrent attention on the Cold War political stage. Accordingly, the topic of Soviet Jewish migration has received ample scholarly attention in terms of the external (international) and internal (Soviet) causes behind the mass emigration movement; the efforts, accomplishments, and significance of the American Soviet Jewry Movement and of Soviet refuseniks; and the economic, social, and psychological characteristics of the Soviet Jewish immigrant population. However, the topic of their transit migration through Austria and Italy has not been explored in depth, despite having been a significant life experience for immigrants, "provid[ing] initial symbolic material by which immigrants unify and then differentiate themselves."[2] There was no "Jewish community" in the Soviet Union; rather, Jews in the Soviet Union tended to be part of close-knit networks of Jewish friends and family without formal Jewish institutions or organizations, which would have been illegal. In transit migration, emigrants for the first time learned of and interacted with the diverse Soviet Jewish population (differences spanned regions, appearances, levels of religiosity, education, wealth, *kultur'nost'*, and so on), creating the beginnings of the Russian-speaking immigrant communities in North America and elsewhere.[3]

This chapter draws on a variety of sources—including archival material, secondary sources, and semi-structured interviews with immigrants conducted by the author in the New York City and Boston metropolitan areas between 2010 and 2014[4]—to examine the experiences and challenges of Soviet Jewish transit migration from the perspectives of both emigrants and JDC staff. The history of JDC's transit migrant program has not been extensively documented nor updated since 1964[5] and deserves further attention for its significance in the lives of immigrants and in the life of the organization. When examined in tandem, the group's transit migration route exposes its historical and structural continuity with other Jewish refugee movements since World War II. This is an important antidote to the historiographical tendency to examine Soviet Jewish migrants and the migration movement as a case sui generis. By focusing on the transit route, this chapter underscores the *experiential* as well as structural continuity[6] among Jewish refugee groups of the twentieth century. Given the upheavals and trauma of the last century for world Jewry, the experience of transit is intertwined with one of the core Jewish dilemmas of the last century: where Diaspora Jewry belongs.

JDC AND TRANSIT MIGRATION

The story of Soviet Jewish transit migration through Vienna and Rome begins with a few families in April 1971. In the three weeks leading up to their arrival in Rome, the combined number of migrants-in-transit in both cities hovered between 150 and 165. Handwritten notes on those three consecutive weekly JDC reports emphatically noted "lowest EVER!," "lowest ever," and again "lowest ever."[7] JDC staff could not have known that they would not again see such low numbers until two decades later.

By 1971, JDC had a well-established program to aid those seeking to resettle. In June 1940, JDC established its Transmigrant Bureau as part of two principal strategies to aid European Jews' escape from Nazism. In both cases, JDC acted as a financial and logistical broker: the Transmigrant Bureau saved 14,000 lives by serving as a "clearing house" for Americans who funded escapees' journeys (with JDC covering overhead costs and funding others with no connections in the United States); another 41,000 German, Austrian, and Czech Jews paid for their journeys by giving local currency to the Jewish welfare organization in their countries of origin in exchange for JDC funding their travel in dollars. After the former strategy was no longer possible following the bombing of Pearl Harbor, the Bureau helped procure false papers; fund individual efforts of large-scale negotiation and rescue; and book passage for refugees, especially by sea. In total, between 1939 and 1944, JDC saved 81,000 persons by assisting in their emigration.[8]

Its work grew in the postwar period. Between 1947 and 1952, 623,000 emigrants from Europe, Asia, and North Africa benefited from JDC aid, including the tens of thousands who left their homes in Muslim-majority countries after the 1948 Arab-Israeli War.[9] Following the closing of the last DP camps in Austria and Germany in 1957, JDC's transit migrant operation remained active in a few key European cities—mainly Vienna, Paris, Athens, and Rome—to facilitate the migration of those Jews who continued to need resettlement from Communist-controlled Eastern European countries, North Africa, and the Middle East. In 1961, about 80,000 Jewish refugees from these regions "were in motion," of whom about half went to Israel and some 30,000 to France; these numbers increased in the following few years.[10] Austria received 18,000 refugees from Hungary in 1956[11] and over 10,000 Poles and Czechoslovakians between 1967 and 1969 during periods of unrest. Not all of these emigrants underwent a stage of transit migration (some traveled directly to their destinations by plane), and not all were aided by JDC. Through the 1960s and 1970s, however, JDC offices in Europe cared for Jews-in-transit leaving all of the following countries: the Soviet Union, Hungary, Romania, Poland, Czechoslovakia, Bulgaria, Yugoslavia, Turkey, Morocco, Libya, Tunisia, Egypt, Ethiopia, Lebanon, Syria, Iraq, Iran, France, the United Kingdom, and other European countries.[12]

Through the postwar period, Vienna had been the primary receiving city of emigrating Eastern and Central European Jews. It was the closest non-Communist capital for Eastern European Jews and hosted a branch of the Jewish Agency for Israel (JAFI, colloquially known as "Sochnut")—ideal for immigrating to Palestine and then Israel.[13] Soviet emigrants arrived in Vienna either with visas issued by the Austrian Embassy, as tourists who would then file for refugee status, or with Israeli-issued documentation already in hand. Beginning in 1968, however, Vienna ceased to be a processing center for those seeking to resettle in other countries. Responding to the Soviet invasion of Czechoslovakia and the political effects of the 1967 Arab-Israeli War in Poland, thousands of Czech and Polish Jews fled to Vienna. Those who sought to continue on to Israel were transferred immediately to JAFI's processing center, a hostel in Schoenau, and flown to Israel within days. Polish Jews, however, preferred to immigrate to the United States,[14] and HIAS began to direct émigrés en masse to Rome.

There seem to be several reasons underlying the decision to make Vienna a transfer city and Rome the processing center, forming the so-called Vienna-Rome pipeline. First, Rome was the location of Western Europe's largest American Embassy with an Immigration and Naturalization Services (INS) department, which could accommodate a larger applicant pool. Second, care and maintenance, especially of migrants needing medical attention, cost roughly half in Italy of what it did in Austria. Third, the Jewish Agency insisted on it, at least partially because of "the great 'visibility' of the transmigrant movement in Vienna," which seemed "dangerous" so close to the Communist border.[15] The Vienna-Rome pipeline became the principal route to aid Jewish refugees from the Soviet Bloc.

Between 1965 and 1971, 21,600 Jews had been allowed to leave the Soviet Union to immigrate to Israel.[16] Emigration from the USSR was illegal, but the Soviet Union began to let Jews trickle out in 1965, ostensibly on the basis of family reunification. Israel's victory in the 1967 Arab-Israeli War led to a reawakening of Jewish consciousness among a sector of Soviet Jewry, which began to demand the right to live as Jews in the Soviet Union or else make *aliyah* (literally "ascend" by immigrating to Israel). Such efforts were amplified by the actions of Soviet dissident refuseniks who captured international sympathy and served as lightning rods for the American Soviet Jewry Movement. The Soviet government sought to resolve the pestering internal protests and garner Western favor by allowing limited emigration, a kind of "bleeding off" of its internal problems.[17] In total, between 1965 and 1991, approximately 775,000 Soviet Jews emigrated from the USSR, the annual numbers fluctuating according to the inclinations of Soviet leadership; Cold War geopolitics; and the desire of Soviet Jews, as a group living with quotidian and institutional ethnic discrimination, to emigrate.

Once movement through the Vienna-Rome pipeline began, it lost momentum only in the years when the Soviet Union "closed its doors" on emigration. Soviet Jewish emigration, to all destinations, adhered to the following pattern over the years: rising steadily through the seventies (with a few small dips), peaking in 1979, and then falling to a trickle until the late eighties, when it again escalated, greater than ever before.

Table 13.1. Emigration of Jewish Citizens from the Soviet Union, 1971–1989

Year	Jewish Emigrants Exiting USSR with Israeli Visas	Of Total Soviet Jews in Transit via Austria and Italy
1971	12,897	58
1972	31,903	251
1973	34,733	1,456
1974	20,767	3,879
1975	13,363	4,928
1976	14,254	7,004
1977	16,833	8,483
1978	28,956	16,866
1979	51,331	34,053
1980	21,648	14,078
1981	9,448	7,687
1982	2,692	1,961
1983	1,314	453
1984	896	556
1985	1,140	792
1986	904	703
1987	8,155	6,083
1988	18,961	16,788
1989	71,005	58,888
Total	361,200	184,967

Source: Fred Lazin, *The Struggle for Soviet Jewry in American Politics* (Lanham, MD: Lexington Books, 2005), 307–8.

Transit migration through Austria and Italy reached its highest point in 1989–1990 before changes in US-Soviet relations and migration policies obviated its need. The route was limited to a small number of migrants-in-transit in 1990.

EXPERIENCING THE VIENNA-ROME PIPELINE

Soviet Jewish emigrants' passage through the Vienna-Rome pipeline entailed a series of formalized steps and the coordination of numerous governments and international aid organizations. Although the process was highly regularized and well organized by JDC and HIAS, for emigrants it was unpredictable and unnerving at every step. No matter who they had been in the Soviet Union, during transit migration they became "nobody, going nowhere"—as many put it in present-day interviews—residing in temporary places and facing transition after transition. Their feelings of loss, status change, uncertainty, and suspended waiting are common among transit migrants. There was, furthermore, a particularly Jewish aspect to their experiences.

The Soviet emigration process and requirements morphed in various ways over the two-plus decades until the dissolution of the Soviet Union, but they remained daunting and punishing throughout: One former INS official noted that "the process and effects of applying to leave were, in themselves, so egregious as to turn almost all Soviet applicants into genuine refugees."[18] Upon leaving the Soviet Union, all emigrants underwent a corrupt and often vindictive customs search, paid the equivalent of $1,000 (an enormous sum for average salaries of about $120 per month) to rescind their Soviet citizenship and obtain an exit visa, and were allowed to exchange no more than 100 rubles (an average of about $90) per person in currency. The strains of departing from one of the Soviet exit points were many, including the frequent malicious delays of Soviet customs officials, the timetables of trains, the colossal burdens of all of one's belongings, the fear of obstructed exit from the USSR, and the anxiety of what lay beyond. They crossed the Soviet border as stateless people, with limited currency and possessions of value and no expectation of returning even to visit; goodbyes were permanent, and departures were treated with the finality of funerals. Immigrants today continue to express bitterness at the Soviet regime for denying them a dignified exit.

Emigrants holding Israeli exit documents[19] traveled to Vienna by train, by plane, or, in the era of blossoming cooperative businesses under Gorbachev, by bus or boat. Even leaving at a time when emigration was being severely restricted by the USSR—as, for example, in August 1980, with only about 193 Soviet Jews arriving in Vienna per week[20] as opposed to more than 2,000 per week at the end of 1989—people experienced the transition as a "sea of people," as "chaos."[21] Raisa Lachman, a seamstress from Kiev, Ukraine, who spent seven months in transit migration described the journey from Chop, Ukraine, through Czechoslovakia to Austria in 1989 with emotion:

> [In Bratislava], there were even _more_ people than in Chop. Because there were people there from all over the Soviet Union. . . . It was such a nightmare, like I've never seen and will never forget. The first train arrived, and _people_ would pass _people_ and luggage alike through the windows. It was _so_ awful! It was the beginning of October, there was already a little snow falling, it was melting, and this route was awful. It was worse than during the [Second World] War. During the War, there wasn't such a thing, or maybe there was, but, either way, it reminded me of the War, the Evacuation, the fear.[22]

Raisa could have only been a small child during the evacuation, when Soviets fortunate enough to obtain passage moved en masse to Central Asia to escape German forces. Still, the analogy speaks to the fear, anxiety, and chaos Raisa experienced during transit, heightened by the collective affective experiences of those around her. Reaching Austria entailed a combination of exhaustion and relief.

At the Vienna arrival points, representatives (_shlichim_) of the Jewish Agency, the only non-Soviet organization to hold a complete list of those exiting with Israeli visas, greeted newcomers. It remains unclear how Soviet Jews first learned in 1971 that they could use Israeli documents to continue to other destinations—perhaps through word of mouth from relatives abroad, perhaps through special circumstances and advice from other organizations or diplomats. Historian Fred Lazin notes that an administrative report by JDC Executive Vice Chairman Charles Jordan dated March 1, 1966, indicates that Soviet Jewish individuals asked to change destinations in Vienna as early as 1966.[23] Lazin speculates that Jewish Agency officials confiscated visas or otherwise prevented Soviet Jewish emigrants from knowing that other options existed.

As more and more emigrants sought to resettle in Western countries over the years, Soviet Jews were greeted at their various points of arrival in Vienna with the question "Israel or elsewhere?" Those answering "elsewhere" were transferred into HIAS's and JDC's care after meeting with a JAFI representative whose job it was to persuade them to change course to Israel. For some, this interview was an uneventful formality; for others, it was a charged and difficult conversation in which they felt guilty for refusing *aliyah* or felt pressured and disrespected by the representative.[24]

In Vienna, JDC conducted initial interviews with families to establish Jewishness[25] and social service needs (later eliminated), and HIAS met with migrants to begin processing visa paperwork. JDC provided transit migrants with rudimentary lodging, which Dr. Akiva Kohane of JDC's European headquarters in Geneva labeled "sub-standard, overcrowded, dirty, and not cheap."[26] To house Soviet migrants during periods of heavy intake, JDC also rented apartments across the city (some of them stunning) and found group lodgings in (beautiful, scenic) towns outside of Vienna. A minority were confined in a refugee camp in Vienna rented by JDC.

Because most JDC accommodations were located among local populations rather than isolated in camps, Soviet Jews experienced the West in full. For nearly everyone, emigration marked the first encounter with the world outside the Soviet Union.[27] The deeply felt stress of being in transit was marked not only by the losses inherent to permanent emigration but also by a deep, jolting encounter with the unknown world outside the Iron Curtain, which immigrants described as coming to the "Moon," to "Mars," or to "another planet."[28] Many Soviet emigrants reacted to the bountifulness of goods in the West with anger at the Soviet Union and sadness for themselves and loved ones for being so deprived, deceived, and even condemned. It made them feel, as fifty-year-old Minsk native Viktor Grobnik said about exiting the USSR in 1989, "inferior, of having lived life without knowing anything, like a half-person."[29]

At the same time, the encounter with the new and the beautiful in Austria—and later in Italy—induced real enchantment for those who opened themselves up to the experience. "Along with the worries about how it will turn out," one elderly woman said of her transit migration out of

A Soviet Jewish client at the Vienna train station about to depart for immigration processing in Rome. Vienna, Austria, 1989. Photo by Doron Bacher, Beit Hatfutsot.

Leningrad in 1989, "there was the joy of seeing something in this world."[30] Emigrants visited historical landmarks, museums, the city zoo. They were awed by wealthy Austrians along the "Street of Millionaires" (Graben Street, the city's main shopping artery); by regular people enjoying pastries in local cafés; by the overwhelming and unimaginable selection and packaging of goods in stores; by the cleanliness, orderliness, and technological advances apparent throughout the city. As one immigrant put it, "We were running around with eyes bulging, like we were crazy."[31]

After three days to a month or longer in Vienna,[32] HIAS arranged for group visas issued directly by the Italian government to cover all HIAS clients traveling to Italy, a process in continuation from the postwar DP program. It also arranged for transfers to Italy on scheduled and specially hired overnight trains, which would last between fourteen and nineteen-plus hours.[33] After a hostage-taking incident in 1973, HIAS also hired armed guards to protect emigrants from their point of departure in Vienna's Südbahnhof station.[34]

Emigrants were told ahead of time by HIAS workers that they would not have long to unload their belongings at their destination, the Orte train station in the Lazio (Rome) region of Italy. Even those immigrants who described their transit migration as quick and easy identify the transition off the train and onto buses at Orte (about an hour from Rome) as the worst, most stressful part of the entire journey. Emigrants' apprehensions were magnified by their knowledge of Soviet and Jewish histories and the general shared affective atmosphere of fear, anxiety, and vulnerability among emigrants. Klara Drob struggled to articulate the surreal and uneasy feeling of entering and experiencing a fundamentally new mode-of-being of an emigrant-in-transit:

> We were told that basically within ten minutes we should throw all our baggage through the windows and detrain. And then—well, there was this feeling, you know, it was—that—that you are in emigration. . . . We didn't know [what was going on]. Here was a moment when you understood that you had arrived nowhere. It was a bit of this unpleasant feeling from, you know, suddenly remembering those awful, frightening stories about things that happened to the Jews. And so this was, of course, distressing. This was the only moment during which they gathered everyone: "quickly, quickly, quickly!"[35]

The transit route that Soviet Jewish émigrés followed had been shared by many Jewish refugees since World War II, and perhaps they sensed this precarious Jewish history intuitively, experientially, without fully knowing it. In a sense, the route itself generated a shared affective experience of being a Jewish migrant-in-transit, moving through chaos and uncertainty.

From Orte, emigrants were transported to JDC-arranged accommodations in Roman hostels for a maximum of ten days, after which they had to find their own housing (JDC required proof of this before dispensing migrants' monthly relief grants). In the early seventies, Soviet Jews sojourned mainly in Rome. As the years passed and the number of families-in-transit rose, emigrants moved to the towns on the Tyrrhenian Sea where working- and middle-class Romans summered (e.g., Ostia, Ladispoli, nearby Passoscuro, Santa Marinella to the north, and Nettuno and Torvaianica to the south). At least half of their monthly grants went to housing—one apartment was usually shared among a few families, especially in the summers when rents in these coastal towns soared. In the late 1970s, most Soviet Jews lived in Ostia, where locals came to call the post office—a main émigré gathering spot—the "Red Square." Then and in the late 1980s, with Ostia "full," it was Ladispoli that became most popular, among as many as twenty other towns. As in Austria, Soviet Jews lived among and mixed with locals; their presence was conspicuous.

As they waited, HIAS processed migrants' paperwork. Before their embassy interviews, migrants underwent a medical examination and submitted a collection of additional documentation (e.g., fingerprints, photographs, signed forms; in the late eighties, some of this was done in Vienna). HIAS worked with the Jewish Federations in North America and Jewish community groups in Australia and New Zealand, all of which bore the economic and social responsibility for immigrants, to identify resettlement cities. Jewish communities accepted families based on distinct criteria— particular professions, education levels, ages, genders, health requirements, available funding, and so on. Once a destination was approved, the International Committee for European Migration arranged for air travel. Given the complex process, the number of organizations involved, and the ever-changing number and backlog of clients in the pipeline, delays were common. (The United States, due to its use of parole authority[36] as an alternative to refugee status, typically had the shortest wait time.)

The duration of the transit period varied. In the first half of the 1970s, it might have lasted just four or five weeks. During the late 1970s and 1980s, when the majority of Soviet Jews exited, the high volume of emigrants meant longer waits. Throughout the two decades of Soviet transit migration, the weekly intake of clients was unpredictable; JDC and HIAS learned of the size and demographic composition of new arrivals only after the Jewish Agency transferred emigrants into their care. From their all-time migrant low in 1971, both JDC and HIAS had to repeatedly and rapidly expand and shrink their resources to accommodate the changes over the course of two decades.

An illustrative circumstance took place in 1979, when the Soviet Union allowed higher rates of Jewish emigration to appease the United States during SALT II negotiations. In January of that year, Dr. Akiva Kohane, director of transmigrant operations in JDC's European headquarters in Geneva, Switzerland, wrote to Ralph Goldman, executive vice chairman of the Joint in New York City: "[W]e never thought we would have such a [large] caseload . . . in Italy."[37] By March, the Vienna-Rome caseload numbered well over 9,000, with a record pace of new arrivals. In a memorandum dated March 9, 1979, Kohane informed Goldman, in dire tones, that JDC may be facing "an unexpected deluge. . . . We may be witnessing the beginning of a movement on an unprecedented scale to reach soon a level of about 5000–6000 arrivals per month"; JDC logistics at the time were based on expected arrivals of 2,000 per month. Kohane describes this as an "apocalyptic picture," "grim," an "emergency situation," and an "avalanche" to be treated by "emergency action." Kohane urged for a high rate of exit from Italy "TO DIMINISH THE PRESENT INTOLERABLE SIZE OF THE CASELOAD."[38] His alarm was palpable, even as he observed the situation from a distance in Geneva. One month later, the Vienna-Rome caseload peaked at over 11,000. In the town of Ladispoli, where half of the Soviet Jews resided at the time, there were 4,000–5,000 Soviet Jewish transit migrants among a permanent Italian population of 11,000.[39] Tensions with Italian locals were high.

At the same time a year later, in April 1980, the caseload in Vienna and Rome was down to 4,343 in Italy and 528 in Vienna.[40] It continued to decrease throughout the year, totaling just 1,773 in December 1980.[41] JDC downsized its offices through the 1980s, only to expand them to their greatest capacity by the end of the decade. By September 1989, the Vienna-Rome pipeline held some 20,000 Soviet Jews in various stages of processing.[42] A period of US INS changes in the adjudication of refugee status resulted in over 5,000 Soviet Jews being denied visas and therefore being left stranded, stateless, in Italy beginning in the fall of 1988 through 1989.[43] In the closing months of Soviet Jewish transit migration, after

October 1989, a staggering 27,000 more Soviet Jews joined the route.[44] The European caseload of JDC and HIAS was 28,000 at the close of 1989.[45]

The logistical complexities of processing and keeping track of so many people at a time—and the corresponding funding problems—are self-evident. In 1980, the cost per person for an average twelve-day stay in Austria came to $144.72; in Italy, it was $512 for an average stay of seventy-five days.[46] The total average cost, then, to JDC for *each* person's care and maintenance in the Vienna-Rome pipeline was $656.72 for eighty-seven days in transit, an average of $7.55 per person per day.[47] These numbers doubled at the end of the decade: In 1988, the average cost of supporting a transit migrant was $15 per day,[48] and the average time spent in transit reached 100 days in 1989.[49] At the $15-per-diem rate, the peak caseload of 28,000 translates to JDC expenditures of approximately $420,000 *per day* for the maintenance of the Soviet Jewry transit migrant program during December 1989. JDC appropriated a total of $64,381,500 to its transit migrant program that year.[50] The entire transit migrant operation required an incredible amount of coordination, energy, and funding, especially when

Staff member Pia Addad (right) with Soviet Jewish transmigrant clients in the JDC Rome office. Italy, 1980.

JDC and HIAS were handling thousands of clients at a time and the number of incoming clients was chronically unforeseeable.

A Community in Transit

Even in the most dire of circumstances, as among Europe's DPs following World War II, people make a life for themselves while their future is being legally and logistically determined. Historical studies of the lives of Jewish Holocaust survivors in DP camps richly depict the ongoingness, the everyday mundanity, and the social effervescence of this temporary community, even in the aftermath of the cruelest form of devastation.[51] Time must be passed, endured, made use of, even when the main activity is waiting for the end of the period of transition.

By administering the route, JDC helped create the infrastructure that allowed the migrant-in-transit community to flourish. JDC provided a number of cultural and educational amenities, such as modest libraries, whose books, many unavailable in the USSR, interested migrants read voraciously; lectures, concerts, shows, and movies; "clubs" and classes for children, teenagers, and adults to learn about Judaism and Israel and connect with each other; and services during Jewish holidays, celebrated by many Soviet Jews for the first time. A cooperating migrant aid agency, World ORT, offered English and computer classes and vocational training for a limited number of migrants chosen by lottery (no more than a few hundred at a time in Italy).

Among Soviet Jews in transit, a vibrant, although temporary and ever-changing, community formed, with its own social dynamics, including reunions of friends and family, regular meeting places, robust networks of information and gossip exchange, self-organized schools, and even self-organized group tours to cities in the north and south of Italy. In JDC's 1975 Annual Report in Rome, Loni Eibenschütz Mayer wrote about Soviet Jewish life in transit: "We are now dealing with a very large group which has developped [sic] its own life pattern, almost its own tradition in Italy."[52] "Old-timers" helped out newcomers with tips on how and where to find housing, where to buy the cheapest and best foods, and where and how to sell the wares they brought along. Relationships were not altogether benevolent: Some emigrants, for example, profited off of newcomers as housing brokers or formed a "gang of thieves."[53]

In Italy, émigrés' time was defined by waiting. People wait in different ways, but during transit, in general, it was waiting accompanied by an unmoving and deep sense of anxiety about the present and future. Almost unanimously, Soviet immigrants talk about the feelings of uncertainty, unpredictability, indeterminacy, and being in limbo. Even without the added strain of refugee status refusals (as took place during 1988–1989), the condition of living in transit migration, of waiting for permission to leave while unfamiliar organizations controlled the conditions of the present and the future, weighed heavily on emigrants' minds and equanimity. Consider Ella Bobrovsky's description of her family's time in transit from the end of July to September of 1989:

> It was a very unpleasant time, in terms of morale. Very unpleasant: the uncertainty. Always thinking, will we get refused refugee status; will we get refused, will we not? Nothing is certain. And everyday those so-called "roll-call meetings," where decisions [about status] were announced. The worst part was that we couldn't buy the kids ice cream or anything. We were there for a short time, didn't have time to work anywhere, and [JDC] didn't give a lot [of relief money]. We had no rights; we were without citizenship. We were saving everything because you don't know what lies ahead. And overall, there was complete uncertainty. In the middle of Europe, with no citizenship, just—stateless, with ailing, elderly parents and young children. So we didn't give the kids [any treats]. The first time we bought them ice cream was when we got our [visa] approval, and it was clear that we would be leaving [Italy]. . . . Before then, nothing was spent, everything was being saved.[54]

What resonates strongly in Ella's description are feelings of anxiety and fear, of life on hold. This is germane to cross-cultural and transhistorical experiences of waiting for permanent immigration status[55]—the period of being "in transit" is almost a misnomer for this experiential state of suspension between leaving as emigrants and settling as immigrants.

Although many suffered from depression and anxiety, various health problems, and difficulties or ruptures in personal relationships as a result of emigrating, the experiences were not all dire. Emigrants took in the beauty, richness, and excitement of Italy with hundreds to tens of thousands of other Soviet Jews, encountering new personal and social freedoms that brought both discovery and upheaval. Boston College Professor Maxim Shrayer aptly describes his two months of transit migration in 1987—the mix of bliss and despair, the stress of making ends meet, and the magic of the everyday—as a "paradisal poverty": the astonishment and full-bodied pleasure of seeing true beauty while feeling comfortable with one's desire for the unattainable.[56] Milana Zillman, who left Odessa, Ukraine, in 1979 at the age of twenty-four and spent two months in transit, described her sensations this way:

> None of [the negative stuff] matters once you broke free from the Soviet Union. There's a panic-laden fear that you won't be able to get where you want to go. There's a panic-laden fear that you won't pass the medical exam [that the INS required] in Italy. You don't know for two weeks and have to wait. You can feel condemned while you're in Italy; you don't know <u>when</u>, you don't know <u>where</u> [you'll go]. . . . My outlook was: every day is a gift.

Then she added quickly with a laugh, "But I have no idea what is going on."[57]

Soviet Jewish Emigration and the JDC Italy Office

Just as these feelings of ignorance, anxiety, and suspended animation that Soviet emigrants experienced are typical for populations waiting for permanent immigrant status, so, too, are misunderstandings between refugee groups and the organizations caring for them. Tensions arise from the fundamental power difference between workers and clients, resulting in negative perceptions—ungrateful, untrustworthy, helpless refugees and indifferent, unfeeling, or neglectful relief workers—and sometimes ending in physical aggression or violence.[58] In the Vienna-Rome pipeline, conflicts arose from the broad fundamental differences between Soviet and Western cultures.

The Italian offices of JDC greeted the first Soviet Jewish transit migrants warmly:

> We welcomed the first families from the Soviet Union in April 1971 with great emotion. We were particularly impressed by the fact that, despite the official propaganda and the impossibility of giving the children a Jewish education, they all, without exception, feel a deep Jewish identification; as soon as they arrived in Rome, they looked for the synagogue, and made a point of celebrating Jewish holidays.[59]

By 1974, however, Soviet Jewish emigrants had become a "very difficult group to deal with and control" in the eyes of the organization, unlike any other transit group in terms of "personality and attitude"[60] and in terms of "social and psychological patterns."[61] JDC documents refer to Czechs fleeing in 1968, for example, as being in true need, not asking for much, and thankful for what they received.[62] Those from the USSR, staff found, acted "more helpless" and showed "less personal initiative" than the Poles and Romanians JDC assisted.[63]

Having come from the Soviet Union, they had particular worldviews, fears, and expectations that made them difficult to accommodate. Eibenschütz Mayer noted the "great deal of tension and hostility the refugee group carries along." They were at once dependent, demanding, and very resourceful, with "unrealistic expectations about living standards and opportunities in the Western world." She attributed this range of behavior to the Soviet way of life: "[T]hey are deeply conditioned by the Soviet life system. They come from a society where everything is pre-planned, and there is little or no space for individual initiative and competition." Moreover, coming from the Soviet system, they have built a very ambivalent relationship with authority, which they fear and challenge at the same time, developping [*sic*] all sorts of devices to deceive it and exercise some independence. . . . They tend to repeat the same ambivalent attitude towards the agency, which they regard as the omnipotent authority on which they depend and expect a solution to their problems, and at the same time need to oppose and deceive.[64]

The results were frustrating for JDC social workers. Migrant transgressions involving the breaking of local laws included the selling of their wares in flea markets and to individuals along the transit route; taking on employment and driving cars in Italy; minor crimes such as pickpocketing; and more serious, isolated crimes such as armed robbery and drug use (which occasionally led to overdose deaths). Suicides also presented difficult situations.[65] Between 1975 and 1980, there were seventy-five cases of deaths, criminal acts (including murders), and many police detentions.[66] Staff in the JDC Italy office also expressed frustration over dissimulations to obtain more relief grant money (e.g., false declarations of having had suitcases lost or stolen, refusals to accept "no" for an answer, and damages made to or unpaid bills left from apartment rentals).[67]

JDC was well aware that this behavior was not all malicious.[68] The toll of the journey on emigrants was immediately apparent to JDC staff. In 1971, Eibenschütz Mayer had already observed that

during the adjustment period [of being in Italy] they show anxiety and insecurity, which is often expressed in difficulty in managing every-day life and in projecting themselves into the future. These feelings tend to decrease and often disappear as time passes, but frequently reappear before departure time.[69]

A few years later in 1975, Eibenschütz Mayer wrote, "Many emotional problems develop in connection with the emigration processing," especially because the "first impact with the [transit migrant's] condition in a totally strange environment can be traumatic."[70]

Observations about "the tremendous anxiety that [Soviet transmigrants] have concerning their future in the West" remained prominent in reports by JDC employees throughout the 1970s.[71] In April 1979, when Soviet Jews in Vienna and Rome numbered 11,000, JDC's medical director, Dr. Sasha Gonik, worried that JDC staff leading the transmigrant program were not concerned enough with "the anxiety [transit migrants] face after having taken the decision to leave their country, the physical and mental stress of the trip, first to Vienna and then to Rome, [and] the insecurity of their future"; he also took issue with the often dismissive way in which Soviet Jewish transit migrants were labeled and discussed.[72] Despite these observations, JDC did not offer adequate psychosocial support for those in transit. Program heads like Dr. Akiva Kohane seemed to minimize such requests for psychological services given the urgency of immediate logistical problems.[73]

In a joint statement carrying thirty-two signatures titled "The Bitter Taste of Charity," published in the leading US Russian-language newspaper *Novoye Russkoye Slovo* on January 15, 1988, recent arrivals aired a number of grievances with the administration of the transit migration process, particularly in Ladispoli, Italy (where, just as in 1979, the majority of emigrants resided at the time).[74] The account begins and ends with a statement of appreciation for the work of the organizations involved but advises them to take heed of the serious problems that the immigrants perceived and experienced. The authors questioned the very selection of Ladispoli as a main outpost for transit migrants, as the town was run mainly by the Communist Party, a point of discomfort and reason for mistrust among ex-Soviets. The statement also expressed particular concern about the difficult conditions that affected small children, the sick, the elderly, and individuals traveling alone, especially in terms of inadequate medical services, the poor quality of JDC-provided lodging, difficulties with housing, and limited access to English courses during a critical time of preparation for onward journeys. The article criticized HIAS and JDC workers for responding to people with hostility, insults, roughness, and humiliation, claiming that such "rotten" attitudes and treatment had resulted in nervous breakdowns, depression, and suicide attempts among emigrants. "Can't anyone understand," the letter asked, "that people coming out of Russia need special, very delicate treatment?" Italians, the authors continued, seem to understand this better than JDC and HIAS.[75]

What rings clear is the authors' sense of entitlement to demand better transit conditions, especially when one considers the desperate conditions of other refugee groups of the past century. It all looked different from the point of view of regular Soviet Jewish emigrants who, despite their eagerness to leave the Soviet Union, were ignorant of the reality that faced them as ex-Soviets and as people now stateless and in transit. Consider the recollections of Maria and Lenny Voron, a married couple from Odessa, based on their observations during the six months they spent in transit migration in 1989.

"At first we didn't know what ['refugee' status] was all about," Lenny said following an interview in 2012. He continued:

> At first we thought we deserve it, we deserve everything, and everyone owes us. I remember people yelling at those volunteers at HIAS: "What are you doing?!" "Do this, do that for me." It wasn't because [Soviet Jewish] people are bad or mean, it was because . . . we totally didn't understand how it all worked, first of all. Second of all, we were used to the government being responsible for everything, and mistook HIAS [and JDC] for government agencies.
>
> "And mistook the organizations' volunteers for government bureaucrats," Maria added. "People totally didn't understand what these [workers] were doing for them."
>
> "For *us*," Lenny continued. "Later we realized that all of that was a complete misconception, once we . . . learned how things work."[76]

As Eibenschütz Mayer immediately observed about the Soviet emigrants, they were at once incredibly resourceful and self-sufficient and also mistrustful and demanding of official organizations. The total psychic and physical burdens of the journey along with their Soviet-bred aversion to following official rules translated into many of the difficulties faced by the Joint, which was at least partially responsible for transit migrants in a legal, monetary, and social sense. Their clashes stemmed from the inherent conflict of interest between humanitarian organizations and their clients as well as the stresses of both organizing and passing through the transit migration process—especially when coming from a closed, authoritarian socialist society.

Soviet Jewish Emigration and JDC Leadership

While the staff of the JDC office in Italy focused on the day-to-day and face-to-face tasks of the transit operation, the senior staff in Geneva and New York coordinated JDC's overarching policies and mechanisms. Although they were working tirelessly to maintain the difficult and over-taxed Vienna-Rome operation, several members of JDC's leadership personally sided with the Jewish Agency's efforts to curtail Soviet immigration to countries other than Israel, most prominently Ralph Goldman, a committed Zionist[77] and chief executive of JDC from 1976 to 1985 and 1986 to 1988. Both HIAS and JDC were part of a broad coalition of American organizations that fought for and funded Soviet Jewish emigration.[78] But whereas HIAS, whose principal work entails aiding immigration to the United States, continuously advocated for emigrants' right to choose their destinations, the Joint's senior staff were more willing to assent to Israel's efforts to increase *aliyah*.[79] In confronting a large population that did not wish to go to Israel, JDC leaders faced a genuine political and ethical dilemma: Who decides where Diaspora Jewry belongs?

By 1974, most likely propelled by fear following the October 1973 Arab-Israeli War, about 18.7% of Soviet Jewish émigrés were choosing to continue to countries other than Israel from Vienna. In 1976, that percentage was at 49.1% and continued to climb. Israel dubbed all Soviet Jews not settling in Israel *noshrim*—"dropouts" from the destination intended for them. *Noshrim* were stereotyped as barely Jewish economic migrants taking advantage of the generosity of world Jewry. This terminology persisted throughout the years of Soviet emigration—used by JDC leadership as well—and still permeates scholarship and popular portrayals of Soviet Jews who settled in countries other than Israel.[80]

There were a number of ways that JDC cooperated with the Jewish Agency to increase Soviet immigration to Israel, including changing the conditions of the transit route. In 1973, the Jewish Agency had already pressured JDC and HIAS to cut off any kind of assistance to those Soviet Jews Israel called *yordim* who had initially settled in Israel but left ("descended") for Rome and other European cities, seeking to immigrate elsewhere. (After initially abiding by the edict, HIAS later reinstated assistance to them.) In 1976, Max Fisher, then chairman of the Jewish Agency's board of directors and a confidant of both Prime Minister Rabin and President Nixon, "proposed that JDC and HIAS stop aiding Soviet émigrés with Israeli visas who 'dropped out' in Vienna" altogether.[81] In 1976, a "Committee of Eight"[82] made up of American Jewish and Israeli leaders was established to accomplish this goal—unsuccessfully, due to US organizations' and Austrian Chancellor Dr. Bruno Kreisky's insistence on emigrants' freedom to choose their destinations.[83] Ralph Goldman's biography suggests that it was he who proposed that a committee review the issue,[84] despite JDC's official policy to aid those in transit.

The next major attempt to curtail the Vienna-Rome pipeline took place under Prime Minister Menachem Begin at the end of the 1970s, but Begin ultimately acquiesced to the principle of freedom of choice, seeking to influence emigrants rather than force them to settle in Israel. By 1980, JDC and HIAS agreed to a plan devised by American and Israeli leaders to aid in Vienna and Rome only those emigrants with first-degree relatives in the United States. The Council of Jewish Federations and Welfare Funds (CJF) blocked this plan.[85]

Undaunted, concurrent with the so-called Begin Compromise, JDC was sketching a plan in cooperation with the Jewish Agency and HIAS that was designed to route Soviet Jewish emigrants from Vienna to Naples,[86] where they would all stay in a single large hostel and receive information about Israel in an effort to increase immigration there: "It was assumed that out of the 13,000 people who will be brought to the hostel, 20% . . . may agree to go on aliyah, 30% . . . would be sent to HIAS" (and so it was hoped that the "Jewish people" would agree to fund this), and the half that opted out and went back to Rome "will be trying to find organizations, people or authorities to assist them and help them get out of Italy (or remain)."[87] Even though such a reality would have placed a considerable amount of *additional* stress on those in transit, Kohane expressed his personal desire to Goldman in July 1980: "I know that you are as anxious as I am to make a success of this program"; they were both "praying that the project should be a success."[88] This attempt also failed, however, given the Italian government's insistence on Soviet Jews remaining in the Lazio province after an earthquake hit Naples in 1980.[89]

The final Israel-led endeavor came in the late eighties. As of March 1988, during a year when 88.5% of Soviet Jewish emigrants arriving in Vienna proceeded to Rome rather than Israel, Israel issued a new letter of invitation (*vyzov*) directing emigrants to pick up their Israeli visas at the Israeli Embassy in Bucharest, Romania (rather than the Dutch Embassy in Moscow).[90] Unlike Austria, Romania would not endorse emigrants' freedom to choose their destinations, and once in Bucharest, Israel would be their only possible destination. This plan, too, failed after hesitation on the part of the Dutch and their American and Soviet ambassadors as well as the subsequent opposition of American Jewish leadership.[91]

The controversial rerouting of emigrants through Bucharest eventually resolved itself with the creation of a new US immigrant legal category for members of historically persecuted groups under the Lautenberg Amendment of November 1989. The American Jewish establishment, at this point overwhelmed by the large numbers of arriving Soviet immigrants, agreed to a yearly maximum of 50,000 Soviet refugees (of whom 40,000 were initially expected to be Jews). Facing this quota and both the opportunity and mounting urgency to leave the crumbling Soviet Union, over a million resettled in Israel in the 1990s by direct flight. As a result of *perestroika*-era overhauls, US INS processing would now take place in Moscow, eliminating the need to maintain the costly Austria-Italy passage. The last trainload of Soviet Jews arrived in Rome from Vienna on February 15, 1990.[92] All Soviet Jews bound for the United States left Rome by June 1, 1990,[93] with the remaining caseload of Canada- and Australia-bound émigrés following suit by the end of 1990.

Ultimately, immigration was not exactly a matter of emigrants' "freedom of choice." Through their political will and enormous outlays of effort and money, it was the powerful, "Free World" Jewish elite (as well as the nation-states involved in the migration) creating the contexts and possibilities for emigrants' decision making. Despite the political views and personal preferences of some of its leaders, JDC's transit migrant program withstood the complexities, challenges, and sheer scale of Soviet Jewish transit migration. JDC helped hundreds of thousands of Jews, not just from the Soviet Union but also from all over Europe, Asia, and North Africa, begin their lives anew during a tumultuous and catastrophic century for Jews. The uncertainties and temporary nature of life in transit made it a difficult period in immigrants' lives but one that was made infinitely more bearable by JDC's and HIAS's provision of legal, social, and material assistance.

NOTES

1. The terms used by JDC and HIAS in all of their documents and literature is *transmigrant*. I use the contemporary academic equivalent *transit migrant* and *transit migration*, defined as the period during which migrants, maintaining unfixed immigration statuses, sojourn in a place other than the one from which they emigrated and in which they will settle as immigrants.

2. Fran Markowitz, *A Community in Spite of Itself: Soviet Jewish Emigres in New York* (Washington, DC: Smithsonian Institution, 1993), 6.

3. Markowitz, *A Community in Spite of Itself*, 127.

4. See Inga Veksler, "'We Left Forever and into the Unknown': Soviet Jewish Immigrants' Experiences of Transit Migration" (PhD diss., Rutgers University, 2014). This is the first academic work to focus on the topic of Soviet Jewish transit migration. All names have been changed to pseudonyms.

5. The principal source for this history is Oscar Handlin, *A Continuing Task: The American Jewish Joint Distribution Committee, 1914–1964* (New York: Random House, 1964).

6. Between the postwar DP period of the 1940s through the 1970s, when Soviet Jews became clients, there was structural continuity along the route, not only

in terms of various logistics but also in terms of personnel. Throughout the postwar period, many of the same staff members had retained their positions in JDC's leadership, including Dr. Akiva Kohane—once the director of Poland's country program, in the 1970s he was the director of transmigrant operations in JDC's European headquarters in Geneva, Switzerland—and Sam Haber, who joined JDC in March 1947 as the director for the American occupation zone of Germany (later taking on responsibility for the remainder of Germany as well as Austria) and who served as JDC's Executive Vice Chairman in New York City from 1967 to 1976. Both Kohane and Haber were major decision makers and coordinators of the Vienna-Rome pipeline through the 1970s, solidifying the process that continued through the 1980s.

7. JDC Archives, Records of the New York Office of the American Jewish Joint Distribution Committee, 1965–1974, Folder 277, Memorandum from Ted Feder and Louis Horwitz to Sam Haber, Subject: Vienna-Rome Caseload, March 5, 1971; March 19, 1971; April 2, 1971.

8. Handlin, *A Continuing Task*, 86–87.

9. Ibid., 99.

10. Ibid., 114.

11. Ibid., 109.

12. JDC Archives, Records of the New York Office of the American Jewish Joint Distribution Committee, 1965–1974, Folder 30, Report on Arrivals, January 1, 1968, to August 31, 1968, September 13, 1968. The majority of these Jewish migrants-in-transit settled in Israel.

13. The Soviet Union, along with countries under its influence, severed diplomatic relations with Israel following the 1967 Arab-Israeli War.

14. JDC Archives, Records of the New York Office of the American Jewish Joint Distribution Committee, 1965–1974, Folder 21, Report on Activities of the JDC Office in Vienna, 1968, April 25, 1969.

15. Ibid.; JDC Archives, Records of the New York Office of the American Jewish Joint Distribution Committee, 1965–1974, Folder 30, Meeting Held between Mr. Haskell of the Jewish Agency, Mr. Seidenman of the UHS, Mr. Horwitz, and Mr. Feder on November 26, 1968, in Geneva by Theodore Feder, November 27, 1968. According to an agreement between the JAFI and HIAS, all Poles emigrating to countries other than Israel

were to be transferred to Rome by June 1968. As of November 1968, about 10% still remained in Vienna, and a representative of the Jewish Agency insisted that they all be moved because "as a group, they were always prepared to meet [incoming] trains [from Poland] and give 'friendly advise' on emigration" (ostensibly on not emigrating to Israel) and because "congregating large numbers of persons having recently come out of the Iron Curtain, so near the Iron Curtain, was dangerous."

16. Fred Lazin, *The Struggle for Soviet Jewry in American Politics* (Lanham, MD: Lexington Books, 2005), 307–8.

17. Zvi Gitelman, "Soviet Jews: Creating a Cause and a Movement," in *A Second Exodus: The American Movement to Free Soviet Jews*, ed. Murray Friedman and Albert Chernin (Hanover, NH: Brandeis University Press, 1999), 89.

18. Gregg Beyer, "The Evolving United States Response to Soviet Jewish Emigration," *International Journal of Refugee Law* 3, no. 1 (1991): 35.

19. Exit visas to other countries were significantly harder to obtain from the Soviet government; only 3,337 such exit visas were issued for the United States between 1971 and 1977, for example. This nevertheless involved third-country processing (TCP), similarly requiring transit through Western Europe.

20. JDC Archives, Records of the New York Office of the American Jewish Joint Distribution Committee, 1975–1989, Folder IT 1134, Telex from Akiva Kohane to Ralph Goldman, September 22, 1980. The weekly estimate is derived by dividing the total number of Soviet arrivals to Vienna in August (770) by four.

21. Diana Kagan, in discussion with the author, New York, NY, August 1, 2012.

22. Raisa Lachman, in discussion with the author, Staten Island, NY, March 9, 2011.

23. Fred Lazin, "'Freedom of Choice': Israeli Efforts to Prevent Soviet Jewish Emigres to Resettle in the United States," *Review of Policy Research* 23, no. 2 (2006): 392.

24. See, for example, JDC Archives, Records of the New York Office of the American Jewish Joint Distribution Committee, 1965–1974, Folder 27, Naomi Feinstein, Vienna Trip Report, April 1975.

25. JDC Archives, Records of the New York Office of the American Jewish Joint Distribution Committee, 1975–1989, Folder 1139, Memorandum

from Akiva Kohane to Ralph I. Goldman, Subject: Rejected Case, October 12, 1979; JDC Archives, Records of the New York Office of the American Jewish Joint Distribution Committee, 1965–1974, Folder 27, Naomi Feinstein, Vienna Trip Report, April 1975; JDC Archives, Records of the New York Office of the American Jewish Joint Distribution Committee, 1975–1989, Eligibility Criteria, December 17, 1987. Unlike HIAS, JDC only served Jewish clients. Jewishness was determined through an interview about Jewish practices with a JDC representative in Vienna. Interviews became especially tricky with emigrants officially registered under a different Soviet ethnicity and those lacking Jewish knowledge. In 1979, JDC policy for transmigrant clients stated that at least one member of the family must be fully Jewish. In 1987, the policy was clarified to account for various family structures (e.g., a half-Jewish child traveling only with a non-Jewish parent), but the principal criterion remained that "a family must have at least one member present who had two Jewish parents." The small number deemed ineligible would appeal to another organization assisting transit migrants such as the Satmar organization Rav Tov, the Russian Orthodox organization the Tolstoy Foundation, the World Council of Churches, the International Rescue Committee, or Catholic Charities, among others.

26. JDC Archives, Records of the New York Office of the American Jewish Joint Distribution Committee, 1975–1989, Folder 1137, Memorandum from Akiva Kohane to Ralph I. Goldman, Subject: Russian Transmigrants, March 10, 1978.

27. Restrictions on international travel loosened slightly in the late 1980s.

28. Veksler, "'We Left Forever,'" 169, 173.

29. Viktor Grobnik, in discussion with the author, Brooklyn, NY, July 10, 2012.

30. In discussion with the author, Brooklyn, NY, November 23, 2011.

31. Valentina Kmelintzky, in discussion with the author, Brooklyn, NY, August 16, 2012.

32. HIAS's task of arranging for visas to Italy for all migrants took at least three days (although in 1978 to 1980 it took as little as one). When emigrants arrived in Vienna too sick to travel, they and their families remained in Vienna without proceeding to Italy, waiting for paperwork to be completed and medical clearance for travel.

33. Beginning in December 1988, to expedite transfers to Rome, some arrived by plane.

34. The incident was referred to as the Schoenau Ultimatum. Two pro-Palestinian actors took three Soviet emigrants hostage off of a train en route to Vienna. They demanded the close of Schönau Castle, the JAFI-run Austrian processing center for Soviet emigrants to Israel. Over the course of the transit migrant program, the offices of the humanitarian organizations and the emigrants themselves were subjected to harassment, numerous bomb threats, and violent attacks, mainly by Palestinian sympathizers, including in 1969, 1972, 1973, 1976, 1978, and 1981.

35. Klara Drob, in discussion with the author, for the documentary *Stateless*, directed by Michael Drob (New York: COJECO, 2014), Brooklyn, NY, April 28, 2013.

36. Lazin, *Struggle for Soviet Jewry*, 267. The US Attorney General has the power to "parole" individuals into the United States. This requires sponsorship by friends, relatives, or federations, who sign an affidavit assuring that the parolee will not become a public charge. Parolees were ineligible for medical benefits, government transportation to the United States, resettlement funding or reimbursement, and permanent resident status. The status of almost all Soviet parolees was ex post facto "adjusted" to conform to that of political refugees.

37. JDC Archives, Records of the New York Office of the American Jewish Joint Distribution Committee, 1975–1989, Folder IT 24, Memorandum from Akiva Kohane, Subject: Russian Transmigrants in Italy, January 30, 1979.

38. See JDC Archives, Records of the New York Office of the American Jewish Joint Distribution Committee, 1975–1989, Folder IT 24, Memorandum from Akiva Kohane to Ralph I. Goldman, Subject: Movement of Russian Transmigrants from Kohane to Goldman, March 9, 1979. This would require arrangements with the US Attorney General to increase parole numbers.

39. Ibid., Folder IT 24, Memorandum, Subject: Vienna-Rome Caseload, April 20, 1979; ibid., Folder IT 24, Memorandum from Alexander Gonik, Subject: Jews from Russia in Transit in Italy, April 17, 1979. Another 9,000 Italians commuted into Ladispoli to work there (Ibid., Memorandum from Akiva Kohane, Subject: Reports from the Field, January 30, 1979).

40. Ibid., Folder IT 23, Memorandum, Subject: Vienna-Rome Caseload, April 25, 1980.

41. Ibid., Folder IT 23, Memorandum, Subject: Vienna-Rome Caseload, December 12, 1980.

42. Piet Buwalda, *They Did Not Dwell Alone: Jewish Emigration from the Soviet Union, 1967–1990* (Baltimore: Johns Hopkins University Press, 1997), 193.

43. See Victor Rosenberg, "Refugee Status for Soviet Jewish Immigrants to the United States," *Touro Law Review* 19 (2003): 419–50. The surge of Soviet emigrants in 1988 led to a budgetary shortfall in the INS, and a year of chaotic refugee admission policy ensued. Whereas the approval rate for refugee status for Soviet emigrants was 99% until September 1988, rejections peaked in April 1989 at nearly 40%, creating a major backlog for the humanitarian organizations and an atmosphere of strain and anxiety among émigrés. All was henceforth resolved by the Lautenberg Amendment of November 1989.

44. Roberta Elliot, ed., *Hebrew Immigrant Aid Society (HIAS) Annual Report of 1990* (New York: Fleetwood, 1991), 4.

45. Roberta Elliot, ed., *Hebrew Immigrant Aid Society (HIAS) Annual Report of 1989* (New York: Fleetwood, 1990), 9, 23. HIAS processed 5,000 emigrants per month in 1990 through the first half of the year.

46. JDC Archives, Records of the New York Office of the American Jewish Joint Distribution Committee, 1975–1989, Folder IT 23, Telex 2824, March 5, 1980; ibid., Folder IT 23, Telex 2827, March 6, 1980.

47. Per diem costs average $12.06 per person in Austria and roughly half of that—$6.83 per person—in Italy.

48. *JDC Annual Report 1988* (JDC: New York, 1989), 25.

49. *JDC Annual Report 1989* (JDC: New York, 1990), 21.

50. Ibid., 19, 50. After US Refugee Program (USRP) reimbursement, the net cost to JDC came to $29,077,200, 58.8% of its budget that year.

51. See especially Atina Grossmann, *Jews, Germans, and Allies: Close Encounters in Occupied Germany* (Princeton, NJ: Princeton University Press, 2007); Hagit Lavsky, "The Experience of the Displaced Persons in Bergen-Belson: Unique or Typical Case?" in *"We Are Here": New Approaches to Jewish Displaced Persons in Postwar Germany*, ed. Avinoam Patt and Michael Berkowitz (Detroit: Wayne State University Press, 2010).

52. JDC Archives, Records of the New York Office of the American Jewish Joint Distribution Committee, 1965–1974, Folder 259, Annual Report 1975 by Loni Eibenschütz Mayer. David Bezmozgis's 2011 novel *The Free World* depicts the darker side—scamming, smuggling, dealings with the Mafia—of life in transit.

53. JDC Archives, Records of the New York Office of the American Jewish Joint Distribution Committee, 1965–1974, Folder 259, Annual Report 1975 by Loni Eibenschütz Mayer.

54. Ella Bobrovsky, in discussion with the author, New York, NY, July 8, 2011.

55. Rebecca Rotter, "'Hanging in-Between': Experiences of Waiting among Asylum Seekers Living in Glasgow" (PhD diss., University of Edinburgh, 2010); Rebeckah Lennartsson, "'You Are Nobody while You Are Waiting': Asylum Seekers' Experiences of Nothingness," *Ethnologia Scandinavica* 37 (2007); Emma Stewart, "Exploring the Vulnerability of Asylum Seekers in the UK," *Population, Space and Place* 11 (2005); Jan-Paul Brekke, *While We Are Waiting: Uncertainty and Empowerment among Asylum-Seekers in Sweden* (Oslo: Institute for Social Research, 2004); Diana Wong, "Asylum as a Relationship of Otherness: A Study of Asylum Holders in Nuremberg, Germany," *Journal of Refugee Studies* 4, no. 2 (1991).

56. Maxim Shrayer, *Waiting for America: A Story of Emigration* (Syracuse, NY: Syracuse University Press, 2007), 215.

57. Milana Zillman, in discussion with the author, Boston, MA, November 12, 2011.

58. See Rahul Oka, "Coping with the Refugee Wait: The Role of Consumption, Normalcy, and Dignity in Refugee Lives at Kakuma, Kenya," *American Anthropologist* 116, no. 1 (2014): 1–15. See also Kierra Crago-Schneider's and Avinoam Patt's chapters in this volume.

59. JDC Archives, Records of the New York Office of the American Jewish Joint Distribution Committee, 1965–1974, Folder 260, AJDC Programme in Italy—1970–71 by Loni Eibenschütz Mayer, November 21, 1971.

60. Ibid., Folder 259, Annual Report 1974 by Loni Eibenschütz Mayer, April 8, 1975.

61. Ibid., Annual Report 1975.

62. Ibid., Folder 30, Public Relations Draft Written by Sophie Lennox, August 30, 1968; JDC Archives, Records of the New York Office of the American Jewish Joint Distribution Committee, 1965–1974, Folder 30, Memorandum for File by Kohane, September 2, 1968.

63. Ibid., Folder 259, Memorandum from Eibenschütz Mayer to Feder, Subject: Increase in Caseload, January 29, 1973.

64. Ibid., Annual Report 1974 and Annual Report 1975.

65. JDC Archives, Records of the New York Office of the American Jewish Joint Distribution Committee, 1975–1989, Folder IT 25, Memorandum from Akiva Kohane to Ralph I. Goldman, Subject: Problems among Russian Transmigrants in Rome, February 17, 1978.

66. Ibid., Folder IT 42, Memorandum from Akiva Kohane to Ralph I. Goldman, Subject: Draft Minutes of Meeting Held at the Office of the Jewish Agency in Rome July 24, 1980, 1, July 29, 1980.

67. JDC Archives, Records of the New York Office of the American Jewish Joint Distribution Committee, 1965–1974, Folder 259, Annual Report 1975; JDC Archives, Records of the New York Office of the American Jewish Joint Distribution Committee, 1975–1989, Folder IT 28, Report from Loni Eibenschütz Mayer, Subject: Transmigrants Programme in Italy 1974–75, October 15, 1975.

68. Moreover, the Soviet Union purposefully used the emigration movement to expel unwanted criminals.

69. JDC Archives, Records of the New York Office of the American Jewish Joint Distribution Committee, 1965–1974, Folder 259, Annual Report 1975; ibid., Folder 260, AJDC Programme in Italy—1970–71, 4, November 21, 1971.

70. Ibid., Folder 259, Annual Report 1975, 5.

71. JDC Archives, Records of the New York Office of the American Jewish Joint Distribution Committee, 1975–1989, Folder IT 25, Memorandum from Zev Hymowitz for the Record, August 30, 1978.

72. Ibid., Folder IT 24, Memorandum from Alexander Gonik, Subject: Jews from Russia in Transit in Italy, April 17, 1979.

73. See, for example, JDC Archives, Records of the New York Office of the American Jewish Joint Distribution Committee, 1975–1989, Folder IT

24, Memorandum from Akiva Kohane to Ralph I. Goldman, Subject: Psychological Aspects of Jewish Immigration, September 18, 1978.

74. Rosset et al., "The Bitter Taste of Charity," *Novoye Russkoye Slovo* (January 15, 1988).

75. In another example of World War II's traces in the Vienna-Rome pipeline, emigrants encountered both Austrians and Italians who wished to offer others the help that they received during the war.

76. Maria and Lenny Voron, in discussion with the author, Hackensack, NJ, July 8, 2012. The Vorons were responding to my inquiries about how they felt and perceived refugee status; their larger point was that they did not know how rare and privileged of a status it was.

77. See Tom Shachtman, *I Seek My Brethren: Ralph Goldman and "The Joint"* (New York: Newmarket Press, 2001).

78. See the extensive literature on the American Soviet Jewry movement.

79. From its very inception, Israel looked to Soviet Jewry as a source of the population surge that would allow it to become a viable state with a particular type of population (e.g., non-Arab, Jewish, Ashkenazi).

80. In contrast, partially because it is linked with a social movement and political struggle, Israel-bound emigration (*olim*) retains a noble and prestigious historical quality.

81. Lazin, "'Freedom of Choice,'" 394.

82. It was later expanded to a Committee of Ten consisting of the leadership of the Jewish Agency, the Israel government, the Prime Minister's Office, the Council of Jewish Federations and Welfare Funds, HIAS, JDC, the United Jewish Appeal, the National Jewish Community Relations Advisory Council, and the United Israel Appeal.

83. Lazin, "'Freedom of Choice,'" 394–95.

84. Shachtman, *I Seek My Brethren*, 124.

85. Lazin, "'Freedom of Choice,'" 399–400. Ironically, the Soviet Union had issued a similar requirement in 1979, triggering mass rejections of emigration applications.

86. Naples is the site of the Jewish Agency's office in Italy. Many transmigrants stayed in Naples under the Jewish Agency's care in the 1960s and probably before then.

87. JDC Archives, Records of the New York Office of the American Jewish Joint Distribution Committee, 1975–1989, Folder IT 42, Memorandum from Akiva Kohane to Ralph I. Goldman, Subject: Draft Minutes of Meeting Held at the Office of the Jewish Agency in Rome, July 24, 1980; July 29, 1980.

88. Ibid., Folder IT 42, Memorandum from Akiva Kohane to Ralph I. Goldman, Subject: Draft Minutes of Meeting Held at the Office of the Jewish Agency in Rome, July 24, 1980; July 29, 1980.

89. See JDC Archives, Records of the New York Office of the American Jewish Joint Distribution Committee, 1975–1989, Folder IT 22, Memoranda dated December 22, 1980; December 23, 1980; January 21, 1981; February 19, 1981; March 23, 1981; March 30, 1981.

90. Romania was the only state in Eastern Europe that maintained diplomatic relations with Israel.

91. Buwalda, *They Did Not Dwell Alone*, 170–179.

92. Elliot, *HIAS Annual Report 1990*, 4.

93. Ibid., 5.

CONTRIBUTORS

Elissa Bemporad is the Jerry and William Ungar Chair in East European Jewish History and the Holocaust and an associate professor of history at Queens College and the Graduate Center—CUNY. She is the author of *Becoming Soviet Jews: The Bolshevik Experiment in Minsk* (Indiana University Press, 2013), winner of the National Jewish Book Award, winner of the Fraenkel Prize in Contemporary History, and finalist for the Jordan Schnitzer Prize in Modern Jewish History. Her new book, titled *Legacy of Blood: Jews, Pogroms, and Ritual Murder in the Lands of the Soviets*, will be published with Oxford University Press in 2019. Elissa is also the coeditor of *Women and Genocide: Survivors, Victims, Perpetrators* (Indiana University Press, 2018). She has recently been a recipient of an NEH Fellowship and a Fellowship at the Center for Advanced Holocaust Studies at the United States Holocaust Memorial Museum in Washington DC. Elissa's projects in progress include research for a biography of Ester Frumkin.

Kierra Crago-Schneider is a Program Officer in National Academic Programs in the Jack, Joseph and Morton Mandel Center for Advanced Holocaust Studies at the United States Holocaust Memorial Museum. She previously served as a historian at the Conference on Jewish Material Claims Against Germany. Dr. Crago-Schneider received a PhD in history from the University of California, Los Angles in 2013, an MA in Jewish history from the University of California–Los Angles in 2007, as well as an MA in European history from the University of California, Riverside in 2004. Dr. Crago-Schneider's publications include: "Anti-Semitism or Competing Interests? An Examination of German and American Perceptions of Jewish Displaced Persons Active on the Black Market in Munich's Möhlstrasse," in *Yad Vashem Review* 1, no. 38 (2010) and "A Community of Will: The Resettlement of the Orthodox from Föhrenwald," *Holocaust and Genocide Studies* 32, no. 1 (2018). Her current manuscript, *From Barter to Black Market: The Re-Criminalization of the Jews in Germany*, is based on one half of her dissertation, "Jewish 'Shtetls' in Postwar Germany: An Analysis of Interactions Among Jewish Displaced Persons, Germans, and Americans Between 1945 and 1957 in Bavaria."

Veerle Vanden Daelen holds a PhD in history from the University of Antwerp. Her dissertation examined the return and reconstruction of Jewish life in Antwerp after the Second World War (1944–1960). She has held fellowships at the Frankel Institute for Advanced Judaic Studies (University of Michigan) and the Herbert D. Katz Center for Advanced Judaic Studies (University of Pennsylvania). Besides numerous articles, she has authored two books, *Vrouwbeelden in het Vlaams Blok* (Ghent, 2002) and *Laten we hun lied verder zingen. De heropbouw van de joodse gemeenschap in Antwerpen na de Tweede Wereldoorlog* (1944–1960) (Amsterdam, 2008). Currently, she coordinates the work package Identification and Investigation for EHRI (European Holocaust Research Infrastructure) at CEGESOMA. She is also affiliated to the University of Antwerp, where she has taught courses on migration history, Jewish history, and other topics.

Kinga Frojimovics, a historian and archivist, is a project researcher at the Vienna Wiesenthal Institute for Holocaust Studies. She is the author of the book *I have Been a Stranger in a Strange Land: The Hungarian State and Jewish Refugees in Hungary, 1933–1945* (Yad Vashem, 2007). Her current research project focuses on Hungarian Jewish forced laborers in Vienna in 1944–45.

Zhava Litvac Glaser is originally from Buenos Aires, Argentina, where her parents immigrated from Eastern Europe. She now resides in New York City with her husband and two children. Zhava earned a Bachelor of Science degree in Judaic Studies from the University of Southern California, a master of arts degree in Intercultural Studies from the Fuller Graduate School, a master of arts degree in Jewish History from the Graduate Center of the City of New York, a master of philosophy degree from Hunter College, and a PhD in Jewish History with a certificate in Medieval studies from the Graduate Center of the City of New York. Her current areas of research are Medieval Jewish history and Jewish rescue and relief during the Holocaust.

Jaclyn Granick is Junior Research Fellow at St. Peter's College and the History Faculty, University of Oxford. She completed her PhD in 2015 at the Graduate Institute of International and Development Studies, Geneva. Her research is at the interface of twentieth-century international history and modern Jewish history. She is currently writing *International Jewish Humanitarianism in the Age of the Great War*, a political and social history which looks at non-state, quasi-state, and state actors in an international framework, connecting North America, Europe, and the Middle East through a thematic history of humanitarian activity undertaken by Jews from 1914 to 1929. As a Newton International Fellow of the British Academy, she is working on a new project to gender Jewish international history in the long twentieth century.

Atina Grossmann is Professor of History in the Faculty of Humanities and Social Sciences at the Cooper Union in New York City. Publications include *Jews, Germans, and Allies: Close Encounters in Occupied Germany* (2007), *Juden,*

Deutsche, Alliierte: Begegnungen im Besetzten Deutschland (2012), *Wege in der Fremde: Deutsch-jüdische Begegnungsgeschichte zwischen New York, Berlin und Teheran* (2012), and *Reforming Sex: The German Movement for Birth Control and Abortion Reform, 1920–1950* (1995); coedited volumes on *Crimes of War: Guilt and Denial in the Twentieth Century* (2002) and *After the Nazi Racial State: Difference and Democracy in Germany and Europe* (2009), as well as *Shelter from the Holocaust: Rethinking Jewish Survival in the Soviet Union* (with Mark Edele and Sheila Fitzpatrick) (2018). She is working, together with Dorota Glowacka, on a brief summary volume (Bloomsbury) on *Gender and the Holocaust*, and her current research focuses on "Remapping Survival: Jewish Refugees and Lost Memories of Displacement, Trauma, and Rescue in the Soviet Union, Iran, and India," as well as the entanglements of family memoir and historical scholarship.

Laura Hobson Faure has been an associate professor in North American studies at the Université de Paris 3 Sorbonne Nouvelle since 2010. A graduate of Bryn Mawr College, she completed a doctorate in history at the École des hautes études en sciences sociales. She recently published *Un plan Marshall juif: la présence juive américaine en France après la Shoah, 1944–1954* (Armand Colin, 2013) and coedited a collection of essays on the Oeuvre de Secours aux Enfants: *L'Œuvre de Secours aux Enfants et les populations juives au XXème siècle. Prévenir et Guérir dans un siècle de violences* (Armand Colin, 2014, with Katy Hazan, Catherine Nicault and Mathias Gardet).

Marion Kaplan is the Skirball Professor of Modern Jewish History at NYU. She is a three-time National Jewish Book Award winner for *The Making of the Jewish Middle Class: Women, Family and Identity in Imperial Germany* (1991), *Between Dignity and Despair: Jewish Life in Nazi Germany* (1998), and *Gender and Jewish History* (with Deborah Dash Moore, 2011) as well as a finalist for *Dominican Haven: The Jewish Refugee Settlement in Sosua* (2008). Her other publications include: *The Jewish Feminist Movement in Germany, Jewish Daily Life in Germany, 1618–1945* (ed.) and *Jüdische Welten: Juden in Deutschland vom 18. Jahrhundert bis in die Gegenwart* (with Beate Meyer, 2005) She has edited several other books on German-Jewish and women's history and has taught courses on German-Jewish history, European women's history, German and European history, as well as European Jewish history, and Jewish women's history. Her newest book, *Jewish Refugees Fleeing Hitler: Hope and Anxiety in Portugal, 1940–45* will be published by Yale University Press in 2019.

Linda Levi is Director of Global Archives at the American Jewish Joint Distribution Committee. The JDC Archives, one of the most significant repositories in the world for the study of modern Jewish history with centers in New York and Jerusalem, includes three miles of text documents, 100,000 photographs, over 6,000 books, and over 1,000–audio-visual recordings including oral histories. A graduate of NYU, she received her MA from Brandeis University in contemporary Jewish studies. Ms. Levi has worked for the organization for over three decades and is an expert on Jewish communities around the world. She served as editor of *In Every Generation: The JDC Haggadah* (2010) and *I Live. Send Help. 100 Years of Jewish History in Images from the JDC Archives* (2014). She has published a number of professional articles and has lectured extensively about the JDC Archives and the history of the organization at academic, professional, and Jewish genealogy conferences.

Maud S. Mandel (Ph.D., University of Michigan, 1998; A.M., University of Michigan, 1993; B.A. Oberlin College, 1989) is President of Williams College and Professor of History and Judaic Studies. Former dean of the college and professor of history and Judaic studies at Brown University, she is author of *In the Aftermath of Genocide: Armenians and Jews in Twentieth Century France* (Duke University Press, 2003) and *Muslims and Jews in France: History of a Conflict* (Princeton University Press, 2014) and co-editor with Ethan Katz and Lisa Leff of *Colonialism and the Jews* (Indiana University Press, 2017). She has been awarded fellowships from the American Council of Learned Societies and the American Philosophical Society. Her most recent article, "Simone Weil: A Jewish Thinker?" was published in the volume *Thinking Jewish Modernity* by Princeton University Press in 2016.

Mikhail Mitsel grew up in Lviv (Ukraine) and in 1978 graduated from Lviv State University. In the 1980s, he worked in the museum Kyiv Fortress as a researcher and tour guide. In the 1990s, he was a researcher at the Institute for Jewish Studies in Kyiv. In 1998 he moved to the United States. He is an archivist, specializing in Eastern European Jewish history at the Archives of the American Jewish Joint Distribution Committee in New York. Mitsel is the author of many articles and books in English, Russian, Ukrainian, and Polish, including *"The Final Chapter": Agro-Joint in the Years of the Great Terror* (Kyiv, 2012), the photo album *The American Brother: The "Joint" in Russia, the USSR and the CIS* (Jerusalem, 2004) (co-authored with Michael Beizer), *Jews of Ukraine in 1943–1953: A Documented Study* (Kyiv, 2004), *Jewish Religious Communities in Ukraine: Kyiv, Lviv: 1945–1981* (Kyiv, 1998), and *List of the 1863 Insurgents Jailed in the Kyiv Fortress* (Przemyśl, 1995).

Avinoam Patt is the Philip D. Feltman Professor of Modern Jewish History at the Maurice Greenberg Center for Judaic Studies at the University of Hartford, where he is also director of the Museum of Jewish Civilization. Previously, he worked as the Miles Lerman Applied Research Scholar for Jewish Life and Culture at the United States Holocaust Memorial Museum (USHMM). He received his PhD in modern European history and Hebrew and Judaic studies from NYU. His first book, *Finding Home and Homeland: Jewish Youth and Zionism in* *the Aftermath of the Holocaust* was published by Wayne State University Press in 2009. Patt is also the co-editor (with Michael Berkowitz) of a collected volume on Jewish Displaced Persons, titled *We Are Here: New Approaches to the Study of Jewish Displaced Persons in Postwar Germany* (Wayne State University Press, 2010). He is a contributor to several projects at the USHMM and is a co-author of the source volume, titled *Jewish Responses to Persecution, 1938–1940* (USHMM/Alta Mira Press, 2011). He is co-editor of an anthology of contemporary American Jewish fiction titled *The New Diaspora: The Changing Landscape of American Jewish Fiction* with Mark Shechner and Victoria Aarons, published by Wayne State University Press in 2015 and finalist for the National Jewish Book Award, Anthologies. He is currently writing a new book on the early wartime and postwar memory of the Warsaw Ghetto Uprising (under contract with Wayne State University Press) and co-editing a new collected volume on *Laughter After: Humor and the Holocaust.*

Suzanne D. Rutland is Professor in the Department of Hebrew, Biblical and Jewish Studies in the Faculty of Arts and Social Sciences at the University of Sydney. Her major history of Australian Jewry, *Edge of the Diaspora: Two Centuries of Jewish Settlement in Australia*, was first published in 1988 and has had two subsequent editions (Collins, 1988; Brandl and Schlesinger, 1997; Holmes and Meier, New York, 2001), and her latest publication is *The Jews in Australia* published in 2005 by Cambridge University Press. She has held numerous leadership positions, including president of the Australian Jewish Historical Society. She has been a convener of the Australian Association of Jewish Studies on a number of occasions. Professor Rutland was awarded an OAM (Medal of the Order of Australia) for service to Jewish education and history through a range of higher education development roles and as an author and academic, and to the promotion of interfaith relations. In 2011 Professor Rutland was listed as one of the fifty most influential Jews in Australia.

Anna Sommer Schneider is Associate Director and Professor for the Center for Jewish Civilization, Edmund A. Walsh School of Foreign Service at Georgetown University. She received her PhD from the Department of Jewish Studies at the Jagiellonian University in Kraków, Poland. She is the author of *She'erit Hapletah: Surviving Remnant. The Activities of the American Jewish Joint Distribution Committee in Poland, 1945–1989* (2014, published in Polish) and co-author of *Rescue, Relief and Renewal: 100 Years of the Joint in Poland* (2014). She is also the author of numerous scholarly and critical articles on Holocaust memory and the history of the Jews in post–World War II Poland, published both in Polish and English.

Inga Veksler received her PhD from the anthropology department of Rutgers University in 2014. Her dissertation, "'We Left Forever and into the Unknown': Soviet Jewish Immigrants' Experiences of Transit Migration," grew out of her own family's experience of transit migration from Odessa, Ukraine, through Austria and Italy during six months in 1989.

Rakefet Zalashik received her PhD in history from Tel Aviv University in 2006, with a dissertation on the development of psychiatry in Palestine and Israel, 1892–1960. Her work focuses on the history of psychiatry in Israel, Palestine, and Germany; immigrant absorption and the integration of Holocaust survivors into Israeli society; the relationship between mental health and gender; and Israeli identity formation. She is the author of *Ad Nafesh: Refugees, Immigrants, Newcomers and the Israeli Psychiatric Establishment* (2008, in Hebrew) and *Das unselige Erbe: Die Geschichte der Psychiatrie in Palästina und Israel* (2012, in German) and is the scientific editor of the Hebrew translation of Freud's *Moses and Monotheism* (2009). Her work has also appeared in journals such as *Science in Context*, *The Journal for the History of Psychiatry*, *Israel Studies*, *Zmanim*, and *Korot: The Israel Journal of the History of Medicine and Science*. In 2013, she co-edited *A Jew's Best Friend?: The Image of the Dog Throughout Jewish History* (with Phillip Ackerman-Lieberman). Dr. Zalashik was a Dorot Post-Doctoral Fellow at NYU and has held positions in the United States at the University of Virginia and in Germany at the Hochschule für Jüdische Studien in Heidelberg and the University of Potsdam's Moses Mendelssohn Center for European-Jewish Studies. She has received fellowships from the United States Holocaust Memorial Museum, YIVO, and the University of Haifa's Bucerius Institute for Research of Contemporary German History and Society, among others.

INDEX

Page numbers in *italics* indicate illustrations.

Zalashik, Rakefet, 7, 21, 304n6
Zawadzki, Stanisław, 347
Zeitinger, Jenő, 427–29
Zelicki, Paweł, 326
Zentral Komitet (ZK)/Central
    Committee of Liberated Jews
    (CCLJ), 361, 366, 371–73, 377,
    380, 406n12
Zillman, Milana, 455
Zionism: DPs in Germany and, 362–
    63, 369–70, 373, 381, 408n32; of
    FSJF, 286; Hungary, retraining
    camps in, 427; Laura Margolis
    and, 169; Polish anti-Zionist
    campaign, 359n57, 359n68;
    Polish Jewish refugees in Central
    Asia and, 213, 219, 220, 223,

240nn36–37; postwar Poland
    and, 328, 331, 337, 355–56n28;
    Rosenberg and Rosen on, 138–39,
    157–58nn17–18, 157n15; transit
    migration of Soviet Jews through
    Austria and Italy (1971–1990)
    and, 460–63
ZK (Zentral Komitet)/CCLJ (Central
    Committee of Liberated Jews),
    361, 366, 371–73, 377, 380,
    406n12
ZRWM (Związek Religijny Wyznania
    Mojżeszowego; Union of Jewish
    Religious Congregations, later
    Religious Association of the
    Mosaic Faith), Poland, 326, 327,
    337, 338, 349

CPSIA information can be obtained
at www.ICGtesting.com
Printed in the USA
BVHW040607270219
541271BV00002B/6/P

9 780814 342343